ANDERSONVILLES
of the NORTH

ANDERSONVILLES
of the NORTH

THE MYTHS AND REALITIES OF NORTHERN TREATMENT
OF CIVIL WAR CONFEDERATE PRISONERS

JAMES M. GILLISPIE

University of North Texas Press
Denton, Texas

10 9 8 7 6 5 4 3 2 1

Permissions:
University of North Texas Press
P.O. Box 311336
Denton, TX 76203-1336

The paper used in this book meets the minimum requirements of the American National Standard for Permanence of Paper for Printed Library Materials, z39.48.1984. Binding materials have been chosen for durability.

Library of Congress Cataloging-in-Publication Data

Gillispie, James M., 1969–
  Andersonvilles of the North : the myths and realities of Northern treatment of Civil War Confederate prisoners / James M. Gillispie.
      p. cm.
  Includes bibliographical references and index.
  ISBN 978-1-57441-255-0 (cloth : alk. paper)
  1. United States—History—Civil War, 1861-1865—Prisoners and prisons. 2. United States. Army—Prisons—History—19th century. 3. Military prisons—United States—History—19th century. 4. Military prisons—Northeastern States—History—19th century. 5. Military prisons—Middle West—History—19th century. 6. Prisoners of war—United States—Mortality—History—19th century. 7. Prisoners of war—Confederate States of America—History—19th century. 8. Prisoners of war—United States—History—19th century. I. Title.
  E615.G55 2008
  973.7'71—dc22
                                    2008018774

CONTENTS

ILLUSTRATIONS

FOUND AFTER PAGE 108

ACKNOWLEDGMENTS

No academic work is ever the sole creation of the author. That may sound cliché but it is true nevertheless; it is certainly the case with this one. I cannot thank Ronald Chrisman, the Director of University of North Texas Press, enough for his help and support in getting this project from raw manuscript to finished book. Many thanks also to Karen DeVinney, the Press's managing editor, for all the work she did to improve the readability of the manuscript. The book is much better for her input. From start to finish my experience with the Press has been nothing but positive.

While doing research for the book many people and institutions provided critical assistance. No one, though, was more helpful and supportive than John Coski, Historian and Director of Library and Research at the Museum of the Confederacy in Richmond. John is one of those rare individuals for whom the term "gentleman scholar" actually fits. On more than one occasion I went to Richmond to do research and discovered that John had found items I had either overlooked or did not know existed and made them available for me. I also want to thank Teresa Roane, Library Manager, and the rest of the staff at the Museum of the Confederacy for all their help during my trips to Richmond. The staff of the Southern Collection at the University of North Carolina was also a tremendous help to me as were those at Carrier Library (James Madison University), J. D. Williams Library (University of Mississippi), the Library of Congress, the State Library of Virginia, Alderman Library (University of Virginia), and Perkins Library (Duke University).

Lastly, but certainly not least, I need to thank my family. My wife Julie had to endure my obsession with this topic for a number of years. There were also many times when our daughter Lauren was a toddler that Julie made sure I had the time and space I needed to work on the manuscript. It is to Julie, really, that I owe the most. And as for Lauren, thank you for understanding when Daddy had to get some work done.

Roseboro, North Carolina
July 2008

INTRODUCTION

IN 1998, JAMES MCPHERSON OBSERVED in *Writing the Civil War* that while the Civil War has been and continues to be the most written-about event in American history, a remarkably small percentage of the literature has focused on the prisoner of war issue. Since that time, about a dozen books on this topic have been published, though rarely by academic presses. This relative dearth of writing on the subject may reflect the belief that William Best Hesseltine's seminal work, *Civil War Prisons: A Study in War Psychology* (1930), set such a high standard that there was little meaningful to add. More likely it reflects an understandable reluctance to tackle a subject that remains highly controversial nearly 150 years after the war ended. Whatever the reason, writing on this topic, whether by lay historians or Ph.D-holding scholars, has rarely shed new light on it or attempted to offer a new interpretation of prisoner of war policies and life inside the war's camps. My intention is to offer a book that does offer a new perspective on Northern POW policies and how Federal officials treated Confederate captives during the Civil War.

From the end of the war until Hesseltine's book appeared, Union officials had been characterized as horribly inhumane when it came to their treatment of Confederate prisoners. Because of a basic lack of Christian compassion in Yankee DNA, postwar Southerners argued, conditions in Federal prisons were excessively harsh and deadly. According to writers from the Lost Cause era, Confederate prisoners were thrust into crowded and filthy pens where they were systematically denied adequate food, clothing, shelter, and medical care. Since Union officials had the resources to provide all of these things but cruelly chose not to, Southern prisoners suffered and died in huge numbers.

Hesseltine took a much more objective view of the situation. While he did think that given the North's resources mortality in Union prison camps was too high, he did not attribute it to some congenital defect in Northerners' basic character. Rather, he suggested they denied vital resources to Confederate prisoners because they suffered from what he called a "war psychosis." After being bombarded with prison atrocity stories by the Northern press, officials decided in 1864 to initiate a retaliation program where supplies such as food and medicine were withheld as a way to dish out to Southern prisoners the same treatment that Union prisoners were believed to be receiving at places like Belle Isle in Richmond and Andersonville in Georgia. Northern officials were not evil, they were misguided.

Since Hesseltine's still-valuable book, there has been a noticeable trend back towards characterizing Northern officials as cruel, vindictive, and negligent in their prisoner of war policies. This has been most true of books published by non-academic presses but university professors have also tended to condemn Federal prison officials and policies as callous and unnecessarily harsh in their writing. In the 1960s one scholar described Union officials as acting towards Southern prisoners with "sadistic apathy." In 2005 the most recent scholarly treatment of this issue, *While in the Hands of the Enemy*, was published by the prestigious LSU Press. In this prize-winning book, Charles Sanders breaks with past writers in that he holds both governments responsible for deplorable conditions in their prisons. But, like virtually every other work, this one is particularly hard on Northern officials. Sanders concludes that by the middle of the war, and especially during its final year, Union policies were "deliberately designed to lower conditions in the camps and increase immeasurably the suffering of the prisoners."

The literature has been almost uniformly negative in its assessment of Federal prison policies and treatment of Confederate prisoners of war. But there have been a couple of books published within the last decade that have broken with this well-established image of cruel and negligent Yankee keepers. In 2000 Northern Illinois University Press published *Rebels at Rock Island* by Benton McAdams. This excellent study of a notorious Northern prison acknowledged that life there was difficult and potentially deadly. But while showing that life there was hard, McAdams did not find any compelling evidence of a Federal conspiracy to lower conditions there. That same year Dale Fetzer and Bruce Mowday's study of Fort Delaware, *Unlikely Allies: Fort Delaware's Prison Community in the Civil War*, was published by Stackpole Books. Like McAdams, these authors show that life there was difficult but find little to indicate that Northern officials systematically mistreated prisoners or denied them adequate food, clothing, shelter, and medical care. These two studies are quite good and offer a very different perspective on Northern prison policies, but they have had little effect (if the writing done since their publication is any indication) on altering or revising the long held, wholly negative image of Union prison policies.

This book argues that the most reliable evidence, wartime records and Southern diaries, supports McAdams' and Fetzer and Mowday's less negative characterization of Federal prison policies and treatment of Confederate prisoners. There is a mountain of eyewitness testimony from former prisoners testifying to how Union officials starved, beat, and generally abused them every chance they got. But as I argue in the first two chapters, postwar writing done about the Civil War's prisons should almost never be taken at face value as reliable primary source evidence. Both Northerners and Southerners in the half-century or so following the war exploited this issue for personal, political, and social reasons. Rarely does one find a postwar narrative, whether it be about Andersonville or Rock Island, that reads like a dispassionate attempt to accurately portray what life was like as a prisoner during the Civil War. The overwhelming majority, from both regions, are virulent polemics that often conflict with wartime records and diaries. I have, therefore, chosen not to rely on eyewitness testimony written after 1865.

Rather I have chosen to rely more heavily on the *Official Records of the War of the Rebellion* and the *Medical and Surgical History of the War of the Rebellion.* These "Northern" sources have their problems but they are far less flawed than postwar narratives. While Union records may not always fully acknowledge the defects in Northern prisons, they also were not intended for popular consumption or created to make sure Union officials came off looking better to historians after the war. Significantly, Southern diaries, more reliable because they were private and not written to achieve any particular agenda, tend to support rather than undermine the Northern wartime records. Thus, this study relies exclusively on wartime sources as the most reliable available.

What these records reveal is that Union policies towards Confederate prisoners were more humane than commonly thought. One of the most important misconceptions about Federal prison policies is that the United States suspended the exchange agreement that existed between the two governments in the spring of 1863 solely out of military self interest. The records clearly show that this decision was prompted by Confederate policies regarding black Union soldiers. When the United States chose to utilize African Americans, the Davis administration responded by declaring that blacks were not legitimate soldiers and if captured they would be treated as either recovered property or as insurrectionists liable to summary execution. Davis and Confederate officials had the right to make any laws they liked regarding African Americans. If they chose not to use black soldiers, that was their right; it was also the right of the United States to utilize this manpower source if they chose. Union officials were violating no law and the notion that they were somehow bound to prosecute the war to suit their enemy's tastes is preposterous. Having chosen to use black soldiers, the United States was obliged to protect them from enslavement and execution, punishments that were recognized by Western nations as illegitimate treatments of soldiers captured in battle. Records show clearly that Northern officials firmly and plainly made it clear to Confederate authorities that until Richmond was willing to recognize black Union soldiers as equally eligible as whites for exchange under the 1862 agreement the cartel would remain suspended.

Not only do the records show that Union authorities did not suspend the exchange cartel out of cold military calculation, but they also show that throughout the war officials generally acted with humanity towards Southern prisoners. In the fall of 1861 United States officials, with no real experience and few international laws to guide them, created a prison system with an officer to oversee it, something Richmond did not do until late in 1864. General Orders No. 100, issued in April 1863, formalized Northern prison policies and were considered humane and enlightened enough to become the model for international laws on the subject later in the century. An elaborate inspection system made sure that General Orders No. 100 was being complied with. Inspection reports and Southern diaries indicate that most of the time food, clothing, and shelter were adequate by the standards of the time. There were, of course, periods when these things were not adequately supplied but they appear to have been episodic rather than chronic or systematic. When it came to medical care, statistics show that Confederate prisoners were often more likely to recover from major killers like dysentery, smallpox, and pneumonia in a Union prison than at the South's largest medical center, Chimborazo Hospital in Richmond. Such evidence strongly suggests that the characterization of Federal officials as cruel, negligent, and sadistically apathetic towards Southern prisoners of war is in need of updating.

Given the highly controversial nature of this topic it is necessary to be as systematic and thorough as possible or risk being pilloried for selective use of the evidence. I have done mini studies of the North's nine major prisons to determine how closely General Orders No. 100 was complied with, placing particular emphasis on the food, clothing, shelter, and medical issues in them. The ultimate result is, I think, a book that significantly broadens our understanding of how Union officials dealt with prisoners during the Civil War. However, that approach is necessarily repetitive and does sacrifice readability, something I hope the reader will understand and forgive.

As a final word of introduction to this study, this attempt to revise and update the image of Federal officials in this area is most emphatically *not* intended to be an apologist piece. Far too often revisionist works go too far, becoming so fixated on revising or updating an existing interpretation that they swing too far in the opposite direction. Ultimately the revised interpretation is often just as distorted and inaccurate as the original model. I have tried to avoid that pitfall here; the reader will have to be the ultimate judge, of course. But I do not argue or even remotely suggest that conditions in Northern prisons during the Civil War were anything other than difficult and dangerous. Prisoners' barracks were often drafty, damp places with leaky roofs; food quality and quantity were not always what they ought to have been; the camps were unsanitary breeding grounds for all sorts of diseases; and Northern officials often took too long to fix serious problems in their prisons. What this book does propose is that difficult living conditions do not by themselves constitute proof of systematic negligence and cruelty and that the most reliable evidence available seriously undermines the widely held idea that Union officials conspired to make their prisons as horrible and deadly as possible. Even if the reader does not accept the idea that the Yankees were considerably more humane and reasonable in their treatment of Confederate prisoners than commonly thought, this author hopes he/she will accept that the traditional, well-established image of cruel Northern keepers can no longer stand alone as *the* interpretation of Northern policies toward and treatment of prisoners during the Civil War.

−1−

SERVANTS OF THE DEVIL AND JEFF DAVIS

THE NORTHERN VERSION OF THE POW EXPERIENCE, 1865–1920

ON APRIL 9, 1865, GENERAL ROBERT E. LEE surrendered the South's principle army and best hope for victory to General Ulysses S. Grant at Appomattox Court House in Virginia and signaled the beginning of the end of the Confederacy. Northerners everywhere were jubilant. The Civil War, which was not supposed to last so long or cost so much in lives and treasure, was finally, mercifully, over. What was not over, what in fact was only beginning, was the work of explaining to themselves, and more importantly, to future Americans, what this late conflagration meant and symbolized. Northern veterans began writing and talking about their experiences in the greatest event in American history since the Revolution almost as soon as the guns fell silent. Between 1865 and 1920 Northern writers churned out a massive body of work about the Civil War. Accounts of battles are, of course, numerous but many veterans also focused on the other aspects of soldier life—camp life, marches, forms of recreation, and the like. One area that received close attention was how Northern soldiers suffered in Confederate military prisons.

Postwar prison narratives written by Northerners between 1865 and 1920 were universally negative. When reading narratives from this era, one discovers quickly that regardless of when written they are virtually indistinguishable from each other. In fact, one will even occasionally find the same illustrations used in different books. Generally the researcher finds several charges leveled against the South. Confederates murdered Federal prisoners in cold blood on a regular basis. Union prisoners were improperly fed, when they were fed at all, and Southern authorities denied them adequate shelter from the elements. Vicious dogs, usually associated with Andersonville, tracked down escapees, mauling them for Confederates' amusement. Finally, guards tortured prisoners by various devices such as suspension by the thumbs and the use of cat o' nine tails.

Most of the postwar writing pertaining to Confederate prison life (and death) is set in the notorious Andersonville in Georgia. Books and articles set in other Southern facilities like Richmond's Libby Prison and Belle Isle in the James River and Salisbury in North Carolina do exist but they were far less popular than those using Andersonville as settings. Even before the war ended, Andersonville had gained a reputation with the Northern public as a black hole of suffering and death. Hanging its commandant, Henry Wirz, as a brutal war criminal gave such impressions the stamp of legitimacy. With Andersonville "proven" to have been a uniquely ghastly place by late autumn 1865, it is not surprising that writers would choose it as the setting for books and articles for the next half-century. These stories placed prisoners on the same plane as veterans who could tell more stories of combat; they proved that a morally corrupt element in the country had been vanquished; and they sold well too.

The notion of cruel Rebel jailors acting on orders from Jefferson Davis and other high-ranking Confederate officials did not emerge from thin air after Appomattox. During the war both sides had accused each other of inhumane treatment of prisoners. Many Northerners became convinced that Union prisoners were mistreated when newspapers published atrocity propaganda during the war's first year as a means of putting pressure on the Lincoln administration to do something to get Northern soldiers out of Confederate hands. Lincoln had been reluctant to negotiate a formal exchange agreement at the time out of fear that doing so would give the Richmond government official recognition, thus opening the door for European recognition and aid. An official exchange cartel was worked out in July 1862 and operated until its suspension in June 1863. From that point on, prison populations increased and stories of Confederate cruelty again became common.

In time of war any and all negative propaganda about one's enemy is generally accepted as unvarnished truth. It also usually follows that the actions of one's own government and soldiers during wartime are perceived as above reproach. Such was certainly the case with the prison issue. Northerners believed that their government ran spa-like resorts for

Confederate prisoners while officials in Richmond fiendishly plotted new ways to increase suffering and death among Union prisoners. Veteran and ex-prisoner Alva C. Roach, writing at the war's close, offers a good example of the average Northerners' opinion about how prisoners of war were treated during the Civil War. "While our men in Southern prisons were dying from starvation and exposure, the rebels in Northern prisons fared sumptuously every day; had good quarters, . . . and received the respect and civility due them as prisoners of war." Roach's claims of Southern cruelty were far from new or unusual. A year earlier, in the spring of 1864, some of the sickest prisoners the South held were paroled by special agreement and sent by flag-of-truce boat to Annapolis, Maryland. Being the worst cases, these parolees were in shockingly poor physical condition; some would live barely a month after their release.[1]

Federal officials were on the scene or arrived shortly after the prisoners' arrival to view their condition and gather first-hand evidence of conditions in Confederate prisons. One of these officials was the chairman of the Joint Committee on the Conduct of the War, Benjamin Wade. What Wade saw understandably horrified and angered him. Many, he commented had "literally the appearance of living skeletons, many of them nothing but skin and bone." Such specimens were not the unfortunate but inevitable by-products of war; these men were reduced to their wretched state, Wade concluded, by wicked, premeditated policy.[2]

Wade, and other Union officials on hand, were mistaken in their conclusion that the 1864 parolees were victims of Confederate cruelty, but under the circumstances it seemed to be the obvious one. Wade scoffed at Southern claims that Union prisoners were fed the same rations as Southern soldiers. How, he asked, was it possible for rations to reduce sedentary Northerners to the state of emaciation he witnessed at Annapolis while the same rations fortify "the rebel soldiers [sufficiently]...to make long and rapid marches and to offer a stubborn resistance in the field[?]" The Secretary of War, Edwin Stanton, did not think the claim that Northern captives starved on the same rations that Southern soldiers seemed to thrive on made much sense either. Even allowing that the Annapolis parolees were the worst cases, Stanton concluded that Union men in Confederate hands were not getting all they were entitled to. He spoke for most Northern officials that spring when he said that there must exist "a deliberate system of savage and barbarous treatment and starvation, the result of which will be that few, if any of the prisoners . . . will ever again be in a condition to render any service, or even to enjoy life." These official ideas about Confederate prison policies did not change after the shooting stopped.[3]

Government officials from Washington were not the only ones to investigate and report on the Annapolis prisoners. The United States Sanitary Commission was in Maryland that spring as well. The Commission's report, published in 1864, confirmed what the newspapers had been printing regularly for at least a year and reinforced officials' conclusions about Southern barbarity towards Union prisoners. The same commission, in a separate investigation in Annapolis of Southern treatment of prisoners, drew the same conclusion. "The best picture cannot convey the reality, nor create that startling and sickening sensation which is felt at the sight of a human skeleton, with the skin drawn tightly over its skull, and ribs, and limbs, weakly turning and moving itself, as if still a living man!" Repeating Wade's query, the Commission asked, "what other deduction can be drawn, than that all was a premeditated plan, originating somewhere in the rebel councels for destroying and disabling the soldiers of their enemy, who had honorably surrendered in the field." The report was never amended and stood as powerful proof of Confederate cruelty in the decades after 1865.[4]

Without a doubt, though, the most decisive act cementing images of Southern barbarity in Northern minds was the trial and execution of Henry Wirz. Union officials would have preferred to try the Confederate prison head, General John Winder, but he had died of natural causes the preceding February. In July 1865 the *New York Times* helped sustain the popular desire to hold someone or some group responsible for Southern prison policies. "The assassins of the president disposed of, the Government will next take in hand the ruffians who tortured to death thousands of Union prisoners. The laws of civilized warfare must be vindicated; and some expiation must be exacted for the most infernal crime of the century . . . ." The following month the *New York Tribune* expressed the opinion; "It is very certain that our soldiers in Southern military prisons were treated with a degree of inhumanity and barbarity that finds no parallel in modern civilization." Another Northerner railed that Andersonville's and other prisons' horrors were directly attributable to "some general design upon the part of the rebel Government . . . ." It was in this vengeance-laden atmosphere that Wirz (and through him the South) went on trial before a Northern military tribunal. Little wonder that Andersonville's most recent and best historian has noted that, "Wirz was a dead man from the start."[5]

One of the first books published after the war detailing Union prisoners' suffering at Andersonville was *The Demon of Andersonville or, The Trial of Wirz*, an abridged, newspaper-style recounting of the trial filled with "evidence" of Southern depravity as personified by Wirz. The book's title page sends the clear message that Wirz was not of this world, but was from an evil nether region. The page sports a color illustration of Wirz in an oval frame with a malevolent glare on his face. Behind the frame is a winged demon with long nails, a barbed tail, and an evil grin. According to the book, it was Wirz's demonic qualities that made him Richmond's choice to run Andersonville. Confederate authorities knew that such a heartless individual would ensure that Yankee prisoners suffered terribly and died in large numbers. General Winder, readers discover, wrote Wirz during the war to tell him, "he was wanted to torture and murder at his discretion the Union soldiers whose fate it was to be captured by the rebels." Wirz, being the fiend that he was, eagerly accepted the position.

Those delving into *The Demon of Andersonville's* "evidence" learned how Southern leaders such as Winder and their henchmen "perfected the plan of murdering the Union soldiers . . . by starvation, by overcrowding, and by exposure to all weathers." Accusations of cold-blooded murder were common in this book and would be repeated numerous times, sometimes verbatim, over the subsequent half-century. In one instance a one-legged wretch pleaded pitifully with Wirz to be let out of the stifling stockade for a little fresh air. Wirz's response was, "Shoot the one-legged Yankee devil!" According to the author, a sentinel eagerly complied by blowing part of the prisoner's head off. When authorities hanged Wirz in November 1865, the event, according to this particular book, and in the North's collective imagination, "ended the career of a faithful servant of the Devil and Jeff Davis." *The Demon of Andersonville's* tone and wild accusations were echoed in numerous memoirs and other writing by Northerners between 1865 and 1920.[6]

Far and away the most common specific charge made against the South's prison camps after the war was that the guards routinely shot prisoners without provocation. One former prisoner wrote, "The guards appear delighted to receive orders [to shoot prisoners] and seem to find real consolation in having the privilege of firing upon us on the most trivial pretext. A thirst for blood seems to characterize them." Published shortly after the war, A. O. Abbott's *Prison Life in the South* revealed how cruelly trigger-happy Southern prison personnel were. While on the way to prison, the train stopped, at which point one poor prisoner stepped out of line to relieve himself and was shot. In his 1865 book, Gilbert Sabre reported that at Belle Isle Union men were shot down for singing patriotic songs. Warren Lee Goss told readers in his 1869 memoir: "Frequently the guard fired indiscriminately into a crowd." At the end of the century another ex-prisoner reported that "prisoners were shot down in cold blood at Macon and Columbia, simply because some of the guards wanted to kill a 'Yankee'." Another claimed in 1912, "Prisoners were frequently shot without cause by the rebel officers and guard, in a spirit of malice or as a vindictive display of power, and often the act was accompanied by the language of hatred and sometimes . . . of levity."[7]

Often one finds the allegation that prison officials rewarded sentinels with furloughs or promotions for killing defenseless Yankees. Robert H. Kellogg, who testified at the Wirz trial and became something of a professional Andersonville survivor in the postwar years, writing and speaking about his ordeals there, was among the first to allege that Southern keepers were rewarded for murdering prisoners. The guard who shot a captive, according to Kellogg, "receives a furlough as a reward for the very *virtuous deed* he has done." According to another, a guard murdered a prisoner and shortly after the incident the perpetrator had new sergeant's stripes, proving that murdering prisoners was rewarded rather than punished by the Confederate government.[8]

According to at least a few Northern writers after the war, armed guards were not the only personnel in Southern prisons doing their part to kill as many Yankees as possible. Some claimed that post surgeons were very active in furthering the Confederate policy to use prisons to incapacitate and murder Union captives. *The Demon of Andersonville* points out in several places that Southern surgeons injected prisoners with poison on the pretext of vaccinating them against the dreaded smallpox. One 1870 memoir claimed that not only were prisoners poisoned, but many were injected with a hereditary disease so that survivors of captivity would return to the North to weaken and kill Yankees for generations to come. Another ex-prisoner claimed shortly after the war that Andersonville doctors ran a "dissecting house" where they conducted "experiments" on human guinea pigs. No details about the "experiments" are provided, probably to allow Northern imaginations to supply images far more gruesome than anything the writer might have been able to conjure with mere words. One narrative must have horrified readers when they read that doctors at Andersonville performed amputations on fully conscious prisoners for fun, not because such terrifying operations were necessary.[9]

Charges that Southern surgeons actively participated in programs to actually induce death were less common than the accusation that sick and wounded prisoners were ignored and/or mistreated. John Lynch of the 13th New York Cavalry painted a very nasty picture of Andersonville's medical personnel. They strolled through the stockade, Lynch said, "apparently more with the view of enjoying the sufferings of their victims than to prescribe for their relief." Augustus Hamlin wrote that Confederate doctors "gloated over the distresses of their fellow men, and delighted in the awful destruction of life which was branding with eternal infamy the manhood of their nation." The notion that a government would permit, even encourage, its doctors to neglect and mock sick and wounded prisoners was truly reprehensible and a good indication of how morally bankrupt the Confederate cause truly was.[10]

To have been murdered by a guard or a surgeon was a terrible fate to be sure, but some Northern writers pointed out that at least such deaths were generally quick. Lessel Long expressed the opinion that it "would have been doing many a poor boy a good service if they had . . . drawn [the prisoners] up in a line and shot them, instead of torturing them by the slow process of starvation and exposure." Speaking at the ceremony to dedicate the memorial to Pennsylvania's dead at Andersonville in 1909, General E. A. Carman echoed Long, saying that the "soldier who is struck down to death or wounds in battle is to be envied when compared with the slow death of exposure and starvation." In *Harper's Pictorial History of the Great Rebellion* readers discovered that thousands of helpless Union prisoners, "from weakness induced by starvation, became idiots." Henry Hernbaker, a member of the 107th Pennsylvania concluded while at Belle Isle that Richmond's policy "respecting us seemed to be to unfit us as much as possible for future service, and in order to secure this object the more speedily, they cut down our scant half rations to one-half the usual quantity. Death began to reap a rich harvest . . . ." An Andersonville survivor in the mid-1870s said rations at Andersonville were as follows:

> One day we received nearly a pint of black stock beans, cooked with a good mixture of worms, hulls, husks, etc., etc., nothing else; next day we were given a small piece of coarse corn bread, poorly baked, with sometimes about two ounces of rotten beef with sometimes a little salt.[11]

Not only were Northern prisoners allegedly denied medical care and adequate food as a matter of Southern policy, cruel Confederate officials, especially at Andersonville, denied them shelter from the elements. At

Andersonville, one survivor reported, all the trees that could have afforded some protection from the summer heat were cut down in order to increase prisoners' discomfort. There were plenty of trees that could have been cut down and given to the prisoners to make shelter with at places like Andersonville but having the inmates bake in the sizzling Southern sun and shiver on cool, damp nights was all part of the diabolical Confederate plot to weaken and kill prisoners of war. George Russell recounted for an 1886 Grand Army of the Republic audience that a lot of the prisoners at Andersonville "had no shelter at all" and had to "lay [lie] down on the pitiless earth at night with no other covering than the clothing on their backs, few of them having any blankets, chilled at night and scorched by the heat by day . . . ." Another claimed that the sun was "scorching hot here, and having nothing to protect us from its burning rays, the whole upper surface of our feet would become blistered . . . ." John Lynch guessed that at Andersonville, due to evil Richmond policies, "fully 80 per cent. of the prisoners had no protection from sun or storm." To have refused to provide even rudimentary shelter at Andersonville, where plenty of building material existed and where, according to one writer, the temperatures routinely reached between 120 and 140 degrees was truly a sign of barbaric character.[12]

Postwar critics also alleged that Confederate officials chose prison sites that were most likely to increase Union prisoners' misery and mortality. One declared that Belle Isle in Richmond "seemed to have been chosen for its capability of adding to the wretchedness to which our brave men were compelled to submit. The ground was low, wet, and flat, and calculated to breed every character of fatal diseases." Ambrose Spencer maintained that Southern officials chose Andersonville's location because the stream that ran through the stockade and served as the prisoners' water supply was "well known in that country [to be] the prolific parent of disease and death . . . ." One Andersonville survivor given to colorful expression described the same stream as "a serpent, breathing death, its mouth full of corrosive poison."

General Winder was well aware of the stream's potential for destruction, according to many Northern writers, and deliberately put Union prisoners in the position of having to rely on a disease-ridden water supply or go without. One ex-Andersonville inmate alleged that Winder had remarked in 1864, "I am going to build a pen here that will kill more Yanks than can be destroyed at the front. That marsh in the center of the pen will help kill them mighty fast." Another quote attributed to Winder in an 1866 piece reads: "I will make a pen here for the d—d Yankees, where they will rot faster than they can be sent!" Twenty-one years later another ex-prisoner claimed Winder said: "We are doing more for the Confederacy here in getting rid of the Yanks, than twenty of Lee's best regiments at the front." How prisoners would have been privy to Winder's conversations is never mentioned and, in all likelihood, never questioned by the readers who were eager for "evidence" to support their belief that the Confederate cause had been morally bankrupt with no redeeming characteristics whatsoever.[13]

In addition to murder, starvation, exposure, and neglect in pens specifically chosen for and designed to maximize suffering and death among Northern prisoners, readers of prison narratives between 1865 and 1920 learned that systematic torture was part of the Southern prison experience. Having been used to abusing slaves, the theory went, Southerners were hardened to human suffering. Consequently they routinely subjected Northern captives to thumb screws and beatings with leather whips. Prisoners were also subjected to the excruciating torture of having their thumbs tied behind their backs and being lifted several inches off the ground with all the prisoner's weight pulling on the thumbs. One prisoner claimed to have seen a fellow prisoner at Andersonville "hung by the thumbs for two hours, nearly killing him for trying to get a little something to eat." Not all postwar prison narratives go into the grisly details of how prisoners were tortured by fiendish rebels, but many do use the term "torture," leaving no doubt in the reader's mind that Union prisoners were abused physically as a matter of Confederate policy during the Civil War.[14]

Many Northerners considered Southern slaveholders' use of dogs to track down runaway slaves particularly uncivilized and cruel. Thanks largely to the description in *Uncle Tom's Cabin* of Eliza attempting to escape across the ice-choked Ohio River with her baby clutched to her breast as hounds brayed after her, nipping at her heels, this theme fit nicely into postwar prison horror tales. Numerous memoirs and books exploited this image to great effect, describing Southern keepers and their fiendish hell-hounds chasing down and mauling Union prisoners. One writer claimed he saw a returning escapee who "was badly torn by [the dogs], and was so weak he could scarcely stand up. He was sent to the hospital that night, where he died from his wounds . . . ." Northern readers also learned from these narratives that Wirz was not exactly upset when a prisoner or group of prisoners made a break for freedom. On the contrary, he purportedly enjoyed escapes, viewing them "as a relaxation from the monotony of his [ordinary] torturing." For Wirz, taking out the dogs to hunt human prey was a delightful and regular diversion. This particular theme worked so well in postwar accounts of Andersonville that some have scenes of fleeing prisoners in rags being chased and/or torn to pieces stamped on the covers or title pages.[15]

While these narratives make fascinating reading, they are not particularly useful as primary source material regarding life in Confederate prison camps during the Civil War. In the overwhelming number of cases, they were written to achieve one or a combination of objectives, which seldom included a desire to provide posterity with an unbiased, objective reporting of the Union prisoner's experience. William Marvel has recently discussed the unreliability of postwar accounts of Andersonville, describing them as full of exaggerations and often offering tales that either lack wartime corroborating evidence or contradict existing wartime records. Social, political, economic, and personal concerns among Northerners, especially veterans, drove Northern writing and played significant roles in shaping how the Union prisoner of war experience was portrayed by the victors. An examination of these factors offers a fascinating and revealing picture of how important the Civil War, or more precisely, the manipulation of its memory, was to postwar Northerners.[16]

For Northerners, victory in the war vindicated antebellum claims of moral and cultural superiority over the benighted South. As one historian has noted, "The final defeat of [the Confederacy] allowed the Yankees to . . . proclaim again their superiority in matters of war, leadership, and culture." Indeed, Northerners fully expected their defeated foemen to offer "a complete repudiation not only of what had been southern mores and beliefs, but also of all that allegiance to the Confederacy implied." White Northerners, like most Americans at the time, entered the war viewing it within a millennial framework—an Old Testament-style trial by ordeal of good versus evil. One Northern minister used that very term, describing the Union as the "New Israel . . . going through the Apocalypse on its way to the millennium, the Kingdom of God on earth."

The message emanating from Northern pulpits just prior to and during the war had been loud and clear: the war was a holy crusade against heretics. Ministers such as Henry Ward Beecher told Unionist listeners not to fear the war because God would intervene on the North's behalf because its cause was the righteous one. "Our only fear," he railed, "should be lest we refuse God's work. He has appointed this people, and our day, for one of those world-battles on which ages turn. Ours is a pivotal period. The strife is between . . . a wasting evil and a nourishing good; between *Barbarism and Civilization*." Dr. Edward Everett Hale told listeners in 1862: "We are to introduce into the South and Southwest, new men, new life, and a higher civilization." Reverend Daniel C. Eddy told one audience, "Argue as we may, our Southern people are a different race . . . . Slavery has barbarized them, and made them a people with whom we have little in common." Prison horror narratives were designed as much as anything else to fit into that prevailing attitude.[17]

In much postwar writing done by Northerners, each government's treatment of its captives (in addition to military victory) proved that the righteous and honorable cause had prevailed. Northern victory achieved more than simply quelling an internal rebellion; it had triumphed over a truly corrupt, inhumane society. In the postwar world, as Marvel has noted, "Andersonville came to signify all that was evil in the hated Confederacy." This also explains why it was discussed so much more than Libby, Belle Isle, Salisbury, and other pens. Union prisoners did not suffer, according to these writers, because of a lack of resources or any other mitigating circumstance; they suffered and died because their jailors were truly barbaric, dishonorable, unchristian people. "[W]ho ever heard before," A. O. Abbott asked in 1865, "of men who called themselves Christians coolly and on principle starving men to death for no other reason than that of fighting for their country?" One ex-prisoner claimed that Southerners were so morally and religiously perverted that they believed that "kindness shown to a Union prisoner was treason to God!" The terrible abuse and neglect of Northern prisoners was, one writer argued in 1886, "nothing but cold-blooded murder, premeditated from day to day, by these curses who were too low down in the scale to be classes in the human family." The theme that the South's mistreatment of defenseless non-combatants spoke loudly and clearly about the character of its citizens and its cause was a common one in postwar writing.[18]

Having heard from Southerners for at least twenty years before Lincoln's election how much more chivalrous, honorable, and Christian they were than Yankees, Northerners seemed to really enjoy attacking that image using Andersonville terror tales for their ammunition. Alva Roach declared that far from being the gracious gentlemen they claimed to be, Confederate officials treated him and his comrades so badly that it "would disgrace the wild Arab of the Sahara." Another survivor spoke for many when he said that Union experiences in Confederate prisons proved "Either the race of F.F.V's [First Families of Virginia] have become sadly degenerated, or they were always inferior to the people of the North." "The South boasted of its chivalry," Lessel Long wrote in 1886, "and yet no tribe of savages was ever guilty of greater barbarity." Another wrote that "The southern press and southern orators have always laid stress upon the chivalrous character of their people. History places some of the greatest crimes of which the human family have been victims at the door of the world's chivalry." Andersonville, according to another, would stand as a monument "to the everlasting shame of those concerned, and to the detriment of the fair fame of the South, its chivalry and its humanity." "Not content," another commented, "to have been the cause of the most needless war ever waged, they have affiliated themselves with crimes which are revolting to every Christian civilization except that of the chivalrous slaveholding South." One ex-prisoner called the treatment dished out by Confederate prison personnel "defiant to the principles of Christianity," which he claimed was unknown in its true form south of the Mason-Dixon Line.[19]

When not using prison narratives to tear down the myth of Southern chivalry and gentlemanliness specifically, Northern writers expended a considerable quantity of ink arguing that this issue proved beyond all doubt that the Confederacy had been generally evil and devoid of any redeeming characteristics. "It seemed that the more bitter our anguish became," one former prisoner wrote, "the more delighted were our fiendish keepers." A Libby Prison survivor said, "the general inhuman treatment we received at the hands of those having us in charge were acts . . . unparalleled in the history of civilized warfare." Such assertions that the South waged a war that violated the rules of civilized war was one of the more common elements found in postwar Northern writing about Confederate prisons. Union prisoners endured, a writer for *The Atlantic Monthly* claimed, "insults, bitter and galling threats, exposure to scorching heat by day and to frosty cold at night, torturing pangs of hunger,—these were the methods by which stalwart men had been transformed into ghastly beings with sunken eyes and sepulchral voices." Southern prison policy, according to a Union veteran, "without exception, from Virginia to Texas, was one of stupendous atrocity." Ambrose Spencer informed readers that the "laws which regulate civilized warfare, and demand kind attention for those taken in arms—were intentionally and cruelly disregarded [by the Richmond government]." When Josiah Brownell entered the Andersonville gates, he said he viewed prisoners who had been "suffering every day misery and woe such as the Evil One himself need not have been ashamed to have imposed upon his subjects."[20]

To further emphasize that the Civil War proved Northerners to be more honorable and chivalrous than their Southern brethren, much of the postwar writing juxtaposed life in Northern and Southern prisons. In a number of books and memoirs Confederate prisoners were supposedly treated with great care and humanity by Northerners. With the war scarcely over, one commentator argued that while "our men in Southern prisons were dying from starvation and exposure, the rebels in Northern prisons fared sumptuously every day; had good quarters,...and received the respect and civility due them as prisoners of war." This same writer went so far as to compare the officers' prison at Johnson's Island in Ohio to "a first class hotel." In the mid-1880s an ex-prisoner claimed that Union prisons were entirely free from "any complaint of inhumanity such as disgraced the cause of the Southern Confederacy." Hoping in 1911 to help ensure that future generations had the facts, a former Camp Morton guard wrote that "our Government dealt with its prisoners with conscientious regard for life" and "abusive treatment of [Confederate prisoners] did not enter into the code of the Union soldier." That Union prisoners did not receive any of the same "magnanimity" Southern prisoners were reportedly showered with made Confederate policies, and through them, the cause itself, seem that much more repugnant in Northern minds, which was rather the point.[21]

Gruesome tales of starvation and torture in the enemy's prisons could also play an important role in making sure that current and future generations never forgot the enormity of Union veterans' accomplishment in the Civil War. They had triumphed over a real evil in the country and in so doing had not merely maintained the Union that had existed in 1860 but had fought hard and suffered terribly to refashion the nation, passing on a new and improved version of it to their descendents. Veterans wanted, indeed they demanded, the gratitude of the country for their crusade, the success of which came at a tremendous amount of sacrifice. Nothing proved better at illustrating the courage, endurance, and patriotism of the Northern soldier of the Civil War than narratives of places like Andersonville. A generation with that level of devotion to God and country deserved, certainly in veterans' eyes, a special and exalted place in society and history.

Two good studies of the Grand Army of the Republic, a powerful veterans' lobby that emerged after the war, point out that many veterans did not think the nation was doing enough for its ex-crusaders. They expected preferential treatment for jobs and pensions as their due for services rendered in the fight of good over evil. They got no preference when it came to job security, however, and President Grover Cleveland vetoed a bill to expand the list of veterans eligible for federal pensions beyond those who had been physically disabled by combat. The GAR and other veteran advocacy groups organized to pressure the government for greater veterans' benefits, especially pensions, which was an increasingly important goal as the war generation reached retirement age. The GAR and other groups encouraged ex-prisoners to relate their experiences to remind public officials in Washington that defeating the evil Confederacy deserved more rewards in the form of pensions and that having been starved and tortured in Rebel prisons was just as physically debilitating as having been hurt on the battlefield. One historian of the era's veteran organizations has noted that a "fascination with the sufferings of prisoners of war permeated the columns of the soldier papers, as indeed it permeated much of the nonveteran discourse about the war." To become a member of the GAR, in fact, the initiate had to kneel before a coffin on which was written the name of an Andersonville victim. It is no coincidence that the last two decades of the nineteenth century saw an explosion of Andersonville narratives. And these stories had their desired effect. One bill introduced in the House of Representatives in 1880 and endorsed by the National Ex-Prisoners of War Association would pay Union veterans who had spent up to six months in any Southern prison a pension of eight dollars per month; the amount would be nine dollars for those who had spent a year or more in such facilities. By the middle of the first decade of the twentieth century pension guidelines had been liberalized to the point that virtually any Union veteran who applied got one. In 1907, for example, one of every three dollars spent by the federal government was spent on veterans' pensions.[22]

As veterans aged they thought not only about larger pensions but also about how the war years and their role in the great event of their lifetime would be remembered by later generations of Americans. They wanted to be remembered as grand heroes who had removed a diseased element from the nation. The emphasis on sectional reconciliation at the end of the century, though, threatened that interpretation. Northern veterans were not unwilling to extend the hand of friendship to ex-Confederates; the GAR even held joint reunions with former enemies. But they did not want handshakes and a general willingness to forgive the ex-Rebels to cause anyone then or later to forget which side had been wholly right and righteous and which wholly wrong and evil. Union veterans were particularly upset at the display of the Confederate flag all over the South as a sacred symbol and the return of dozens of captured flags to the South. A columnist for the *New York Tribune* captured that feeling well in 1881 when he wrote:

> As ensigns of an unholy cause the Confederate flags are, and of right ought to
> be, odious to the eyes of loyalty; but as the exponents of manly daring, forti-

tude, and devotion to an idea (although a wrong one) they are entitled to the respect of all men and well worthy the reverence of those who upheld them so bravely on the field of martial strife.

One veteran lamented that school textbooks were not doing their job at the end of the century to teach American children that the North had fought a righteous war against a sinful and traitorous enemy, being "content . . . to give the causes on each side which led up to the Rebellion, leaving the reader to his own conclusion as to the right or wrong of it." The Northern cause and the Northern one alone deserved veneration and stories of Confederate-run prison pens like Andersonville were partly designed to remind the younger generation and those that would come after the veterans were long dead that the Southern cause had been wholly and utterly wrong.[23]

Northern Republicans eagerly made prisoners' suffering part of their "bloody shirt" campaigns, which were so much a part of the political landscape of the late nineteenth and early twentieth centuries. Republicans, with a great deal of help from the powerful and active GAR, successfully painted Democratic opponents, even those with solid war records, with the Confederate/Andersonville brush. During the 1868 election year, for example, one Republican partisan reminded a crowd that their choice was between patriotic saviors of the Union and "the late Confederate army of the South, and their more treacherous allies, the Copperheads of the North." The GAR called Democrat and former Union general Francis P. Blair a "servant of the lost cause," and denounced the Democratic-controlled House of Representatives of the 1870s as the "Confederate House." Such allusions were quite damaging when being associated with the Confederacy in any way was to be associated with Davis, Wirz, and Andersonville.

In an attempt to garner the veteran vote, James G. Blaine roared in an early 1870s political debate that "neither the deeds of the Duke of Alva in the Low Countries, nor the massacre of Saint Bartholomew, nor the thumb screws and engines of torture of the Spanish Inquisition begin to compare in atrocity with the hideous crimes of Andersonville." James Garfield, a former Federal officer, was yet another politician who recognized the political hay to be made by exploiting the prisoner of war issue along with other "bloody shirt" themes. While campaigning in Toledo, Ohio, in October 1879 he addressed a group of Andersonville survivors, praising the ex-prisoners as noble heroes while hinting that his opponent ran under the standard of those who had inflicted such suffering upon them in Georgia some fifteen years earlier. "We can forgive and forget all other things before we can forgive and forget [Andersonville]." Of course the last thing Garfield wanted was for veterans and other voters to forget anything about the war that Republicans might find useful in pressuring voters to support them. John Lynch, an Andersonville survivor, railed that if you vote for Democrats "you mock the maimed forms of our numerous comrades throughout the land, and then, indeed you mock the spirits and mortal remains of the martyrs of Belle Island, Salisbury, Florence, and Andersonville."[24]

Finally, hair-raising tales of prison misery served to place former inmates on the same heroic plane as other veterans who could boast of participating in exciting, historic battles. Former prisoners did not want to be remembered by later generations as soldiers who sat out the war (possibly because they ran from it) far from harm's way, contributing nothing significant to the grand crusade to preserve and purify the Union. When reading former prisoners' memoirs one is often reminded that Federal prisoners could have escaped their terrible suffering by taking the oath of allegiance to the Confederacy. Instead, they said bold and intensely brave things like, "You can starve my body, but you shall not stain my soul with treason!" In 1914 A. J. Palmer told a gathering of former prisoners and others at Belle Isle, a stop on their journey to Andersonville to dedicate the New York monument, "I look upon these comrades that have lain here in unmarked graves so long as the supreme heroes of the war. Every single one of them had a way to escape. All you had to do was to walk out to the gate and hold up you hands and say you were ready to take the oath of allegiance to the Confederacy, and you would have walked out scot free." He then asked rhetorically, "How many of them did it? In the city of Richmond, not eighty of them, all told, but six thousand of them lie dead about our feet *rather than do that*." Martha A. I. Burdick wrote a poem for the Union prisoners that built on that theme, which read in part:

They died, and yet they might
have lived—
Might have escaped their awful
lot—
If they had bartered loyalty
for their release, but they would not.

Being a prisoner was thus just as honorable and brave as having endured the battlefields' perils, perhaps more so. Survivors' medals presented to the New Yorkers in 1914 had on one side an image of the infamous stockade with the noble words, "Death Before Dishonor" above it, making the point clearly that these prison veterans preferred risking a slow painful death to joining immoral traitors. One former prisoner argued that Andersonville "was the greatest battlefield of the war. On no other field is there any record of such mortality. As to those heroes who lived and died here in indescribable torment and misery, a grateful country will some day give credit due for unexampled loyalty under unexampled circumstances." These New Yorkers were certainly not expressing any new views on the matter. Maine's monument, for example, erected a decade earlier in 1904, reads: "In grateful memory of those heroic soldiers of Maine who died that the Republic might live, and of those who daring to live, yet survived the tortures and horrors of Andersonville Military Prison, 1864–1865."[25]

Exaggerating and fabricating tales of life in Southern prisons and then using them to pursue a variety of ends may have been very well and good for Federal veterans and Republican politicians, but white Southerners deeply resented Northerners' manipulation of the prisoner of war issue to brand them, their region, and their cause as immoral, barbaric, and dishonorable. While condescending and insulting attitudes from the North were nothing new, former Confederates felt their sting more acutely in the wake of defeat. White Southerners reacted to postbellum insults as they had to the antebellum variety, by turning them on their heads. If Northerners would use the treatment of prisoners as the litmus test to prove which side embodied noble, Christian characteristics, Southerners would do the same. Between 1865 and 1920 Confederate veterans and other Southern writers put out their side of the prison issue, one where Confederate prisoners languished in a number of Northern Andersonvilles.

Endnotes

1. Alva C. Roach, *The Prisoner of War, and How Treated* (Indianapolis, IN: Railroad City Publishing House, 1865), 67; William B. Hesseltine, *Civil War Prisons: A Study in War Psychology* (Kent: The Ohio State University Press, 1930; repr., New York: Frederick Ungar Publishing Co., 1971), 247–48; William Fletcher Thompson, *The Image of War: The Pictorial Reporting of the American Civil War* (New York: Thomas Yoseloff, 1959), 86–94.

2. House of Representatives, 38th Congress, 1st Session, "Report #67: Returned Prisoners, May 9, 1864," in *U.S. House of Representatives Reports: Fort Pillow Massacre and Returned Prisoners* (New York: Johnson Reprint Co., 1970), 1–5 (hereafter cited as *Report #67*).

3. United States War Department, *War of the Rebellion: Official Records of the Union and Confederate Armies* (Washington, D.C.: Government Printing Office, 1899; repr., Harrisburg, PA: Telegraph Press, 1971), Series II, Volume 7, 110–11 (hereafter cited as OR with all citations being from Series II unless otherwise indicated); *Report #67*, 1–5; Hesseltine, *Civil War Prisons*, 172–209; Hesseltine, ed., *Civil War Prisons* (Kent, OH: Kent State University Press, 1962), 5–8.

4. United States Sanitary Commission, *Narrative of the Privations and Suffering of United States Officers and Soldiers While Prisoners of War in the Hands of the Rebel Authorities* (Philadelphia, PA: King and Baird, 1864), 25, 68, 92–95; "Privations and Sufferings of U.S. Soldiers in Rebel Prisons," *The Atlantic Monthly* (December 1864): 777–78.

5. Quotes from the *Times* and *Tribune* in Hesseltine, *Civil War Prisons: A Study in War Psychology*, 238–39; William Marvel, *Andersonville: The Last Depot* (Chapel Hill: University of North Carolina Press, 1994), 243.

6. N.A., *The Demon of Andersonville or, The Trial of Wirz* (Philadelphia, PA: Barclay and Co., 1865), 50–51, 56, 60–63, 72, 89–90, 118–19.

7. Gilbert Sabre, *Nineteen Months a Prisoner of War* (New York: The American News Company, 1865), 58–59; A. O. Abbott, *Prison Life in the South* (New York: Harper and Brothers, 1865), 51–53, 141–43, 202–3, 314; "At Andersonville," *The Atlantic Monthly* (March 1865): 285–97; Ambrose Spencer, *A Narrative of Andersonville* (New York: Harper and Brothers, 1866), 58–59, 82; Willard W. Glazier, *The Captive, the Prison Pen, and the Escape* (Hartford, CT: H. E. Goodwin, 1868), 123–24, 186–87, 319–22, 336–39; Warren Lee Goss, *The Soldier's Story of His Captivity at Andersonville, Belle Isle, and Other Rebel Prisons* (Boston: Lee and Shepard, 1869), 85–86; Samuel S. Boggs, *Eighteen Months a Prisoner Under the Rebel Flag* (Lovington, IL: by author, 1887), 19, 38–41, 54, 65; T. H. Mann, "A Yankee in Andersonville," *The Century* (July 1890): 447–58; Asa B. Isham, *Prisoners of War and Military Prisons* (Cincinnati, OH: Lyman and Cushing, 1890), 82–84, 298; Thomas Sturgis, *Prisoners of War, 1861–1865* (New York: Knickerbocker Press, 1912), 305.

8. Robert H. Kellogg, *Life and Death in Rebel Prisons* (Hartford, CT: L. Stebbins, 1865), 146–47; Roach, 130–32; Josiah C. Brownell, *At Andersonville* (Glen Cove, NY: "Gazette" Book and Job Office, 1867; repr., Glen Cove, N.Y.: Glen Cove Public Library, 1981), 9–10, 22; Samuel J. M. Andrews, *Sufferings of Union Soldiers in Southern Prisons* (Effingham, IL: Register Print, 1870), 11; George G. Russell, *Reminiscences of Andersonville Prison: A Paper Read by Comrade Geo. G. Russell Before Post 34, GAR, Tuesday, June 22* (Salem, MA: Observer Steam Book and Job Printers, 1886); Lessel Long, *Twelve Months in Andersonville* (Huntington, IN: Thad and Mark Butler, 1886), 55; Joseph S. Keen, *Experiences in Rebel Military Prisons at Richmond, Danville,*

Andersonville (Detroit, MI: Detroit Free Press Printing Co., 1890), 191; Glazier, 120–24; Goss, 86–87.

9. Norton P. Chipman, *The Tragedy of Andersonville: Trial of Captain Henry Wirz, the Prison Keeper* (Sacramento, CA: by author, 1911), 240–353; *The Demon of Andersonville*, 61–62, 89–90; Kellogg, 253–56; Andrews, 7, 13.

10. Augustus C. Hamlin, *Martyria; or, Andersonville Prison* (Boston: Lee and Shepard, 1866), 105; Henry Hernbaker and John Lynch, *True History. Jefferson Davis Answered. The Horrors of the Andersonville Prison Pen* (Philadelphia, PA: Merrihew and Son, 1876), 11; Long, 100–3, 195–97; Boggs, 10; Goss, 23–25; Keen, 18.

11. *Harper's Pictorial History of the Great Rebellion, Volume II* (Chicago: McDonnell Brothers, 1868), 795; Eudora Clark, "Hospital Memories," in *The Atlantic Monthly* (August 1867): 144–57; Sergeant Oates, *Prison Life in Dixie* (Chicago: Central Book Concern, 1880), 203–4; Abbott, 314–15; Kellogg, 73–74; Roach, 67; Mann, 454; Glazier, vi; Goss, 168–70; Keen, 5–7, 11; Isham, 398; Hernbaker and Lynch, 4, 10.

12. *Pennsylvania at Andersonville Georgia: Ceremonies at the Dedication of the Memorial* (C. E. Aughinbaugh: Printer to the State of Pennsylvania, 1909), 25, *Harper's Pictorial History of the Great Rebellion*, 795; Long, 46–48, 57, 103, 194–95; Sabre, 23–24; Boggs, 48–49; Spencer, 20; Andrews, 16; Chipman, 240–53; Roach, 67, 212–18; Hamlin, 43–44, 54.

13. Quartermaster General's *Office, General Orders #70. The Martyrs Who, For Our Country, Gave Up Their Lives in the Prison Pen in Andersonville*, Ga. (Washington, D.C.: Government Printing Office, 1866), 8; *Harper's Pictorial History of the Great Rebellion*, 795; Long, 46–48, 57, 103, 194–95; Sabre, 23–24; Boggs, 48–49; Spencer, 20; Andrews, 16; Chipman, 240–53; Roach, 67; Hamlin, 43–44, 54.

14. Hesseltine, *Civil War Prisons: A Study in War Psychology*, 240–52; Boggs, 22, 31–32, 41–42, 61–63; Hernbaker and Lynch, 5, 11; Sabre, 50–52; Abbott, 48–50; Kellogg, 331–35, 385; Roach, 51; Clark, "Hospital Memories," in *The Atlantic Monthly* (September 1867): 324–37; "At Andersonville," 287; Hamlin, 10–11, 150; Spencer, 68–70, 78, 152; Goss, 222–23; Andrews, 7–9; Boggs, 5, 20, 38, 48–49, 55, 71–75; Isham, 278–81, 358; *Pennsylvania at Andersonville*, 26–27; Chipman, 240–353.

15. Sergeant Oates, *Prison Life in Dixie* (Chicago: Central Book Concern, 1880); Isham, 275–78; Spencer, 78; Kellogg, 63–64; Long, 172–78; Hamlin, 65–67; Abbott, 131.

16. Marvel, 243–46; Hesseltine, *Civil War Prisons: A Study in War Psychology*, 247–52.

17. Nina Silber, *The Romance of Reunion: Northerners and the South, 1865–1900* (Chapel Hill: University of North Carolina Press, 1993), 13–18; Avery Craven, *Reconstruction: The Ending of the Civil War* (New York: Holt, Rinehart, and Winston, Inc. , 1969), 67; W. Fletcher Thompson, Jr., *The Image of War: The Pictorial Reporting of the American Civil War* (New York: Thomas Yoseloff, 1979), 36; David B. Chesebrough, ed., *"God Ordained This War:" Sermons on the Sectional Crisis, 1830–1865* (Columbia: University of South Carolina Press, 1991), 2, 56–63, 88–89, 90–92, 94–102; Terrie Dopp Aamodt, *Righteous Armies, Holy Cause: Apocalyptic Imagery and the Civil War* (Macon, GA: Mercer University Press, 2002), 1–49; Steven E. Woodworth, *While God is Marching On: The Religious World of Civil War Soldiers* (Lawrence: University Press of Kansas, 2001), 93–144; Randall M. Miller, Harry S. Stout, and Charles Reagan Wilson, eds, *Religion and the Civil War* (New York: Oxford University Press, 1998), 110–30.

18. Long, 55; Abbott, 48, 315; Marvel, xi, 243.

19. Sabre, 17; Abbott, 316; Kellogg, 63–65, 363, 384; Roach, 3–4, 62; Hamlin, 10–11, 30, 43–44; Spencer, 32–35, 108; *Harper's Pictorial History of the Great Rebellion*, 792–95; Goss, 13–15, 100, 257; Andrews, 7–11, 16–17; Long 44, 55, 195, 198–99; Boggs, 5–6, 26, 48–49; Keen, 3–4, 34; Isham, 486; *Pennsylvania at Andersonville*, 91–93; Chipman, 299–300; Sturgis, 275–78; Deborah B. West, "Image of the South: As Presented by Select Northern Magazines, 1865–1880," Master's Thesis, Florida State University, 1959, 9–13, 54–74; Douglas Gibson Gardner, "Andersonville and American Memory: Civil War Prisoners and Narratives of Suffering and Redemption," Ph.D. Dissertation, Miami (OH) University, 1998, 3.

20. *A Pilgrimage to the Shrines of Patriotism: Being the Report of the Commission to Dedicate the Monument Erected by the State of New York, in Andersonville, Georgia* (Albany, N. Y.: J.B. Lyon, Printers, 1916), 108; *Pennsylvania at Andersonville*, 40–41, 71, 91–93; Sturgis, 275; Chipman, 240–353; Isham, 398; Keen, 3–4; Boggs, 5; Long, 44, 179; Andrews, 6, 16; Goss, 100; Brownell, 7; Spencer, 147; Hamlin, 150; Clark, "Hospital Memories," *The Atlantic Monthly* (August 1867): 147; Roach, 51; Abbott, 201; Hesseltine, *Civil War Prisons: A Study in War Psychology*, 238–40, 251–58.

21. Sabre, 25–26; Abbott, 206; Kellogg, 73–74; Roach, 67–69; Oates, 203–4; Long, 198–99; Isham, 134–46; Sturgis, 270–78; *A Pilgrimage to the Shrines of Patriotism*, 94, 133; Hernbaker and Lynch, 7.

22. Stuart McConnell, *Glorious Contentment: The Grand Army of the Republic, 1865–1900* (Chapel Hill: University of North Carolina Press, 1992), xi–xv, 15–21, 94–97, 123–53, 167, 179; Mary R. Dearing, *Veterans in Politics: The Story of the G.A.R.* (Baton Rouge: Louisiana State University Press, 1952),

50–79, 86, 278–84, 309–16, 334–38, 439–42, 466–69; Hesseltine, *Civil War Prisons: A Study in War Psychology*, 247–51.

23. McConnell, 182–87, 190–92, 225–26; Dearing, 117, 408–11; *Pennsylvania at Andersonville*, 46–48.

24. Gardner, 105–17; McConnell, 15, 123–53; Dearing, 16, 50–79, 116, 131, 149–51, 160, 186, 230, 278–84, 334–38; Hesseltine, *Civil War Prisons: A Study in War Psychology*, 248–50; Oates, 199–205; Lynch, 13–14.

25. Gardner, 70, 232–45; *A Pilgrimage to the Shrines of Patriotism*, 44, 99–102, 120–21; *Pennsylvania at Andersonville*, 19, 30–32, 57, 71, 91

–2–

THE LOST CAUSE AND THE SOUTHERN SIDE OF THE POW DEBATE

1865–1920

IN APRIL 1865 THE CONFEDERACY DIED for all intents and purposes when Generals Robert E. Lee and Joseph E. Johnston surrendered the South's principle armies to Generals Ulysses S. Grant and William T. Sherman respectively. While white Southerners grieved for their lost cause, Northerners celebrated wildly. Their joy came not only from victory and the chance to finally return home to loved ones; it came also from the conviction that right had triumphed over wrong. The idea that the Confederate States of America had been a morally bankrupt society received official and public legitimacy during Andersonville commandant Henry Wirz's trial and subsequent execution before the year was out.

Ex-Confederates did not want to be remembered as traitors or as members of a degraded society who were defeated by a righteous foe. Many, probably most, white Southerners feared that the victors' history would become the official version of the Civil War—a concern not without precedent. Jefferson Davis expressed the concern many in his region harbored, warning, "Men live in the estimation of posterity not by their deeds alone, but by their historians also." To make sure the victors' history was not the only one that would be available, Davis wrote his massive version of events, *The Rise and Fall of the Confederate Government*. He made no claims about historical objectivity; this was going to be the pro-Confederate side of the story. By his own admission the project was undertaken to do "justice to the cause and add wherever I could another leaf to her crown of glory."[1]

That Davis and other Southerners would attempt to portray the Confederate era as a romantic and glorious crusade is not surprising. Nobody wants to be associated with a losing side that lacked any redeeming qualities, which was precisely how Northerners were portraying the former Confederacy and its supporters. An additional burden was the understanding and acceptance by both sides that the war had been a conflict where God would grant victory to the righteous side. Throughout the war, Confederates never doubted ultimate victory because they never doubted their moral superiority to the Yankees. As minister Benjamin Palmer put it in a June 1861 sermon, "at the very opening of our separate career, we bend the knee together before God—appealing to his justice in the ajudication [*sic*] of our cause, and submitting our destiny to his supreme ajudication."[2]

Throughout the war, Davis called for fast days and days of prayer to insure God's continued support for the Confederacy and its armies in the field. An Atlanta newspaper reminded readers, "our cause is just, and a righteous Judge and God of Battles will decide in our favor." J. W. Tucker, a minister in Fayetteville, North Carolina, maintained, "God is with us . . . . He is on our side . . . . Our cause is just." Tucker went on to tell listeners that the Civil War was "a conflict of truth with error—the Bible with Northern infidelity—of pure Christianity with Northern fanaticism—of liberty with despotism—of right with might." The Baptist minister J. William Jones spoke to his congregation of the "God of Israel, God of the centuries, God of our forefathers, God of Jefferson Davis and Albert Sidney Johnston and Robert E. Lee and Stonewall Jackson, and the God of the Southern Confederacy." Methodist bishop George Foster Pierce proclaimed in the spring of 1863 that "The triumph of our arms is the triumph of right and truth and justice. The defeat of our enemies is the defeat of wrong, malice, and outrage." By October 1864 Confederate victories were harder to come by, causing Brigadier General Stephen Dodson Ramseur's brother-in-law to doubt the possibility of ultimate Southern victory. "Don't give up," Ramseur told him. "We are bound to succeed. The God of Justice will order all things for the good."[3]

While not all Southerners were able to rally around the idea that no matter how bad things appeared God would come through for His people, most did, even when their fortunes looked bleakest. To General Sherman such a state of affairs seemed wholly illogical and he commented on this to his wife in 1864. "No amount of poverty or adversity seems to shake their faith," he wrote. "Wealth and luxury gone, money worthless, starvation in view within a period of two or three years, are causes enough to make the bravest tremble, yet I see no sign of let up—some few deserters—plenty tired of war, but the masses determined to fight it out." What Sherman failed to understand was that Southerners simply but fervently believed that they and their cause were righteous and no amount of earthly war materiel from the North could defeat a people protected by Providence.[4]

At the end of the Civil War, the South was faced with a rather serious intellectual dilemma. On the one hand there seemed to be evidence that God had not looked favorably on the South after all and that the Richmond authorities, if the testimony given at the Wirz trial was to be believed, had been quite brutal and unchristian towards helpless prisoners of war. On the other hand, ex-Confederates did not want to accept that God favored the Yankees over themselves or that Southern honor had been forever sullied by its gross mistreatment of Northern prisoners during the war. Southerners resolved the crisis by creating a model for interpreting the Civil War era that came to be known as the Lost Cause. This model allowed Southerners to take pride in their Confederate past in part by denying that God had played much, if any role, in the military outcome and by arguing that the true story of how prisoners were treated showed that the South had been humane and Christian in its care of prisoners while Northerners had been the true demons. How each side prosecuted the war and conducted itself in battle became more important in the Lost Cause school than ultimate victory or defeat. That model taught, among other things, that losing carried no stigma and could even be called heroic if one fought nobly and chivalrously against a huge and unprincipled foe who thought no barbarity outside the boundaries of civilized warfare.

Part of the multi-pronged battle plan for creating a pro-Confederate version of the war was proving that military victory was not a Divine condemnation of the South. This was critical since Southerners had spent the war years attributing victory and defeat in battle as signs of God's approval or lack thereof. Besides, Southerners could not continue to view themselves as superior to Yankees if Appomattox were accepted by the South as God's will and His statement about the region's moral inferiority vis-à-vis the North. Richmond editor Edward A. Pollard worried that if defeat were not attributed to more earthly factors Southerners would feel the need to abandon their traditional and distinctive culture to become more like their Northern superiors. "It would be immeasurably the worst consequence of defeat in this war," he wrote in 1865, "that the South should lose its moral and intellectual distinctiveness as a people, and cease to assert its well-known superiority in civilization . . . and in all the standards of individual character over the people of the North."[5]

Southerners, the Lost Cause taught, could continue to hold their heads high and look Yankees defiantly in the eye because they had fought well and honorably and had been defeated *only* because the Federals had had more men and supplies. The region's inhabitants accepted readily the sentiment expressed in the little verse that went,

The Yankees did not whip us boys,

No, never let it be said,

We wore ourselves out whipping them,

And stopped for want of bread.

In the years after the war, Edward McCrady summed up many Southerners' feelings about how they lost the Civil War. He explained, "the war was one of machinery against chivalry, in which the knight-errant was bound to be run over by the locomotive." Another Confederate veteran told an ex-foeman at a reunion: "Your people whipped us because you had five times as many men as we had, and all the money and rations you wanted, and I don't think I ever heard that God gave one half-starved man the strength to whip five fully-fed men." Such expressions were common in the region after the war and were not entirely lacking evidence to support them. However, they were less attempts to objectively explain the war's outcome than they were attempts to show that Northerners had won primarily because they possessed advantages the South lacked, giving the former something of an unfair advantage in their fight.[6]

Ex-Confederates made the case in the postwar years that they lacked the might to win the Civil War but that did not mean that they and their cause had been wrong. As Wade Hampton told a gathering of the old Washington Artillery in 1878, "right shall make might my friends. We may not see it here on earth, where truth so often goes down before falsehood . . . but in the last great reckoning . . . you who have stood by this right shall on that day find that right shall prevail." Another former Confederate echoed the idea that "the sword in and of itself never made any cause right, and the outcome of battles does not affirm the truth of political or even religious questions." Occasionally one even finds that defeat was not a negative verdict from Heaven on the South's society and its people but actually was proof that He still favored them over the Northerners. "Defeat," Richmond's Second Presbyterian Church's pastor said at the 1875 dedication of the Stonewall Jackson monument there, "is the discipline which trains the truly heroic soul to further and better endeavors." Of course such sentiment was completely at odds with wartime rhetoric, but then the Lost Cause was not about accuracy; it was about building a pro-Southern version of the Civil War era.[7]

One theme commonly found in Lost Cause "history" is that how each side conducted itself in battle and prosecuted the war proved who was right and who was wrong. A contributor to *Confederate Veteran* in 1921 made a point that by that time was very familiar to Southerners. "It has been said," he wrote, "that 'war is one of the strongest evidences in the world of the imperfections of modern civilization,' and the manner in which it is waged is an evidence of the degree or character of the civilization attained by those engaged in it." Having been Crusading Christian Confederates, to borrow Charles Wilson's apt characterization, was far more laudable than having been a victor who, while having won, did so by dishonorable and immoral methods. Much was made (and still is among many Southerners) of Sherman's March to the Sea and Lee's Pennsylvania raid. "To [Southerners'] everlasting honor," claimed one, "stands the fact that on their march through the enemy's country they left behind them no ruined homes, no private houses burned, no families cruelly robbed . . . ." *The Land We Love*'s masthead proclaimed, "No nation rose so white and fair, or fell so pure of crimes." A postwar song entitled "The Sword of Lee" described it as, "shrouded now in its sheath again, it sleeps the sleep of our noble slain, defeated, yet without stain . . . ."

The idea that the Confederates, in stark contrast to the Yankees, had fought a purely honorable and chivalrous war was extremely common in Lost Cause literature. In the early twentieth century a veteran told a group of fellow ex-Confederates during a ceremony presenting them with the Southern Cross of Honor that "The rising generation will stand with uncovered heads in your presence and thank God that our South land can produce such chivalric manhood." The great Confederate heroes like Lee, Jackson, and others were portrayed not simply as great war leaders; they were also paragons of virtue and Christian morality. On one of Jackson's monuments in Richmond was inscribed, "Warrior, Christian, Patriot." Lee became one of the "Christian heroes of the ages." The message was made so often that it was impossible to miss; the South had fought an honorable war and played by the rules of war while the Yankees "had set at defiance the plainest laws of civilized warfare."[8]

The prisoner of war issue figured prominently in the battle for how the Civil War would be remembered in the South just as it was in the North.

Andersonville atrocity stories, along with Wirz's execution for gross cruelty, potentially called Confederate character and conduct during the Civil War into serious question. Yankee accusations of Southern barbarity at Andersonville had to be thoroughly refuted if Southerners were to effectively drape their cause and their region with the mantle of moral superiority over the Yankees. Moreover, Andersonville's stigma had to be removed lest it give credence to the Northern version of the war and make future generations of Southerners feel shame at having descended from dishonorable ancestors. In 1869 Joe Barbiere made it quite clear that his book, *Scraps from the Prison Table*, was designed to teach the rising generations that writing by Northerners about Andersonville was not to be believed.

> I hope every true child of the South—who love their ancestry and their heroic deeds—will read carefully, and when the lying histories of a fanatical party, speaks of the so-called horrors of Andersonville, let the youth of the South know, that it is written, to hide the cruelties practiced by our enemies upon Confederate prisoners.[9]

Postwar Southerners were extremely concerned and angry about Northern exploitation of Andersonville because it cast the Confederacy and its supporters in such a terrible light. Losing the war had been bad enough, but portraying Southerners as fiendish, immoral, un-Christian barbarians was too much salt for Southern wounds. Andersonville literature motivated a number of writers to destroy the "web of falsehood" woven by Union veterans and other Northerners regarding Andersonville and other Confederate prisons during the Civil War. John William Jones, writing in 1876, made no bones about his motivation for writing. He was outraged over the numerous Northern reports and memoirs about Andersonville that he branded as attempts "to asperse the honor of the [South by charging it] with deliberate and willful cruelty to prisoners of war." Reuben Clark of Tennessee, himself a former prisoner of war, wrote, "We have heard much of Andersonville Prison, and doubtless the privations and sufferings of prisoners at that place were very great; but great as they were, they have been much exaggerated . . . ." It seemed to one Southerner at the end of the century that the region's officials and writers "have never been able to satisfy the minds of the people of the Northern States in regard to the treatment of Federal prisoners confined in Southern prisons, and especially in the prison at Andersonville, Ga. They have always held it as a blot on our record, and we have been unable to inform them fully of the facts."[10]

To provide a lasting and tangible reminder to future Americans that Andersonville left no dishonorable stain upon the Confederate cause, an effort was made to erect a monument to Henry Wirz at the site of the former prison. Northern states' erection of monuments to Andersonville victims there played a major role in the decision to make sure a pro-Confederate rebuttal monument had a place as well. In December 1905 *Confederate Veteran* applauded the work of the United Daughters of the Confederacy in rallying support and money for the erection of a monument "to our Southern martyr, Capt. Wirz, in solemn protest against the unjust calumnies of the monuments erected at that place by the North regarding the treatment of their prisoners at that prison. Too long have they gone unrefuted, while eternal truth demands their refutation." The following month the magazine published the resolutions of the Georgia Division of the UDC's which concluded that Wirz had been "judicially murdered under false charges of cruelty to prisoners," and that a monument was necessary because Yankees kept making "after an interval of forty years these false charges . . . on signboards, in private places, from the pulpit, and on monuments . . . ." This idea that Wirz was an innocent victim of Yankee injustice, one that would eventually end up written in stone, was less about making sure an innocent man's name was cleared than it was about clearing the Confederacy's name. Rarely, if ever, does one find in the Lost Cause-era's literature about Andersonville and Wirz a piece that does not directly tie Wirz's innocence to the South's.[11]

One method Southerners employed to refute Northern assertions that the Confederacy treated Union prisoners rather brutally, as evidenced by Andersonville, was simple inversion: claiming that the opposite was true. According to Lost Cause-era writers Southern prisons were relatively healthy places and Northern prisoners were treated very well despite the difficulties imposed by the North's blockade and destruction caused by the war. During the war, these writers argued, 26,436 of the 220,000 Confederates held by the North died, a mortality rate of 12%. That statistic became an important weapon in the Lost Cause arsenal because it was higher than the mortality rate among Union prisoners in Confederate care. Southern writers after the war often claimed that despite serious shortages only 22,576 of the 270,000 Union prisoners held by the Confederacy died, a mortality rate of 8.36%. Unlike the well-supplied North, one Southerner wrote in 1898, "the Confederate Government did all that could possibly be done for the well-being of Federal soldiers . . . ." This idea was expressed often by Southern writers in the postwar era; it seemed to be cold hard evidence that the Confederacy had acted with utmost humanity towards Federal prisoners at all times thus refuting Northern accusations and actually turning them on their heads.[12]

The problem is that the numbers given here and used quite often by Southern writers after the war was that they were contained in a report by Federal Surgeon-General Joseph K. Barnes that was lost—if it ever existed. Not only is evidence lacking that this report ever existed, the numbers are not supported by any other wartime documents, official or otherwise. Furthermore, they conflict with those provided by the *Official Records* published at the end of the century, which indicate that a greater percentage of Union prisoners died in captivity, not the other way around.

For Southerners to have tried to get away with presenting an argument that made Confederate prisons sound like relatively pleasant places would have been going too far and they realized that. After all, the mortality figures and photographs of emaciated Andersonville victims were powerful counterarguments. Southerners did not attempt therefore to claim that no suffering existed in their camps. Rather they presented the suffering and mortality that occurred in Confederate military prisons as ultimately the North's responsibility. Postwar Southern writers absolved Confederate prison officials, and by extension the South, of wrongdoing by claiming that necessary supplies were denied to the Southern officials because the North waged an unnecessarily destructive war. As the war dragged on, the Confederacy, due to Yankee armies that burned foodstuffs and destroyed crops and livestock as they marched, had difficulty feeding its troops and citizens. That situation, combined with an increasingly effective naval blockade, created serious supply crises in the South; the capital city itself experienced food riots during the war. Given that situation, Southern writers argued that nobody should be surprised that Federal prisoners suffered right along with Confederate soldiers and civilians. Had the Confederacy had access to the necessary provisions, this argument concluded, officials would have made certain that prisoners received them.[13]

That argument had several attractive qualities to recommend it to postwar Southerners. For one thing, like many Lost Cause myths, it was not without a kernel of truth. The Confederacy did suffer from supply problems that worsened as the war progressed and Southern diaries document those serious shortages. Further, those shortages were caused by Federal policies that had hardened, especially after 1862, towards the Rebels and broadened significantly the list of legitimate targets for destruction. And last but certainly not least, it rinsed Southern hands clean of Union prisoners' blood and transferred it to Northern hands. Postwar writers in the South thus declared often that their officials did all they could under the circumstances for Yankee prisoners but callous Federal policies and actions precluded their doing more to mitigate suffering and mortality in places like Andersonville.[14]

In a classic case of what sociologists would label "blaming the victim," some writers after the war actually blamed the Andersonville inmates themselves for their mortality, or at least a good bit of it, in an attempt to absolve the Confederacy of any wrongdoing. The Yankees were animalistic in every sense of the word and created an environment at Andersonville highly conducive to disease mortality. According to one postwar propagandist, Andersonville prisoners exhibited such an "abominable disregard" for all sanitary regulations "that if a conspiracy had been entered into by a large number of the prisoners to cause the utmost filth and stench, it could not have accomplished a more disgusting result." The post's chief surgeon, R. Randolph Stevenson, reinforced that argument in 1876, stating that the Yankee prisoners "seemed to become indifferent to the ordinary decencies of life, and many of them grew filthy and disgusting in their habits . . . [as those] with whom there is no sense of shame or moral restraint." Federal prisoners, according to Stevenson, who "paid a strict regard to personal cleanliness escaped the pestilence [diarrhea and dysentery]." The conclusion was obvious to Southerners: Wirz and other officials (like Stevenson) were not responsible for forcing dirty Yankees to get clean if they preferred to remain filthy. Had the prisoners at Andersonville simply taken some personal responsibility for their own hygienic needs they would not have perished in such numbers.[15]

The Northerners' propensity for living in filth was not the only reason some Southern writers suggested caused the bulk of their sickness and mortality in Confederate prisons. Allegedly the Yankees had weaker stomachs and digestive tracts than Southerners. Federal prisoners certainly got the same rations as Southern soldiers; they just had problems digesting them. The staple Confederate ration was corn meal and Union prisoners at Andersonville either refused to eat it or it made a painfully quick trip through digestive tracts used to softer wheat bread. The famous photographs and woodcuts of Andersonville survivors who more closely resembled skeletons than healthy human beings did not support Northern propaganda about Confederate cruelty, but rather reflected the general Yankee inability to adapt to Southern food ways. This particular claim was not common, but it did provide one more argument to prove that the South had nothing to be ashamed of in its treatment of Union prisoners during the Civil War.[16]

Yankee prisoners were also alleged to have been quite irresponsible with the "wholesome and nutritious" rations they received. Some claimed after the war that Andersonville inmates sold their food rations to buy whiskey and tobacco. Northern prisoners were even said to have sold their clothes to obtain these articles they were so addicted to. Neither Wirz nor any other official could have done much about Northerners' willingness to sell and barter away vital necessities in order to indulge in certain fleeting pleasures. If Union prisoners went hungry or strolled about the compound in rags the fault lay with the prisoners. No doubt there was some truth to these reports. However, the wildly exaggerated claim made in some post-war accounts that a significant number of Andersonville prisoners regularly gambled themselves into starvation was over the top.[17]

The claim was also made that prisoners at Andersonville were victimized by fellow inmates rather than by Southern officials. If food was sometimes scarce at the prison, thanks to the Yankees' methods of prosecuting the war, the situation was made worse because Federal prisoners stole food from one another. Thus if some prisoners did starve to death or suffer from malnutrition at Andersonville, the fault was again on the Federal side. This argument that, once again, the blame for Union prisoners' suffering lay in a more northerly direction was not without some basis in fact. There was a group of prisoners who called themselves "Mosby's Raiders," after the Virginia guerrilla, that preyed on other prisoners, especially newcomers and the weak. The "Raiders" were eventually caught and Wirz allowed the prisoners to mete out whatever punishment they deemed just to this group of six. The prisoners tried them and sentenced them to death and Wirz allowed those condemned to be hanged within the stockade.

There can be little doubt that the despicable group was responsible for increasing suffering among some prisoners and were responsible for some deaths at Andersonville. The implication that six rogues were responsible for the suffering and deaths of hundreds, even thousands, is difficult to accept, however. Besides, mortality did not suddenly decline after the "Raiders'" executions. That did not matter in the years following Wirz's trial as Southerners grasped at any argument that would exonerate the Confederacy of wrongdoing regarding prisoners of war. When arguments managed to put the blame on the Yankees, so much the better.[18]

The argument Southerners relied on most often, however, was to place the blame for prisoners' suffering and death on Washington officials for suspending the prisoner exchange cartel in the spring of 1863. In July 1862 both governments agreed to a general exchange cartel after months of debate on the subject. Neither side had expected to have to care for large numbers of prisoners and neither particularly wanted to do so. The main obstacle had been Lincoln's concern that an official agreement would constitute recognition of the Confederacy as an independent nation by the United States, potentially opening the door for more direct European aid to the South. The Federal government, under considerable public pressure, relented and an agreement based on the one made between the Americans and the British during the War of 1812 went into effect and virtually emptied both sides' prisons to the delight of prisoners and their families.[19]

In May 1863, though, Washington suspended the cartel indefinitely and exchanges, with limited exceptions, ceased. The cartel's suspension led to mushrooming prison populations in both regions and overcrowding, disease, and death resulted in large numbers in many military prisons. Thousands of Union and Confederate soldiers who had hoped to serve their respective countries on the field of battle wound up fighting for their lives in prisoner of war camps. Tragically, thousands of them lost that battle. Had the cartel remained in effect it is likely that most of those would have lived— if only to die of disease in their own army or on the battlefield. It is indisputable that halting exchanges led to conditions in both sides' prison facilities that were highly conducive to a wide variety of deadly microbes. Given that reality, Southerners during the half-century or so after the war placed the mortality in *all* Civil War prison camps on the North's doorstep because the Yankees were the ones who decided to quit exchanging prisoners.

As with the other arguments Southern writers made during the postwar period to deflect blame away from Richmond and redirect it northward, there is some basis for this conclusion. The Federal authorities *did* suspend exchanges in the spring of 1863, a decision that had dire consequences for soldiers unlucky enough to find themselves in any of the war's military prisons. However, as will be discussed more fully in the fourth chapter, the North had legitimate reasons for doing so. The most important reason exchanges were halted was that the Confederacy refused to treat African American soldiers as entitled to all the rights and privileges as whites. Official Confederate policy stipulated quite clearly that black soldiers captured in combat could be sold into slavery or put to death along with their white officers. To protect those soldiers and officers, the Federals decided that exchanges would not resume until Richmond rescinded that policy, which it never did.

Sometimes Southern writers of this period simply ignored the reason Federal officials gave for suspending the cartel, preferring to point out that the North halted exchanges and allow readers to infer that no justifiable basis could have existed for condemning thousands on both sides to extended periods of uncomfortable, potentially lethal, confinement in enemy prison pens. Those who did address it claimed it was not the real reason the cartel was suspended. By 1863 the North held more prisoners than the South, making it in its best interest at that point to quit exchanging prisoners. With this in mind, Union officials, one writer claimed, "invented every possible pretext" to keep from exchanging prisoners. The issue of black troops was nothing more, another informed readers, than a "subterfuge to prevent exchanges." For the Yankees, humanitarian considerations were secondary to winning the war.[20]

Lost Cause writers portrayed the Confederate leaders as being horrified by the North's decision to stop exchanging prisoners. Southern officials realized that the decision would doom thousands to the experience of trying to survive in miserable conditions and in many cases death. Moved solely by Christian compassion for their fellow men, Confederate officials began negotiating with Washington to get the 1862 exchange agreement reinstated in order to spare soldiers on both sides "the necessity of prison life with all its attendant horrors." An 1896 contributor to *Confederate Veteran* told readers that Southern officials had begged Union officials to lift the cartel's suspension out of a "sense of honor and common humanity" during the last two years of the war only to be coldly rebuffed at every turn. "The South was clamorous and persistent for a fair exchange," another partisan reported in 1905, "but was denied by the United States government." Even when Richmond officials explained to Union authorities in 1864 and 1865 that supply shortages were increasing the suffering of Northern prisoners, Washington turned a deaf ear. Secretary of War Edwin Stanton, the best example of hard-hearted Yankees, is supposed to have replied to humanitarian pleas from Richmond by saying: "No, we will make no exchanges; our men in your hands must suffer." Another summed up Southern opinion on this question very well, writing in 1894 that "The milk of human kindness seemed to have been squeezed out of Uncle Sam's official heart."[21]

Having tried to do the right thing only to be blocked by Northern officials lacking any sense of Christian humanity, Lost Cause-era writing concluded that prisoner mortality during the Civil War, all of it, was the North's fault. In his book, *The Confederate View of the Treatment of*

Prisoners, John William Jones asked rhetorically: "since the Federal Government turned a deaf ear to all of these appeals [to resume exchanges], are *they* not responsible before God and at the bar of history *for every death that ensued?*" (emphasis in original). Jefferson Davis and Alexander Stephens both wrote that the North's suspension of the 1862 exchange cartel was the root cause of all prisoner mortality during the war. Davis explained that he never dreamed the Federals would stoop to halting exchanges. Washington officials, he argued, made prisoner of war policy with a "marked . . . degree of cold-blooded insensibility which we had not anticipated." Therefore, "On them rests the criminality for the sufferings of these prisoners." As late as 1916 contributors to *Confederate Veteran* were still hammering this theme. One writer that year repeated the by-then familiar argument that halting exchanges was the key factor in prisoner suffering and death and since the North had halted exchanges, "the suffering and death of every wretched prisoner, not only in the Andersonville 'hell hole,' but everywhere North and South" was to be laid squarely on Northern heads.[22]

While arguments that Northern policies caused prisoners' suffering and death were common in the postwar South, far more popular were hair-raising tales of unspeakable cruelty Southern prisoners endured in Federal captivity. Showing that Yankee prison officials actively took a role in increasing suffering and death offered the most solid proof that victory had not gone to the righteous or morally superior side in the Civil War. A Rock Island survivor declared in 1912, "There are no words adequate to depict or describe the terrible suffering and the outrageous cruelties and barbarities that were inflicted upon the prisoners there by those in charge. It is almost beyond belief. The arch fiend himself could not have devised a more diabolical scheme of cruelty." According to Mississippian Lamar Fontaine, "The acts of our so-called humane heads of the most powerful, civilized and enlightened government on earth, through their treatment of us, has [*sic*] put a foul blot upon our country's history that time cannot efface."

Most Southerners were uninterested in effacing such blots. They were actually far more interested in bringing them to light and dwelling on them in vivid detail. Hundreds of writers in the fifty years after Lee's surrender embarked on a mission to prove "that the sufferings of the Confederate prisoners in Northern 'prison pens' were terrible beyond description; that they were starved in a land of plenty; that they were frozen where fuel and clothing were abundant; that they suffered untold horrors for want of medicine, hospital stores, and proper medical attention; that they were shot by sentinels, beaten by officers, and subjected to the most cruel punishments upon the slightest pretext . . . ." Tragically, as Confederate prisoners discovered, "a fiendish love of suffering" drove Northern prison policy.[23]

A favorite theme in Southern writing on the prisoner of war issue was that Confederate prisoners starved to death in a land of plenty. One writer described the North, accurately, as a place "flowing with plenty" while, not so accurately, "our men died by the thousands from causes which the Federal authorities *could* have prevented" (emphasis in original). "The Federal Government," another argued, "was rich, its resources unlimited, and it had all the world to draw upon. If there was an exercise of inhumanity, the Confederate government may have had an excuse. The Federal government had none."

A 1905 article printed in *Confederate Veteran* informed readers, "Though in a land flowing with plenty, our poor fellows in prison were famished with hunger, and would have considered half the rations served Federal soldiers bountiful indeed." A former inmate at Johnson's Island said that "to be hungry, night and day for six months, and that too, in the midst of plenty, was hard, to say the least of it." Robert Little claimed he saw grown men "cry like children because they were hungry." Speaking to a group of veterans and others at the Stonewall Camp of the United Confederate Veterans in 1904, James Crocker related that being hungry in Federal prisons "was a cruel, bitter treatment, and that too, by a hand into which Providence had poured to overflowing its most bounteous gifts." This theme even made it into songs like "I'm a Good Old Rebel," which went, in part,

> I followed old mas' Robert
> for four years near about,
> got wounded in three places,
> and starved at Pint Lookout.

A poem about Fort Delaware told veterans,

> Oh, speak out, young soldiers, and let your country hear
> All about your treatment at Fort Delaware—
> How they work you in the wagons, when weary and sad,
> With only half rations, when plenty they had.

The theme of starvation amid plenty is quite common in Southern writing about the prisoner of war experience during the Lost Cause era. Yankees appear particularly dastardly and dishonorable because they had the means to mitigate greatly Confederate prisoners' suffering and death but chose to withhold them. Not coincidentally, the theme dovetailed nicely with the Lost Cause interpretation of Confederate defeat wherein the South was not beaten but overwhelmed by a well-supplied foe who refused to fight according to the rules of chivalry and civilized warfare.[24]

Related to the common complaint that Federal authorities refused to adequately feed Confederate prisoners was that they refused to supply Southern inmates with adequate protection from the elements. Former prisoners often complained in postwar memoirs and testimonials that they were robbed of blankets and other clothing and forced to survive in unheated barracks or tents. This uncomfortable situation was presented as part of a premeditated plan originating in the Northern War Department. The historian researching this topic will not have to dig long to find stories of prisoners freezing to death or losing limbs and digits to frostbite for want of adequate housing, blankets, and fuel. The conclusion Southern readers reached was that the Federals could have saved hundreds, perhaps thousands, of Confederate prisoners' lives had they not been so cruel as to withhold wood and coal during harsh Northern winters. Such supplies were available in great abundance but Union officials simply preferred that prisoners in their care suffer as much as possible. The result was more suffering and mortality among Confederate prisoners than ought to have occurred given the North's resources.[25]

Postwar Southern writing about the treatment of prisoners, like Northern writing, contended that Confederate prisoners were routinely subjected to a variety of physical abuse worthy of the Middle Ages. In these narratives Northerners became psychotic beasts who beat and tortured helpless prisoners for the sick pleasure they derived from it. Guards were portrayed as beating prisoners with sticks, belts, fists, or anything that happened to be handy at the moment. Prisoners attempting to defend themselves from such unprovoked and cowardly attacks were certain to get shot in these stories.

The most commonly cited torture was suspension by the thumbs for long periods of time. Never pointed out in these stories by Northern or Southern writers was that this particular form of punishment was fairly common in the military at that time. This punishment consisted of tying a man's thumbs to a string draped over a tree limb or a spike driven into a pole or some other stationary object so that only his toes touched the ground. By modern standards such treatment is brutal and unnecessary but by mid-nineteenth century American standards it was viewed as an effective means of making sure rules were obeyed. Suspension by the thumbs in the manner just described may have been used in Northern prisons and likely was (just as it was in Confederate prisons) as a way to ensure conformity to regulations in facilities where a comparatively small group armed with single-shot weapons had to maintain order and security.

According to Lost Cause-era writing, the Yankees made some modifications in order to inflict a great deal more pain. A number of former prisoners claimed that Northern guards suspended prisoners entirely off the ground by their thumbs. One said he witnessed prisoners at Johnson's Island suspended in such a manner and that the poor victims "would grow so deathly sick that they would vomit all over themselves, their heads [would] fall forward and almost every sign of life [would] become extinct . . . ." Not only that, but "the ends of their thumbs would burst open; a surgeon standing by would feel their pulse and say he thought they could stand it a little longer." Others, unfortunately, could not. A former Fort Delaware resident alleged that officials there hung prisoners by the thumbs until they died.

In addition to sadistic thumb suspension, there were other forms of physical abuse in the camps. At Camp Chase, one commentator said, prisoners who had been caught attempting to escape "were taken out in the presence of the garrison and tortured with the thumb screw until they fainted with pain." Occasionally the Yankees got creative with their sadism as when, according to one ex-prisoner, "prisoners were buckled hands and feet and rolled onto a stone pavement and left for hours, though the thermometer was at zero." Physical abuse and torture was a common theme in postwar accounts of the Confederate prisoner of war experience. It was a wonderful way to prove how truly cruel and immoral the Yankees had been during the war and it reinforced the Lost Cause mantra that unlike the Confederates, Northerners had conducted themselves with extreme dishonor during the war.[26]

Just as Northern writers did, Southern authors accused former Yankee prison officials and guards of cold-blooded murder. The most common way Union sentinels dispatched their defenseless enemies was simply to shoot them down for no reason other than doing so meant one less Rebel in the world. One writer gave his opinion after the war that "the practice of firing on our prisoners by the guards in the Northern prisons appears to have been indulged in to a most brutal and atrocious extent." Another ex-prisoner asserted that Yankee officials ordered guards to shoot "without hesitation or challenge." His conclusion was that Federal Secretary of War

Edwin Stanton had issued those orders and that they were eagerly followed in every Union prison so far as he knew. Some claimed that Northern guards took out their frustrations with the war's progress, or lack thereof, on the prisoners. One ex-prisoner said he noticed "that the shooting was most violent after a Confederate success." Another made the especially inflammatory charge "that Negro soldiers were promoted to corporals for shooting white prisoners at Point Lookout." Accusations that Union guards murdered helpless prisoners and received rewards from Federal officials for doing so circulated throughout the South for decades after the war and were believed by many, probably most, of the region's inhabitants.[27]

A more insidious means of killing Confederate prisoners, one again that mirrors Northern accusations, was a clumsy form of germ warfare adopted by the Yankees. This particular allegation was considerably less common than charges of gunning Southerners down in cold blood but can be found nonetheless without too much effort. Union officials committed what one writer termed an "unnatural atrocity" by intentionally putting prisoners in camps where smallpox was raging. The more common germ warfare technique supposedly used was to inject Southern prisoners with poison on the pretext of vaccinating them against smallpox. One prison camp survivor wrote, a "Poisonous virus of a loathsome disease was used, and this soon manifested itself among those who had submitted to this diabolical outrage. Many of these victims died with a complication of diseases superinduced by the vaccination, many lost arms and legs and eyes, and those who recovered were maimed for life." A so-called civilized, honorable people could sink no lower than to trick prisoners into lining up to be poisoned.[28]

To many Southerners, Jefferson Davis's imprisonment became yet another way to illuminate Yankee vindictiveness and brutality. Federal mistreatment of Davis during his two-year imprisonment should have led Northerners "to blush," according to one writer. Davis's imprisonment, in fact, made him more beloved in the South than anything he did while president of the Confederacy. He bore the Yankees' punishment on his shoulders for his people. As Allen Tate noted many years ago, Davis "became the sacrifice for the Southern people to the passions of the Northern mobs . . . ." A poem written during his captivity captured that fact perfectly, reading in part,

> Manacled! O, word of shame!
> Ring it through all the world!
> My countrymen, on you, on you,
> This heavy wrong is hurled.

We flung our banners to the air;
We fought as brave men fight;
Our battle-cry rang through the land;
Home! Liberty! and right!

For this I am here,
clanking the prisoner's chain
And standing proud in conscious worth,
I represent my land,
And that Lost Cause for which she bled
Lofty, heroic, grand.

Davis's experience at Fort Monroe, Virginia, was portrayed as an awful experience endured bravely for a noble people and a holy cause. In Southern minds, that captivity revealed just how malicious Northerners were. Not content with winning a war by uncivilized means, they felt compelled to kick the South while it was down by inflicting a harsh prison experience on the personification of the South. Davis's endurance of the ordeal made him an almost Christ-like hero to Southerners during the postwar period. During one of his speaking tours the railroad car in which he was traveling was adorned with a wreath bearing the inscription, "He Was Manacled for Us."[29]

Defeat presented Southerners with the added burden of dealing with hundreds of thousands of deaths in a lost cause. Having lost so many loved ones was difficult enough without adding the idea that they had died in vain. Southern suffering and death had to have meaning. By making honorable and brave conduct in the war more important than ultimate victory, Southerners were better able to accept their personal and collective sacrifices. Southerners could console themselves by believing that had the Yankees fought by the rules of civilized war, total victory would have been theirs. Tales of Northerners' horrible abuse of Confederate prisoners proved to be a powerful means of transmitting the idea that the Union played dirty pool during the war. Thus, those who paid the ultimate price fighting a doomed crusade to protect home and family from such a venal enemy became particularly venerable rather than tragic wastes of life.

Finally, as for Northerners, active contribution to the glorious cause became a mark of distinction. Those who boasted being on the great battlefields performing and witnessing great deeds were men of great honor in the region. Confederate veterans, though, who spent as much as half the war in prison camps did not want others to suspect that they were less heroic or less willing to sacrifice for the sacred cause because they were removed from the din of battle. Hair-raising tales of captivity in Union prisons were useful ways to prove that those whose lot it was to spend time in Yankee prison camps sacrificed as much, if not more, for the Southern cause as any other veteran.

It is easy to see that postwar writing about the prison issue in the South fit very snuggly and securely into the Lost Cause-era's portrayal of the Civil War as a morality play between knightly Christian Confederates and unprincipled Yankee thugs. Excellent histories of postwar Southern thought and culture by historians such as Charles Reagan Wilson, Gaines Foster, Thomas Connelly, Barbara Bellows, and Karen Cox have offered compelling evidence that in order to deal with the trauma of defeat and maintain what Robert Penn Warren called their "mystique of prideful difference," Southerners created a pro-Confederate/anti-Yankee model for interpreting the Civil War. The possibility that late-nineteenth/early twentieth-century Southern writers tackling the prisoner of war issue, which was *exceptionally* explosive, were not trying to achieve certain unhistorical goals with their writing while other writers in their region were busily covering the Civil War with a shroud of myth and legend seems, at best, remote. Furthermore, there is no compelling reason to think that Southerners at this time would have been purely objective in their handling of this issue while Northerners certainly were not. Researchers of this topic need to understand the atmosphere in which writing on this subject between 1865 and 1920 was done and realize that it is essential to view this era's evidence with an especially critical eye.

As has been shown in these first chapters, the prisoner of war issue became an oft-used tool by both Northerners and Southerners after the war to accomplish a variety of goals. Unfortunately for researchers seeking to find the truth about the Civil War's military prisons, objective recording was rarely among postwar writers' motives for taking up the pen. This has seemingly been recognized in Northern narratives but much less so with those written by Southerners during the Lost Cause era. While Union veterans argued loudly and often that they were abused and neglected in Confederate prisons as a matter of policy, few if any historians in the twentieth/early twenty-first centuries would accept their writing as reliable eyewitness evidence, and with good reason. Oddly, Southern writing from the same period complaining that Union officials neglected and abused Confederate prisoners as a matter of policy has been regularly cited as reliable primary source evidence in modern writing dealing with Federal military prisons. As will be shown in the next chapter, the Lost Cause interpretation of the prisoner of war issue wherein Union officials stand convicted of increasing prisoners' suffering and mortality because they unjustifiably suspended the exchange of prisoners in 1863 and then refused to take proper care of Confederates who fell into their care despite having adequate resources, has remained the dominant model for understanding how Northerners treated Southern prisoners during the Civil War.

Endnotes

1. William J. Cooper, Jr., *Jefferson Davis, American* (New York: Alfred A. Knopf, 2000), xiii, 554–56, 614–26.

2. David B. Chesebrough, *"God Ordained this War": Sermons on the Sectional Crisis, 1830–1865* (Columbia: University of South Carolina Press, 1991), 1–10, 202, 221–28; James McPherson, *Battle Cry of Freedom* (New York: Oxford University Press, 1988), 649, 691; Drew Gilpin Faust, *The Creation of Confederate Nationalism: Ideology and Identity in the Civil War South* (Baton Rouge: Louisiana State University Press, 1988), 22–32, 42.

3. Gary Gallagher, *The Confederate War: How Popular Will, Nationalism, and Military Strategy Could Not Stave Off Defeat* (Cambridge, MA: Harvard University Press, 1997), 49–51, 77, 106; Randall M. Miller, Harry S. Stout, and Charles R. Wilson, eds, *Religion and the American Civil War* (New York: Oxford University Press, 1998), 4–5; William J. Cooper, Jr. and Thomas E. Terrill, *The American South* (New York: Alfred A. Knopf, 1990), 455–57; James W. Silver, *Confederate Morale and Church Propaganda* (New York: W.W. Norton, 1957), 14–18, 25–41; Chesebrough, 193–95, 221–28.

4. Charles Reagan Wilson, *Baptized in Blood: The Religion of the Lost Cause, 1865–1920* (Athens: University of Georgia Press, 1980), 1–17; Richard E. Beringer, Herman Hattaway, Archer Jones, and William N. Still, Jr. *Why the South Lost the Civil War* (Athens: University of Georgia Press, 1986), 92–99; Gallagher, 51–57; Silver, 14–18, 25–41, 82–92.

5. Edward A. Pollard, *The Lost Cause* (N.P., 1866; repr., New York: Gramercy Books, 1994), 699, 751; Wilson, *Baptized in Blood*, 69–78; Gaines M. Foster, *Ghosts of the Confederacy: Defeat, the Lost Cause, and the Emergence of the New South, 1865–1913* (New York: Oxford University Press, 1987), 79–87; Richard M. Weaver, *The Southern Tradition at Bay: A History of Postbellum Thought*, ed. George Cove and M. E. Bradford (New Rochell, N.Y.: Arlington House, 1968), 149–66; Robert Penn Warren, *The Legacy of the Civil War: Meditations on the Centennial* (New York: Vintage Books, 1964), 3–14; Frank

E. Vandiver, "The Confederate Myth," in *Myth and Southern History*, vol. 1, *The Old South*, 2nd edition, ed. Patrick Gerster and Nicholas Cords (Urbana: University of Illinois Press, 1989), 148–49; Rollin G. Osterweis, *The Myth of the Lost Cause, 1865–1900* (Hamden, CT: The Shoe String Press, 1973), 12–14; Cooper, Jr. and Terrell, 455–56; Cooper, Jr., 325–419.

6. Thomas L. Connelly and Barbara L. Bellows, *God and General Longstreet: The Lost Cause and the Southern Mind* (Baton Rouge: Louisiana State University Press, 1982), 7–8, 21–38, 73–106; Susan Speare Durant, "The Gently Furled Banner: The Development of the Myth of the Lost Cause, 1865–1900" (Ph.D. dissertation, University of North Carolina-Chapel Hill, 1972), 105–45, 361–70; Theodore H. Jabbs, "The Lost Cause: Some Southern Opinion between 1865 and 1900 About Why the Confederacy Lost the Civil War" (master's thesis, University of North Carolina-Chapel Hill, 1967), 54–75; Wilson, 23, 40–49, 69–78, 126–27; Foster, 47–61, 91, 101, 117–25, 157; Osterweis, 30–65.

7. Connelly and Bellows, 7–8; Foster, 47–61, 117–19; Wilson, 10–11, 18–25, 40–57; Cooper, Jr., 614–16; Cooper, Jr., and Terrell, 455–56

8. Mary L. Williamson, *A Confederate Trilogy for Young Readers* (n.p.: 1895; repr., Harrisonburg, VA: Sprinkle Publications, 1989), 66; Pollard, 256–60, 490–506, 596–97, 606–15, 662–70; Durant, 105–45; Cooper, Jr., 615–26; Vandiver, 148–49; Weaver, 67–68, 149–53; Connelly and Bellows, 28–38, 70–101; Foster, 47–61, 123–26, 142.

9. Joe Barbiere, *Scraps from the Prison Table at Camp Chase and Johnson's Island* (Darbytown, PA: W. W. H. Davis, 1868), 288, 292, 320–21; *Confederate Veteran* (December 1905), 542; (January 1906),181–82; (June, 1906), 267; R. Randolph Stevenson, *The Southern Side; or, Andersonville Prison* (Baltimore, MD: Trumbull Brothers, 1876; repr., New Market, VA: John M. Bracken, 1995), 121; J. William Jones, *Southern Historical Society Papers* (March 1876): 113, 162–70 (hereafter cited as *SHSP*).

10. *SHSP* (March 1876), 113; (April 1876), 226; (April 1877), 201–14; *Confederate Veteran* (December 1898), 584; (March 1905), 105–19; (October 1906), 437; Reuben G. Clark, *Valleys of the Shadow: The Memoir of Confederate Captain Reuben G. Clark, Company I, 59th Tennessee Mounted Infantry*, ed. William B. Clark (Knoxville: University of Tennessee Press, 1994), 53–54; John Henry King, *Three Hundred Days in a Yankee Prison* (Atlanta, GA: J. P. Davis, 1904), 3–5; Pollard, 628, 641; Stevenson, 30.

11. *Confederate Veteran* (February 1896), 52; (December 1898), 584; (March 1900), 122; (August 1900), 364-367; (December 1905), 542; (January 1906), 10-11, 181–82; (June 1906), 267; (October 1906), 445–46, 448–53, 473; (December 1906), 558–59; (January 1907), 14–16; (April 1907), 156; (May

1908), 199–200; (May 1909), 200; (June 1910), 267–68; (May 1919), 178–80; (December 1929), 445; *SHSP* (March 1876), 113–14, 184–207; (April 1876), 226; Jefferson Davis, "Andersonville and Other War Prisons," in *Belford's Magazine* (January 1890), 166–70, 174–78; Griffin Frost, *Camp and Prison Journal* (Quincy, IL: Quincy Herald Book and Job Office, 1867; repr., Iowa City, IA: Press of Camp Pope Bookshop, 1994), x–xix; J. Ogden Murray, The *Immortal Six Hundred: A Story of Cruelty to Confederate Prisoners of War* (Winchester, VA: The Eddy Press Corporation, 1905), 10–11, 120; J. W. Minnich, *Inside and Outside of Rock Island* (Nashville, TN; Dallas, TX: Publishing House of the M. E. Church, South, 1908), 3–5, 11–12, 23, 36–37; Mark E. Neely, Jr., Harold Holzer, and Gabor S. Boritt, The *Confederate Image: Prints of the Lost Cause* (Chapel Hill: University of North Carolina Press, 1987), 171; Thomas J. Pressly, *Americans Interpret Their Civil War* (Princeton University Press, 1954; repr., New York: The Free Press, 1966), 101–2; Barbiere, 292, 299–307, 320–21; Stevenson, 101–21; Durant, 105–6, 134–35; Osterweis, 92–101.

12. *Confederate Veteran* (March 1898), 118–20; (January 1906), 181–82; (October 1906), 449–53; (March 1912), 113–14; (August 1916), 348–52; (May 1917), 240; (April 1918), 147–49; (November 1918), 470; (April 1929), 157; *SHSP* (March 1876), 116–22, 216–17; (April 1877), 197–200; (December 1906), 69–74; Alexander H. Stephens, *Recollections of Alexander H. Stephens*, ed. Myrta Lockett Avery (New York: Doubleday, Page, and Company, 1910; repr., New York: Da Capo Press, 1971), 233–36; Jefferson Davis, "Andersonville and other War Prisons," in *Belford's Magazine* (February 1890), 348–49; Davis, *The Rise and Fall of the Confederate Government*, abridged (New York: Collier Books, 1961), 495–96; Samuel Lewis, *The Treatment of Prisoners of War, 1861–1865* (Richmond, VA: William Ellis James, Book and Job Printer, 1910), 3–13, 507–8; John William Jones, *Confederate View of the Treatment of Prisoners* (Richmond, VA: Southern Historical Society, 1876), 123–24, 216–17, 326; Hunter McGuire and George L. Christian, *The Confederate Cause and Conduct in the War Between the States* (Richmond, VA: L. H. Jenkins, 1907), 135; James Huffman, *Ups and Downs of a Confederate Soldier* (New York: William E. Rudge's Sons, 1940), 107; William Henry Morgan, *Personal Reminiscences of the War of 1861–5* (Lynchburg, VA: J. P. Bell and Co., 1911), 255–56; Pollard, 640–41; Stevenson, 15–30, 233.

13. Ibid. all.

14. Marcus B. Toney, *The Privations of a Private* (Nashville, TN: by author, 1905), 85–86; Anthony M. Keiley, *The Prisoner of War* (Petersburg, VA: by author, 1866), 141–42; Clark, *Valleys of the Shadow*, 53–54; Lamar Fontaine, *The Prison Life of Major Lamar Fontaine* (Clarksdale, MS: Daily Register Print,

1910), 4–12; Davis, *The Rise and Fall of the Confederate Government*, abridged version, 495; Davis, "Andersonville and Other War Prisons," in *Belford's Magazine* (February 1890), 337–40, 343; Stevenson, 71–86; Barbiere, 304–305; King, 3–12; *Confederate Veteran* (October 1906), 449–53; (July 1911), 341–43; (February 1916), 74; (November 1918), 470, 501; (May 1921), 168; *SHSP* (March 1876), 196, 218; (December 1906), 69–74.

15. Pollard, 626; Stevenson, 21, 28.

16. Stevenson, 71–86.

17. Pollard, 626; *SHSP* (March 1876), 161.

18. Pollard, 626; Stevenson, 162–70.

19. This issue will be discussed more fully in Chapter Four.

20. *SHSP* (April 1876), 315–18; Jones, 116–17, 317–18; McGuire and Christian, 109–36.

21. *Confederate Veteran* (August 1894), 242–43; (January 1896), 10–13; (October 1896), 348; (October 1905), 155–56; (March 1910), 113; (August 1916), 348–52; (October 1919), 410–11; *SHSP* (March 1876), 125–31, 156–58, 196; (April 1876), 315–18; Murray, 87; Clark, 53–54; Davis, *Rise and Fall of the Confederate Government*, abridged, 482–96; Stephens, 233–36; Morgan, 255–57; Pollard, 625; Stevenson, 22–28, 227–40.

22. Davis, "Andersonville and other War Prisons," in *Belford's Magazine* (January 1890), 161–63; (February 1890), 337–44; Davis, *The Rise and Fall of the Confederate Government*, abridged, 493–94; Stephens, 233–36; Pollard, 616–28; *Confederate Veteran* (February 1916), 74–75; SHSP (March 1876), 116, 121–31, 184.

23. Fontaine, 59; *Confederate Veteran* (September 1905), 401–5; (February 1905), 65–69.

24. Robert H. Little, *A Year of Starvation Amid Plenty* (Belton, TX: n.p., 1891; repr. Waco, TX: Library Binding Co., 1966), 18; William L. Fagan, ed., *Southern War Songs* (New York: M. T. Richardson and Co., 1890), 361–62; Brian Temple, *The Union Prison at Fort Delaware: A Perfect Hell on Earth* (Jefferson, NC: McFarland and Co., 2003), 73; James F. Crocker, *Prison Reminiscences* (Portsmouth, VA: W. A. Fiske, 1906), 2–24, 143–47; John J. Dunkle [pseudonym: Fritz Fuzzlebug], *Prison Life During the Rebellion* (Singers Glen, VA: Joseph Funk's Sons, Printers, 1869), 5–37; *Confederate Veteran* (August 1894), 242–43; (October 1896), 387; (March 1898), 118–22; (February 1898), 71–73; (March 1900), 121–22; (February 1900), 62–64; (March 1905), 105–10; (January 1906), 27–32; (July 1908), 346–47; (June 1912), 294–97; (February 1919), 68–70; *SHSP* (March 1876), 115–16, 235–43; Barbiere, 5–6; Keiley, 143–47; Jones, 243–73; Pollard, 641.

25. *Confederate Veteran* (September 1897), 467–70; (February 1898), 71–73; (September 1905), 401–5; (January 1906), 27–32; (December 1907), 565–66; (October 1910), 471–72; (February 1912), 65–69; (June 1912), 294–97; (July 1912), 327; (August 1926), 295; *SHSP* (March 1876), 162–70, 226, 239, 261; Keiley, 57–58, 60–61, 68–69; Barbiere, 190, 288; Jones, 123, 326; Murray, 124; Shepherd, 16–17; Fontaine, 5–6.

26. *SHSP* (March 1876), 235–38, 240–41, 264, 276; (July 1879), 324–29; *Confederate Veteran* (December 1898), 571; (February 1900), 62–64; (March 1905), 105–10; (November 1910), 516; (February 1912), 65–69; (June 1914), 268–70; (February 1919), 68–70; (April 1919), 130–31; Pollard, 490–506, 596–97, 606–15, 640–43, 662–70; Davis, "Andersonville and other War Prisons," in *Belford's Magazine* (February 1890), 337–43; King, 83–84; Keiley, 134–35; Barbiere, 289–90; Little, 11, 15–17; Fontaine, 4–6; Stevenson, 145–79; Jones, 326; Cooper, Jr. and Terrill, 455–56; Weaver, 67–68.

27. *SHSP* (March 1876), 235–39, 241, 281–89; *Confederate Veteran* (September 1897), 467–70; (December 1898), 571; (March 1900), 121–22; (October 1900), 442; (March 1905), 105–10; (January 1906), 27–32; (March 1906), 128; (November 1907), 495; (December 1907), 565–66; (July 1908), 346–47; (February 1912), 65–69; (June 1912), 294–97; (June 1914), 268–70; (August 1926), 295; Barbiere, 78, 129, 198–99, 289; Little, 9–10, 14, 23–24; King, 80–82; Murray, 95, 145; Jones, 138–39, 243–73, 276–79; Stevenson, 145–79, 227–40.

28. *Confederate Veteran* (February 1912), 65–69; Jones, 145.

29. Allen Tate, *Jefferson Davis: His Rise and Fall* (New York: Minton, Balch, and Co., 1929; repr., New York: Kraus Reprint Co., 1969), 297–99; Jefferson Davis, "Fiction Distorting Fact": *The Prison Life, Annotated by Jefferson Davis*. ed. Edward K. Eckert (Macon, GA: Mercer University Press, 1987), xi–xivii; *Confederate Veteran* (February 1893), 49–50; (October 1896), 348; (September 1921), 333–35; Foster, 96.

–3–

CONTINUITY AND CHANGE

MODERN WRITERS AND THE ISSUE OF FEDERAL
TREATMENT OF CONFEDERATE PRISONERS

SINCE THE WAR GENERATION and its immediate descendents left the stage in the first third of the twentieth century, fewer people were willing to deal with the controversial issue of prisoners of war. Many probably thought there was little left to say on the topic given the rather large amount of material Northern and Southern writers produced in the half-century after the war's conclusion. Some were probably reluctant to reopen old wounds. Others likely had an understandable reluctance to touch a topic that continued to generate heated debate by partisans on both sides of the issue. It was far more comfortable to leave such issues alone.

Over the past century, though, a few writers have stepped forward and addressed this particular topic. Most of the writing is fairly recent, perhaps a response to James McPherson's 1998 comment in *Writing the Civil War* that this topic has been neglected relative to the voluminous attention other aspects of the war years have received. "Although good books and articles on individual prisons (especially Andersonville) have appeared in recent years," McPherson wrote, "only one general study of this important matter has been published since 1930." Since then two general studies have been published, the most recent, *While in the Hands of the Enemy*, on a major academic press. Still, compared to other aspects of the war this area remains an under-explored topic.[1]

Modern treatments of the subject, at least regarding Federal treatment of Confederate prisoners, has tended to reinforce rather than seriously challenge the Lost Cause-era interpretation that Union prison camps were unduly harsh and lethal. Some commentators have approached the issue of Confederate prisoner mortality far more dispassionately than their Lost Cause predecessors did but reached basically the same negative conclusions about Northern motives and actions towards Southern captives. Others have accepted the Lost Cause interpretation completely and have added their voices to their ancestors'. But a small handful of writers have begun to question seriously the premise that Confederate prisoners were mistreated as a matter of policy and died in inexcusably high numbers. They are, however, in such a minority that they have made little if any impact on the thinking in this area.

Surprisingly the beginning of the twentieth century saw two historians, James Ford Rhodes and Holland Thompson, try to bring a level of objectivity to this issue that had been glaringly absent in most writing up to that point. Rhodes warned researchers that veterans' accounts and many of the postwar treatments were highly suspect. He described most postwar narratives and second-hand writing as "entirely polemical." "In no part of the history of the Civil War," Rhodes added, "is a wholesome skepticism more desirable, and nowhere is more applicable a fundamental tenet of historical criticism that all the right is never on one side and all the wrong on the other." Researchers needed to be especially wary, he said, because in the "mass of material the man with a preconceived notion can find facts to his liking." Rhodes tried very hard not to fall into the traps others had of taking postwar writing at face value and using it to castigate the era's officials.[2]

That is not to say he did not find fault. He found quite a bit of mismanagement on both sides but no convincing evidence that Federal or Confederate officials designed their prisons to produce as much suffering and death as possible or that those authorities were woefully derelict or negligent in their duties. The closest Rhodes came to indicting Union officials was to suggest that it was a bit surprising to him that mortality statistics between Northern and Southern prisons were so close given the North's vastly superior resource capabilities. He viewed that as a topic for further investigation, though, and did not conclude that the comparable numbers constituted de facto proof of Yankee misconduct towards Confederate prisoners.[3]

At about the same time, Holland Thompson was reaching similar conclusions. In 1911 he wrote, "We must believe that the greatest horrors—for there were horrors—arose from ignorance or apparent necessity, rather than from intention." Thompson had interviewed dozens of former prisoners and discovered that there was a wide range of experiences, even among those who had been at the same prisons at the same times. He also discovered that many of the stories told by the interviewees did not match up very well, and often not at all, with wartime evidence found in the *Official Records*. Like Rhodes, Thompson warned other researchers to be extremely careful when evaluating their evidence and to ignore the more vitriolic accounts by both region's veterans. Many veterans and regional partisans were writing to achieve certain goals, none of them remotely related to providing an objective accounting of their experiences, making such sources highly unreliable.[4]

Rather than try to gain an ex post facto conviction of Federal officials for criminal neglect, Thompson suggested that Confederate prisoners' suffering often resulted from mismanagement on the part of inexperienced officials. Southern prisoners also likely suffered, he thought, because unscrupulous government contractors sought to pad their profit margins and did so at the prisoners' expense whenever they could get away with it. Since contractors' providing substandard goods was known to be a serious problem for the Federal government, one that had detrimental effects for Union soldiers during the war, the possibility that the same thing happened in Union prisons seemed reasonable to Thompson. This willingness to consider factors beyond miserly and/or vindictive Northerners when examining Confederate prisoners' experiences and mortality had been missing in the literature and promised to point the writing on the subject in a more objective direction.[5]

Both of these historians deserve a great deal of praise and credit for attempting to bring some objectivity and reason to a topic that had been approached solely with emotion up to that time. Either because they were so far ahead of their time or because their works were not highly detailed, book-length studies, they were virtually ignored. Most writing about prisoners during the Civil War, especially that done by Southerners, continued to be highly critical of Northern policies and actions towards Confederate captives. Despite Rhodes's and Thompson's work, the Lost Cause image of Union prisons and their officials retained its dominance in the literature and through the combination of repetition and a lack of alternative images remained one of the facts of the Civil War. Modern writing (defined as that done since the publication of William B. Hesseltine's seminal and highly influential work, *Civil War Prisons: A Study in War Psychology* in 1930) has run the spectrum from wholly endorsing the Lost Cause interpretation of how Confederate prisoners were treated to seriously questioning that model.

Several themes developed during the postwar era in the South can still be found in modern writing. One of the more prevalent is that the North could have done a whole lot more than it actually did to mitigate suffering and death in its prisons given the abundant resources it could tap into. Unfortunately for Southern captives, the Federal Commissary-General of Prisoners, Colonel William Hoffman, was a tight-fisted old skinflint who only grudgingly allowed Northern resources into his prison system. Many have also argued that Washington bears primary responsibility for suffering and mortality in the war's prisons because it unjustifiably halted prisoner exchanges in the spring of 1863. Some have argued that Secretary of War Edwin Stanton was to blame because he was a vindictive and vengeful individual. Others have argued that General Ulysses Grant bears much responsibility for coldly calculating that halting exchanges and keeping them halted was a huge boon to the Northern war effort. Ultimately, whatever evidence is used, a lot of modern writing reinforces the Lost Cause interpretation of Union treatment of Confederate prisoners.

Mauriel Joslyn has written and lectured quite a bit on this issue and has reached the conclusion that Northern officials had no business halting exchanges and that they engaged in a vindictive retaliation program that caused unnecessary suffering and mortality among Confederate prisoners. At a seminar hosted by the Museum of the Confederacy in Richmond in 2004, Joslyn maintained that prisoner suffering and mortality could have been significantly mitigated had the exchange cartel remained in effect. Southern officials, adhering to a "chivalric code," begged to have the exchanges resumed. They wanted to ease unnecessary suffering and death and emptying the prisons was a major step in that direction. Unfortunately for prisoners on both sides, Yankee officials did not recognize any sort of "chivalric code" and therefore the exchange cartel remained suspended, dooming thousands of Americans to slow deaths in prisoner of war facilities.[6]

Joslyn has also been among those recent writers who have concluded that the Federal government had all the resources it needed to properly care for Southern prisoners but chose not to use them. The North was, she points out, "gorged" with supplies, which, if properly utilized, could have significantly mitigated suffering and death among the prisoners. Tragically, Confederate prisoners would not have access to the North's bounty. Union officials were not negligent or inexperienced. They were, rather, engaged in a program of "ethnic cleansing."[7]

In the only book about Point Lookout, Edwin Beitzell also took a very dim view of Federal policies towards Rebel prisoners. Point Lookout was crowded, unsanitary, and potentially lethal. There can be no question that Union officials were not as quick as they should have been dealing with the bad water supply at the camp which caused high rates of diarrhea, weakening many to the point that they contracted one of the various lethal diseases found in virtually all sedentary camps of the era and died. Beitzell's book, like the Lost Cause-era sources he relied on so heavily, concluded that Federal officials were guilty of far more than failing to fix the water problem in a timely manner. Yankee officials intentionally made Point Lookout as uncomfortable and lethal as possible. Northerners had all they needed to care for the prisoners but actively chose not to. He concludes, as have others, that "the prisoners at Point Lookout died from lack of sufficient food, clothing, blankets, shelter, and medical attention that the Federal Government could have provided." Again, this was not due to inexperience or simple mismanagement. The suffering and death at Point Lookout was the inevitable result of "vindictive directives from the high command in Washington," especially from Secretary of War Edwin Stanton. Union guards who indulged in an orgy of "brutality and senseless killings" were never punished because that was all part of the Yankees' plan for Southern prisoners.[8]

A website dedicated to Point Lookout's prison camp days paints as dismal a picture as Beitzell. The Federals "deprived" the prisoners of adequate clothing and they "often had no shoes in winter or, only one blanket among sixteen or more housed in old, worn, torn, discarded union sibley tents." The prisoners' diet was so minimal that one prisoner was suffering so badly from starvation that he "devoured a raw seagull that had been washed ashore." Confederate captives also routinely ate trash to keep hunger away, according to this site. In addition to the poor living conditions and starvation rations, prisoners at Point Lookout "were . . . randomly shot during the night as they slept, or if they called out from pain."[9]

In 2002 Michael Horigan published a book about the North's most infamous prison, Elmira in New York. His study, *Elmira: Death Camp of the North*, was praised by both William C. Davis and especially James I. Robertson. Robertson in fact captured the tone of the book very accurately when he said that it "points several fingers of guilt at Federal authorities . . . ." The book lacks the Lost Cause-era's shrillness, but makes many of the same arguments of Southerners writing after the war. Ignoring the role Richmond's policy towards African American soldiers played in the exchange cartel's breakdown, Horigan follows the well-worn path that General Grant recognized that by the spring of 1863 the South benefited disproportionately from continued exchanges and essentially ordered them halted—not that Grant had that kind of sweeping authority in April 1863. Grant's arguments about Confederate violations of the agreement may have been valid, but they hid the true reason and Grant's "cold, brutal logic of a policy forbidding the exchanging of prisoners would culminate in the physical and psychological destruction of thousands of human beings . . . ." Secretary of War Edwin Stanton is also blamed for the callous and unjustified policy. But Horigan also blames Lincoln as well, something few modern writers have done. "President Lincoln," he wrote, "agreed that an end to the prisoner exchange would curtail the South's ability to carry on the war. The cartel was now a dead letter."[10]

The idea that Northern officials, due to their resource capability, could have done a great deal more to mitigate suffering and death at Elmira but chose not to is also clear in Horigan's account. The Commissary-General of Prisoners, Colonel William Hoffman, insured that Confederates suffered and died because he was a miser and preferred saving a nickel to caring for prisoners properly. In mid-1864 the Union government, after having been convinced by atrocity propaganda in the Northern press, implemented a retaliation policy that reduced the amount of food and other necessities Southern prisoners received. By May 1864, Union officials "sailed by [the] fixed star" of retaliation. Overall the book gives a good idea of how miserable it was to be at Elmira during the Civil War. Unfortunately, while Horigan recognizes the tense postwar atmosphere in which writing about prisons was done, the citations are exclusively from that era and tend to reinforce the Lost Cause interpretation of Union prison policies.[11]

Lonnie Speer has recently written on the subject in a general way. His first book, *Portals to Hell: Military Prisons in the Civil War* was fairly well-received and is a good book overall. Speer pointed out that the Confederacy's refusal to accord black troops equal status to whites played a major role in the Federal decision to suspend the exchange cartel. But he also said that other motives may have come into play. "Confederate soldiers released from Union prisons," he suggested, "returned to service in far greater numbers than did Union soldiers released from the South." In fact he argued that Union soldiers sometimes surrendered more easily in order to get out of service. Consequently the North was not benefiting from the exchange program as much as the South was, so Union officials suspended it. He also suggested that by 1863 the North held more prisoners than the South so prisoner exchanges disproportionately benefited the Confederacy leading to the suspension of the exchange agreement.[12]

Speer also argued, as so many before and since have, that the North had the resources to supply Confederate prisoners with all they could possibly need but failed to do so as a matter of policy. Part of the problem was that Hoffman was "a methodical, budget-conscious administrator" who would never spend a penny on a prisoner until that prisoner was in dire need—at which time it was too late for many to do any good. The real problem, though, was the Union authorities became convinced, through newspaper propaganda, that Northern prisoners were being starved and tortured in Southern prisons. That led to the institution of a retaliation program by Federal authorities in mid-1864 thought up by Hoffman and "backed by [Quartermaster General Montgomery] Meigs and Edwin M. Stanton, intended to treat Confederate prisoners of war as they believed the Confederate government was treating Union captives." Ration reductions and mail restrictions, which were the major parts of this program, led directly to increasing disease and death in Northern prisons.[13]

In his follow-up book, *War of Vengeance: Acts of Retaliation Against Civil War POWs*, Speer is much more critical of Union officials, falling into the older Lost Cause interpretation of Federal prison policies. For example, on the crucial question of exchanges, Speer portrays Confederate officials as willing to do anything to get the exchanges resumed. Southern officials, he argues, "even offered to resolve the controversy concerning black soldiers as POWs." Unfortunately, "no matter what the Confederate authorities offered or agreed to in proposing an exchange, Union authorities were determined to find some excuse to refuse." Confederate authorities come across as chivalrous humanitarians on the exchange question while their Northern counterparts are portrayed as calculating individuals with so little regard for human suffering that they would refuse to alleviate their own soldiers' despair by agreeing to the Confederates' most generous terms.[14]

Philip Burnham, whose work on this subject has appeared in a volume with such Civil War scholars as Gary Gallagher and James McPherson, is another recent writer that tends to reinforce the more traditional and negative model of Federal treatment of Confederate prisoners. Burnham, like many others who preceded him, blamed the Federals for halting the exchange cartel, which "doomed thousands of POWs to death." He concedes that Southern policies towards black prisoners played a role but also has pointed out that suspending the cartel "coincided, it turned out, with its own pragmatic designs of winning the war." "Badly undermanned," Burnham has written, "Richmond stood to gain more from prisoner exchanges than did Washington. With superior numbers, the North could afford to have the cartel suspended—all prisoners frozen in military limbo—and watch the South founder for lack of recruits." Not only were exchanges perhaps actually halted because officials like Grant knew it benefited the North's war effort, but Grant, according to Burnham, "also feared that the existence of regular exchanges encouraged Federal soldiers to desert, seeking through capture and parole to find an easy way out of the war. So the prisoner cartel was left to collapse." Apparently Yankees had less passion for their cause than did Southerners—an argument that is traced back directly to Lost Cause-era sources.[15]

As for conditions in the camps, Burnham has recognized that the war's scope played a role in the poor conditions found in both regions' camps. The war was far larger than anyone could have anticipated and inexperience and honestly poor planning played significant roles in making Civil War prisons miserable places. But, he writes, "since Union authorities were better able to supply food, clothing, and shelter" the suffering and death in their prisons is "far less excusable." Federal decisions to withhold food and other necessities during the implementation of a misguided retaliation program doomed an untold number of Southern prisoners to their graves when they might have lived.[16]

While there have been writers who have carried on (usually without intending to) the Lost Cause interpretation of how Confederate prisoners were treated during the Civil War, a significant amount of the modern writing has taken a more balanced approach. Writers such as Hesseltine, Frank L. Byrne, Michael Gray, James Robertson, and others have explored this controversial issue with the sort of objectivity that Rhodes and Thompson hoped would be applied by later historians. However, while this group's writing lacks the Lost Cause style's accusatory (and often shrill) tone, it tends to retain rather than question the foundation of earlier writers' case against the Yankees, which was that they could have done more to mitigate Southern prisoners' suffering and mortality and failed to do so. The result has been a body of well-researched, well-written pieces that has tended to support (again, likely inadvertently) the Lost Cause interpretation's contention that Confederate prisoner mortality was higher than it should have been because of policies pursued by Union officials.

In 1930, Hesseltine's seminal and still useful and influential book was published. In his introduction Hesseltine noted that because of the topic's controversial nature scholars had too long ignored this particular issue. Echoing Rhodes and Thompson, Hesseltine concluded that most of the postwar writing, even that done by former prisoners, was "indeed polemical" and therefore of dubious reliability.

Hesseltine discovered, for example, that in the late nineteenth century former Union prisoners found it nearly impossible to secure disability benefits from the government because it was extremely difficult to link their current physical problems to their prison experience. Most people could understand and accept that years of living in the field and participating in arduous campaigns and combat could take a permanent toll on one's physical well being. It was more difficult for people to accept that those who had spent much of their service in a prison and not endured as many long marches or as much combat had been permanently damaged by their experiences. The Andersonville atrocity propaganda served notice that having spent time in Southern prisons during the war was dangerous and debilitating. The campaign was highly successful. In 1880 a bill was introduced in the House of Representatives to grant eight dollars a month to veterans who had been incarcerated in Rebel prisons for at least six months and nine dollars if they had spent at least a year in them. Having discovered that many postwar writers took up their pens for reasons other than to educate others about their experiences, Hesseltine set out "to examine, without being swayed by these accounts, the true conditions in regard to prisons and prisoners in the Civil War."[17]

In keeping with his desire to pursue the topic of Civil War prisons and prisoners with more reason and objectivity than previous writers, Hesseltine determined not to pass judgment on either side for the mortality that occurred in their prisons. He was not interested in proving that one side was more humane or chivalrous than the other as others had been so eager to do. After consulting mortality statistics he found it surprising, as Rhodes had, that the numbers seemed closer than one would expect given the resource disparity between the North and the South. Previous Southern writers argued that such evidence was de facto proof that inhumane Northerners were guilty of overt mistreatment of prisoners by withholding their bounty. Hesseltine rejected that kind of broad character assassination.

He did conclude, though, that suffering and mortality in Union prisons could have been mitigated given the North's greater ability vis-à-vis the South to materially provide for prisoners. In Hesseltine's view, Union officials such as Stanton and Hoffman were not so much evil as they were overly eager to believe atrocity stories printed in Northern newspapers. Horrible conditions in places like Libby Prison, Salisbury Prison, and Belle Isle "being reported in the North created the belief that the prisoners were ill treated through a deliberate purpose; the inevitable hatred engendered by the war made such a belief readily credible. The result of this psychosis was that prisoners in the Northern prisons were forced to suffer in retaliation for the alleged Southern cruelty." From the summer of 1864 until the early weeks of 1865, Confederate prisoners endured a "retaliation program" in which their rations were cut, sutlers were restricted severely in what they could sell to prisoners, and relief packages from friends and relatives were restricted as well. This policy unnecessarily increased suffering and death in Northern prisons.[18]

The "war psychosis" theory was a breakthrough in the literature. It seemed to explain double-digit prisoner mortality in the resource-rich North without impugning Northern character as Lost Cause-era writing had done. Yankees in Hesseltine's model were not vindictive brutes. Rather, they were simply led astray by irresponsible journalists, what would be labeled "yellow" or "tabloid" journalists by later generations. The theory was not offered as an apology for the suffering and mortality in Union prisons. It was simply put forth as a more objective and scholarly explanation for it.

In many respects Hesseltine's 1930 work is a shining example of everything good historical writing should be. He recognized the problems of sources written years after the fact and treated them with the skepticism they deserve. And he had no interest in building a case for one side being a paragon of chivalry and virtue while the other lacked any redeeming qualities whatsoever. The fact that this book remains the standard source on the subject and has been reprinted in its original form for over seventy years is an accomplishment few works can boast.

When it came to the critical question of who was most responsible for the cartel's suspension, Northerners wind up bearing most of the blame. The Union's position that black troops and their white officers should be treated under the agreement's terms the same as any other prisoners is portrayed as unnecessarily legalistic. The "Confederates," on the other hand, "were eager to continue the exchange of [white] noncommissioned officers and privates." Hesseltine also suggests that Grant's motives for insisting that no distinctions be made between black and white troops were more military than humane. Grant understood that his side was benefiting from the cartel's suspension and Richmond's intransigence on the black prisoner issue provided a nice justification for keeping the door shut on prisoner exchanges.[19]

Also, even though Hesseltine did not overtly attempt to laud the Confederacy and berate the Union, Confederate officials are not really held responsible for conditions in their prisons. The destruction of Southern lands during the war and the increasingly effective Northern blockade caused acute shortages in the Confederacy, which severely hampered Richmond's efforts to take proper care of Yankee prisoners. While there is a lot to recommend that conclusion, Hesseltine never addressed the possibility that at least some of the poor conditions might be the result of a Confederate "war psychosis." To date nobody has ever asked why Northern officials lapped up atrocity propaganda and made policy decisions based on it while similar tales were published in Southern newspapers seemingly with little effect on Confederate prison policy. Readers are left to assume that Richmond officials were blocked by wartime circumstances from properly caring for prisoners while officials in Washington could have done more but did not.[20]

A number of writers since Hesseltine have followed his commendable example and attempted to explore the prisoner of war issue with greater objectivity and depth, having no interest in using the issue to point out the moral differences that supposedly existed between Yankees and Rebels. Reflecting the enormous influence Hesseltine has had on this topic, most have tended to reinforce the "war psychosis" theory of Confederate prisoner suffering and mortality. Thus despite better researched and better written studies of this topic, the basic theme that Confederate prisoners were victimized by callous, vindictive, and negligent Federals has remained largely intact or at least unchallenged.

James I. Robertson is a good example of this group of writers. In the early 1960s he wrote about the truly terrible conditions that existed at Elmira in an article entitled, "The Scourge of Elmira," which appeared in *Civil War Prisons*, a collection of essays edited by Hesseltine. In 1995 Kent State University Press republished the collection. Reading the article the reader comes to understand why a Texan expressed the opinion years after the war that "If there was ever a hell on earth, Elmira prison was that hell."

In his article Robertson concluded that the suffering and mortality at Elmira were due to Hoffman's orders to reduce rations "in retaliation for deprivations suffered by Federal prisoners in the South" to the point where Elmira inmates subsisted on bread and water. The post's surgeon, E. L. Sanger, is described by Robertson as "mistreating and neglecting ill Confederates as retaliation for the sufferings of Federal soldiers in Southern prisons." Between the retaliation measures enforced at Elmira and what he called the "almost sadistic apathy" Hoffman and other Union officials displayed towards Confederate prisoners, the captives never had a chance.[21]

A little over twenty-five years later in *Soldiers Blue and Gray*, Robertson again argued that Confederate prisoners suffered and died in unnecessarily high numbers. Prisoners' deaths during the Civil War, he argued, were due to a number of factors. When boiled down, the factors led to the following conclusion: "A combination of wartime shortages [in the South] and wartime psychoses [in the North] accounted for much of the suffering that prisoners had to endure." "In truth," he wrote, "conditions of Southern soldiers incarcerated in a land of plenty were as inhuman as those for Union soldiers imprisoned in a land being systematically destroyed." In this particular chapter, Confederate authorities are presented as doing the best they could despite being overwhelmed by circumstances beyond their control. Northerners, on the other hand, enjoyed a veritable cornucopia of material resources that were kept from Southern prisoners. Not surprisingly, Hoffman comes in for a thrashing. Robertson described him as a "dollar-conscious administrator whose miserly qualities bode ill for Confederate prisoners." Robertson did not attempt to make an overt comment about Northern character, or lack of it, in his writing. Indeed, he recognized that "Neither side started out with the intention of abusing prisoners of war." Unfortunately for Confederate prisoners, the Yankees abandoned their good initial intentions for various reasons and many died who would have otherwise lived.[22]

In 1964 Dr. Phillip Shriver of Kent State University and a graduate student, Donald J. Breen, published a study of Ohio's Civil War prisons. In their overview of prison policies, they said the exchange cartel was only agreed to by the Lincoln administration in 1862 because the South held more prisoners, making it in the North's military interest to exchange captives. When the North gained the greater number of prisoners, Union officials suspended the cartel because that was now in their best military interest. Richmond's policy on black troops is addressed but is portrayed as secondary to military calculation. Stanton had "shrewdly concluded" that a continuation of exchange would be of greater benefit to the South than to the North and ordered it halted. Stanton was fully supported by General Grant on that front. "As Grant sized up the situation, the North by 1864 held far more Confederate prisoners than the South held Unionist" so the cartel would remain suspended despite humanitarian concerns. Prisoners on both sides would languish with no hope for exchange until February 1865. At that point exchanges began to be resumed only because Grant "was finally convinced that the defeat of the Confederacy was in the offing . . . ." The authors show that conditions in Ohio's prisons were not all that terrible during the first half of the war but deteriorated considerably after that. They attribute the decline to the overcrowding halting the exchanges caused and to the hold the "war psychosis" had on Union officials, which caused them to withhold food and other provisions "despite the more abundant larder upon which [the North] could draw." Overall this is a good study of Ohio's Civil War prisons, and remarkably the only one available forty years later that reinforces the theme that the Yankees pursued policies that directly increased suffering and death in their prisons.[23]

One of the best recent studies of a Union prison is George Levy's *To Die in Chicago*, which is about Camp Douglas. Levy's book is definitely not intended to excuse the South while condemning the North. He makes the excellent point that the Confederacy cannot be completely exonerated for conditions in its prisons because it had more resource difficulties, because "The South had the means to carry on the war [for four years]." Conditions at Camp Douglas were often not what they should have been for many reasons Levy says. At times the problem was unscrupulous government contractors. At various points Levy chronicles how these parasites, unfortunately so common in wartime, shorted the prison on food, especially beef. Part of the problem stemmed from Hoffman's unwillingness to part with a dollar—not an entirely invalid argument. But a major problem was that Union authorities, believing that the Confederacy was intentionally harming Federal prisoners, implemented a harsh retaliation policy where rations were reduced and Southerners did not get all the clothing and protection from the elements that they needed to survive. The result was exceptionally high sickness and mortality rates at Camp Douglas.

While Levy's book does leave plenty of room for readers to conclude that the Yankees were, once again, the bad guys, this is anything but a neo-Lost Cause treatment. Levy does a very good job pointing out that Chicago itself suffered terribly from diseases such as scarlet fever during the Civil War. He also shows that prisoners were not any sicker at Camp Douglas than they were in the field, though they were more likely to die of their disease in Chicago than in the field.[24]

Another recent study of an individual prison that is far more balanced than previous writing is Michael Gray's one of the infamous Elmira. This is the best and by far most balanced look at Elmira currently available, and likely to be the standard on the prison for some time. Gray does not see Federal officials as evil brutes at all. One of the biggest problems with Elmira was its location and unhealthy conditions. That, and certain officials were far too slow in improving those conditions. Hoffman is described as "tight-fisted," an individual "whose thriftiness did not help alleviate the suffering of Elmira prisoners." But Hoffman's well-known concern with economy was not the only problem. Federal officials still were too eager to believe atrocity propaganda that they read in the newspapers and withheld supplies vital to survival. There is the subtle hint here and there in the book too that Northern officials bear more responsibility for mortality in their prisons than their Southern counterparts. For example, Gray points out that the mortality at Andersonville was twenty-nine percent and 24.4 % at Elmira, "a small variant when the unequal quantity and quality of resources possessed by each government was considered."[25]

One of Hesseltine's students, Frank L. Byrne, has written a number of pieces about Civil War prisons with an admirable amount of objectivity. Byrne criticizes Northern and Southern officials for conditions in their prisons. "Even in a nineteenth- century civil war," he has argued, "prisons might have been much less fatal." Neither side did a particularly stellar job caring for prisoners but conditions became much worse after the cartel was suspended in mid-1863, something he sees as the result of both Richmond's refusal to treat black soldiers as legitimate prisoners and Grant's belief that the suspension aided the North's war effort. "The deterioration of conditions in the South was worse, in part because of a reaction to the problem that was almost a nonresponse." Confederate officials did little because they put all their hope in a resumption of exchanges. Northern officials insured miserable, lethal conditions would prevail in their prisons because they implemented a harmful retaliation program in mid-1864 that denied prisoners adequate food, clothing, and shelter. Employing a tightwad like Hoffman to oversee the prisons did not help either. The money Hoffman saved during the war (two million dollars) "represented the unacknowledged price of many prisoners' lives."[26]

William C. Davis has written on this topic as well. Like the other, more objective writers, he does not attempt to use this issue to prove that the Yankees should be recognized as having been guilty of knowingly pursuing policies designed to increase suffering and death in their military prisons. Davis has made the rather astute observation that prison commandants were rarely the best officers available. The best and brightest preferred the more honorable and glorious positions in the field. He sees a lot of the problems found in the war's prisons being the result of "incompetence of the men put in charge of the prisons. It was not, after all, the kind of position which tended to attract either the most gallant or the most able of officers." He also warns that many of the postwar atrocity stories cannot be taken at face value and must be treated with a great deal of care before using them. A major problem for Confederate prisoners was that Hoffman and other officials, reacting to atrocity propaganda, called for ration reductions that increased suffering during the last two years of the war. Also, Hoffman refused to spend adequately on his prisons and that "made the plight of his prisoners worse." Thus, while Northern officials could have done more for their prisoners, Davis tends to portray the suffering and death in the war's prisons as resulting from tragic incompetence more than from malice or apathy.[27]

The most recent scholarly treatment of the prisoner of war issue, Charles Sanders's *While in the Hands of the Enemy*, tends to reinforce more strongly than writers like Byrne, Levy, and Gray the traditional image of Northern officials acting overtly to increase suffering and death in their prison camps. Sanders is not a neo-Lost Causer, though. His book is not intended to be a diatribe against fiendish Yankees. Sanders argues that both Union and Confederate officials made conditions in their respective prisons worse and more lethal than they need have been. He writes at the beginning of his book,

> . . . although difficulties such as organizational incompetence, inexperience, and chronic shortages of essential resources certainly contributed to the horrors in the camps, these factors pale into insignificance when compared to the devastation wrought by Union and Confederate leaders who knew full well the horrific toll of misery and death their decisions and actions would exact in the camps.

For Sanders, prisoners became pawns in the hands of officials who used them and this issue to pursue certain goals that had nothing to do with humanity. Sanders portrays Northern and Southern officials in 1863 as introducing much harsher policies towards captives in their custody. "Military and civilian leaders," he argues, "with full knowledge of the consequences of their actions, began to implement policies that dramatically increased the incidence of sickness and death among the captives under their control." While conditions began to deteriorate in 1863, it was in 1864 that life in Union prisons became "the darkest of the war." At that point, according to Sanders, increasingly harsh retaliation "orders signaled nothing less than the advent of a new and far more determined effort to develop and implement a policy of successive rounds of retaliation, deliberately designed to lower conditions in the camps and increase immeasurably the suffering of prisoners." The book is well written and, refreshingly, is not an attempt to excuse one side and excoriate the other. Valuable as it is, there is little that is new in the evaluation of Northern officials and their camps, however. Their suspension of the cartel is portrayed as driven mostly by its military value and Union authorities refused to provide adequate food, clothing, shelter, and medical care as a standard operating procedure for their prisoner of war depots.[28]

There have been a handful of historians within the last decade or so who have suggested that the traditional paradigm wherein Northern officials knowingly did everything they could to maximize suffering and mortality in their prison camps is not accurate. At least one is a major Civil War scholar and another has published a major study of a Union prison on a university press. These historians' work in this area has not made much of an impact in the literature, however, as the most recent scholarly contribution to it clearly shows.

James McPherson dedicated several pages in larger works to this issue. McPherson has described life in the war's prisons, whichever side one is talking about, as miserable. But he also says that conditions in Northern prisons were better than they were in the South. He also has pointed out that medical care in Federal prisons was no worse than it was in the field, but by modern standards that is not saying much. But, "Confederate prisoners were 29 % less likely to die in Yankee prisons than to die of disease in their own army, while Union prisoners were 68 % more likely to die in Southern prisons than in their own army." Such a statistic is a major blow to those who argue that Northern officials induced death through intentionally harmful policies. McPherson also has argued that the halting of exchanges had everything to do with Richmond's policies towards African American soldiers and nothing to do with military calculation on Grant's part as has been so often asserted. Despite his extraordinary scholarly stature in the era for a generation, he has not convinced too many people that the Yankees were not vindictive captors.[29]

In *Civil War Prisons and Escapes*, Robert E. Denney briefly touches on the issue of Union treatment of Southern soldiers in the beginning of his book. Denney points out how complex the task of feeding, clothing, and sheltering thousands of prisoners was for Northern authorities. "While the concept of receiving prisoners of war may sound easy to understand, imagine for a minute what your reaction would be to suddenly be responsible for food, housing, clothing, medical care and control of [about a quarter million] people, be they military or civilian." Rather than holding Northern officials responsible for not doing all they could to mitigate Confederate prisoners' suffering and mortality, Denney suggests that most officials associated with Union military prisons were "hard-working, diligent, and honorable people who were doing their best in a bad situation." In fact, "As the war progressed, the camps in the North improved, while those in the South worsened." Confederate prisoners' mortality was often the result, he says, of their condition upon arrival rather than of deliberate cruelty or neglect. "Usually if [prisoners] survived for the first two weeks, their life expectancy improved." His few words at the beginning of a larger work may be argued to paint a bit too rosy a picture of Union officials and their prisons, but Denney deserves recognition as one of the few willing to go against a widely held interpretation of Northern prison officials.[30]

In 2000 *Unlikely Allies*, a study of the infamous Fort Delaware, was published. This book is also something of a break from the writing that casts Union officials as at least partially responsible for killing thousands of helpless prisoners. Dale Fetzer and Bruce Mowday make the important point that much of Fort Delaware's reputation rests on unreliable postwar narratives. In one example they show that the Reverend Isaac Handy's postwar diatribes against Northern officials and Fort Delaware often part company with historical records. Handy claimed, for example, that Federal officials heartlessly denied him and other inmates at the prison any communication with loved ones. The records clearly show, however, that Handy's wife visited him at Fort Delaware on several occasions. The authors also document the important fact that most of the mortality that occurred at the prison cannot be attributed to the famous retaliation program of 1864–65. They show that the "period of July–December 1863 proved to be the worst for the inhabitants of Pea Patch Island. Almost one-half of all the deaths in the POW population occurred in that time period . . . ." The culprits were not Yankee neglect or malice, though. Smallpox hit this prison with a vengeance, as it did others, and despite taking all known actions against this frightening and lethal disease, prisoners died by the dozens during those months. This is a very well-researched book and certainly casts doubt on the traditional image of Northern prison officials. Unfortunately, the authors failed to analyze the period of 1864–65 with the same detail as 1861 to 1863, leaving the book open to the charge that it does not address conditions during the time when retaliation regulations were in effect.[31]

That same year one of the better studies (probably the best) of a Northern prison was published. Benton McAdams's *Rebels at Rock Island* is a truly excellent piece of scholarship. He argues that incarceration at that prison was anything but pleasant, but comparisons to Andersonville are completely unjustified. Rock Island has been saddled with a rather nasty reputation as particularly lethal, thanks in no small part, McAdams noted, to Margaret Mitchell's placing the dashing Ashley Wilkes there in *Gone with the Wind*. While suffering and death were certainly tragic realities at Rock Island, he argues convincingly that most of the suffering "was not the result of policy and inhumanity but rather of accident, incompetence, and the inability to cope with a war larger than any the nation had ever before endured." The book challenges the image of commandant Colonel Adolphus J. Johnson as a cruel jailor and even has a few kind words for William Hoffman. "Hoffman," McAdams says, "served his government well during the war. He had almost single-handedly constructed a prisoner of war apparatus that cared for a quarter of a million prisoners, and he kept most of them alive." True, Hoffman was overly concerned about saving money. But he does not deserve the reputation as "an inhuman fiend who intentionally denied care the Union was perfectly capable of providing."[32]

With so many conflicting interpretations, the difficulty for the historian of this topic is sorting through the evidence to create an accurate picture of Union policies and treatment of Rebel prisoners. Most of the writing over the last 140 years has tended to hold Northern officials guilty of causing unnecessary suffering and death by creating conditions in their prisons conducive to those things. Many modern writers have gotten away from the Lost Cause interpretation of Union prison policies, at least to the point of not accusing them of murder. Few, though, have seriously challenged the traditional idea that Northern officials pursued policies that inflated the suffering and death tolls in their prisoner of war facilities. They could have at least mitigated the death in their prisons but, as many writers continue to contend, consciously chose not to do so. Even though a few brave writers have tried to challenge that traditional image in recent years, they remain largely ignored in favor of the more traditional view of Union prison policies, which is published in much greater quantity. The following chapters attempt to show conclusively that recent writers like McAdams, McPherson, Fetzer, and Mowday have the stronger case.

Endnotes

1. James M. McPherson and William J. Cooper, Jr., eds., *Writing the Civil War: The Quest to Understand* (Columbia: University of South Carolina Press, 1998), 4.

2. James Ford Rhodes, *History of the United States*, Volume 5, *1864–1865* (New York: The Macmillan Company, 1912), 483–509.

3. Rhodes, 483–509.

4. Holland Thompson, ed., *The Photographic History of the Civil War*, Volume 4: *Soldier Life and Secret Service and Prisons and Hospitals* (n.p.: 1911; repr., Secaucus, NJ: The Blue and Grey Press, 1987), 14, 16–18, 48, 168.

5. Thompson, 14–18, 48, 168.

6. Mauriel Joslyn, *Immortal Captives: The Story of the 600 Confederate Officers and the United States Prisoner of War Policy* (Shippensburg, PA: White Mane Publishing, Co., 1996), xiii, 32–33, 41; Joslyn, "The U.S. Policy of Retaliation on Confederate Prisoners of War," in *Andersonville: The Southern Perspective*, ed. J. H. Segars (Atlanta, GA: Southern Heritage Press, 1995), 133–45; Joslyn spoke along with myself on this subject as part of the Museum of the Confederacy's evening lecture series on March 31, 2004, where she reiterated her position that the Federals' unprincipled refusal to continue exchanges after the spring of 1863 resulted in unnecessary suffering and death.

7. Joslyn, "The U.S Policy of Retaliation on Confederate Prisoners of War," 133–42.

8. Edwin W. Beitzell, *Point Lookout Prison Camp for Confederates* (n.p.: by author, 1972), 176–83.

9. "Point Lookout Prison Camp for Confederates" at http://members.tripod.com/PLPOW/prisonhis.htm. Accessed 12/23/1990.

10. Michael Horigan, *Elmira: Death Camp of the North* (Mechanicsburg, PA: Stackpole Books, 2002), vii, 16–19.

11. Horigan, 16–20, 22–45, 52–53, 65–93, 100–19.

12. Lonnie Speer, *Portals to Hell: Military Prisons in the Civil War* (Mechanicsburg, PA: Stackpole Books, 1997), xiv–xix, 104–5.

13. Speer, 11–15, 291–92.

14. Speer, *War of Vengeance: Acts of Retaliation Against Civil War POWs* (Mechanicsburg, PA: Stackpole Books, 2002), 131–40.

15. Philip Burnham, "The Andersonvilles of the North," in *With My Face to the Enemy: Perspectives on the Civil War*, ed. Robert Cowley (New York: Berkley Books, 2001), 367–81; Burnham, *So Far From Dixie: Confederates in Yankee Prisons* (New York: Taylor Trade Publishing, 2003), 55–64.

16. Ibid.

17. William Best Hesseltine, *Civil War Prisons: A Study in War Psychology* (Ohio State University Press, 1930; repr., New York: Frederick Ungar Publishing Co., 1971), viii, 249–50.

18. Hesseltine, viii, 7–34, 172–209.

19. Hesseltine, 67–113, 219–24.

20. Hesseltine, 172–209. See also Hesseltine's introduction in *Civil War Prisons*, ed. William B. Hesseltine (1962; repr. Kent, OH: Kent State University Press, 1995), 7.

21. James I. Robertson, "The Scourge of Elmira," in *Civil War Prisons*, ed. William B. Hesseltine (repr. Kent, OH: Kent State University Press, 1995), 88–92.

22. Robertson, *Soldiers Blue and Gray* (Columbia: University of South Carolina Press, 1988), 190–203.

23. Phillip R. Shriver and Donald J. Breen, *Ohio's Military Prisons in the Civil War* (Columbus: Ohio State University Press for the Ohio Historical Society, 1964), 4–5, 15–19, 38–39.

24. George Levy, *To Die in Chicago: Confederate Prisoners at Camp Douglas, 1862–1865* (Evanston, IL: Evanston Publishing, 1994), 65, 125–36, 149–60, 180–87, 247.

25. Michael P. Gray, *The Business of Captivity: Elmira and Its Civil War Prison* (Kent, OH: Kent State University Press, 2001), 29, 87, 92, 161.

26. Frank L. Byrne, "Prison Pens of Suffering: Simple Names Like Johnson's Island and Andersonville Come to Mean Hell," in *Civil War Album: Complete Photographic History of the Civil War, Fort Sumter to Appomattox*, ed. William C. Davis and Bell I. Wiley (New York: Tess Press, 2000), 590–608; The article appeared earlier in *Fighting for Time*, Volume 4: *The Image of War, 1861–1865*, ed. William C. Davis (Garden City, NY: Doubleday and Co., 1983), 396–451.

27. William C. Davis, *Rebels and Yankees: The Fighting Men of the Civil War* (New York: Salamander Books, 1989), 168–83.

28. Charles W. Sanders, Jr., *While in the Hands of the Enemy: Military Prisons of the Civil War* (Baton Rouge: Louisiana State University Press, 2005), 2–5, 142–96, 200–65, 272, 298.

29. James M. McPherson, *Ordeal by Fire: The Civil War and Reconstruction*, 3rd Ed. (Boston, MA: McGraw Hill, 2001), 485–92.

30. Robert E. Denney, *Civil War Prisons and Escapes: A Day-by-Day Chronicle* (New York: Sterling Publishing Co., 1993), 9–12.

31. Dale Fetzer and Bruce Mowday, *Unlikely Allies: Fort Delaware's Prison Community in the Civil War* (Mechanicsburg, PA: Stackpole Books, 2000), 59–62, 92–93, 115–19, 148.

32. Benton McAdams, *Rebels at Rock Island: The Story of a Civil War Prison* (DeKalb: Northern Illinois University Press, 2000), xiii, 203–13.

$-4-$

UNION POLICIES
REGARDING PRISONERS
OF WAR

1861–1865

TO LOOK AT MOST OF THE WRITING DONE BETWEEN 1865 and the present, the evidence against Northern officials regarding how they treated Confederate prisoners during the Civil War appears to be pretty damning. Ex-prisoners and modern writers have agreed, with some very limited, very recent exceptions, that the Federal government could have done considerably more than it actually did to mitigate Southern prisoners' suffering and mortality. Many have contended that the North had everything it wanted, materially speaking, but failed to share its bounty with Southern captives out of a spirit of vindictiveness. Others cite a misguided retaliation policy wherein vital supplies were intentionally kept from prisoners in Northern pens for the supposed misdeeds of the Richmond government. Still others have preferred the lesser charge of simple negligence. Whatever the reasons offered by writers discussing Union treatment of Confederate prisoners, most have stated explicitly or implied strongly that Southern prisoners' suffering and mortality were excessive.

Modern writers often accept that medical ignorance and the enormity of the job of caring for prisoners between the summer of 1863, when the exchange cartel was suspended, and 1865 were variables affecting mortality in Northern prison camps. However, most also assume that the North's military, financial, and material resources should have been adequate to have overcome those difficulties. In fact, anyone researching this topic will find quickly that the idea that given the North's material abundance Confederate mortality was inexcusably high has become cliché.

This chapter reexamines that old and remarkably durable negative perception of Northern prisoner of war policies through official military records and wartime Southern diaries written by prisoners before the postwar axes were brought out for grinding. Evidence from these sources reveals that while Union prisons were most certainly uncomfortable and potentially lethal places, Northern officials tried more often than not to provide adequate food, clothing, shelter, and medical care for Confederate inmates. That their efforts to take proper care of those prisoners failed to keep mortality below 12% is tragic, but that statistic says far more about life in military camps of that time period than it does about the character of the Northern people and their government during the Civil War.

One concept that is critical to understand when trying to assess whether Union officials were unduly negligent and/or abusive toward Confederate prisoners is that notions of rules regulating treatment of military prisoners captured in battle were in their infancy when the Civil War began in 1861. Charles Sanders asserted in a 2006 article that Northern policies regarding prisoners of war "stood in direct contradiction to the provisions of international law," suggesting that a body of law in this area existed. The fact is that no body of international law, no Geneva Conventions, in short, nothing remotely close to the modern and extensive body of international laws existed in the 1860s to inform Northern officials about how Southern prisoners were to be fed, clothed, sheltered, and cared for medically. Further muddying the water was the fact that Confederate prisoners were not, at least in eyes of Northerners and the eyes of the international community, soldiers from a legal nation; they were rebels, outlaws. While Western nations by the middle of the nineteenth century tended to accept that they had certain humanitarian responsibilities for prisoners from enemy nations, it was far less clear that rebels or internal enemies were entitled to the same rights and privileges as combatants from legally recognized states. Most likely such captives wound up in the category of traitors, outlaws who had forfeited their right to expect the protection of the law and were therefore at whatever mercy the legitimate authorities chose to bestow.[1]

The idea too that when prisoners have surrendered and thrown down their arms that they are to be treated as humanely as possible is very modern. Prior to the Enlightenment in the West, those unfortunate enough to be captured in battle were ransomed, enslaved, or killed. While exceptions no doubt existed, wars prior to the Enlightenment had not been romantic jaunts fought between groups who harbored chivalric ideas about war as some sort of lethal tournament fought according to rules and regulations. Western history is full of examples prior to the Enlightenment of prisoners and civilians who happened to be in the area being slaughtered wholesale in the wake of a battle. Soldiers had good reason to fight to the death because they knew they could expect little humanitarian mercy from their opponents if the battle did not go their way and they had to surrender. Fortunately for soldiers, particularly the poorer ones who would not bring a ransom, the Enlightenment introduced in the West ideas that promoted minimizing wars' destructiveness and increasing respect for human life. Only then did prisoners' plight begin to improve.

Two of the Enlightenment's more influential figures, Montesquieu and Jean-Jacques Rousseau, urged that when wars were fought they ought to be prosecuted in such a way as to cause as little death and destruction as possible. In Rousseau's view, wars were fought between nations and not between individuals. Nations' soldiers are enemies by accident or because of circumstances beyond their control. However soldiers became enemies, Rousseau accepted that it was legitimate for them to try to kill their opponents in combat; such is the nature of war after all. Once an opponent had surrendered and laid down his arms, though, his status immediately changed. By quitting the fight and throwing down his weapons a soldier went from being fair game for injury or death to a prisoner. Civilized warfare demanded, according to the period's philosophers, that unarmed prisoners not be slaughtered, tortured, enslaved, or abused in any way that might amuse the victors.

Civil War-era Americans tended to accept the more generous ideas and practices of the eighteenth century. During the American Revolution each side assumed that captors were responsible for feeding, clothing, and sheltering prisoners. They also agreed that prisoners were not to be killed or harmed intentionally for being on the wrong side. That does not mean that prisoners' experiences were pleasant during that war; the point to be understood is that overtly mistreating prisoners was, by common agreement, forbidden. In 1785 the new United States and Prussia worked out a treaty wherein both nations agreed that captors assumed responsibility for prisoners' basic maintenance. These vague guidelines, based more on custom than on an existing body of binding international agreements, were all officials had to guide them during the Civil War. By the end of the war, Union policies regarding Confederate prisoners would be considered humane and enlightened enough by Western nations to form the basis for international treaties on the subject in the last quarter of the nineteenth century.[2]

1861–1863

When the Civil War began, few in the nation gave much serious thought to the idea that it might be a long, drawn-out affair. Most thought the war would be over after one or two major battles with their side gaining overwhelming victory. For Northerners such ideas began to dissipate quickly on the plains of Manassas, Virginia, in July 1861 when their great army was sent scurrying back to the safety of Washington's defenses. In the wake of what would come to be First Manassas or Bull Run, Union officials began planning for a longer conflict. More men were called to serve and the call was for three-year enlistments rather than the original ninety-day deals the first wave of volunteers had made. And preparations were made to deal with prisoners captured in what was shaping up to be a longer war than many had anticipated or wanted.

That July, the Union's Quartermaster-General, Montgomery C. Meigs, urged the Secretary of War at the time, Simon Cameron, to appoint a Commissary-General of Prisoners to create and administer a prison system to deal with enemy captives. It is quite likely that Meigs did not make this request because he wanted to ensure that Southern prisoners were well taken care of; at least that was likely not his sole or even driving motivation. Enemy prisoners, he realized, would fall under his jurisdiction in the absence of some other official specifically designated to deal with that particular aspect of the North's war effort. He did not want it. Such a job was sure to be a thankless one and he had been given the daunting job of provisioning the Northern war machine, the largest military force by far that the United States had ever created. The last thing he wanted was the additional burden of looking out for hundreds, perhaps thousands, of Confederate prisoners. Whatever his motivation, he got his wish and in October 1861 Colonel William Hoffman was appointed Commissary-General of Prisoners.[3]

Hoffman's job was to oversee the North's military prisons to ensure humane and uniform treatment of Southern prisoners. During the previous summer Meigs had told Cameron that the Commissary-General of Prisoners, whoever that ultimately was, should be guided by the principle that prisoners of war "are entitled to proper accommodations, [and] to courteous and respectful treatment." In early October 1861, for example,

Meigs and Hoffman were working to find a location for a prison in Ohio. Hoffman had authority for final approval of a site but Meigs pointed out to him that he should choose a location that would not sit at a higher latitude than the west end of Lake Erie "in order to avoid too rigorous a climate." Towards the end of the same month Hoffman was informed that he had the authority to provide prisoners with all that "may be absolutely necessary for the comfort and health of the prisoners." In fact Hoffman was given considerable authority over Northern prisons that October. Meigs let Hoffman know that he would leave much to his "discretion and knowledge, and [that Meigs believed] that your appointment will alleviate the hardships of confinement [for] those erring men." There was certainly nothing said among key officials at the beginning of the war to suggest that Union authorities had anything but the best of intentions for Southern prisoners' welfare while in Northern hands.[4]

But while Meigs was describing Hoffman's duties to him, explaining that the government expected decent treatment for prisoners, Meigs also expressed a concern about spending. As Quartermaster-General, Meigs certainly had every right to worry about having the necessary funds to perform his gargantuan duties. However, he made it very clear to Hoffman that the new Commissary-General was to strike an acceptable balance between saving money and taking proper care of Confederate prisoners. "In all that is done," Meigs told him in October 1861, "the strictest economy consistent with security and proper welfare of the prisoners must be observed." Essentially Hoffman was told that defining what was and was not a necessary expenditure was up to him. As it turned out, Hoffman was discovered to be a man whose definition of necessary was extremely narrow.[5]

Hoffman has taken a beating in the literature as an unfeeling skinflint whose miserly qualities doomed thousands of Southerners to premature graves. That is not entirely fair or accurate. Rock Island's historian, Benton McAdams, has provided the best description to date of the Union's Commissary-General of Prisoners. Hoffman was raised by a father who "scratched for every penny," McAdams has pointed out, making Hoffman cheap, to use a modern term. When Meigs told Hoffman to watch his spending, Hoffman understood that to mean that a major part of his job description was not to part with a nickel if he could help it—and he never did. Given Hoffman's childhood and his specific instructions to watch his spending it is not surprising that, for him, it often happened that "financial concerns outgrew their proper place . . . ." But, as McAdams has convincingly argued, "Hoffman was not evil; he was narrow. He was unimaginative, humorless, hidebound . . . . He had extremely strict ideas of duty, obligation, and his own career, and he followed those tenets blindly. From that came suffering."

Hoffman's financial ideas would, over the course of the war, hinder attempts to take proper care of Confederate prisoners, but that does not automatically indicate a plan to neglect or abuse them. McAdams also has shown that the record "clearly shows that Hoffman, albeit grudgingly, often acted with humane concern."[6]

An important point to make here is that Federal officials, who have been so often accused of negligence, took the initiative before the war was a year old to create a prison system and appoint a chief administrator for it. There was no immediate pressing need to do so and in the fall of 1861 the South actually held the bulk of the war's prisoners. Yet in order to be ready for future prisoners the United States began to prepare for them. That suggests very clearly that Union officials at the war's opening intended to assure humane treatment of enemy captives. While the North was making such preparations in 1861, Richmond officials were making far more limited plans for prisoners. The Confederacy, for example, would not appoint General John Winder to be its chief prison administrator until late 1864.[7]

During the war's first half, the wartime evidence suggests that when Southern soldiers fell into Northern hands they had little cause for complaint. In January and February 1862 the War Department's position was that prisoners in Union hands would not be mistreated. "Besides the rations allowed by regulations [full Union ration] without regard to rank," Meigs told Hoffman in late February, "the United States will supply such blankets, cooking utensils and clothing as are necessary to prevent real suffering." In Tennessee that same month, Major General Henry Halleck ordered his Chief of Staff, Brigadier General George Cullum: "Give [Southern prisoners] everything necessary for their comfort. Treat them the same as our own soldiers." Cullum apparently did as he was told. In a report made shortly after giving Cullum his instructions, Halleck boasted to the War Department that all soldiers in his department were "cared for without distinction of states or counties, friends or foes." A Confederate soldier, James Conrad Peters, who had been captured at Fort Donelson, backed up Halleck's report that all soldiers were cared for regardless of uniform. "We have been well treated," Peters recorded, with he and his fellow prisoners having "plenty to eat of bacon, pork, and beef, light bread, beans, etc." Two months later Peters remained in Yankee hands and after some eight weeks in captivity he wrote, "I am still well and hearty" in his diary.[8]

As Peters suggested, food does not appear to have been a serious problem for Rebel prisoners, at least not during the first half of the war. Indeed, even the most vitriolic Lost Cause pieces suggest that the starving of prisoners was something that evolved and was common during the last half of the war as Northern methods for prosecuting the war hardened. In March 1862, Hoffman instructed officials at Camp Chase near Columbus, Ohio, to have "regularly issued to each mess the same rations that are allowed our private soldiers." This order was not unique or restricted to Camp Chase but was intended for all Northern prison camps. That being the case, Southern prisoners fared well by the standards of the time in terms of food. As Bell Wiley showed in his excellent studies of Civil War soldiers decades ago, soldiers receiving the full United States ration (over 4,500 calories) were the best fed in the Western world and likely on the planet, in terms of sheer bulk. With their minimal understanding of the importance of a varied diet in preserving health combined with the general definition that a good ration was one that filled the belly, Union officials had every reason to view the amount of meat and bread (the bulk of the ration's food calories) issued to soldiers and prisoners as perfectly adequate, especially for relatively inactive prisoners. The major problem, of course, was that vegetables were only a small part of the Federal ration and fruit was not provided at all. The important point to make here, though, is that supplying prisoners with the full official Federal ration during the first half of the war does not constitute negligence; Southern prisoners between 1861 and 1863 were not receiving any less food than Northern soldiers in the field from Union officials and such rations were abundant by contemporary standards.[9]

During this same period, those prisoners not satisfied with the monotonous rations were permitted to supplement their diet through private camp sutlers. These private merchants sold all sorts of items (usually at exorbitant rates) to prisoners and were certainly a boon to those who could afford to patronize them. A February 1863 list of non-contraband items sutlers were allowed to sell in Northern prisons included "hams, flour, molasses, canned fruits, apples, pies, cakes, raisins, nuts, clothing, boots and shoes . . . ." It is difficult and likely impossible to determine with any accuracy what percentage of prisoners could afford better diets through post sutlers, but it is safe to assume that a significant enough number of prisoners either entered prison with funds or received money through the mail (which was permitted with some brief interruption in 1864) to make doing business worth the merchants' while. Sutlers also helped the prisoners indirectly by paying a fee for the privilege of doing business in the prisons. Hoffman saw the obvious advantage of sutlers' fees defraying prisons' expenses but he also expected that they were to be used "for the health and comfort of the prisoners." As he told one commandant in July 1862: "The sutler is entirely under your control and you will see to it that he furnishes proper [legal] articles and at reasonable rates, and you will impose a tax upon him for the privilege . . . . This tax will make part of the fund available for the prisoners' benefit."[10]

The very existence of the prison funds has been cited as evidence that Confederate prisoners suffered and died in higher numbers because Hoffman and other Northern officials went too far to save money. Always looking for ways to save his government money, something he viewed as a major part of his duties as Commissary-General of Prisoners, he authorized commandants to withhold food and other rations they considered in excess of what prisoners needed to be healthy. As he explained to Colonel James Mulligan, Camp Douglas's commandant, in March 1862: "The regular ration is larger than is necessary for men living quietly in camp, and by judiciously withholding some part of it to be sold to the commissary a fund may be created with which many articles needful to the prisoners may be purchased and thus save the expense to the Government."[11]

Hoffman's decision to allow commandants to save money by withholding rations likely did lead to actual suffering in some cases. Commandants were given rather vague guidelines and that could certainly have led to withholding more than was wise or judicious—whatever that may have meant. But to leap upon the existence of funds as de facto proof that Southern prisoners literally starved in Yankee prisons because Hoffman was a miser who specifically told commandants to hold back large amounts of food to save money would be going too far. Recall that sedentary prisoners were receiving rations designed for combat soldiers making long marches and fighting great battles. Hoffman, not unreasonably, assumed that the same abundant caloric intake necessary to sustain soldiers in the field was not necessary for prisoners who did little more than stand or lie around all day. It should also be understood that when the term "rations" is used, it applies not only to food but to things like soap and candles. Also, "rations" included items that were not vital to prisoners' health like coffee, tea, sugar, salt, and molasses. So ration reductions implemented to increase prison funds did not automatically mean that meat, bread, and vegetables were being slashed to save money and defray expenses.

Hoffman doubtless felt vindicated in his decision to encourage camp commanders to help defray expenses by holding back some of the rations when he received reports like the one he got from Camp Chase in late July 1862 stating that "a considerable portion [of the prisoners' ration is] daily finding its way to the slop tubs." Believing the official ration was overly generous, combined with the prisoners' being permitted to patronize camp sutlers and receive food from family and friends through the mail, Hoffman did not think there would be any undue suffering for want of food. And, as most of the inspection reports he received during the first half of the war indicated, prisoners' food rations seemed to be of sufficient quality and quantity to assure that captives were not going hungry. He therefore had every reason to believe the prison fund was a good idea, one that saved money without sacrificing the prisoners' health.[12]

Clothing for prisoners was also a responsibility that Union officials took on during the first half of the war. Meigs told Hoffman that the government viewed this as a duty to prisoners and that "clothing not good enough for troops has by fraud of inspectors and dealers been forced into our depots. This will be used." The condemned clothes were indeed unsuitable for combat troops that would put a lot of stress on them, but Northern officials concluded that they would work just fine for relatively immobile captives. In many cases the condemned Federal clothing was an improvement over what the Southern prisoners arrived in as Hoffman noted in a report saying that "it will be desirable to throw away many of the filthy garments which prisoners will have on when they arrive . . . ." The inspection reports from Northern prisons from 1861 to 1863 indicate that most prisoners were at least basically clothed—hat, jacket, shirt, drawers (underwear), trousers, socks, and shoes. While not all Confederate prisoners required new clothing items upon arrival or at any time during their stays in Yankee prisons at this point in the war, they could get them in a variety of ways. The Federals could supply them as they did, for example, in February 1863 at Camp Douglas where "620 pairs of shoes, 597 overshirts, 303 flannel shirts, 12 cotton shirts, 312 woolen blouses, 1,980 knit socks, 1,846 pairs of cotton drawers, 60 flannel drawers, 148 hats, 101 pairs of pants, [and] 3 gray overcoats" were issued to needy prisoners. Or they were allowed to buy higher quality items at the camp sutlers. Or they could have friends and relatives send them clothing through the mail. Ultimately there is no compelling wartime evidence to suggest that Southern prisoners during the first half of the war were wandering about Northern pens in rags or nearly naked.[13]

From 1861 to 1863 Union officials also provided adequate shelter from the elements for prisoners of war. The accommodations to be found in those facilities were certainly far from luxurious, but then again living quarters in most military camps at that time were pretty rough and intended to do little more than keep soldiers somewhat drier and warmer than they would be if they had no shelter at all. Northern prison shelter included wooden barracks and, though far less common, army tents. These were often drafty and leaky, not insulated, and minimally waterproofed. Living in Union prison barracks was, without question, uncomfortable when the weather was particularly cold or wet. Claims that the water in prisoners' canteens froze if they were more than a couple of feet from the barracks' stoves are likely not exaggerations. But the Federal position was that the prisoners' comfort was not a valid concern. In July 1862 Meigs made that point quite clear to Hoffman when the commissary-general had requested funds to better seal prison barracks against the rain and snow. Meigs told Hoffman that "the department will approve the reasonable repair of [barracks] to make them waterproof. If the prisoners have as good quarters as our own soldiers in the field can be supplied with it seems all that humanity requires . . . ." Arguing that enemy prisoners were somehow entitled to snug, watertight accommodations while the soldiers in the field dutifully protecting that government could not be given the same seems difficult, if not impossible.[14]

While the barracks and tents did not offer a lot of comfort, particularly in severe weather, they were not substantially different, and certainly not inferior, than those the prisoners were accustomed to in the field. In July 1862, for example, the prisoners at Camp Butler in Illinois were reported as living in tents that "were generally provided with board floors." The tents were also described as having prisoner-constructed fireplaces and chimneys with wood provided regularly to fend off the cold. The amount of wood allotted to prisoners was not always sufficient, especially during particularly cold spells, to keep the tents' interiors 10 to 15 degrees above freezing, but it was provided. Such would not have been found very often in the Rebel armies in the field, especially during the campaigning season. Confederate soldiers spent the war years living in unfloored tents or, while in winter quarters, makeshift cabins, the quality of which varied greatly depending on the occupants' building skills. Often while they were on campaign and traveling light, a rubber poncho and a blanket were their only shelter. To these men, and this would have been particularly true of veterans, wooden barracks or tents with board floors and wood or coal stoves would not have been seen as unduly sparse or as evidence of unacceptable negligence.[15]

Critics of Federal policies towards prisoners can, and generally do, point to evidence indicating that living quarters were in terrible shape. Such evidence exists because it was true; living quarters often left quite a bit to be desired. Confederate prisoners did have to live in barracks with roofs that leaked. They did live in quarters constructed hastily of green wood that split and warped as it dried out, causing holes in the walls that let the cold in and the heat out. The question to be answered, though, is whether such evidence indicates or proves Yankee negligence or callousness. The Yankees' critics have uniformly answered the question with a resounding "yes." But the fact that Union inspectors reported these problems and made requests for funds to remedy them indicates that official policy was that such conditions were not supposed to exist for prisoners' barracks. And the evidence that positive steps were usually taken to remedy the problems also indicates that Northern officials did not purposely build leaky, drafty barracks to increase suffering and death among Southern prisoners. Because problems such as leaky roofs and holes in walls had to be reported, justified, and go through the official approval process, fixing them in a timely manner was out of the question. Ultimately, the evidence that Confederate prisoners' barracks were sometimes cold and wet indicates that the Union government was inefficient and that fixing enemy prisoners' living spaces was low on the official "to do" list.

If it is difficult to argue that providing shelter for Southern prisoners that was comparable, if sometimes admittedly crude by modern standards, to what Civil War soldiers on both sides lived in constituted negligence, the case gets harder to make when one sees that the records show how often Northern officials worked to enlarge and repair prisoners' living quarters during the first half of the war. At times crowding became a problem at several prisons and when it was reported to Hoffman additional space was generally ordered and built. At other times barracks were reported as needing repairs and these too were usually approved (though with warnings to keep an eye on spending) and made during this period of the war. In fact, the records from this period indicate that barracks floors in many prison facilities were raised off the ground to aid ventilation (and prevent tunneling), repaired to make them reasonably warm and dry, and expanded to ease crowding.[16]

Northern efforts to take humane care of Southern prisoners during the first half of the war can also be seen in their attempts to see to it that adequate medical care was available for captives. Following the Battle of Fort Donelson, Halleck reported to the War Department that "Humanity required" that prisoners receive the same medical treatment as soldiers. Hoffman agreed. In March 1862 he instructed Camp Chase officials that "all sick must be properly and kindly treated." He also informed them: "It is supposed that ample surgical aid will be found among the prisoners; but if not you will notify the department, when the deficiency will be promptly remedied." That same month he ordered additional hospital buildings for Camp Morton near Indianapolis so that ill prisoners would be more comfortable and not have to remain in the barracks where they could infect others. From 1862 through 1863 Hoffman regularly approved expenditures for clean sheets, pillow cases, and underclothing for sick prisoners. In fact, for all Hoffman's concerns about spending, he did not appear to hesitate when it came to medical costs during this period.[17]

One of the more difficult things to do was to find competent medical personnel for prisons. The best and brightest tended to prefer treating the country's loyal soldiers and the government certainly wanted their soldiers to have them too. That did not mean, though, that Hoffman did not want to have reasonably competent medical men to treat Southern prisoners. In March 1862 there was a lot of illness at Camp Butler and Hoffman contacted Halleck, who was in overall command of that military department, about getting "an energetic medical officer" for the camp to "alleviate the sad condition of the sick." Usually Hoffman hoped that, in order to save the government the expense of providing them, doctors could be found among the prisoners themselves, and this was the case sometimes. But as he instructed Camp Chase officials, if Confederate medical personnel could not be found among the inmates they were to notify him immediately. In the spring of 1862, Camp Morton's chief medical officer was a Dr. Bobbs. Hoffman contacted Meigs about replacing Dr. Bobbs because he felt that Bobbs lacked the experience to carry out his duties towards the prisoners effectively. The results, according to official inspection reports from 1862 and early 1863, were decreasing death rates and improving health among the prisoners. In April 1863 Hoffman responded to a report from a former prisoner that he had been ill treated while in Union care by boasting: "The sick and wounded have been as well and as promptly attended to as our own soldiers and all have been furnished with an abundant supply of rations, even including what may be called luxuries." The "luxuries" claim certainly went too far, but the records do seem to support his claims about the sick and wounded. His response also indicates that the Northern policy for treating ill and injured prisoners was to provide all the medical care that was available, primitive as it may have been at that time.[18]

The wartime records point strongly towards the conclusion that Union officials during the first half of the Civil War took their humanitarian duties towards Confederate prisoners seriously. Northern authorities provided prisoners with the same rations Union soldiers received and insured that they received basic clothing, shelter, and medical care. That Federal officials provided prisoners with the same rations and comparable clothing to that of Union soldiers was a decision ahead of its time and influenced later international laws on the subject of how to treat prisoners. Not until 1874 at the Brussels Conference were capturing nations required to provide prisoners of war with the same quality and quantity rations as that nation's soldiers. And while the policy to allow prisoners to supplement their rations and clothing via sutlers and the mail system reflected the desire to shift the financial burden of caring for prisoners away from Washington as much as anything else, Yankee officials could have denied those options to the prisoners. The right to such options was not spelled out in any body of international law or custom dealing with prisoners of war in the early 1860s.[19]

It is remarkable that Confederate prisoners during the first half of the war received the considerations that they did from Northern officials in Washington. The United States was not legally or customarily obligated to treat Southerners as legitimate prisoners of war. The general understanding, as reflected in most international agreements and treaties indicated, was that enemy prisoners from legally recognized states were due certain rights and privileges. This was not firmly established for soldiers fighting for a state or nation that was not recognized by anyone on the planet but their own government, which certainly was the legal reality for Confederates. The highly debatable presumption that states had the legal right to secede/destroy the United States is moot here. The United States and the rest of the world treated the Civil War as an internal rebellion, not a conflict between two separate, independent nations. Union officials would have been within their legal and constitutional rights to define Confederate soldiers as rebels guilty of treason; as article III, section III of the Constitution clearly says, treason is "levying war against [the United States], or in adhering to their enemies, giving them aid and comfort." Fortunately for thousands of Confederate prisoners, Union officials did not take such an extreme position during the war's first two years and chose to bestow rights and privileges on Southern prisoners despite any legal requirement that they do so.[20]

While the records for the first half of the war undermine the position that Northern officials neglected and/or abused Southern prisoners, a major reason Confederate captives had little cause to complain was that for most of that period they did not have to remain in Yankee prisons for extended periods of time. After initially balking at requests by Confederate officials for an official agreement between Washington and Richmond to exchange prisoners, the Lincoln administration approved such a deal in July 1862. Northern officials had been concerned that such a formal and legal agreement would prove that Washington recognized the Confederate States of America as a separate nation, something Southern officials were fully aware of and understood would help boost their chances for foreign recognition as well as ease the hardship of prisoners of war. A fairly simple agreement was worked out wherein a mathematical formula stipulated that privates were exchanged man for man with privates, and so many privates were worth a corporal, sergeant, lieutenant, and so on until one general required the exchange of 60 privates. The excess prisoners on either side would be paroled (let go) with the understanding that they would not rejoin their respective units until formally notified of their exchange. The exchange cartel, until its suspension in the spring of 1863, virtually emptied the war's prisons. The result was that crowding was rarely a problem and administering the prisoners' needs was more efficient. This probably explains why researchers can expend tremendous amounts of time and energy sifting through Confederate testimony (even from the Lost Cause era) and still find very little describing the "horrors" of prison life prior to the summer of 1863. The question to be answered, then, is whether the dedication to humane treatment of Confederate prisoners was abandoned by Northern officials during the second half of the war as has been so often argued.[21]

According to the most recent scholarly treatment of the subject, that is precisely what occurred. Charles Sanders has argued that 1863 would see "a new and decidedly darker chapter in the history of prisoner of war treatment in Union camps" written by hard-hearted, vindictive officials like Edwin Stanton and Ulysses S. Grant. Prisoners would be starved in Northern pens, with draconian cuts in rations producing "frightful [scurvy] epidemics in most Union camps." "Put simply," he argues, "the longer the war continued, the more terrible the camps of the Union and Confederacy became." Such may well have been the case in Southern prisoner of war facilities, but there is a significant amount of compelling evidence that such a characterization of Union prisons between 1863 and 1865 is, generally speaking, not so much inaccurate as it is exaggerated.[22]

1863–1865

One important piece of evidence suggesting that Union officials intended to continue treating Southern prisoners with humanity and as legitimate prisoners of war is General Orders Number 100, written by the famous lawyer Francis Lieber. These orders were made official in April 1863 to insure uniformity in the treatment of prisoners and to reiterate that Northern policy was not to neglect or abuse Southerners who were captured in battle. One important thing General Orders 100 did was clearly define a prisoner of war as "a public enemy armed or attached to the hostile army...[who was] exposed to the inconveniences as well as entitled to the privileges of a prisoner of war." They also articulated the North's official position regarding how these "public enemies" were to be treated if captured, stipulating in article 56, section 3: "A prisoner of war is subject to no punishment for being a public enemy nor is any revenge wreaked upon him by the intentional infliction of any suffering or disgrace, by cruel imprisonment want of food, by mutilation, death or any other barbarity."

According to another section: "Unnecessary or revengeful destruction of life is not lawful." Helping one's self to prisoners' private property was also officially designated as "dishonorable and ... prohibited." Significantly, and despite recent arguments to the contrary, it appears that at the war's midpoint when Washington officials were beginning to fight a "hard" war where the destruction and confiscation of private property were embraced as legitimate, the same Yankee authorities chose not to take a "hard" line towards captured Rebels.[23]

And yet, within mere weeks of the publication of General Orders 100 the Federals up and decided to quit exchanging prisoners, dooming thousands to extended periods of uncomfortable, potentially deadly confinement. For generations and in the most recent treatment of the issue, General Ulysses S. Grant has been held largely, if not solely, responsible for the North's decision to suspend the exchange cartel. Even though both sides screamed about violations of the agreement before the ink on it was dry, it was Grant's understanding that halting the exchange of prisoners by 1863 would give the Northern war machine an even greater numerical superiority in the field than it already possessed. Charles Sanders recently put it quite bluntly, saying that Grant "prohibited the resumption of general exchanges" and that "the general's refusal was . . . based on simple, ghastly arithmetic." He goes on to say that although "Grant acknowledged that refusing to permit general exchanges was tantamount to a death sentence for the thousands of Union boys wasting away in southern camps, he was convinced that this strategy would ultimately yield victory at the least cost in Union blood and treasure." Had Grant been motivated to consider the issue from a humanitarian standpoint rather than being fixated on "a more direct, and decidedly military, objective" historians have and still tend to argue, exchanges could have been resumed and hundreds, probably thousands, of Confederate prisoners (and Union ones for that matter) would not have had to have suffered painfully slow deaths from disease and starvation while in the hands of the enemy.[24]

Often dismissed in the major scholarly treatments of this issue is the Union explanation that the South's refusal to recognize black soldiers as legitimate prisoners of war subject to exchange on the same basis as white soldiers lay at the heart of the decision to suspend the 1862 agreement. This dismissive attitude is clearly expressed in the most recent scholarly work, which points out that while "Grant publicly proclaimed that his decision was prompted by the South's refusal to exchange black soldiers under the same terms as whites, the general's refusal was actually based on simple, ghastly arithmetic." In fact Sanders has gone so far as to allege that a conspiracy existed to lie to the public by telling them that the North was refusing to exchange to protect its black soldiers from execution and/or enslavement when the "real" reason was Grant's "ghastly arithmetic." Citing Benjamin Butler's postwar memoirs, Sanders relates that Butler (whose personal and political relationship with Grant by war's end was strained) "recalled" conversations with Grant while Butler was the North's exchange agent wherein Grant laid out his military reasoning for not exchanging prisoners. Butler remembers that he agreed with Grant's assessment but that if the Northern public realized that their loved ones were suffering and dying as part of some sort of cold-blooded attrition strategy that it "would spawn a public relations nightmare for the Lincoln administration and would play directly into the hands of the Peace Democrats in the upcoming presidential and congressional elections." Thus the black prisoner issue was trotted out as political window dressing to make the government's non-exchange policy more politically palatable. It certainly was not the primary motive for suspending exchanges in 1863 despite what was said and written at the time.[25]

There are some serious flaws with this characterization and Grant's role in the decision. One major problem with laying the issue at Grant's feet is that the decision was made without any input from him. At the time Grant had his hands quite full with the siege of Vicksburg and it is highly unlikely that he shifted his focus at this critical and decisive moment in the war to make prisoner of war policy changes. More importantly, there is not a scrap of wartime evidence to suggest or prove that he had any direct or indirect effect on the 1863 decision. Grant may well have understood the military advantages of halting exchanges, and no doubt he did, but at that point in the war he was strictly a field officer without much, if any, influence over policy decisions. In fact, Grant did not get that kind of authority over military policy until well into 1864. So the cartel was suspended independently of Grant and his input in prisoner of war policy was indirect and limited until the final months of the war.[26]

Grant's thinking and actions in this area have also been presented in a very one-dimensional way. Too often he is shown as the hard-headed militarist who said things like "We have got to fight until the Military power of the South is exhausted and if we release or exchange prisoners captured it simply becomes a War of extermination." But this quotation, often used by Grant's detractors, was far from the only thought he ever expressed on the prisoner of war/exchange issue. Too often overlooked or dismissed is that in Grant's mind any exchange agreement between the two governments had to be at least reasonably equitable for both sides and in 1864 he believed that exchanges, at least on the basis of the 1862 cartel, benefited the Confederate war effort far more than they did the Northern one. For a variety of reasons conditions in Southern prisons had been deteriorating and many of the prisoners paroled from them at that point were returning incapable of returning to active duty. In August 1864 Grant told Butler, then acting as Union Agent for Exchange, "I am opposed to exchanges being made until the whole matter is put on a footing giving equal advantages to us with those given to the enemy." Here, then, is some evidence that suggests that Grant's lack of support for resuming exchanges was not based exclusively on the desire to undermine Confederate military strength. Grant appears concerned, at least partly, with making sure that prisoner exchanges did not strengthen the South while doing little to nothing to benefit the Northern war effort. Like many in the North, Grant believed that exchanged Confederates would be ready to return to the field immediately while exchanged Federals were often broken-down wrecks of humanity totally unfit for service. Thus, Grant's unsupportive attitude towards resurrecting the 1862 cartel reflects more than the simplistic desire to deny soldiers to the Confederate armies. Rather, Grant appears in this correspondence to be willing to support exchanges if, and only if, his side got as much from the deal as the enemy, which certainly seems to be a reasonable position to have taken.[27]

Grant was not opposed to all exchanges. He did not have a problem, for example, with battlefield exchanges because both sides benefited equally. In a letter to General Marcus Canby in New Orleans in September 1864, General Henry Halleck answered Canby's questions about whether or not he could exchange prisoners recently taken since the 1862 agreement had been suspended officially. Halleck informed him that he was authorized to permit post-battle prisoner exchanges, telling him:

> I presume that General Grant's order to make no more exchanges of prisoners was based on the fact that they gave us only such men as they have utterly broken down by starvation, receiving from us men fit for duty. Every exchange, therefore gives them strength, without a corresponding advantage to us. Not so, however, with exchanges made on the battle-field or immediately after an engagement. Exchanges of this kind made man for man, as provided for in the cartel, General Grant did not intend to prohibit. You and the officers under your command are therefore at liberty to continue the exchanges in the field as provided for in the last clause of article 7 of the cartel of July 22, 1862.

Thus, while Grant certainly recognized the military benefits gained by the cartel's suspension, the premise that "ghastly arithmetic" was the only factor considered when Grant and other officials suspended the exchange cartel in 1863 is oversimplified. Other factors, like equality of benefits, were present and must be acknowledged if a fuller, more accurate picture of this decision is to be seen.[28]

In October 1864 the most direct evidence that Grant was not opposed to exchanging prisoners and was perfectly willing to consider post-battle exchanges is found in correspondence between him and General Robert E. Lee. With his Army of Northern Virginia needing all the men it could get, Lee contacted Grant about exchanging prisoners recently taken by both sides during Grant's Overland Campaign. Lee's communication did not address the cartel in any broad sense; he was asking for an exchange of prisoners recently taken by each army, something Grant was known to favor. Grant acknowledged Lee's proposal, responding, "Among those lost by the armies operating against Richmond were a number of colored troops. Before further negotiations are had upon the subject I would ask if you propose delivering these men the same as white soldiers?" Lee told Grant that he was personally willing to exchange all troops on an equal footing, but he had to abide by his government's position that "negroes belonging to our citizens are not considered subjects of exchange and were not included in my proposition. If there are any such among those stated by you to have been captured around Richmond they cannot be returned." Regrettably then, Grant informed Lee, no prisoners would be exchanged unless *all* were eligible. He told Lee on October 3: "I have to state that the Government is bound to secure to all persons received into her armies the rights due soldiers. This being denied by you in the persons of such men as have escaped from Southern masters induces me to decline making the exchanges you ask." The result was that those prisoners wound up on trains for Northern prisons and Andersonville.[29]

As Grant's communications with Lee indicate, he was not opposed to the idea of exchanging prisoners so long as he felt his side benefited equally. The correspondence also reveals that the issue of assuring equal protection and treatment for black Union soldiers was not political propaganda. Historians such as Frank L. Byrne and James McPherson have acknowledged that Richmond's inequitable policies towards black troops were critical to the cartel's collapse. But these writers have not done lengthy studies and the larger, more recent, works on the subject have dismissed those policies as not having anything more than a peripheral relationship to the decision to suspend the agreement in 1863. As a result, the prevailing interpretation that the black prisoner issue was not the "real" reason for the suspension has been the prevailing one in the literature.

On the one hand the idea that the North's decision was not based solely or primarily on Southern policies to execute and/or enslave captured African American soldiers has some plausible aspects. For one thing, the North was certainly far from a racial utopia where black men were accorded equal treatment. Because black people were about as welcome in Northern communities as the plague, the idea that protecting black soldiers was the key reason the Lincoln administration halted exchanges does sound difficult to believe. Additionally, black soldiers were often mistreated in the service and for many months were not paid the same wage as white soldiers. That blacks' protection and welfare was a major concern to white Northerners does appear to be difficult to support. But, that Northern whites were far from racial egalitarians is not the same thing as proof that when Union officials cited the black prisoner issue as the reason the cartel was suspended and would remain so until Richmond altered its policies on the subject they were lying or misleading the public and historians to hide their "true" logic.

The overwhelming hard wartime evidence indicates that the key issue that led the Northern War Department to suspend the prisoner exchange agreement was indeed Richmond's policy regarding African American soldiers and prisoners and their white officers. The Federals' concern that these men would not be treated as legitimate prisoners of war was hardly an idle one. Jefferson Davis was outraged in January 1863 that officials in Washington had decided to allow blacks into the Union forces where they would be trained and "encouraged to a general assassination of their masters." To resort to calling "several millions of human beings of an inferior race" was not legitimate war, Davis believed, but servile insurrection—the white South's worst fear unleashed. He went on to say that the decision was "the most execrable measure recorded in the history of guilty man" and that black soldiers and their white officers would be treated not as legal United States soldiers and officers. The Davis administration's policy was that when captured these soldiers and officers "may be dealt with in accordance with the laws of those States providing for the punishment of criminals engaged in exciting servile insurrection." They were not to be protected by the 1862 cartel.[30]

Southern officials could not bring themselves to recognize black prisoners as legitimate captives due the protections of the 1862 cartel because that would have conferred a level of equality upon them that Confederate authorities would not do under any circumstances. As Alexander Stephens made crystal clear in his 1861 "cornerstone" speech, the Confederacy was founded upon the great natural truth that the black man was inferior to the white man. If they decided in 1863 to exchange blacks and whites equally under the terms and conditions of the 1862 agreement they would have been repudiating their nation's most sacred principle, the cornerstone of white supremacy. Neither could Confederates agree to surrender the right to control their property (slaves) simply because that property had run off, donned a blue uniform, and was called a free man by a foreign enemy. Treating blacks as entitled to all the rights and privileges as whites under the 1862 agreement was, to Confederates' way of thinking, to give away everything they had seceded to maintain. As one Rebel put it, Southerners would "die in the last ditch" before they surrendered what they viewed as their sacred rights. So, black prisoners would be treated as recaptured property to be returned to slavery or punished as insurrectionists.[31]

Whether or not the fiery language heard in official circles about what to do when and if black soldiers were taken in arms would be actively enforced in the field remained to be seen. But when African Americans began to be captured it seemed that they would indeed be treated like recaptured slaves. In April 1863 General Pemberton contacted the War Department from Vicksburg about what to do with a captured black soldier. Secretary of War

James Seddon told Pemberton to put him to work anywhere Pemberton thought he could be most useful to him. In fact he could put any captured blacks to work because the government, Seddon informed him, "has determined that negroes captured will not be regarded as prisoners of war." Three months later General P. G. T. Beauregard asked for clarification on the government's position regarding black prisoners who claimed to have been free when the war started. Several members of the famous 54th Massachusetts were being held in South Carolina at the time and protested, correctly, that they were neither escaped slaves nor insurrectionists. Seddon told Beauregard to make no distinction; all African Americans taken in uniform would be assumed to be runaway slaves. Richmond's official position, he went on to say, was that "*all* negroes taken in arms . . . are to be handed over to the authorities of the State where they are captured to be dealt with according to the laws thereof [emphasis mine]."[32]

With Confederate officials sending the clear and unmistakable message that they would refuse to accord black Union prisoners the same protections as white ones, Union authorities moved to suspend the exchange cartel as a way to force Richmond to rescind its policies towards African American prisoners wearing the United States uniform. Certainly a major part of Union officials' motivation came from concerns that if black men feared enslavement and/or execution as the risks of signing on for the Union that they would not do so, or at least not in significant enough numbers to have the positive impact on the war effort officials hoped for. Just as certainly, though, Northern officials had a duty to protect all of their soldiers' welfare to the best of their ability. To insure that black prisoners were treated as legitimate prisoners, the War Department declared in May 1863 that Southern prisoners would be retained "in order to be in a position to check the rebel Government and restrain the execution of its avowed purpose [to sell blacks and/or execute them and their white officers] in violation of the cartel." A few weeks later Lincoln himself weighed in to make his government's reason for suspending the cartel perfectly clear to all. In General Orders 252 he said, "It is the duty of every Government to give protection to its citizens, of whatsoever class, color, or condition, and especially to those who are duly organized as soldiers in the public service. The law of nations and civilized powers, permit no distinction as to color in the treatment of prisoners of war as public enemies." In November 1863, Secretary of War Edwin Stanton informed General Butler that he was to make no agreement to resume exchanges unless *all* United States soldiers were included in Confederate proposals. He told the General:

It is known that the rebels will exchange man for man and officer for officer, except blacks and officers in command of black troops. These they absolutely refuse to exchange. *This is the point on which the whole matter hinges.* Exchanging man for man and officer for officer, with the exception the rebels make, is a substantial abandonment of the colored troops and their officers to their fate, and would be a shameful dishonor to the Government bound to protect them. *When they agree to exchange all alike there will be no difficulty* [emphasis added].[33]

Confederate officials fully understood that the cartel was a dead letter so long as they clung to their right to enslave or execute black prisoners and their officers. But cling to it they did. Seddon informed Davis in February 1864 that the government's orders to send captured blacks to depots in the various states so that they could be claimed by former owners or sold at public auction "have been duly promulgated through all the departments and districts of the Army." A couple of months after that, Braxton Bragg told North Carolina's governor, Zebulon Vance, that black prisoners captured at the Battle of Plymouth were to be held until their owners could reclaim them. Since the issue of black prisoners was the major reason the Federals were giving for suspending the 1862 cartel, Davis told Bragg to inform Vance to announce the captures as quietly as possible to keep the Yankees from hearing about it. As Bragg told Vance, Davis's wishes were "to take the necessary steps to have the matter of such disposition kept out of the newspapers of the State, and in every available way to shun its obtaining any publicity as far as is consistent with the proposed restoration."[34]

Late in the summer of 1864 General Butler, whose appointment as the Union's Agent of Exchange thoroughly outraged Confederate officials, reiterated his government's position to his opposite number, Robert Ould. The Northern government would not consider resuming prisoner exchanges under the conditions of the 1862 agreement until Confederate officials agreed to include black soldiers as eligible for exchange the same as white prisoners. "If you are willing," Butler told Ould, "to exchange these colored men claimed as slaves, and you will so officially inform the Government of the United States, then, as I am instructed, a principle difficulty in effecting exchanges will be removed." Butler said he would like nothing better than to begin exchanging prisoners again. Like most Northerners he believed that the Confederacy was not treating Federal prisoners well at all, moving him, he told Ould, to be willing "to consent to anything" the South demanded to rescue Union prisoners from the "wrongs, indignities, and privations" they suffered in Confederate prison pens. But he would not consent to and he was not permitted, "to barter away the honor and faith of the Government of the United States which has been so solemnly pledged to the colored soldiers in its ranks." Not being a particularly good diplomat, Butler could not resist needling Ould by accusing Confederate officials of preferring to allow their soldiers to languish in prison rather than risk sacrificing their sacred right to treat black people any way they liked, telling him: "You certainly appear to place less value upon your soldier than you do upon your negro." But he had a point.[35]

Confederate officials, however, could not be persuaded or needled into changing their views about black prisoners, at least not in any meaningful way. In August 1864, more than a year after exchanges were halted, Seddon announced in what Sanders has termed "a dramatic concession to northern demands": "It has been considered best . . . to make a distinction between negroes . . . who can be recognized or identified as slaves and those who were inhabitants of the Federal States." Those not identified as free by Confederate authorities (whose dedication to making the correct designation was certainly questionable) would continue to be "returned" to slavery or forced to work on Confederate fortifications while those determined to be free would be "held in strict confinement" rather than sold. They were still not eligible for exchange on an equal footing with white prisoners according to the 1862 cartel and as Washington officials were demanding. With less than a year left in the war the cartel remained in limbo because, as one Union agent pointed out, the Richmond government had still not "as yet formally recognized [blacks]...as prisoners of war."[36]

Finally, in February 1865, the Confederate Congress repealed its policy allowing the states to try and execute black prisoners and white officers as insurrectionists. That body did not, however, rescind its policy that black prisoners whom Confederate officials deemed were fugitive slaves were liable to re-enslavement. In fact, black soldiers continued to be enslaved and forced to work on Confederate forts and breastworks until the end of the war. With their soldiers' lives thus guaranteed (and securing the lives of the white officers was of greater concern), Union officials were more willing to consider resuming exchanges. The issue of black prisoners was not effectively resolved so much as it was sidestepped by the agreement that those prisoners held the longest would be the first exchanged. That insured that for weeks, perhaps months, those processed and released would be white, leaving the controversial issue of black captives to be dealt with at some vague future time, presumably after Union victory was already secured. Indeed, at this stage in the war, with Confederate manpower, territory, and resources dwindling down to virtually nothing, Union authorities could afford to think in such terms and loosen, though not repudiate, their position on black equality. With victory seemingly on the horizon and the chances of blacks being taken prisoner dramatically decreasing with each passing day as Grant and Sherman chased Lee and Johnston more than fought them, it seemed reasonable to secure the release of hundreds of long-suffering prisoners by easing the stand on an issue for which little practical need remained. And during the final eight or so weeks of the war exchanges did slowly resume. Unfortunately, by that time each side's prisons were so full that thousands were unable to be processed and released until the war was over, remaining prisoners despite the resumption of the cartel.[37]

With all the correspondence demonstrating that Richmond's policy was at the center of the controversy, it is difficult, if not irresponsible, to blithely dismiss that policy because Northern whites were racists and could not have really meant what they repeatedly said. Union officials like Butler, Grant, and Lincoln himself made it very clear that if Southern officials did not treat black Union soldiers the same as white ones that the Confederacy would not get its men back. That this was mere pretext or a bluff, while not out of the realm of possibility certainly, would be more convincing if the South had called the bluff in some way and Union officials then scrambled around for other reasons to keep exchanges suspended. If there was something concrete in the wartime records to indicate that Northern officials were merely putting on a moral front to hide their true motives for halting exchanges, then perhaps the evidence given above could be taken at something other than face value. But in the absence of such evidence, and with the existence of a significant amount of evidence to the contrary, then the possibility that Northern officials meant what they said about the reasons for the cartel's suspension in 1863 needs to be taken more seriously.

Part of the reluctance, and it is understandable, to accept at face value the demands that black prisoners be treated equally lies in the fact that it portrays the North as more racially enlightened than it actually was and certainly makes Confederates look more bigoted vis-à-vis the North than was the case at the time. It could well be that there is a middle ground here. On the one hand it is perhaps too much to conclude that humanitarian protection for black Union soldiers was the sole reason for the cartel's suspension. But it is certainly not out of the realm of possibility that Northern officials had to make certain that black soldiers would be treated the same as white soldiers by Confederate officials because they wanted and needed that manpower for their war effort. Before the war ended, over 200,000 black soldiers would serve the Union cause. They certainly played a role in securing ultimate Northern victory and no doubt officials in the North knew that. It was why, after all, the Emancipation Proclamation contained a section that accepted blacks into Federal service. They must have understood how difficult it would be to recruit black soldiers and get the most out of those men if they understood that the government did not "have their back." Few indeed, would enlist and fewer still would not take the first chance to go AWOL if they knew that joining and fighting meant risking enslavement or execution as a rebel slave. If the Federals wanted these men, and they did, they could not hope to have them if they abandoned them in the field to the mercy of the Confederates. So they did not—not, perhaps, solely for the fine moral reasons modern officials would, but for more selfish reasons. And yes, even for more military reasons, just not ones based on attrition tactics as many have concluded.

Furthermore, not only did the North have every right to halt prisoner exchanges as a way to protect its soldiers, the suggestion that Union officials were unreasonable for doing so brings up an interesting and overlooked point. While it is unquestionably true that Confederate officials viewed black soldiers with fear and loathing and thought they were not proper combatants due the rights and privileges of legitimate soldiers, it does not follow that the North was obligated to prosecute its war to suit Southern sensibilities on the topic. The North's decision to use a particular race of men as soldiers, which had been suggested by some in the South (General Patrick Cleburne for one) well before Richmond approved that very same policy in March 1865, was not illegal or unreasonable. Black soldiers did not constitute some new diabolical military weapon deemed too terrible and uncivilized for modern war. Many outside the South and the United States no doubt found it a distasteful decision, but that is not the same as defining it as an illegal or illegitimate one. Confederate leaders' decision to view black soldiers as unprotected by the vague but oft-used term, "rules of civilized war" and the 1862 cartel was theirs alone. They were free to make that choice, of course, but they had no legal or customary right to expect that the United States government would abide by it. They must also be held responsible for making a choice that played a starring role in the cartel's suspension rather than let off the historical hook as people helplessly forced into a corner by unreasonable and unconscionable Yankee demands.

For the first half of the Civil War, Union officials' actions and policies regarding prisoners of war cannot very well be depicted as cruel or negligent. With the war barely opened they began preparing a military prison system and appointed an officer to administer it. They participated in discussions with Southern leaders to create the 1862 exchange cartel despite serious misgivings that doing so would constitute official recognition of the Confederacy and open the door to foreign nations doing the same. By most Northern and Southern accounts the prisoners held by the North were fed, clothed, and sheltered in an acceptable manner and given any medical treatment they may have needed. They created a uniform code for dealing humanely with prisoners of war in General Orders 100 that was considered so enlightened that it became the template for later international agreements on the subject. And their decision to suspend exchanges was a sanction imposed on Richmond to protect its soldiers and officers from being killed or enslaved if captured in battle. The question is whether the ruling sentiment to treat captured Rebels humanely changed at some point during the war's second half.

Hesseltine and quite a few historians since have, of course, suggested that the North did become more vindictive and cruel thanks to a propaganda-induced "war psychosis." There are a number of problems with accepting that some sort of mental instability, resulting from sensationalized newspaper stories, caused Northern officials to institute a program to increase suffering in their military prisons. One is that while there is no question that Federal officials did truly believe that their prisoners were not treated nearly as well as they believed they treated the Rebels, this idea was accepted much earlier than mid-1864. As early as July 1862 Meigs said he thought that Southern prisoners got all they needed from the Federals and were as comfortable as circumstances allowed, which was, he said, "much more than our men, prisoners [in the] South, get." The following spring Hoffman echoed the sentiment, boasting that Confederate captives had all they needed materially speaking but that such "has by no means been so with our troops whey they have been captured." From 1862 through half of 1864 Union authorities believed that their boys were not cared for by the Rebels as they should be but no records exist that prove that a policy was created to treat, or mistreat, Southern prisoners in a like manner.[38]

That changed in the summer of 1864, but the so-called retaliation policy was not a knee-jerk reaction to newspaper propaganda. In the spring of 1864 Federal officials conducted an official investigation into how Union prisoners were treated by interviewing prisoners returned by special truce agreements at Annapolis, Maryland. These prisoners were not representative of the typical prisoner, though. They were the most weak and ill, which was why they were granted special paroles in the first place. The parolees were in shocking states; several would not live more than a few days after their return. These prisoners would be interviewed to get an idea from eyewitnesses (rather than relying on what the newspapers said from afar) as to how the Confederate authorities were actually treating Union soldiers. Once the investigation was complete they would determine what, if any, changes needed to be made in their own policies towards prisoners of war.

Not surprisingly, what they saw and heard horrified them. Howard Leedom of the 52nd New York testified before Congress that he lost several toes to frostbite on Belle Isle in Richmond because the guards there took his shoes and replaced them with old Confederate shoes that were "all cut and split open." Proper rations, according to the prisoners, were not to be had in Southern pens. "I was so starved," a member of the 8th Tennessee Cavalry testified, "that when I was down I could not get up without catching hold of something to pull myself up by." Charles Gallagher, a soldier in the 40th Ohio, told Federal officials that Southern prison authorities "give [prisoners] a half a loaf of bread, and tell you that was your day's rations; you could take that or nothing." Other parolees came through Congress in April and May 1864 telling stories that were very similar, leading to the conclusion that some policy must exist to deny Union prisoners the basic material necessities to survive in prison.[39]

Confederate officials had been claiming for some time that Union prisoners were not mistreated as a matter of policy, but that they got all that Southern officials could supply under the circumstances—hinting strongly that the North's blockade, destructive methods, and refusal to exchange were the reasons their soldiers suffered in Southern prisons. But even despite serious supply shortages, Richmond argued, Union prisoners got everything, rations included, that Southern soldiers got. During the 1864 investigations a physician, Dr. B. A. Van Derkieft, testified that he did not see how such claims could be true. He did not see how it was physically possible "that the rebels could fight as well, or make such marches as they have done, upon such small rations as our prisoners have received." Dr. William G. Knowles agreed, arguing that if Southern soldiers were eating the exact same rations as Northern prisoners, "multitudes of them would have died" and the war would have ended already. Congressman Benjamin Wade, who chaired the controversial Joint Committee on the Conduct of the War, also found it difficult to believe that the same rations that reduced

Northern men to little more than "living skeletons" fortified Southern men to where they could "make long and rapid marches and . . . offer a stubborn resistance in the field." Hoffman did not believe the claim either and in his report to the Secretary of War he wrote:

> Can an army keep the field, and be active and efficient, on the same fare that kills prisoners of war at a frightful percentage? I think not; no man can believe it; and while a practice so shocking to humanity is persisted in by the rebel authorities, I would respectfully urge that retaliatory measures be at once instituted by subjecting the officers we now hold as prisoners of war to similar treatment.[40]

One cannot discount entirely the revenge motive here. Certainly Northern officials, like the rest of the public, seethed at the thought of their soldiers being starved and otherwise mistreated by the South. Accepting that is not especially helpful, though, in evaluating Northern policies towards prisoners of war. What needs to be dealt with, since Northern officials have been so long accused and convicted of negligence and hard-heartedness, is whether a retaliation program by itself (the severity of the policy will be dealt with later in the chapter) constitutes proof that the Federals became rather cold-blooded towards Confederate prisoners in the latter half of 1864.

Adopting a retaliation policy may sound harsh, but that is only the case to modern ears attached to people who have lived in a world where treaties barring retaliation have been the norm, which was not the case in 1864. Both governments during the Civil War accepted the idea that retaliation was a legitimate means of getting the enemy to alter certain policies. As early as 1861, for example, Confederate officials seeking to protect their privateers from execution for piracy by the United States threatened to retaliate by executing a Union prisoner taken at First Manassas/Bull Run for every Southerner executed for piracy—a threat that ultimately proved completely successful. At the beginning of May 1863 the Confederate Congress proposed and Jefferson Davis signed a resolution endorsing the use of retaliation. Outraged by the North's decision to arm black troops, the Confederate government defined that decision as "inconsistent with the spirit of . . . modern warfare [that] prevail among civilized nations; they may therefore be properly and lawfully repressed by retaliation." On the Union side, General Orders 100 also specified that retaliation was permissible when a "reckless enemy . . . leaves his opponent no other means of securing himself against the repetition of barbarous outrage." But, it should be noted, those Orders reminded officials that retaliation should be used only as a last resort, otherwise the belligerents would be led "by rapid steps . . . nearer to the internecine wars of savages." Retaliation, therefore, they instructed, "shall only be resorted to after careful inquiry into the real occurrence and the character of the misdeeds that may demand retribution." Since both sides recognized retaliation as legitimate and since the Confederacy had threatened it and endorsed it in official documents, the North cannot reasonably be accused of acting recklessly towards Confederate prisoners by discussing and proposing retaliatory measures in 1864. Thus the important question is whether the retaliatory measures were draconian enough to have caused or significantly exacerbated the suffering and mortality in Northern prisons.[41]

The first charge to address should be that of reducing rations for Southern prisoners to the point that they starved, at least during the war's final year and a half. Until June 1864 Confederates in Northern prisons were to receive the standard Federal ration, which as has been pointed out, was quite generous if nutritionally sub-par. So generous were Federal rations that officials were getting reports that prisoners and soldiers were throwing significant portions of them away. To curb what seemed to Northern officials to be wasting money, money the government did not have to waste, rations were reduced *for Union soldiers and Confederate prisoners* in June 1864. Federal soldiers' cuts were not all that significant, declining from roughly 4,600 calories to a little over 4,400 calories, while the cuts were deeper for prisoners because they were nowhere near as active as combat soldiers. Hoffman specifically pointed out in May 1864 that while he advocated cutting rations, he urged that officials do so "without depriving them of the food necessary to keep them in health." This seems to suggest that Union officials did not intend to place Confederate prisoners on "starvation rations" as so many would claim after the war and continue to argue in recent literature on the subject. Modern prisoners, beneficiaries of a slew of protective legislation and who are larger than their Civil War-era counterparts, receive between 2,500 and 2,700 calories per day.[42]

Part of the 1864 retaliation program was to restrict sutlers from selling food items and to disallow food from family and friends through the mail. While solely dependent on the Federal government there can be no doubt that prisoners did not always get their full ration, but not because officials were trying to starve them. As will be seen in later chapters, prison officials dealt with private contractors for food and other items and these contractors were often far more interested in increasing their profit margins than they were in delivering what they promised at the proper levels of quality and quantity. This was the case with contractors supplying the troops as well so it should come as no great shock that prisoners were sometimes victimized by unscrupulous contractors. While investigations of conniving contractors went on the prisoners would have gone hungry and no doubt would have attributed their discomfort to malevolent Northern policies. That belief would be reflected in the numerous Lost Cause memoirs that related tales of terrible, gnawing starvation caused by callous Yankees. However, those postwar stories are not supported very well by wartime records.

The worst part about having to rely solely on the Federal ration was that it was skimpy on vegetables and neglected fruit entirely. The result of a monotonous diet that did not include adequate fruit and vegetables was malnutrition and scurvy. Officials at the time did vaguely understand that there was a connection between scurvy and fruit and vegetables but they treated those items like medicine rather than as necessary preventatives. During the Civil War, the adage "an ounce of prevention is worth a pound of cure" was not followed. When scurvy became a problem in Northern prisons officials ordered increased levels of fruit and vegetables for the prisoners to bring the problem under control. Unfortunately, when scurvy cases did abate, officials tended to think they had solved the problem and went back to doling out the official ration. Thus cases of scurvy in Federal prisons do not represent de facto proof of "starvation rations" so much as they reflect the lack of importance placed on prevention of illness at the time and the poor nutritional state of the official ration, which most inspection reports say the prisoners received regularly from 1864 through the end of the war.[43]

In the most recent work on Civil War prisons, though, the charge is once again made that scurvy cases represented proof of "starvation" policies in Yankee prisons. By late summer 1864, Sanders asserts, the inhumane policy to starve Southern captives "produced frightful epidemics [of scurvy] in most Union camps." There are several problems with this recent, sweeping charge. No definition of "frightful" is provided and no statistics are provided to prove that the number of scurvy cases in Union prisons were "frightful" or occurred in such numbers as to constitute an "epidemic." The official medical history of the war shows that scurvy numbers varied greatly depending on the camp. At places like Point Lookout and Fort Delaware, the numbers of reported scurvy cases were in the thousands during their history. On the other hand, at places like Alton and Johnson's

Island scurvy was a very minor problem. During the war, in fact, fewer than 60 scurvy cases were recorded at Johnson's Island—1.5% of the cases of sickness reported for that facility during its history. Even at the infamous Elmira, scurvy accounted for only about 3.5% of the total reported illnesses there. In most Northern prisons, according to official records, scurvy numbers ranked well below those for numerous other diseases. Of the ten specific disease categories, scurvy is usually at around seventh (among the third or fourth least common) in reported cases. So the sweeping claim that "frightful epidemics" of scurvy was the norm is far too general and unsupported to be accurate. Finally, there is virtually no way to say with anything approaching certainty that Union ration policies in 1864 "produced" scurvy epidemics. Though Sanders and others have tended to assume that most prisoners "were perfectly healthy when they entered the stockades" only "to sicken and die within the space of a few weeks—victims of...[things like] starvation," there is no way to prove that prisoners reported as having scurvy did not arrive suffering from it. Scurvy did, after all, exist in Confederate armies; as the war went steadily against the Confederacy in 1864 and 1865, rations for Southern soldiers deteriorated in both quality and quantity making it likely they had serious nutritional problems when captured; and it was far from uncommon that prisoners taken represented ill and/or wounded soldiers taken from towns overrun by the enemy and not "perfectly healthy" specimens.[44]

What is often not considered when discussing food rations is that not all prisoners had to rely solely on the Federals, at least not for all that long. The sutler and mail restrictions were apparently relaxed significantly in late summer and early fall 1864 because prisoners' diaries often refer to buying food from the sutler and receiving food through the mail. George Washington Nelson recorded in the summer of 1864: "I did not suffer. My friends supplied me with money, and I purchased from the sutler what I needed." North Carolinian E. L. Cox noted in August 1864 that plenty of food was coming to the prisoners through the mail and that "the general health of the prisoners is very good." Two months later, John Washington Inger boasted that after being a prisoner at Johnson's Island for over a year he still weighed 147 pounds. That is not surprising. When reading Inger's journal one finds numerous references, in the midst of a retaliation program, to "splendid dinners" that included such items as "boiled ham, beef, corn, and flour bread, onions, lettuce, and beets, pound cake, tea, strawberry preserves and butter." At Point Lookout on Christmas Day 1864, Barlett Yancey Malone wrote in his diary of witnessing an eating contest where a five-dollar wager had been made that a prisoner from the 11th Alabama could not eat five pounds of bacon and three two-pound loaves of bread at a single sitting. Those prisoners with friends and relatives willing and able to send money and food, and quantifying this would be difficult, if not impossible, beyond the general conclusion that this applied far more to the officer class, were never in danger of starving at any point in their captivity. Those without such resources probably did suffer, having to rely as they did on rations that were sometimes of substandard quality and quantity and that offered little vegetable matter and no fruit. But as Edmund DeWitt Patterson reminds us, soldiers, especially combat soldiers, form extremely tight bonds of affection with their comrades. When some 200 boxes came in with food and Christmas gifts in December 1863, Patterson was not one of the lucky recipients. But he noted that his brothers in arms did not let him go without. Rather, he wrote in his journal, "thanks to my Mississippi friends I have had a nice dinner, as any one could wish anywhere . . . ." Without wholly discounting the possibility that Confederate prisoners did suffer from hunger from time to time in Union prisons, there is enough wartime evidence from the prisoners themselves to, at the very least, question the long-standing charge that Confederate prisoners lived on little more than bread and water while guests of the Yankees between 1863 and 1865.[45]

Complaints of insufficient clothing and blankets are also difficult to find during this period. While it is always risky to use lack of evidence as evidence, rarity of complaint is striking in light of the fact that so many postwar Southern writers referred to ill-clad inmates who had been robbed of all decent clothing and blankets by unscrupulous Yankees. Southern prisoners' diaries seem to suggest that they were able to procure adequate clothing and blankets from the Union government, the sutlers, or friends and family through the mail.

In late summer 1863 a Confederate prisoner at Johnson's Island recorded in his diary that he had just received "a nice pair of cavalry pants & two good shirts" as well as socks, underclothing, and a vest, leading him to note, "thus I am pretty well clothed." At Point Lookout in October 1863 Scott Peters wrote that he received through the mail two pairs of shoes, two pairs of socks, two pairs of pants, two pairs of drawers, and four shirts. In December 1863 an inmate noted that his friend, a Captain Robert Brown, was "in bed with his overcoat on, and rolled up in three or four blankets." According to an inmate at Rock Island, in February 1864: "Liberal donations of clothing continue to be made by the good ladies of KY. Ten. and by kind friends who do not reside far from this place." Henry Dickinson's diary shows how short-lived the mail restrictions were in practice, writing in his diary from Point Lookout in the summer of 1864: "The amount of clothing, food, etc., received by us from friends was very considerable. Boxes . . . generally sent by express and received by, or rather issued to, us twice each week." Having received reports that with winter setting in, some 1,166 prisoners at the infamous Elmira were in need of blankets, Federal officials issued nearly 4,000 blankets to the prison in December 1864 for the prisoners in need as well as to have enough on hand for those who may arrive needing one. In addition to the blankets, 2,500 jackets, 2,000 pairs of pants, 3,011 shirts, 1,216 pairs of drawers, and 6,065 pairs of socks were issued to Elmira's prisoners. The wartime evidence from Northern and Southern sources seems to suggest quite strongly that the notion of Confederate prisoners being forced by Union officials to stroll about prison compounds half naked and shivering for want of clothing and blankets on a regular basis, as a matter of Northern policy, is, as with the "starvation rations" accusation, open to serious question.[46]

When it came to shelter during the second half of the war, wooden barracks heated by coal or wood stoves continued to be the norm for most Northern prisons. Point Lookout, Maryland, was the only prison where prisoners were sheltered year-round in tents and at Elmira prisoners were housed in tents until the end of 1864 when they were moved into wooden barracks. Given the relatively mild climate of Maryland, housing soldiers at Point Lookout in tents, the same as soldiers in the field, did not constitute inadequate shelter. The prisoners had makeshift fireplaces or stoves for winter and many had wooden floors. One prisoner there recorded in his diary in the spring of 1864 that he and his comrades were "quartered in large Sibley tents," which he described as "quite comfortable." The same cannot be said for housing prisoners at Elmira in tents until after winter had set in, though. This climate was far different from Maryland's and Federal officials had no business sending prisoners to Elmira without making certain that by the time cold weather set in they would be in more substantial wooden structures. While housing prisoners in tents during late fall and winter seems to reveal a negligent or callous attitude towards prisoners, it must be pointed out that Elmira was the only Northern prison where such a situation existed. More significantly, the bad planning at Elmira adversely affected Union guards as much as it did the prisoners as the latter also had to endure life in tents until their quarters were constructed. The guards' quarters were, not surprisingly, finished first but the fact that

Northerners and Southerners at Elmira were inadequately housed as winter set in reflects supremely bad planning at a single prison rather than a broad policy to supply Confederate prisoners with as little as possible to survive in captivity.[47]

That is not to suggest that prisoners' quarters during the second half of the war were comfortable, at least by modern standards. When prisoners arrived at Northern prisons after 1863 they often found barracks that were increasingly crowded, a situation made worse in the winter months when all huddled inside and fought for space near the stoves, often drafty, and sometimes with leaky roofs. While nobody would book a vacation to such quarters, Union officials would point out that they provided four walls and a roof with stoves in the winter and bunks with straw to sleep in. Such quarters were at least as good as troops in the field lived in and, as Meigs said early in the war, that was all humanity required of the Northern government—a position that is difficult to argue against. The point to be made is not that Union officials provided prisoners with snug, comfortable quarters where rain, snow, and cold did not occasionally intrude. Rather, as is made in more detail in later chapters and by the photographs and drawings in this book, the point is that the shelter they provided through the end of the Civil War was considered adequate enough for that era for researchers to seriously question it as evidence in the negligence and abuse case against Federal officials like Hoffman and Stanton.

Ultimately the more objective wartime evidence from Northern and Southern sources indicates that Union policies towards Confederate prisoners cannot be defined as vindictive or inhumane. Postwar charges of abuse and more recent ones of systematic neglect and "sadistic apathy" do not appear to be supported by pre-1865 sources. The major pieces of evidence against Union officials like their decision to halt exchanges in 1863 and implement a retaliation program in 1864 simply fail to hold up under close examination. The decision to halt exchanges had valid and reasonable justifications. The retaliation program does not appear to have been as draconian as often portrayed. Its short-lived duration also makes it difficult to accept that the policy was responsible for all or most of the mortality found in Union prisons. The following three chapters examine how prisoners were fed, clothed, sheltered, and cared for medically in the North's nine major camps, revealing that the humane intentions articulated in General Orders No. 100 were not scrapped during the second half of the war.

Endnotes

1. Charles Sanders, " 'A Most Horrible National Sin': The Treatment of Prisoners in the American Civil War," *North and South* 9, no. 5 (October 2006): 12–29.

2. Perhaps the best discussion on POW laws before, during, and after the Civil War is William E. S. Flory, *Prisoners of War: A Study in the Development of International Law* (Washington, D.C.: American Council on Public Affairs, 1942), 15–23, 39–41, 53–54.

3. United States War Department, *War of the Rebellion: A Compilation of the Official Records of the Union and Confederate* Armies (Washington, D.C.: Government Printing Office, 1894; repr., Harrisburg, PA: Telegraph Press, 1971), Series II, Volume 3, 8, 121 (hereafter cited as *OR* with all citations being from Series II unless otherwise indicated).

4. *OR*, Volume 3, 8, 49, 121–23.

5. *OR*, Volume 3, 122–23.

6. Benton McAdams, *Rebels at Rock Island: The Story of a Civil War Prison* (DeKalb: Northern Illinois Press, 2000), 4, 100, 203–4; William C. Davis, *Rebels and Yankees: The Fighting Men of the Civil War* (New York: Salamander Books, 1989), 172.

7. *OR*, Volume 3, 8, 122–23; Holland Thompson, "Prisoners of War," in *The Photographic History of the Civil War*, Volume 4: *Soldier Life and Secret Service and Prisons and Hospitals*, ed. Holland Thompson (n.p.: 1891; repr., Secaucus, NJ: The Blue and Grey Press, 1987), 32–40.

8. *OR*, Volume 3, 270–71, 281, 316–17; *Diary of a Confederate Sharpshooter: The Life of James Conrad Peters*, edited and annotated by Jack L. Dickinson (Charlestown, WV: Pictorial Histories Publishing Co., 1997), 55–61.

9. *OR*, Volume 3, 32, 11–14, 270–71, 316–17, 344–45, 359, 361; Volume 4, 202, 304–6, 352–53, 366–67; Volume 5, 305–6, 358, 391–92, 487; *James Taswell Mackey Diary*, Eleanor Brokenbrough Library, Museum of the Confederacy, Richmond, Virginia (hereafter cited as MOC); Bell I. Wiley, *The Life of Billy Yank* (Baton Rouge: Louisiana State University Press, 1952), 224–27; McAdams, 215.

10. *OR*, Volume 3, 513, 549–50; Volume 4, 103, 112–14, 178–84.

11. *OR*, Volume 3, 361; Lonnie Speer, *Portals to Hell: Military Prisons of the Civil War* (Mechanicsburg, PA: Stackpole Books, 1997), 14; James I. Robertson, *Soldiers Blue and Gray* (Columbia: University of South Carolina Press, 1988), 190–213; Frank L. Byrne, "Prison Pens of Suffering: Simple Names Like Johnson's Island and Andersonville Came to Mean Hell," in *Civil War Album:*

Complete Photographic History of the Civil War, Fort Sumter to Appomattox, ed. William C. Davis and Bell I. Wiley (New York: Tess Press, 2000), 591–92, 596.

12. OR, Volume 3, 526–27; Volume 4, 102–3, 178–84, 203, 341–42, 366–67, 369–71, 698–99; Volume 5, 358.

13. OR, Volume 3, 122–23, 221, 231, 241–42, 260, 316–17, 522, 542, 607; Volume 4, 112–14, 185, 192, 252, 273, 318, 352, 378, 406, 457–58; Volume 5, 239, 349, 282, 305–6, 316–18, 343–45, 376, 477–78, 487, 509.

14. OR, Volume 3, 375, 383–84, 405, 620–21; Volume 4, 112–14, 238.

15. OR, Volume 4, 262–63, 304–6.

16. OR, Volume 3, 122–23, 345, 348–49, 360, 366, 375, 383–84, 400-401, 405, 513, 620–21; Volume 4, 110, 112–14, 166, 238, 262–63, 304–6, 341–42; Volume 5, 227–28, 239–40, 343–45, 391–92, 500–2, 523, 569–70, 768.

17. OR, Volume 3, 32, 344–45, 348–49, 360, 375.

18. OR, Volume 3, 270–71, 281, 344–45, 359, 360, 366–67, 370, 375, 392, 400–1, 526-527, 607, 647–48; Volume 4, 130–31, 343–44; Volume 5, 487.

19. Flory, 19–23, 29–30, 57–58.

20. Flory, 19–23, 29–30, 57–58; Thompson, 16–18, 24, 32, 39–40, 48; Constitution cited from David M. Kennedy, Lizabeth Cohen, and Thomas A. Bailey, *The American Pageant*, Volume I: *To 1877*, 12th ed. (New York & Boston: Houghton Mifflin Co., 2002), Appendix page 28.

21. William B. Hesseltine, *Civil War Prisons: A Study in War Psychology* (Columbus: Ohio State University Press, 1930; repr., New York: Frederick Ungar Publishing Co., 1971), 7–34, 67–113; Davis, 177; Byrne, 592.

22. Charles W. Sanders, *While in the Hands of the Enemy: Military Prisons of the Civil War* (Baton Rouge: Louisiana State University Press, 2005), 164, 167–68, 179–80, 237–49, 272.

23. OR, Volume 5, 674–76; Flory, 18–23.

24 Hesseltine, *Civil War Prisons: A Study in War Psychology*, 219–24; Sanders, 4, 142–62, 215–18.

25. Sanders, 3–4, 142–62, 167–68, 179–80, 217–18, 274–75.

26. OR, Volume 7, 988–89.

27. OR, Volume 7, 606–7, 614–15, 662, 895.

28. OR, Volume 7, 606–7, 614–15, 662, 687–91, 895, 988–89.

29. OR, Volume 7, 909, 913–14, 1010–11.

30. OR, Volume 5, 795–97, 807–8, 940–41; McPherson, 791–94.

31. *OR*, Volume 5, 807–8, 940–41.

32. *OR*, Volume 5, 455–56, 469–70, 484, 844–45, 855, 867, 966–67; Volume 6, 132, 134, 139–40, 146, 159, 169, 187–88.

33. *OR*, Volume 5, 67; Volume 6, 159, 163, 169, 528, 594–96.

34. *OR*, Volume 6, 226, 913; Volume 7, 46, 78–79, 703–4, 966–71, 1010–11, 1015–16, 1022–23, 1206, 1234.

35. *OR*, Volume 7, 687–91; McPherson, 790-800; Richard F. Hemmerlein, *Prisons and Prisoners of the Civil War* (Boston: The Christopher Publishing House, 1934), 111–13; Robert E. Denney, *Civil War Prisons and Escapes: A Day-by-Day Chronicle* (New York: Sterling Publishing Co., Inc., 1993), 8; L. Gilbert Ferguson, "A Study of Civil War Prisoner Policy," (master's thesis: Mississippi College, 1994), 95–105.

36. *OR*, Volume 7, 33–34, 46, 93, 155–56, 174, 203, 409, 583, 687–91, 703–4, 988, 990–93, 1010–11, 1116, 1206; Volume 8, 26, 153–54, 175–76, 316–17, 355, 361–63, 471; Sanders, 215–16.

37. *OR*, Volume 8, 197, 317; McPherson, 800–1.

38. *OR*. Volume 5, 487; Hesseltine, 172–209; Sanders claims the "retaliation" began much earliear than 1864, *In the Hands of the Enemy*, 3–4, 164.

39. House of Representatives, 38th Congress, 1st Session. "Report #67: Returned Prisoners, May, 1864," in *U.S. House of Representatives Reports: Fort Pillow Massacre and Returned Prisoners* (New York: Johnson Reprint Co., 1970), 6–7, 9–10, 13, 20–21 (hereafter cited as "Report #67").

40. "House Report #67," 1–5, 19–21, 25–28; *OR*, Volume 7, 110–11.

41. *OR*. Volume 4, 238; Volume 5, 487, 674–79; Volume 6, 34–35, 73, 163, 523–24, 868, 892–93; Volume 7, 110–11; Hesseltine, 7–13, 67–113, 172–209; Flory, 43–45.

42. *OR*, Volume 7, 150–51; Sanders, *While in the Hands of the Enemy*, 195–265; McAdams, 215; Patrick Howe, "Cash-Strapped States Slash Calories for Prison Inmates," in *The Fayetteville (NC) Observer* (May 14, 2003), 3A; Bell I. Wiley, *The Life of Billy Yank* (Baton Rouge: Louisiana State University Press, 1952), 224–25.

43. *OR*, Volume 6, 112–13, 149, 265, 479–80, 625–26, 661–63, 967–70, 1014–15; Volume 7, 142–43, 183–84, 466, 484–87, 495, 573–74, 580–81, 682–83, 785, 1017–18, 1104–5, 1184–87, 1240, 1251, 1266; Frank L. Byrne, "Prison Pens of Suffering," in *Fighting for Time*, Volume 4: *The Image of War, 1861–1865*, ed. William C. Davis (Garden City, NY: Doubleday and Co., 1983), 594–95, Hemmerlein, 106; Wiley, *The Life of Billy Yank*, 224–25; McAdams, 94–96, 215; Thompson, 48, 166.

44. Sanders, 5, 172–73, 237, 249; United States Surgeon General's Office, *Medical and Surgical History of the War of the Rebellion, 1861–1865*, (Washington, D.C.: Government Printing Office, 1875), Volume I, Part III, 30, 46–47.

45. *George Washington Nelson Diary*, Virginia Historical Society, Richmond, Virginia (hereafter cited as VHS); *E.L. Cox Diary*, VHS; John Washington Inger, *The Diary of a Confederate Soldier*, ed. and annotated by Mattie Lou Teague Crow (Huntsville, AL: The Strode Publishers, 1977), 88–94; *Paul Agalus McMichael Papers*, Southern Historical Collection, University of North Carolina-Chapel Hill (hereafter cites as SHC); *Joseph Mason Kern Diary and Papers*, SHC; *James Robert McMichael Diary, SHC; John K. Street Diary*, SHC; *D. E. Gordon Diary*, Eleanor Brockenbrough Library, Museum of the Confederacy, Richmond, Virginia (hereafter cited as MOC); *Joseph W. Mauck Diary*. MOC; *Thomas Pickney Diary*, MOC; *Diary of Lafayette Rogan*, MOC; *John A. Gibson Diary*, VHS; *Samuel Horace Hawes Diary*, VHS; *Diary of Capt. Henry C. Dickinson, CSA* (Denver, CO: The Williamson-Haffner Co., 1910/1919), 45, 87, 90, 99, 102, 113; Charles W. Turner, ed., *Captain Thomas D. Houston Prisoner of War Letters* (Verona, VA: McClure Printing Co., 1980), 33–34; McAdams, 94–96.

46. Dickinson, 45, 87, 90, 99, 102–13; *Wilbur Wrightman Gramling Diary*, Elmira Prison Camp Online Library, *John Dooley, Confederate Soldier, His War Journal*, ed. Joseph T. Durkin (Washington, D.C.: Georgetown University Press, 1945), 134–68; Benjamin E. Caudill, *Surrender Hell: The Diary of Col. Benjamin E. Caudill, CSA* (The Dalles, OR: Shirley Combs, 1997), 4–5, 13, 15; *"For the Sake of My Country:" The Diary of Col. W. W. Ward*, ed. R.B. Rosenberg (Murfreesboro, TN: Southern Heritage Press, 1992), 25–30; OR, Volume 5, 343–45; Volume 6, 47480, 778–98, 819; Volume 7, 1184–85, 1213, 1240.

47. OR, Volume 5, 343–45; Volume 6, 215–16, 235, 244–45, 291, 309–10, 492–93, 607, 628–29, 703–4, 809, 878–80; Volume 7, 108–9, 496–98, 554–56, 693–95, 764–65, 804, 840–41, 913, 959–60, 994–96, 1026–27, 1104–5, 1242–43; Volume 8, 44, 113–14, 209–10, 310, 442; Dickinson, 26.

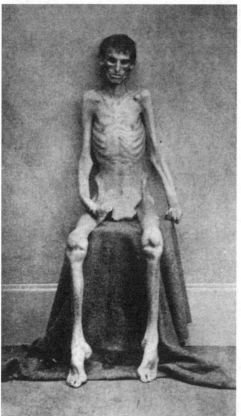

Above: Andersonville Prison as it appeared in August 1864. *Courtesy Library of Congress.*

Left: A returned prisoner from Andersonville. To date, no comparable photo of Confederate prisoners has surfaced. *Courtesy Library of Congress.*

Left: These drawings, copied from photographs, appeared in Frank Leslie's Illustrated Newspaper in June 1864. These extreme cases were used during and after the war to illustrate Southern barbarity. *Courtesy Library of Congress.*

Below: Confederate Winter Quarters, Manassas, Virginia, 1862, showing the living quarters of soldiers in the field. When on active campaign the soldiers would have had only tents. *Courtesy Library of Congress.*

Opposite upper: A Union regiment establishing winter quarters along the James River. Union Quartermaster-General Montgomery Meigs did not see why Confederate prisoners' quarters should be superior to what U.S. soldiers occupied. *Courtesy Library of Congress.*

Opposite lower: Commissary-General of Prisoners, Colonel William Hoffman, 1865. *Courtesy Library of Congress.*

Left: Commandant of Camp Morton in 1862, Colonel Owen was so respected by prisoners that they commissioned this bust as a tribute to him after the war. *Courtesy Indiana Historical Society, P130.*

Below: Union prisoners being marched to exchange point, Aiken's Landing, South Carolina, February 1865. Exchanges never entirely ceased. Sick and injured prisoners were sometimes exchanged. *Courtesy Library of Congress.*

Opposite upper: Wharf on the James where lucky prisoners were exchanged. *Courtesy Library of Congress.*

Opposite lower: Confederate prisoners being marched to the rear, then to Union prison camps. Notice the injured man in the foreground. Thousands of prisoners who entered the camps were either sick or injured, contributing to the mortality found in them. *Courtesy Library of Congress.*

Confederate prisoners awaiting transport to Northern prisons, Chattanooga, Tennessee, 1864. *Courtesy Library of Congress.*

1864 drawing of Point Lookout, Maryland. *Courtesy Library of Congress.*

Aerial view of Pea Patch Island and Fort Delaware, a major depot for Confederate prisoners during the war. *Courtesy Library of Congress.*

Camp Morton, Indiana. Prisoners here lived in wooden barracks heated by stoves in the winter. Contrary to Lost Cause tales, these prisoners were not robbed of blankets or forced to do without proper clothing. *Courtesy Indiana Historical Society, P388.*

Wartime artwork done by a Confederate prisoner showing something of the condition of the inmates and their living quarters at Camp Chase, Ohio. *Courtesy Museum of the Confederacy, Richmond, Virginia.*

Elmira was the most lethal of the Northern prisons and was sometimes called "Hellmira." This photo of prisoners at roll call in late 1864 contrasts sharply with those of Andersonville. The tents were replaced for guards and prisoners with wooden barracks by the first of the year. *Courtesy Museum of the Confederacy, Richmond, Virginia.*

FEDERAL POLICIES AT THE FOUR MAJOR PRISONS IN ILLINOIS AND INDIANA

TO THIS POINT THE ARGUMENT HAS BEEN MADE that Union officials enacted policies that cannot accurately be termed negligent or abusive. Their policies towards captured Confederate soldiers and officers were well within the boundaries of the rules of war as defined and accepted by both sides during the Civil War. Yankee regulations were designed to provide prisoners with the basic necessities for survival: food, clothing, shelter, and medical care. Of course, setting policies and actually having them implemented adequately can be two completely different things, as anyone familiar with government bureaucracies will readily confirm. Therefore a brief examination of major individual Northern prisons is necessary to determine whether or not the charges of negligence and abuse leveled at Yankee authorities are as irrefutable as many commentators have maintained for over a century.

Alton

Alton prison, located in Illinois on the banks of the Mississippi River, was opened in 1833 as Illinois's first state prison. For nearly thirty years Alton served the state in that capacity until a newer facility was built at Joliet. By 1860 Alton was empty, all of its prisoners having been released after serving their debts to society or being transferred to Joliet. The prison would not remain unoccupied for long, however. When the Civil War erupted and failed to end in a single climactic battle as many had hoped, the unforeseen problem of what to do with prisoners of war became an increasingly thorny issue for both governments. As early as December 1861, Union officials began looking at Alton as a place to house Confederate prisoners. The idea made perfect sense because the prison was already there, it was unoccupied, and the government would not have to spend a great deal to get Alton ready to receive Southern prisoners. Beginning in February 1862, Confederate prisoners began arriving at Alton, where the population would range from between 500 and 1,800 at its most crowded in January 1865. Generally the average was between 1,000 and 1,400 prisoners.[1]

Perhaps because Alton was one of the smaller prisons and one that lacked the notorious reputation of an Elmira or Fort Delaware, this Northern prison was not singled out very often by Lost Cause-era polemicists. That certainly was not because Alton was comfortable or healthy compared to other larger and more notorious prison camps. In fact, during the Civil War, nearly 1,500 Southern prisoners died at Alton, which works out to roughly one prisoner per day. Such a statistic shows that life at Alton could be precarious, but the more meaningful thing to determine is whether that statistic reveals Federal negligence and abuse of Alton prisoners.

Prisoners' experiences at the prison would have varied quite a bit between 1863 and 1865, running from pretty decent to utterly deplorable. The reason lay largely with the rather large amount of turnover in the facility's commandant position. Between the exchange cartel's suspension in the spring of 1863 and the war's end, no fewer than four officers ran the post with varying degrees of skill and efficiency. The result was a lack of continuity in leadership during the war's final two years that adversely affected living conditions at Alton.

At the time the cartel was suspended, Alton was run by Major T. Hendrickson, who showed commendable concern for the prisoners' welfare. In April and May 1863 he was in constant contact with Colonel William Hoffman about soliciting estimates and approval for fixing the hospital's leaky roof. He explained to Hoffman that he would need to spend $2,000 to replace the existing roof "in order to have a good tight roof upon [the hospital.]" In June of the same year, Hendrickson expressed his concern that Alton was getting far too crowded. That month the population shot up to over 1,700 prisoners. Surgeon Augustus M. Clark, Hoffman's prison inspector and his eyes and ears at the various prisons, said that Alton's absolute maximum should be no more than 1,200 inmates, making Hendrickson's concerns very valid. During that summer the population was reduced at the site by between 300 and 400 prisoners—not ideal but certainly a step in the right direction. But perhaps the best evidence that Major Hendrickson took seriously his duty to care for the prisoners according to General Orders 100's guidelines is found in Clark's October 15, 1863, inspection report. "In this prison more than any other which I have yet visited," Clark told Hoffman, "regard seems to be paid to the comfort as well as security of the prisoners." Prisoners' food, clothing, shelter, and medical care were all well administered by Hendrickson and while the site remained more crowded than he would have liked, Clark gave Alton and its commandant very high marks that fall.[2]

Unfortunately, Hendrickson did not remain at Alton, leaving the prison in the late fall or early winter of 1863–64. A December inspection report from Brigadier General William Orme described the camp as crowded but otherwise the prisoners had plenty of food, clothing, and medical care and the sanitary condition was "very good." But Hendrickson's replacements would not prove to be nearly as skilled and efficient. Immediately after Hendrickson's departure, the position was held briefly by Colonel G. W. Kincaid until early 1864 when Colonel William Weer assumed command at Alton. Neither officer seemed to post a particularly good record as the prison's commanding officer but Colonel Weer was so poor at his job that conditions at Alton deteriorated rapidly during his administration. At the end of February 1864, Hoffman contacted Weer, expressing concern over conditions at the prison and offering some advice for the new commandant. "I have just received a report from Surg. A. M. Clark, . . . of the Alton military prison, from which I learn that it is not in a very satisfactory condition. Though many things are in a commendable shape, there are others where much reformation is needed." To get Alton back in the reasonably decent shape it had been in under Hendrickson's guidance, Hoffman told Weer to appoint an officer to inspect the camp weekly and submit a report each Sunday to be forwarded to Hoffman with Weer's comments regarding the prisoners' "personal cleanliness, clothing, bedding, quarters, messing, sinks, yards, . . . the hospital and all connected with it. Let nothing pass unnoticed."[3]

Though Hoffman made it clear to Weer that he and the government expected living conditions at Alton to improve, the records reveal that Weer was either unwilling or unable to meet those expectations, and the prisoners ultimately paid the price. One major problem at Alton was the prison's extremely unsanitary condition. In February Clark reported that the sewer pipe that took material from the sinks and latrines to the Mississippi River froze, causing severe and noxious problems with disposing of the waste of over 1,000 men. This clogged and choked pipe was not attended to by Weer who, even if he had not been informed of it by Clark and other inspectors, could not have failed to notice the tremendous stench. At the end of April, Clark complained to Hoffman that the drain remained broken and ineffective, "permitting the fecal matter and urine to exude to the surface . . . ." The overflowing sinks were, he reported, "a pregnant source of disease." Worse, Clark noted that this horribly unsanitary matter was oozing up through the ground and pooling around the hospital kitchen! Weer apparently did not pay any attention to the prisoners' personal sanitary condition either, Clark describing them in the same report as "dirty both in person and clothing. Their bedding is foul and full of vermin, being seldom washed or properly aired."

This was just the tip of the iceberg, though. Hoffman would also learn in April that Weer was not only negligent in making sure the prison and the prisoners were reasonably clean, but he made things difficult for the surgeon and hospital staff as well. Apparently Weer did not get along with the surgeon at Alton, a Dr. Worrall, and for that reason, Clark informed Hoffman, "they do not work together." There were times when Weer refused to sign requisition orders for the hospital, reducing rations and medicines for the patients there, for no other reason than that he did not like dealing with Dr. Worrall or any of his assistants. And to top things off, reports from Clark as well as Lieutenant-Colonel John F. Marsh, another inspector, indicated that Weer was a drinker to the point that he could not do his duty. Marsh's opinion of Weer was that he "is an intelligent but very intemperate man. He was drunk when I saw him, and in my opinion is entirely unfit to hold any position in the military service of the United States. I cannot too strongly urge his removal from the command of [Alton]." From Clark came: "It appears to be the evidence of nearly all the officers at the post that the commanding officer is frequently so much under the influence of liquor as to be utterly unfit for duty." He urged Hoffman to get rid of Weer and put someone else in charge of Alton because "matters are going from bad to worse." Before the month of April was out, Weer was replaced by Brigadier General Joseph T. Copeland.[4]

General Copeland was a definite improvement over Weer, but then there is no way he could not have been. At the beginning of August 1864 Surgeon Charles Alexander inspected Alton and many important improvements had been and continued to be implemented since Copeland assumed command of the post. The prisoners' personal hygiene and living quarters were described as "good for prisoners" where earlier that spring they had been described as "filthy" while Weer was in charge. The sick were much better provided for now that Alton's commander and medical staff were not feuding. Probably the most important improvement, however, was that the sewage situation had finally been brought under control. Conditions at Alton certainly were not perfect; Alexander noted that the prison was still too crowded and garbage removal was not as good as it should have been. But taken as a whole, Alton was improving at summer's end in most areas.[5]

Without question, Southern prisoners at Alton endured some harsh and unpleasant living conditions between 1863 and 1865. The question, though, is whether or not Northern officials actively disregarded Alton prisoners' needs, thereby increasing their suffering and mortality. The existence of a meaningful inspection system suggests that Union authorities intended to assure humane treatment of Confederate prisoners. The inspectors appear to have taken their jobs very seriously, not failing to point out major problems at Alton, as reports filed during Colonel Weer's tenure clearly show. Most compelling is that when Weer was exposed by inspectors in 1864 as utterly incompetent (and perhaps a raging drunk), he was removed from his position, which he had held for a very short time, less than six months. Colonel Weer was an awful choice for commandant and prisoners suffered from his administrative incompetence. But the key thing to note given the long-standing negligence charges against Union officials is that the mistake was recognized and genuine efforts were made by those oft-maligned officials to remove the problem and repair the damage he had caused at the prison.

Little evidence points to starvation rations at Alton. In the postwar years, ex-prisoners often complained bitterly about the food at every other Northern military prison but one will be hard pressed to find articles about starving at Alton in the *Southern Historical Society Papers* or *Confederate Veteran*. True, Alton was one of the smaller prisoner of war facilities with an average population of about 1,000, but the fact that negative reports of the food there are practically non-existent in the postwar period is remarkable. By itself the lack of postwar complaining means little. Official inspection reports, though, observed consistently that until the summer of 1864 Alton prisoners received the same quality and quantity rations as Federal guards. In mid-October 1863 surgeon Augustus M. Clark, whom Hoffman trusted to be his on-site representative at the individual prisons, reported that the food was of sufficient quantity and to help ensure proper quality, "the food . . . is frequently inspected by the surgeon in charge." The prison's water supply was a major problem. Water had to be brought in daily in casks from the Mississippi River. Otherwise, inspection reports throughout the war do not note any problems with the rations issued by the Federal government and for most of the depot's history express packages and a sutler were available to prisoners as a means of supplementing that supplied by the Federals. Finally, the fact that only six prisoners died of scurvy between September 1862 and June 1865 indicates that Alton prisoners were not reduced to walking skeletons.[6]

The accommodations or shelter provided for the prisoners at Alton were better than at other prisons in some respects. The inmates never lived in tents or out of doors at Alton. All the prisoners lived in barracks where they slept in bunks and were provided with hay or straw to sleep on. The barracks were also fitted out with stoves for the winter months. Prisoners' quarters, unlike at other camps, were rarely in need of repairs according to inspection reports. The major problem in this area had more to do with crowding than anything else. This was a problem inspectors reported throughout the prison's history. Alexander had noted at one point that 1,200 was really the most the prison should house but that it could handle 2,000 in a pinch and for a very short time. There were months, however, when Alton's population swelled to over 1,500 for weeks at a time and in early 1865, as Southern prisoners poured in from a dying Confederacy, the number was closer (for a short time) to 1,900. Records indicate that the population rarely remained in excess of 1,500 for more than a few weeks as prisoners were exchanged or transferred to other depots to ease crowding at the prison, but rarely did the number dip below 1,100, which would have been a more comfortable and manageable number for Alton.[7]

As for medical care for the prisoners at Alton, Clark had nothing but positive things to say about the hospital personnel. The hospital, except during Weer's time in command, had all the necessary supplies to care for sick prisoners and was very clean. Clark described the surgeon as "skillful and energetic" and a person who had done all he could "to promote the comfort of the sick and health of the well." A smallpox hospital existed and all prisoners and new arrivals were vaccinated against the disease that took more lives at Alton than any other single malady. Overall, Clark gave Alton a positive review in October, one that was supported two months later by Orme in every particular. Clark told Hoffman, "In this prison more than any other which I have yet visited, regard seems to be paid to the comfort as well as security of the prisoners."[8]

This evidence is inconsistent with the image of negligent Yankee officials—at least at Alton. Certainly crowding was a problem and conditions there were far from ideal. However, the requirement of regular, meaningful inspections and Union officials' insistence on and approval of measures to ensure that Confederate prisoners confined there had about as good food, clothing, shelter, and medical care as most Union soldiers had indicates that Southern captives were not to be ignored or mistreated. Weer's removal for dereliction of duty at the same time a retaliation policy was being planned says a great deal about how seriously Federal officials took their obligations toward prisoners of war. The generally favorable inspection reports made from mid-1864 through the end of the war also indicate that there was more continuity than change in conditions at Alton during the war's final year.

Of course the deaths that occurred at Alton do require some explanation and discussion to illustrate that the prisoners' mortality was not because of vindictive Northern policies. That discussion must begin with smallpox. That particular infectious disease (discussed in greater detail in Chapter Eight) took more Confederate prisoners' lives at Alton than any other. Between September 1862 and June 1865, 537 of the 1,455 (36.9%) disease deaths at Alton were attributed to "eruptive fevers," which were mostly smallpox but included chicken pox and measles. In January 1863, Captain H. W. Freedley inspected the prison and reported to Hoffman that he had authorized the employment of an additional doctor because "smallpox is raging terribly there, having increased within the past week from 6 to about 100 cases." Prisoners at Alton were vaccinated against smallpox and new arrivals were duly treated against the disease. Prisoners who broke out with the rash were quarantined.

These measures were inadequate to deal with the problem, however. Smallpox vaccines were of little if any value because they were often prepared in unsterile environments or were too old when administered to be effective. Quarantine procedures, no matter how vigilant, were also of extremely limited use since officials and doctors at the time did not realize that smallpox victims are actually most contagious in the period between contraction of the disease and the appearance of the tell-tale rash. Quarantine procedures were actually more difficult to enact at Alton than at other sites because the local populace was so frightened of the disease that they fought to keep a smallpox hospital for the prisoners from being established outside the prison walls. That hurdle was overcome, but it took time. Thus the report made in July 1863, which read, "Smallpox has become an almost established disease in the prison. It first appeared in December last, since which time the prison has scarcely been free from it" is not surprising. Union officials battled smallpox with every tool known in mid-nineteenth century America but records indicate the malady remained a problem until the first third of 1864. After that smallpox appears less frequently in inspection reports.

Smallpox victims at Alton were treated as successfully as they were at Chimborazo Hospital in Richmond. At Alton 537 of the 2,632 smallpox cases resulted in death for a 20.40 % mortality rate per reported case. In the Richmond hospital, 166 of the 760 cases or 21.84 % resulted in death. Thus over one-third of the disease deaths at Alton occurred despite Northern officials' best attempts to mitigate mortality from smallpox.[9]

Pneumonia was the second leading killer of Confederate prisoners at Alton, taking 276 (18.96 %) of those who died of some disease there. The charge that Federal negligence caused all or most of these deaths is difficult to sustain. Pneumonia was also a leading killer of Confederate soldiers in the field. A contributor to the *Medical and Surgical History of the War of the Rebellion* pointed out that while Confederate medical records were scanty, "pulmonary affections, exceedingly prevalent in both armies, were more prevalent among the southern troops." At Chimborazo Hospital in Richmond, pneumonia was the second leading killer behind "continued fevers." In fact, pneumonia accounted for a higher percentage of deaths at Chimborazo than at Alton. At the Confederate facility 583 of the 2,717 deaths (21.45 %) were caused by pneumonia compared to the 18.96 % at Alton. It does not seem reasonable to hold Union officials responsible for these unfortunate prisoners' deaths since they do not appear to constitute an unusual statistic for the armies at the time.[10]

Finally, the omnipresent diarrhea/dysentery category claimed an additional 229 lives (15.73 % of the total disease deaths) at Alton between September 1862 and June 1865. Since physicians at the time could not distinguish between the symptom and the disease, diarrhea and dysentery were lumped together into a single category. This was such a common problem during the Civil War that an entire volume of the *Medical and Surgical History* is dedicated to it. This category of illness actually increased in prevalence in both armies during the war and constituted a major health problem during the Civil War in camps and prisons. Again, negligence played no part here. Physicians dutifully treated the conditions but the known "cures" of the day exacerbated the problems more often than they alleviated them. Soldiers' and prisoners' best chance for recovery was to steer clear of the surgeon and hope for the best. In many cases victims' afflictions did clear up on their own but in thousands of cases they did not.[11]

Smallpox, pneumonia, and diarrhea/dysentery alone accounted for 1,042 (71.59%) of the 1,455 disease deaths recorded at Alton. These afflictions were poorly understood at the time meaning that the weapons available to fight them were limited at best. In the cases of pneumonia and diarrhea/dysentery they were also diseases that were extremely common in Civil War-era military camps. Thus, to say in any sort of definitive way that Northern policies were exclusively, or even primarily, responsible for these deaths is problematic.[12]

Statistics seem to support the conclusion that the "retaliation" program proposed and implemented in the early summer of 1864 did not play a role in prisoner mortality at Alton. Most of the disease mortality—972 deaths (66.80%)—occurred prior to June 1864. Up to that point, prisoners at Alton received the same food as Federal soldiers and were apparently adequately supplied with clothing and decent medical care according to inspection reports. Living quarters were not ideal, thanks, apparently, to Weer's inattention, but Southern prisoners did not live in conditions that compared all that unfavorably with an untreated canvass tent in the field (which was not always available) or makeshift cabins for winter quarters.

Furthermore, the records show that during the "retaliation" summer and fall of 1864, mortality at Alton was lower than it was before Yankee officials inaugurated allegedly draconian policies. Six prisoners died in May 1864 and thirteen died in June and July respectively. From August through October monthly deaths registered in the single digits with twenty-six prisoners dying over that three-month period. Those numbers increase in November and are quite high in January 1865 (122) before decreasing steadily from February through June.

The winter increases probably do not point to "retaliation" measures finally taking their toll at Alton, though. For one thing the increases came at a time when many of the mail and sutler restrictions were being eased significantly. Those numbers also occur at a time when Union forces were taking more prisoners and experiencing problems with where to put them all. In October 1864 Alton's population had actually dipped below 1,000 to 975 by transferring prisoners from Alton to places like Point Lookout. Beginning in November, though, the population shot up to 1,747 and so did the number of deaths, which increased from nine to forty. In January 1865 there were nearly 1,900 prisoners at Alton, way too many for that facility. To make matters worse, many of the new arrivals were malnourished and injured men from the field whose susceptibility to camp diseases was more acute. That prisoners had to endure intense crowding for a few weeks at the end of the war was also less a reflection of "sadistic apathy" and more a reflection of the difficulty of finding places to put the increasing flood of Rebel prisoners.[13]

Certainly life was never ideal for prisoners at Alton. In fact, spending any amount of time there had to have been uncomfortable, depressing, and generally miserable. Seeing dead comrades carried out almost daily must have been as frightening as it was sad. Such, though, was the lot of the Civil War prisoner whichever side's prison camp he inhabited. Evidence that Yankee officials made a bad situation worse through negligence or via harmful, retaliatory policies is flimsy at best and tends to be outweighed at Alton by evidence suggesting that officials did all they knew to do to ensure a reasonably safe place of confinement.

Camp Douglas

In the June 1914 edition of *Confederate Veteran* R. T. Bean wrote of his "Sixteen Months in Camp Douglas." Not surprisingly, his article was a scathing diatribe against the Yankees and all things Northern. He told readers, "It was shocking, horrible, monstrous, and a disgrace to any people who permitted such conditions to exist. Since our Spanish war I have been led to believe that there was a great deal of Spanish blood flowing in the veins of those who had charge of us at Camp Douglas. English or German blood would have revolted at such barbarity." Cornelius Hite certainly agreed, but had to amend Bean's opinion a bit because by 1924, when he wrote his anti-Yankee article for the same magazine, World War I had been fought and the Germans were not so highly thought of. Hite railed that the Yankees' treatment of Confederate prisoners at Camp Douglas "was paralleled only by the brutal Germans in the World War." The prison's most recent and ablest historian has also remarked on a 1907 article from *Confederate Veteran* where a poor helpless prisoner was chained up outside in sub-zero weather for the amusement of the guards. More so than Alton, Camp Douglas was cited by the Lost Cause-era writers as a place where Southern prisoners were starved, beaten, and generally neglected by Union officials as a matter of policy during the Civil War.[14]

Camp Douglas was a deadly place, with nearly 4,000 Confederate soldiers dying there between February 1862 and June 1865 of disease. While that number is certainly depressing and tragic for the families of those prisoners, it does not prove negligence or abuse by Northern officials. One of the reasons, probably the leading one, that so many prisoners perished at

Camp Douglas was the location of the prison itself. Located just outside Chicago, the prison was established in one of the sickliest areas of the country. In August 1862 Colonel Joseph Tucker, the prison's commanding officer, lost his own son, Captain Lansing Tucker, to disease at Camp Douglas. In the winter of 1863–64, 475 civilian residents died of scarlet fever and 215 of smallpox with cholera, typhoid, dysentery, and diphtheria all putting in appearances. Not surprisingly, Camp Douglas reported serious health problems and disease mortality during the same period. Adding to the unhealthy environment was the fact that the camp sat on the flat prairie and "could not absorb the human and animal waste generated by thousands of men and horses." It was, to put it mildly, a sickly place in a sickly town. [15]

The choice of locations initially reflected the need to have some place to send the some 15,000 prisoners taken from the battles for forts Henry and Donelson and Camp Douglas seemed appropriate. The grounds had originally been a training center for Union soldiers so it was ready to house soldiers. In light of the severe lack of alternatives, Camp Douglas seemed a reasonable and obvious choice. Besides, negotiations were being conducted to exchange prisoners, making it doubtful that prisoners would be there all that long. To further underscore the point that Federal officials did not choose Camp Douglas to increase Southern suffering, they used the camp once the exchange cartel was in effect as a place to house their own paroled Union soldiers until they were formally exchanged. Thus when Union officials sent Confederate prisoners to Camp Douglas they sent them to a facility they considered good enough for their own soldiers.[16]

For much of the prison's history the camp's major health problems stemmed from its location. Because it was situated on completely flat land, drainage was a problem and Camp Douglas was a muddy bog for extended periods of time. The lack of a system to take large amounts of human waste away from the camp allowed the malodorous matter to accumulate, which made for a very unhealthy atmosphere. In June 1862 Henry W. Bellows, the president of the Sanitary Commission, told Hoffman that conditions at Camp Douglas were "enough to drive a sanitarian to despair." Bellows thought the site was so unwholesome that the only remedy was to abandon it altogether. Hoffman thought Bellows was overreacting but he did consider the idea of abandoning Camp Douglas. Ultimately he decided to recommend against it, it being more cost effective to improve the existing state of affairs.[17]

Since the inspection reports and Bellows's comments showed that sewage removal was the principle sanitation problem affecting prisoners' health, Hoffman urged the War Department to allocate the funds necessary to build a sewer system in the summer of 1862. In several communications Hoffman emphasized to Montgomery Meigs the importance of a sewer system for the prison only to be turned down by the Union's Quartermaster-General. Hoffman has often been accused, and not without justification, of being tight with a dollar but in this case he was begging for money to spend but was denied the funds by his superiors. The decision was not the result of miserliness, though. Meigs was dead set against spending a lot of money, and Hoffman had told him the sewer system would cost between $10,000 and $15,000 on major building projects in Northern prisons just when it appeared that an agreement was due to be completed that would empty them. With the prospect that Camp Douglas would be emptied in the near future, Meigs took the position that the prisoners could be made to dig a few more sinks, which if kept clean and covered would mitigate the sewage issue for the few more weeks the prison would be in operation. A July 1862 communication to Hoffman supports this interpretation. "As there is now," the message read, "a probability that an arrangement for the general exchange of prisoners will be soon made it will be necessary to defer any measures for increasing our prison accommodations for the present." However, it must be noted, the same message stated: "Should those arrangements fail provision must of course be made to meet the necessities of the case."

Meigs's decision was not unreasonable or unduly harsh, though he did fail to fully appreciate the magnitude of the sewage problem at Camp Douglas. Had the camp been emptied and never used again as a prison it would appear less short-sighted and stingy. With the money not forthcoming, Hoffman informed the prison's officials that they were going to have to do the best they could with what they had, at least for the time being. New, deeper sinks were to be dug as quickly as possible and they were to be covered by sheds to mitigate the unhealthy effects of the open, overflowing sinks currently in use.[18]

Despite the failure of Hoffman to secure funds to effectively deal with sewage issues, prisoners during 1862 appear to have been generally provided with decent food, clothing, shelter, and medical care. One prisoner said in 1862 that in his opinion he and his fellow inmates were being treated "a ___ sight better than we had a right to expect." There were even a few slaves serving their masters at the prison until Lincoln found out and put a stop to it. First-sergeant Edwin Taylor of the 20th Mississippi recorded that he had plenty to eat at the prison, having been issued:

"Crackers, Baker's bread, chip beef-fresh beef, Coffee already ground, sugar, beans, [and] cheese . . . ." In May one prisoner wrote home: "I am as fat as I ever was. My weight is 163 lbs." Camp Douglas inmates were also allowed to receive food packages from friends or family and to get money to use at the post sutler who sold food and other items to the prisoners and guards. Colonel Tucker was dressed down by Hoffman in the summer of 1862 for reports of scurvy "where there is an abundance of vegetables and antiscorbutics," which he said "is a novel state of things to me, and I fear grows out of a want of attention . . . ." But scurvy was far less serious than diseases like pneumonia and smallpox and it is impossible to determine if the cases reported originated at the prison or reflected pre-existing conditions.[19]

Since barracks already existed the prisoners were housed in them until exchanged, a process that was completed by the end of September 1862. The barracks had stoves to keep the cold out and the bunks slept two men where body heat and blankets could be combined for warmth. Hay was also provided for comfort to sleep on and helped better insulate the sleepers. G. L. Wells of the 7th Texas recorded that the stoves in his barracks in 1862 "had been heated red hot and the barracks had been fitted with new hay. A more comfortable place under the circumstances I never saw." Wells's opinion may have been rosier than others'; many barracks had leaky roofs and needed other repairs to make them more weather tight by that summer. But, it should be noted, Meigs did approve spending to fix the barracks. On the other hand, a roof and walls fitted out with stoves and straw bedding in bunks up off the ground were better living quarters than most soldiers in either army could hope for in the field at the same time.[20]

The prisoners at Camp Douglas between the battles for Fort Henry and Fort Donelson and September 1862 when the prison was emptied by exchanges were apparently able to get decent medical care. In March Hoffman visited the camp personally and was glad to see the sick prisoners being adequately cared for. Local doctors, according to the prison's most recent historian, were said to have commented on how well the sick at Camp Douglas were treated. Three months after his visit Hoffman contacted Colonel Tucker telling him that if the post required additional doctors, to let Hoffman know so that they could be found and assigned to the camp. The problem was that the unsanitary atmosphere increased the number of ill inmates beyond the hospital's capacity. Only the most severely debilitated were admitted, which meant that some prisoners had to remain in the general population where they spread their germs and bacteria among their comrades. Furthermore, with bed space at a premium, sick prisoners who appeared to be on the mend were returned to the barracks though they were not fully recovered and possibly still infectious.[21]

Clothing was not a serious issue at this time. Prisoners' uniforms were barely a year old when the exchange cartel went into effect and had not been subjected to hard campaigning or battles. Indeed, many prisoners had been taken in their first fight at Fort Henry or Fort Donelson. Those who were in need, though, were given cast-off Federal clothing in June and prisoners were permitted to get non-uniform clothing through the mail. The post sutler also carried clothing articles that the prisoners were allowed to buy.[22]

Unfortunately the exchange cartel did not remain in effect for even one year and Camp Douglas was pressed into service as a prison once again in the spring of 1863. When it became clear that the facility would be used as a prison depot for an extended period of time, Meigs finally approved spending for a water works project to deal with the camp's most serious problem, the effective removal of human waste, that June. The system was quite sophisticated, using running water through the sinks to containers that would be taken from the camp and washed out regularly. According to one historian, the approved project was so state-of-the-art that it "exceeded the standard of living for most civilians in the area."[23]

However as sometimes happens, there was a serious gap between officials' expectations and implementation by the officers on-site. Meigs and Hoffman clearly wanted the sewage problem dealt with; funds for the project were requested and approved and the system was built. Clark's inspection of Camp Douglas in early October 1863 reveals that Colonel Charles De Land had not been doing a very good job making sure the new system was used and kept in good working order. In a blistering report, Clark complained that De Land was doing an awful job keeping the camp clean since assuming command in August. When it came to waste management Clark told Hoffman there had been "apparently no management at all," because the sinks were in "filthy condition." When Hoffman finished reading Clark's report he contacted De Land, telling him in no uncertain terms on October 24, 1863, that such negative reports were unacceptable and that all the problems Clark mentioned were to be fixed. In a fairly lengthy letter Hoffman listed the many problems to be addressed and in which order De Land was to proceed in dealing with them. By no later than the end of November De Land was to submit a report to Hoffman in which he was to "report what has been done to carry out the instructions contained in this letter on the several points above mentioned, taking them in the order mentioned." The sewage problem was at the top of the list.[24]

During the first week of November, De Land wrote to Hoffman describing his efforts to improve the sanitary conditions at the prison, which had disgusted Clark and angered Hoffman. "I have caused," he told Hoffman, "ten new sinks to be constructed over the sewer, with forty funnels each, leading into a soil box, which is washed and cleaned every day by an adjusted hydrant. These will be ready for use in two or three days, when the old ones will be cleansed and covered. I regard this as one of the most important improvements made in the camp." Apparently De Land followed through as a December inspector reported: "The sanitary condition of this camp is very good. The sinks are well arranged and kept clean and pure." In January 1864 Surgeon Edward Kittoe inspected the prison and described the sinks as "clean and well kept. They are so arranged over the large sewers recently constructed that the 'soil box,' which receives the ordure, is emptied and thoroughly washed out every twenty-four hours."[25]

But while certain important improvements were made while De Land was in charge, he was the source of several rather serious problems. Colonel De Land does not appear to have harbored any animosity towards Southern prisoners but he was extremely concerned, obsessed may not be too strong a word here, with preventing escapes from Camp Douglas. To keep prisoners from tunneling out under their barracks, De Land ordered all the floor boards taken up so that tunnel entrances could not be concealed. As Surgeon Kittoe noted in January, the result was that "in the place of dirty boards [there] is a mass of mud and filth." Clark remarked on the problem in February, saying many prisoners' "floors are . . . constantly wet and muddy." That De Land could have accomplished his purpose by raising the barracks off the ground and avoided creating damp and filthy conditions in prisoners' quarters never dawned on him. Clark, however, did see this possibility and assured Hoffman that he had "suggested that the barracks be raised on posts two or three feet high, so as to afford a clear view beneath them and allow the prisoners the advantage of a floor." Work began at once to get the prisoners' barracks up off the ground making living quarters a bit more comfortable and healthier.[26]

De Land also did not issue clothing during the fall of 1863 because of his worry over security, which did not sit well with Hoffman at all. In October Hoffman contacted De Land, informing him, "Surgeon Clark reports that you do not issue the clothing furnished by the quartermaster's department because it will facilitate escapes." Those prisoners needing clothes and lacking friends or family able to mail clothes to them may have recalled after the war how they went without at Camp Douglas and attributed it to Yankee malice or neglect. Hoffman's dismissal of De Land's concerns and his instructions to cut "the skirts of the coats short and cut off the trimmings and most of the buttons, which will sufficiently distinguish them from Federal soldiers," reveal the true reason clothing was not given to those in need at that point in 1863.[27]

Where De Land's poor leadership was most glaring was in failing to make sure that the prisoners' rations were all they were entitled to. In late fall or early winter 1863, Brigadier-General William Orme, who was in overall command of the post while De Land was apparently in charge of the prisoners only, discovered that the prisoners had been complaining of their meat ration routinely being inferior in quantity and quality. Interviews with Confederate sergeant-majors in charge of drawing the rations for the prisoners indicated that the meat supply was insufficient and often of poor quality and Captain Levant C. Rhines, Commissary of Prisoners, told Orme in December 1863: "I most fully believe the prisoners have been shamefully treated by the contractor for fresh beef." After receiving Orme's report and supporting evidence that government contractors may be short- ing the prisoners and the government on the meat ration, Hoffman con- tacted Orme, telling him,

> It appears from these papers that the rations usually issued to prisoners have
> habitually fallen short in weight, particularly in beef and bacon, and that some
> of the articles are of an inferior quality. I have therefore to request that you will
> have the whole matter of rations thoroughly investigated, to ascertain how far
> and in what articles the provisions furnished have been inferior in quality to
> what is required by the contract . . . .[28]

By the middle of February 1864 Hoffman had all the evidence he needed that De Land had let the prisoners' meat ration be of inferior qual- ity and quantity, something some prisoners may have recalled and attrib- uted to Northern vindictiveness rather than to an unscrupulous contractor, which was the reality of the case. General Orme knew about the problem and there was no reason De Land should not have as far as Hoffman was concerned. That was too much; Hoffman was done with De Land, who had not done all that spectacular a job to begin with. One may choose to see Hoffman's anger as stemming from De Land's neglect of the prisoners under his, and by extension Hoffman's, care or as rooted in believing that De Land had been responsible for wasting the government's money. The ultimate result for De Land was that he lost his job and found himself in rather serious legal trouble. Hoffman had informed Orme in late February that he was recommending that De Land "for his neglect of duty as commanding officer and . . . [for] permitting his command to receive rations which were deficient in quality and quantity, be brought before a courtmartial for trial."[29]

With De Land gone and General Orme running things for the prisoners more directly in early 1864 Hoffman had every reason to believe conditions would improve. Orme had, after all, shown himself to be a man who took his duty very seriously, finding out that prisoners and the government had been cheated and following through to find those at fault and fixing the situation. Unfortunately an April inspection report revealed that he was not going to live up to expectations as Camp Douglas's commandant. "General Orme," Hoffman was informed, "gives very little personal attention to his command at Camp Douglas." While the "health, food, and clothing is satisfactory. The barracks are in bad condition . . . the bunks are filthy, and the blankets not properly aired. The grounds are without proper drainage and badly policed." Though this was not exactly a scathing report, April was the last month General Orme was in charge of the prison. He was succeeded by Colonel Benjamin Sweet under whom significant improvements took place at the prison.[30]

Within weeks of Orme turning over command to Colonel Sweet many things about Camp Douglas began to improve. Surgeon Alexander was especially pleased about sanitary improvements. In early July he described the post as in "excellent condition," a phrase he rarely employed. He went on to tell Hoffman: "I saw this camp last April. The change since then for the better is astonishing." The sinks were much cleaner and more closely managed and the prisoners' personal hygiene and living areas were much cleaner as well. Throughout 1864 vastly improved sanitation reports were the norm. In August, Captain E. R. P. Shurly reported: "The grounds of the rebel camp are [now] always clean." An inspection report filed in mid-September stated that Camp Douglas inmates swept their areas daily and were "obliged to carry all slops and dirty water to the sinks." The sinks, often singled out as a leading environmental hazard in pre-1864 reports, were routinely described as in very good condition. In November the sinks were described as being "placed over a sewer and cleaned daily." Such had been expected in 1863; it was just not effectively done until Sweet took over the post. Finally, to help keep the prisoners cleaner, six new boilers had arrived by early October to be used in the recently completed wash-house.[31]

As for food, there is little wartime evidence to indicate that prisoners at Camp Douglas were ever placed on "starvation rations" between the time the post reopened as a prisoner of war site in 1863 and the end of the war. Except for the time in late 1863 when a sub-contractor was holding back beef and supplying cheap, inferior cuts of meat, inspection reports show prisoners getting the full Federal ration, which was shown in the second chapter to have been the most generous (in terms of bulk) on the planet. The quality of the rations were the same as for Camp Douglas's guards, the meat ration being the only exception for a short while. In November 1864 the ration was described as the "same as issued to [the Federal] garrison." For most of the time between 1863 and 1865 there existed "a sutler's shop, containing nearly everything (except liquors), including cider, butter, eggs, milk, canned fruits, boots, &c., underclothing, and all the minor articles usually found in a sutler's stock, of which the prisoners are allowed to purchase." Prisoners were allowed to receive money to use at the sutler and to receive food in the mail. These outside supplementary food sources were briefly interrupted in the summer of 1864 but never halted or restricted entirely. It should also be noted that the vague "ration reductions" often referred to non-food items and edibles not necessary for maintaining prisoners' health and welfare. Candle rations, for example, were eliminated partly to put money into the prison fund and because "the main use made from them [was] to tunnel out at night." Coffee, tea, sugar, and vinegar were also targeted for sharp reductions at Camp Douglas. In May 1864 Colonel Sweet eliminated the hominy ration because "it has been and is entirely wasted [by the prisoners]." These items by 1864 were virtually unknown luxuries to Confederates in the field and were not vital or necessary to sustain health. The money saved from these reductions, though, was used to increase the prison's operating budget to procure things far more important for the prisoners' comfort and general welfare such as cooking utensils, wash tubs, fruits and vegetables, medicines, and building materials to expand barracks and hospital space.[32]

The prisoners' living quarters at Camp Douglas were something of a mixed bag. On the one hand they had walls and a roof along with bunks to sleep in and stoves to help keep the cold away. One inmate recorded in his diary in January 1864: "The night was very cold, but the guards kept the coal stoves red hot all night, which kept the barracks warm, and we slept well." On the other hand they were hardly oases. The barracks (originally built for Northern recruits) were rather flimsily constructed and were neither plastered nor ceiled inside. Roofs were of wood strips and tar paper. Many of these were in bad shape, having been badly damaged by Union soldiers while the post was a parole camp, when Confederates began arriving again in 1863. De Land certainly made things worse when he ripped up the floors. And, as with most Union prisons, especially as the war came to a close, crowding was a problem.[33]

Had Northern officials in Washington and at Camp Douglas not moved forward to reform the prisoners' living quarters the abuse charge might stick better. But the records indicate clearly that improvements in this area did take place, and at a time when Union authorities were supposed to have been retaliating against Southern prisoners. The barracks were elevated off the ground, making them considerably drier and cleaner. Barracks were whitewashed inside and out in the spring of 1864 and repairs to existing quarters as well as the construction of new ones were well under way that fall. An October inspection report noted that "the roofs and floors of many of the barracks are in bad condition, but will doubtless soon be in good order, as workmen are daily employed in repairing them." A week later a report was filed relating that "[n]ew barracks are being built and old ones repaired . . . . The roofs of most of the barracks have been repaired." By November most of the repairs appear to have been completed and the prisoners' barracks in 1864 were probably superior to those provided for the Union recruits in 1861.[34]

So what killed Confederate prisoners at Camp Douglas by the thousands? Pneumonia, which took 1,296 inmates according to *The Medical and Surgical History of the War of the Rebellion* between February 1862 and June 1865, was the leading killer. That figure represents 32.98% of the 3,929 disease fatalities recorded for the prison. Pinning those deaths on Union negligence is difficult to do with anything approaching certainty. As will be discussed more fully in the last chapter, even if conditions at the camp were cold and damp at times such conditions do not cause pneumonia. Perhaps more importantly, with pneumonia being a major killer of Confederate soldiers in their own armies' camps it is highly probable that significant numbers of Southern captives had contracted pneumonia before ever setting foot in Camp Douglas. Some compelling evidence does exist to support that supposition. In late 1864 and early 1865 deaths at Camp Douglas spiked sharply with nearly 900 prisoners dying between December and February. Inspection reports specifically mention new arrivals, especially from General John Bell Hood's command, as in "prostrate condition" in very poor overall physical shape. That many of the "prostrate" could have already had pneumonia seems perfectly plausible and if they did not, their broken condition made them particularly vulnerable to becoming pneumonia victims.[35]

A far better method of determining how good or bad a job Federal authorities did caring for Confederate prisoners than raw mortality statistics is how effectively sick prisoners were treated in prison hospitals. At the South's largest hospital, Chimborazo Hospital in Richmond, Confederate pneumonia patients died at a fairly high rate. According to available records, 37.18% of pneumonia cases ended in death at the Richmond hospital. At Camp Douglas on the other hand, 27.84% of the pneumonia cases resulted in the patient's demise. Since the records clearly show that a Confederate soldier was more likely to recover from pneumonia at Camp Douglas than in his own capital, arguing that medical treatment was substandard or neglected seems to be a stretch at least as far as pneumonia deaths are concerned.[36]

The second leading killer at Camp Douglas was smallpox, which was lumped into the category of "eruptive fevers" in *The Medical and Surgical History of the War of the Rebellion*. Though not all eruptive fever cases were smallpox, this affliction was a major problem at the camp, as it was in every Northern prison camp and in many of each army's camps in the field, taking 823 prisoners' lives during its history. Camp officials and Yankee authorities made every effort to deal effectively with smallpox, if for no other reason than to protect Federal personnel and Northern civilians living nearby. A smallpox quarantine structure was constructed at Camp Douglas and prisoners were "vaccinated as speedily as possible" in 1863 and 1864. When existing quarantine areas were insufficient, a new structure was built in 1864 to get the victims away from the general population. For reasons discussed in detail in the final chapter, these procedures, state-of-the-art at the time, were unable to prevent significant smallpox mortality, which accounted for slightly more than one in five (20.94 %) disease fatalities.[37]

The negligence case is hard to make with smallpox for the same reason it is hard to make it with pneumonia; recovery rates were better at Camp Douglas than at Chimborazo. In Richmond 21.84% of the "eruptive fever" cases concluded with the victim's death. According to *The Medical and Surgical History* morbidity for this same category at Camp Douglas was 17.61%, not as big a difference in recovery rates as with pneumonia but still significant. With records showing that smallpox patients were dealt with as effectively as possible at that time through quarantine and vaccination procedures and with greater success than in the Confederate capital, Federal officials cannot be held guilty in causing or neglecting to treat adequately those afflicted with this dread disease, which seems to let them off the hook to a significant degree for slightly over 20% of the disease fatalities at Camp Douglas.[38]

The same holds true for the third most lethal category, diarrhea/dysentery. This was an extremely common problem in Civil War armies and one that actually increased in prevalence as the war dragged on. This category of illness was simply too common during the American Civil War to claim that prison conditions caused it. That significant numbers of prisoners arrived suffering from diarrhea/dysentery (contemporaries were unable to distinguish between the symptom and the disease, which was why they were lumped together) is extremely likely and since the "cures" usually made the condition worse, being neglected in this case would have been a blessing. At Camp Douglas 698 prisoners died of diarrhea/dysentery, 17.76% of the total disease deaths listed in *The Medical and Surgical History*. But those who were recorded as having the problem were more likely to recover at Camp Douglas, where 5.18% of sufferers died compared to a 9.80% morbidity rate at Chimborazo.[39]

If a definitive connection between Federal actions or inactions and the deaths from the three categories just discussed is lacking, proving that Yankee policies were totally responsible for the majority of Camp Douglas's mortality is difficult to do. Equally difficult to prove is that Northern officials were responsible for the 308 deaths attributed to "other diseases" or the 80 fatalities from wounds and injuries (likely sustained on the battlefield). If these two groups are added to the 2,817 from the other three categories, the evidence suggests strongly that Yankee officials were not responsible, directly or otherwise, for the deaths of 3,205 (81.57 %) prisoners at Camp Douglas.[40]

Camp Morton

In 1891, Robert H. Little published a book, *A Year of Starvation Amid Plenty*, in which he undertook to tell readers how horribly he had been treated as a prisoner at Camp Morton near Indianapolis, Indiana. The book, little more than an extended essay, painted a very grim picture of life at the prison. Accusations of starvation were brought up as they were in most Lost Cause-era writing. During the summer of 1864 prisoners were portrayed as on half-rations as a matter of fiendish Federal policy to increase suffering and mortality among Southern prisoners of war. "I have seen men . . . cry like children," Little wrote, "because they were hungry." Murder and physical abuse at the guards' hands were portrayed as common events in this story of Camp Morton. In one anecdote a guard, distraught over the loss of a brother on the battlefield, murdered two prisoners in a fit of revenge for which he was never punished. Complaints of hunger or mistreatment to those in command would only get a prisoner beaten for being a malcontent. Seven years later the same basic picture of Yankee inhumanity and abuse at Camp Morton was painted in the pages of *Confederate Veteran* by J. K. Womack.[41]

In the last sixty-five years only one book about Camp Morton has been published, James R. Hall's *Den of Misery*, which reaches essentially the same conclusions about Camp Morton and Northern officials that Little and Womack did over a century earlier. This book, which relies almost exclusively on postwar Southern accounts and does not cite such important contemporary sources as the *Official Records* or *The Medical and Surgical History of the War of the Rebellion* or list them in the bibliography, is a long overdue attempt to provide readers and historians with a more accurate vision of life at this particular prison and of the Union's prisoner of war policies. Predictably, given the sources used, the book's thesis is that Camp Morton is an excellent example of Union negligence and abuse towards Confederate prisoners of war. The evidence, according to the book, proves that "in a land of plenty, poor clothing, little food, and lack of medication were used as tools to punish prisoners."[42]

When the contemporary records Hall did not choose to look at are consulted, one finds that Little and Womack were not entirely making things up in their accounts, though they did indulge in a good bit of exaggeration. Prisoners at Camp Morton were never, for example, placed on half-rations. In fact, the food situation was one of the few areas that received consistently positive comments in official inspection reports for the war's final two years. But at times conditions at the prison were about as bad as they could get in many respects. Little and Womack lived in crowded, dirty quarters in an enclosed area where drainage and sewage problems were quite serious. They may have also remembered seeing comrades without blankets and shoes as well. At times medical care was woefully inadequate. Looking back on their captivity they recalled and shared memories of their negative experiences, which did happen, but they often exaggerated them and reached the erroneous conclusion that the discomfort they endured was part of a Northern conspiracy to make the prisoner's lot as miserable as humanly possible. Though Camp Morton was one of the worst places to have been a prisoner during the Civil War, there is little compelling evidence that Confederate prisoners confined there were systematically neglected or punished.

Upon consulting the *Official Records*, one finds quickly that those prisoners sent to Camp Morton after the exchange cartel broke down in the spring of 1863 were destined to endure some hard, uncomfortable times. Surgeon Augustus M. Clark visited the prison in late October 1863 and did not have much good to say about the facility. The prisoners there were getting adequate food of the proper quality but otherwise the camp was in miserable shape in every conceivable area. Camp Morton was in such a sorry state, in fact, that he made the shocking statement that "this camp is a disgrace to the name military prison." One of the biggest problems, one directly impacting the camp's sanitary condition and thus prisoners' health, was that the drainage ditches were permitted to become garbage pits. Not only did the garbage keep the ditches from doing the jobs they were designed to do, "refuse of all kinds" piled up in them creating a very unhealthy atmosphere. The sinks/latrines were another major health hazard at the prison. They were nothing more than uncovered pits that were used until they were full when new ones were dug. Not surprisingly Clark described the sink situation as "exceedingly faulty" and "very foul." Policing, the general cleaning of the camp's grounds and living quarters, was reported to be "very bad." The prisoners' barracks were "dilapidated" and because of a lack of laundry facilities the prisoners were utterly filthy.[43]

For a man of medicine like Clark, the condition of the hospital was horrifying. The main hospital ward "is in so dilapidated a condition that the patients are obliged to fasten their blankets along the wall for partial protection from wind and weather, and are thus deprived of necessary covering." Rations for the sick were cooked in an area Clark complained was "in filthy condition." The policing of the hospital areas was inadequate. No program or plan to prevent sickness seemed to exist at Camp Morton as far as Clark could tell. All of these problems and more he laid squarely on the shoulders of Surgeon Funkhauser. Funkhauser, he told Hoffman, "has a large outside practice, and that he usually (and sometimes omitting even this) visits the camp not to exceed half an hour daily . . . ." With the surgeon attending to his presumably more lucrative private practice, the sick at Camp Morton were looked after by "an enlisted man, who, though he has paid some attention to the study of medicine, and endeavors to do his best, is entirely unequal to the proper discharge of these duties." In order to make sure the prisoners got the medical attention they needed, Clark recommended strongly "that this officer be at once removed and a competent man assigned in his stead."[44]

As Clark's report that fall makes very clear, Camp Morton was, to be blunt, a hell hole. There was reason to hope, though, that conditions there would improve. The same day Clark made his report to Hoffman, he pointed out that the prison had just gotten a new commandant that very day—Colonel A. A. Stevens. Clark and Hoffman hoped that a new administration would change things for the better at Camp Morton. Given the scathing indictment of Dr. Funkhauser, before the month was out Hoffman moved to get a new chief medical officer for the prison. In October 1863 he contacted surgeon-general Colonel Joseph K. Barnes, "to request that a competent surgeon with an assistant be ordered for duty at the camp without delay." Hoffman's request was noted and acted upon. The result was that medical conditions began to improve significantly by the end of 1863.[45]

At the end of January 1864, Clark again visited Camp Morton to see what, if any,improvements were under way at the prison. Prisoners' rations were still reported to be "abundant and of good quality" and the water supply was sufficient quantitatively and qualitatively. When it came to heating for the prisoners, Clark said all "tents and huts" had stoves and plenty of wood for fuel. And on the plus side, Clark did inform Hoffman that the camp's sanitation was being improved in some respects.

Drainage remained a problem but Clark commended Stevens's efforts to remedy the situation. Clark described drainage at Camp Morton as "imperfect, but much better attended to than at last inspection." The same applied to policing the prisoners' part of the camp, which Clark said was now "tolerably well attended to." As for the sinks, they were still open pits and were "not well attended to, though, in very much better condition than at last inspection." The report was not exactly a ringing endorsement but it was a marked improvement over what he had seen three months earlier. These changes for the better alone would have been enough to earn the comment in Clark's report that the "present commandant . . . is rapidly improving the condition of the camp." But there were other notable improvements in Clark's January 1864 report revealing that Union officials were working to remove the unenviable title of "disgrace to the name of military prison" from Camp Morton.[46]

Getting rid of Dr. Funkhauser in favor of Dr. W. A. Johnson began paying off immediately. Clark was impressed, telling Hoffman that Johnson "is an energetic and skillful officer, and has succeeded in working a very great change for the better in this hospital since he assumed the charge . . . ." Food for the sick was better inspected and prepared in cleaner conditions. The wards were clean for a change. They were also sturdier and warmer than they had been in October. Then Clark noted prisoners tacking up sheets and blankets to keep out the cold, something he did not record in January. There was still not enough room in the hospital for all the ill prisoners at Camp Morton but those admitted to the wards were getting much better treatment and had much better accommodations than they had several weeks earlier. Most importantly, the medical personnel were reported as actually doing all they could to prevent and treat illness at the prison, a marked improvement over the lackadaisical attitude that had prevailed during Funkhauser's tenure.[47]

This is not to suggest that Stevens and Johnson had miraculously transformed Camp Morton into Shangri-La. That would certainly be going too far. The barracks for the prisoners, for example, were quite crowded and built on the ground with no flooring; the inevitable result was damp, muddy, unhealthy atmosphere in the prisoners' living quarters. Not only were the barracks crowded and muddy, they were also, in many cases, still in need of significant repairs to improve what had been described as their "dilapidated" condition the previous October. Living in dirty quarters, the prisoners were also quite filthy themselves, many with clothing that needed replacing. And while food rations were plentiful and of decent quality, Clark wanted to see the prison erect central cooking houses so that the rations could be prepared properly—properly cooked in reasonably clean areas rather than in frying pans, canteen halves, and tin cups over open fires. Thus there was plenty of room for improvements in early 1864.[48]

In a number of key areas living conditions at Camp Morton did improve throughout 1864, though not evenly or in every area. In April Lieutenant-Colonel John Marsh, the camp's on-site inspector, filed a report giving Colonel Stevens a lot of credit for his management of the prison. Marsh described Stevens as "intelligent, of good habits, and competent to fill the position which he occupies . . . ." The hospital was in good condition, and the clothing, food, and health of the prisoners were all described by Marsh as "good." A major problem Marsh did note, however, was that Stevens did not insist that the prisoners clean their living quarters and the grounds around their barracks regularly, if at all. "There is not," Marsh noted, "that order, discipline, and cleanliness within the prison quarters which is desirable . . . ." The barracks areas were the worst, primarily because they were still without floors and were not elevated off the ground. Clark in January and now Marsh in the spring had complained of the filthy damp living spaces that inevitably resulted. Stevens had failed to remedy this problem, either because he had had his hands more than full trying to deal with the numerous problems he had inherited from the former commandant or because he thought the prisoners ought to assume primary responsibility for how clean or dirty the space around their barracks were—that they should at least pick up the trash better. There is perhaps some merit in both justifications, but these were important areas in need of more direct and active change and supervision on the commandant's part.[49]

Clark also inspected the camp in April and provided Hoffman with a much more detailed image of what was going on at Camp Morton since Stevens took over. New drainage ditches around the camp were nearing completion and the stream running through the camp "has been well. policed and is now an advantage to [the prison] instead of being as before a nuisance, as the receptacle of all the refuse and filth of the camp. At present, at least, it furnishes a sufficiency of water for washing purposes." The rations were of "good" quality and sufficient quantity though he recommended more vegetables because scurvy was a problem. Clothing and blankets were provided for all but most were in filthy condition owing to a lack of laundry facilities, which had been ordered but not completed yet. The main concerns were, as they had been at his last visit, the dirty barracks and disgusting sinks. The sinks remained "simply open excavations without screens and not filled up with sufficient frequency or properly disinfected." Clark wanted portable receptacles like those in use at Rock Island to remove the human waste from the camp daily to a large latrine some distance from the prison. Otherwise, Clark said he thought the prisoners' overall condition could be called "generally good if [they were] cleaner."[50]

The hospital and its new surgeon, C. J. Kipp, who took over on March 1 when Johnson retired at the end of his contract, were much praised by Clark. The "two main wards," he informed Hoffman, "are models of neatness, thoroughly whitewashed, and in admirable order and police." Sick prisoners "are well clad in U.S. Army hospital clothing and are clean and comfortable. The bedding is in ample quantity, obtained from the Medical Department, U.S. Army, and is clean and in good order." The food, kitchen, and eating areas for the ill inmates were all found by Clark to be in very good order. The hospital's sinks were, unlike in the prisoners' section of the camp, "well screened, whitewashed, and disinfected" though he wanted portable boxes of the type recommended for the prison's central latrines.[51]

The damp and dirty conditions of the prisoners' barracks and sinks remained a problem at the camp through the spring and into the summer of 1864. While improvements had been made from the previous fall, Clark and Hoffman made it clear to Stevens that making things better than they had been in these areas when Camp Morton had been called a "disgrace" was a good start but was not enough to satisfy either of them. In early August Dr. Charles T. Alexander, the Acting Medical Inspector for Prisoners, inspected the prison and found the sanitary condition of the camp "in anything but a favorable condition." The sinks had still not been provided with daily receptacles to take the waste from the camp and the two cesspools at the western end of the camp, which were ten feet long and about four feet wide with boards over them with holes cut into them for seats, were so foul that Alexander exercised his authority and ordered them "to be filled [in], plenty of lime being used, and in their stead two sinks to be built, with boxes on wheels to receive the excrement, the boxes to be emptied and washed daily." Garbage removal was still not as effective as it should have been, especially around the prisoners' living spaces. The prisoners' barracks were still un-floored and on the ground, assuring that wet and filthy conditions would prevail in them. Many of the other things about the prison continued to get good remarks, like the hospital facilities, but Alexander insisted to Hoffman that so long as the prisoners' sinks and barracks were allowed to remain in such unsanitary states, sickness and disease mortality would continue to be serious issues for Camp Morton. He therefore recommended that Hoffman impress upon Stevens the need to improve the policing and sanitary practices at the prison and to enlarge the camp to ease the crowding. With sickness a problem and new prisoners arriving, he also recommended that additional hospital space be created.[52]

Hoffman was not pleased with the things he was hearing about Camp Morton that August. He had assumed that Stevens's improvement program would continue and expand; Alexander's report suggested Stevens felt he had done all he needed to do back in the early spring to satisfy his superiors. He was wrong. In mid-August Hoffman contacted Stevens, informing him that he was quite upset to see that Alexander's report from the prison "shows the camp to be in a much less satisfactory condition than I have been led to expect. You will immediately take measures to make the improvements suggested by Surgeon Alexander . . . ." Hoffman wanted estimates from Stevens as soon as possible for expanding the camp and building additional hospital facilities as per Alexander's recommendations. To make certain things were progressing properly, Hoffman further instructed Stevens to make "weekly reports of what you are doing in this matter so that I may understand the condition of the camp."[53]

During the fall and winter of 1864 Camp Morton underwent more changes for the better as most of Alexander's and Kipp's recommendations were implemented. The camp was enlarged to ease crowding, barracks were repaired, and additional hospital space was constructed (with Hoffman's grudging approval). Clothing and shoe shortages that had been noted in inspection reports in late August were remedied in September and October. Rations were never complained of in the inspection reports and vegetables were issued in greater quantity when scurvy was reported as a problem. Most importantly, from a sanitary standpoint there were several important improvements made. For one thing, prisoners were made to police the camp more regularly, something Stevens should have insisted upon much earlier. In early September Lieutenant J. W. Davidson, Camp Morton's local inspector, reported to Stevens that "the general condition of both prison and prisoners is being improved each day in the way of cleanliness." The sinks were better attended to and the cesspools were gone entirely. New drainage ditches were dug. Even the prisoners themselves were forced to keep their clothes and their bodies cleaner—though that was a relative term here. A December report noted that many prisoners were not remotely interested in bathing, some taking the soap issued to them and "[throwing] it around the barracks" rather than using it for its intended purpose.[54]

One problem that inspectors complained of constantly and apparently never got remedied was the barracks being built on the ground and not supplied with board floors. Lieutenant Davidson called Stevens's attention to the need (again) to raise the barracks and provide floors at the end of August 1864. He appealed to the commandant:

> The quarters occupied by the prisoners are and have been kept in as good condition as quarters built as they are can be kept, but it is impossible to keep them in a perfect state of cleanliness for the reason that they are built low and on the ground, making a ground floor, which, by being constantly in use as they are by the filthiest set of men in the world, becomes perfectly saturated with saliva and other nuisance that is constantly being committed, and is damp all the time, especially in wet weather; and there being no undercurrent of ventilation, there is an offensive odor constantly arising from the floor, which must . . . cause more or less sickness . . . .

Raising them two to three feet, Davidson suggested, would go a long way to improving the sanitary conditions in the prisoners' quarters. The following month he pointed out to the commander again that if the barracks were raised and provided with plank floors they could "be kept thoroughly cleansed and in a good, healthy condition by washing them out each day, which is impossible to do at present." October 1864 found Davidson again appealing to Stevens to realize that raising the floors was important. This time, though, he changed his approach. Hoping to have more luck appealing to Stevens' security concerns, Davidson urged that the quarters "be raised from the ground to prevent them from tunneling out of camp, which they are constantly trying to do as the barracks now stand . . . ." The records do not indicate that Stevens ever took the issue of raising the prisoners' quarters as seriously as he should have and left their inhabitants to dwell in the damp and the mud, a serious blunder that increased misery and sickness at Camp Morton.[55]

On the back of Hall's book about Camp Morton the rather serious accusation is made that withholding medicines and, presumably, medical care were used "as tools to punish prisoners." After consulting the *Official Records* and *The Medical and Surgical History of the War of the Rebellion*, that charge does not seem to be supported by the more reliable wartime evidence. The leading killer of Confederate prisoners at Camp Morton was pneumonia, which between June 1863 and June 1865 took 495 prisoners' lives. That number represents 42% of the 1,175 deaths from disease recorded at the prison during that span of time. The key question is to what extent can Union officials be held accountable for pneumonia fatalities at the site? There can be no doubt that the prisoners' barracks were excellent environments for the disease. Pneumonia is often associated with damp, chilly, and dirty living spaces. To claim, though, that Union officials', especially Colonel Stevens's, failure to raise the barracks or at least provide flooring *caused* all or most of these deaths is not really possible, at least not with any sort of precision. For one thing, damp and dirty conditions do not cause pneumonia. People contract the disease when their immune systems are compromised to the point their body cannot fight the virus causing it. No doubt wounded and malnourished prisoners coming from armies rife with respiratory problems were quite vulnerable to pneumonia in prison. Ultimately what can be concluded is that prisoners' quarters did contribute to increased numbers of pneumonia cases but whether those conditions contributed lightly, moderately, or greatly is virtually impossible to determine with the data available.[56]

More helpful in determining if Confederate prisoners were denied medical care at Camp Morton as "punishment" as its most recent historian has asserted is to look at the mortality rates per reported cases of the major killers at the prison. Pneumonia took 495 prisoners between June 1863 and June 1865, which was 36.6% of the 1,351 reported cases of the disease. That is certainly not a death rate to brag about. On the other hand, it is slightly lower than that posted at Chimborazo Hospital. At the Richmond center 583 of the 1,568 pneumonia patients died of the disease for a death rate of 37.18%. While Confederate records are incomplete, what is available suggests that pneumonia patients did as well in Camp Morton's hospital wards as they would have done in Richmond. Thus it would seem fair to conclude that Union officials did not increase pneumonia mortality by neglecting prisoners or denying them adequate medical treatment.[57]

The second leading killer at Camp Morton was the diarrhea/dysentery category. This problem accounted for 315 deaths and that number represents 14.0% of the 2,241 reported cases. Here a discrepancy seems to exist between the mortality rate per reported case at Camp Morton and Chimborazo, where only 9.8% of these patients died of this particular category of illness. Medical negligence here seems unlikely, though. With pneumonia patients and, as will be shown below, malarial fever patients recovering at nearly the same rates as they did in Richmond it seems odd that diarrhea/dysentery patients would be singled out for substandard care. What is more likely is that with diarrhea/dysentery being such a huge and common problem during the Civil War, many prisoners arrived with advanced cases, though it is impossible to prove that. Furthermore, being treated with the best available remedies at the time would not have been such a good thing for these patients. Standard treatments for this problem were ineffective, if the patient was lucky, and often exacerbated the problem, if he was not so lucky. Holding Union officials at Camp Morton responsible for the 315 deaths, over one-fourth of the total disease deaths, from the most common illness in Civil War camps is unjust. This seems even more true when one considers that a patient was arguably better off not receiving professional medical treatment for this problem in the mid-1860s.[58]

The two categories just discussed, pneumonia and diarrhea/dysentery, accounted for 68% of the total disease deaths recorded at Camp Morton between June 1863 and June 1865. More importantly, most of these deaths cannot justifiably be laid on Union hands. That percentage goes up to nearly 80% when the third killer, malarial fevers, is factored in. During the last two years of the war, 119 prisoners died from "malarial fever." This represents only 10% of the 1,175 disease deaths and it is probable that most of them were recorded prior to Stevens's efforts to improve drainage at the camp. Unfortunately that is difficult, if not impossible, to say with certainty. What can be proven is that prisoners who contracted malarial fevers recovered as quickly from their illness as they would have in Richmond. The 119 deaths were out of 1,954 reported cases for a mortality rate of 6%. That is slightly better than that posted at Chimborazo where 125 of the 1,988 patients treated for this disease died, a 6.29% mortality rate.[59]

In the final analysis was Camp Morton the death camp postwar writers like Little and Womack and the site's most recent historian have argued that it was? The not-so-simple answer is "yes" and "no." For most of 1863 after the camp reopened, Camp Morton was a filthy and malodorous "den of misery" where medical care and facilities were wholly inadequate. Throughout much of the camp's existence the sanitary state of the sinks in the prisoners' portion of the site was substandard. Allowing the latrine problems to remain until the middle of 1864 definitely contributed to increased sickness at Camp Morton. Finally, the prisoners' living quarters were neither raised off the ground nor supplied with flooring, which contributed to increases in cases of sickness and, probably, death. So "yes" this prison was indeed a pestilential hell hole.

On the other hand, that is not necessarily evidence or definitive proof of abusive Union policies being in effect. During 1864 and 1865, when Northerners were presumed to have been treating prisoners as badly as possible, conditions were improving at Camp Morton. Latrine and general camp sanitation steadily improved. The camp was enlarged to ease overcrowding. Additional hospital space was built and, most importantly, Union officials got rid the inefficient and derelict Dr. Funkhauser in favor of more competent medical officers. It is significant, too, that Camp Morton inmates recovered from their maladies at rates that compared very favorably to those posted in the largest Confederate hospital in operation. Thus, while Camp Morton was a terrible place to reside, especially from mid-1863 to mid-1864, Confederate prisoners were not systematically punished there as a matter of United States policy towards Southern prisoners of war.

Rock Island

In 1936 Margaret Mitchell introduced a new generation of white Southerners to the Old South and the Civil War era in a way that would surely have made contributors to *Confederate Veteran* and the *Southern Historical Society Papers* absolutely beam. All the Lost Cause elements were present in her famous, widely read book—beaux and belles, happy slaves, chivalrous and courageous Confederates, and Yankees lacking any redeeming qualities whatsoever. Like Lost Cause advocates who had gone before her, Mitchell utilized the prisoner of war issue to distinguish which side represented good and which side evil. She placed the dashing Ashley

Wilkes at Rock Island and when Scarlett and wife Melanie received the news they were appropriately horrified. "For even as Andersonville was a name that stank in the North," Mitchell wrote, "so was Rock Island one to bring terror to the heart of any Southerner who had relatives imprisoned there." Readers learned that "at no place were conditions worse than at Rock Island. Food was scanty, one blanket did for three men, and the ravages of smallpox, pneumonia and typhoid gave the place the name of a pesthouse." Mitchell did not create the image of "Northern Andersonvilles"; she simply borrowed and reinforced one that already existed in many Southerners' minds—one that has gone virtually unchallenged until very recently.[60]

Of course there was plenty of material produced during the Lost Cause era to draw on to "prove" that Rock Island was a hell on earth. In 1876 Charles Wright of Tennessee wrote a piece for the *Southern Historical Society Papers* chronicling the hardships he endured at Rock Island in 1864 and 1865. He claimed that prisoners were shot for sport and that food was so scarce that it produced a "continued gnawing anguish." In 1898 D. C. Thomas informed *Confederate Veteran* readers that prisoners at Rock Island were poisoned and generally neglected. Eight years later, also in *Confederate Veteran*, Kate E. Perry Mosher argued that prisoners at Rock Island "were shot, frozen, [and] starved . . . ." In 1908 J. W. Minnich published *Inside and Outside of Rock Island* detailing the brutality he witnessed at the prison. In it, he claims, among other things, that guards were promoted for shooting prisoners and that Yankee officials starved prisoners in an attempt to force Confederate captives to switch sides. *Confederate Veteran* immediately recommended Minnich's book as required reading for all Southerners seeking a "fair and balanced" commentary on Northern treatment of prisoners during the Civil War. In 1912 Thomas E. Berry described the Rock Island officials as "terrible and barbarous" and called the commandant an "imp of Satan." "There are no words," Berry wrote, "adequate to depict or describe the terrible suffering and the outrageous cruelties and barbarities that were inflicted upon the prisoners [at Rock Island] by those in charge. It is almost beyond belief. The arch fiend himself could not have devised a more diabolical scheme of cruelty." Taken at face value, there does appear to be some rather damning evidence against those overseeing Rock Island and for well over a century that is exactly how the evidence has been taken.[61]

Until 2000 nobody seriously challenged this image of Rock Island. In that year Benton McAdams published the definitive history of the prison, challenging the notion that Rock Island was a "Northern Andersonville." Conditions there may have been far less than ideal but they never even approached those found at Andersonville. "In truth," he argued, "there were smallpox and hunger at the prison. But also in truth, they have been exaggerated. Most of the suffering was not the result of policy and inhumanity but rather of accident, incompetence, and the inability to cope with a war larger than any nation had ever before endured. Events outran experience, and the prisoners paid the price." The records indicate that McAdams is exactly right. Suffering there was, but Federal officials made dutiful attempts to minimize suffering and mortality at Rock Island as they did at other military prisons.[62]

To judge by the postwar writing of former prisoners and Lost Cause partisans, Rock Island was a true hell on earth. However, when wartime records are consulted, Rock Island offers one of the better examples of the gulf between what Union intentions towards Confederate prisoners actually were and how they were portrayed in the decades after the war. Opened as a depot for prisoners in December 1863 on an island in the Mississippi River, Rock Island was never an oasis, as the deaths of nearly 2,000 Southern prisoners clearly prove. But the wartime records show just as clearly that the prison was not the sort of Black Hole of Calcutta postwar commentators claimed it was.

The possibility that prisoners were brought to tears from hunger seems highly unlikely at Rock Island. Inspection reports from the other prisons often complained that either the quantity or quality of the prisoners' food rations was at times substandard. This concern is almost never mentioned in reports from Rock Island. One exception was when Surgeon Clark reported in April 1864 that the corn bread ration was "poorly prepared" and made prisoners sick. On April 16, Hoffman contacted the prison's commandant, Colonel Adolphus Johnson, about the corn bread situation. Hoffman instructed Johnson to only issue corn bread once per week "and then only after an inspection of it by a medical officer and found to be of a wholesome quality." Colonel Johnson assured Hoffman that those orders would be "strictly carried out" and apparently they were as no complaints are to be found about inferior corn bread or any other part of the food rations in inspection reports filed for Rock Island.[63]

In his excellent study of Rock Island, McAdams found that charges that prisoners at the site were systematically starved are difficult to sustain. Breaking down the official ration for prisoners, he found that they received some 4,000 calories, which, though unbalanced and monotonous, was certainly bulky enough to satisfy the pangs of hunger for the average sedentary prisoner. "If by chance," he noted, "a man's appetite was so voracious that 4,000 calories of bread and beef failed to satisfy him, there was yet more food available [via the sutler and express packages]." As was the case at other Federal prisons, a sutler operated at Rock Island who was permitted to sell food and other items to prisoners for a fee that went to the prison's operating budget. Some prisoners had money upon arrival that was taken (lest they use it to bribe the guards) and put into an account for them that they could draw on to use at the sutler. In January 1864 prisoner Lafayette Rogan described a meal of "Meats, cake, pickles, pies, cheese, oysters, fruits, and milk" thanks to the sutler. Others were lucky enough to have family and friends who could send money to be used at the sutler. Those who arrived broke and without outside allies who could send money could volunteer to work on various prison projects for extra cash. In June 1864 regulations stipulated that skilled workers toiling on the camp's sewer line project would get ten cents per day and unskilled laborers would receive five cents. Enough prisoners had funds that in June and July the post sutler did a brisk business, taking in $2,700 and $5,500 respectively.[64]

It is significant to note as well that scurvy does not appear in the inspection reports from Rock Island. That is not because it did not exist there, but it was never a significant problem as it was, say, at Point Lookout. According to *The Medical and Surgical History of the War of the Rebellion*, between February 1864 and June 1865 there were 439 cases of scurvy reported at the prison. That number accounts for 3.26% of the 13,453 diseases reported at Rock Island during that span of time and the fourteen deaths attributed to scurvy were less than 1% of the 1,589 disease fatalities. Given scurvy's relatively low numbers it seems that prisoners were not being systematically starved.[65]

Just as wartime records indicate that Rock Island prisoners had little to complain of where food was concerned, living quarters were structurally as good as could be expected, though crowding was often an issue. In February 1864 Clark inspected the camp and described the prisoners' barracks as "well built" structures that were from one to three feet off the ground. These were already better than accommodations at Camp Morton. Two coal-burning stoves were provided for each building and placed at either end of the barracks. Under normal conditions the stoves would have been sufficient to minimize the winter chills but the winter of 1863–64 was one of the coldest on record. Since Colonel Johnson could not control the weather, he made sure the prisoners had as much coal as possible to keep the stoves at maximum warmth. McAdams determined that "Johnson never rationed coal; the prisoners could burn all they wanted day and night. In fact, when [a] blizzard made it impossible for him to hire teams to haul coal, Johnson sent troops in to town and impressed eleven teams so he could keep his prisoners from freezing." With temperatures staying well below freezing for extended periods, the prisoners, especially those furthest from the stoves, endured many a cold evening that winter despite a virtually limitless supply of coal. Later they perhaps recalled those frigid nights and mistakenly attributed those hard conditions to Yankee callousness.[66]

A lack of clothing and blankets is rarely mentioned in reports from the prison. Since deficiencies in this area were mentioned by inspectors like Clark and Alexander at other facilities, not pointing out such shortages reveals that there was probably no reason to do so. In early April 1864 Clark told Hoffman that the "prisoners are well supplied with blankets, and as a general thing are well clothed." In July Lieutenant-Colonel A. P. Caraher, who also inspected the prison numerous times, informed Colonel Johnson that the "general appearance of the prisoners is clean and tidy and they are usually comfortably clad." Alexander reported the same when he inspected the camp at the end of July. If prisoners were not satisfied with Federal clothing, they were free to have clothing sent to them through the mail. In January 1864, for example, Rogan recorded in his diary that he received "socks, shirts, pens, ink" and the next month he noted, "Liberal donations of clothing continue to be made by the good ladies of Ky., Ten. and by kind friends who do not reside far from this place."[67]

As was the case at other facilities, drainage was a problem noted very early in inspection reports filed from Rock Island. After heavy rains, standing water was a problem contributing to a muddy, damp environment that was a wonderful breeding ground for all sorts of nasty germs and bacteria. Worse, though, was a marshy swamp area in the camp's southwestern corner, which Clark noted in February 1864 would "be productive of miasmatic disease" if it was not drained. He was especially concerned with getting rid of that significant body of stagnant water before warm weather arrived and increased the dangers it posed to the prisoners and guards alike.[68]

That same month Clark told Hoffman that efforts to improve the camp's drainage by grading the prison streets and providing surface drains leading to a main sewer would begin right away. He also let Hoffman know that the "marsh is to be drained into a natural ravine running to the river on the south side of the island." This was a very commendable start but grading the camp did not commence for several weeks. Approval from the

Quartermaster-General for the plans was not approved until late March or early April causing Clark to comment in April that "the drainage for the camp is entirely unprovided for . . . ." He did assure Hoffman, though, that work would commence immediately in order to improve the sanitary condition of the camp.[69]

Once the governmental red tape had been gone through, work began to drain the camp. On April 18, 1864, Lieutenant-Colonel John Marsh reported that the grounds about the prisoners' barracks were "being constantly improved by grading and drainage." Eleven days later Caraher reported the same kind of improvements in this area, noting "that the avenues of the prison have been for the past three weeks and are still under going a thorough course of grading, and with the recently adopted system of surface drainage . . . promise to soon become hard, dry, and easily kept free from filth." At the end of July Alexander described the camp's drainage situation as "good," an improvement from his previous reports in this regard.[70]

Clark's report from early February 1864 also mentioned that the sinks were in poor condition. Because of rock below the soil the sinks were very shallow, only from two to six feet deep. Not being able to dig the pits any deeper, Clark noted that it was "absolutely necessary to employ movable sinks or build them over the river, otherwise all the spare ground within the inclosure will soon become a seething mass of filth." Plans to construct an "open sewer of masonry, over which are to be built the sinks, allowing the soil to be carried off by a stream of water constantly flowing . . . through the sewer" were worked up and proposed formally throughout February and March. Until the running water sewer was up and running, portable boxes to catch the human waste were used to remove the problem. In early April Clark reported,

> The excavated sinks have been . . . entirely abandoned within the prison inclosure and movable receptacles substituted. A main privy has been constructed for each block of barracks, so arranged that the excrement is received in barrels provided with handles for moving, which are emptied and cleansed in the river twice in the twenty-four hours. These privies are well arranged for the prevention of an accumulation of filth and are kept in good police. They will answer their purpose very well until the permanent privies over the main sewer can be constructed.

At the end of May, work was under way on the sewer and by the end of July Caraher reported that the sewers were kept clean with an "almost constant flow of water through them . . . ." Thus authorities had two effective ways of dealing with the massive and malodorous problem of disposing of the waste that between 5,000 and 7,000 humans produced on a daily basis at the prison.[71]

The improvement efforts at Rock Island had a positive effect on the prisoners' mortality. The *Official Records* and *The Medical and Surgical History of the War of the Rebellion* both show that mortality among Southern prisoners clearly declined over time at Rock Island. Between February 1864 and June 1865, 1,589 prisoners died of some disease, many of them during the first months of the camp's existence. Between February and April 1864 the *Official Records* show that 770 prisoners died at Rock Island, which constitutes 48.45% of the 1,589 deaths enumerated in *The Medical and Surgical History*. From April 1864 through the end of the war disease mortality declined. It is significant to note that just at the time most writers argue that Union prison policies got significantly harsher, Confederate mortality at Rock Island declined. In fact, virtually the same number of prisoners died in the three-month period between February and April 1864 (before the retaliation program was officially discussed and implemented) as perished during the period between May 1864 and June 1865. The prison's population throughout its history remained fairly constant at between 6,000 and 8,000 prisoners until it dropped to just below 3,000 in April 1865 for obvious reasons.[72]

Prisoners at Rock Island were cared for about as well as they would have been at any other camp during the Civil War for most of the time the camp operated. Most of the mortality occurring at the depot was recorded in the first five or six months of operation. A lot of the deaths were attributable directly and indirectly to smallpox problems that erupted almost as soon as the gates opened. Records from February 1864 indicate that prisoners were transferred from the military prison in Louisville, Kentucky, who had the dreaded disease. The surgeon there, J. C. Welch, and his commanding officer, Captain Charles B. Pratt denied that prisoners were sent to Rock Island carrying smallpox—at least they were not sent there deliberately. No doubt they were telling the truth when they said that all prisoners were examined by the doctor before leaving Kentucky. The problem is that victims in the first phases of the disease, though highly contagious, often do not appear to have the disease at all. They may have no fever and the rash could have been a day or two away from appearing on the victim. The ultimate result was that Rock Island experienced a serious health crisis just as it was opening for business.[73]

Initially the medical officers at the prison were not doing an efficient job treating the smallpox cases. They were especially remiss, according to Clark in February 1864, in getting smallpox patients out of the barracks, a situation he rightly called "inexcusable." Existing facilities to quarantine those with the illness filled quickly and while additional smallpox wards were being built prisoners afflicted with the deadly disease remained inside the prison fence, though separated as much as possible from the other prisoners. Work on additional smallpox hospital facilities moved forward relatively rapidly and on March 1, 1864, Clark reported: "Every man now suffering from the disease has been removed from the prison inclosure, and every possible precaution is being taken to prevent the spread of the contagion." One of the most important precautions taken was vaccinating existing and newly arriving prisoners to minimize the death toll from smallpox. No doubt Union officials were concerned about their own welfare and that of the guards. Unfortunately, the vaccines at the time, prepared in unsterile environments and often with expired material, were far from a panacea. Another precaution was to treat the prisoners' clothing before they returned to the general population. In April 1864 Clark reported that

> the surgeon in charge has attempted to purify and disinfect the clothing brought by [the prisoners] to the pest-house. This is done by thoroughly boiling the clothes, then subjecting them in a close apartment to the fumes of burning sulphur, followed by a second boiling. This is said to have been effectual in destroying the infection, as no new case has yet been traced to the use of this clothing.

With those precautions in place, smallpox did decline in the spring and summer of 1864 but Rock Island, like other prisons, never entirely defeated this enemy that continued to raise its ugly head from time to time though never with the virulence and deadly results of those early weeks of 1864.[74]

When it came to treating smallpox the doctors there, after some necessary corrections and direction from Surgeon Clark, did about as well as doctors did at Chimborazo Hospital. Between February 1864 and June 1865 there were 1,797 cases of "eruptive fever," most of which were smallpox, treated at Rock Island. Of those, 436 died for a mortality rate among reported cases of 24.26%. In Richmond the mortality rate among reported cases in the "eruptive fever" category was 21.84%, not significantly lower than at the Illinois prison. Despite the precautions taken and despite treating smallpox victims as well as they could at that time period, this disease was the leading killer of Confederate prisoners, accounting for 27.43% of the 1,589 disease deaths recorded in *The Medical and Surgical History*.[75]

Pneumonia was the second leading killer at Rock Island, taking 397 prisoners' lives: 24.98% of the disease death total. The smallpox epidemic may have also contributed to pneumonia totals as prisoners' immune systems were taxed fighting smallpox, making them more vulnerable to contracting pneumonia. Certainly the living quarters were conducive to the spread of pneumonia. Dozens of men lived in the close quarters of prison barracks, quarters made even closer in the winter as they crowded around the stoves and slept two to a bunk. Sharing germs and bacteria in such an environment was inevitable. While little could be done about barracks housing, officials treated the illness as well as they knew how at the time. According to the records, that was reasonably effective for the period. At Chimborazo, 37.18% of pneumonia patients died from the illness. Rock Island's record was significantly better than that. At the Illinois pen, 397 of the 1,464 cases ended in death, which was only 27.11% of all those reported, a full 10% better than the recovery rate posted at the Richmond hospital.[76]

Finally, as at all military camps and facilities during the Civil War, the diarrhea/dysentery category accounted for a significant amount of illness and death at Rock Island. Nearly 4,000 prisoners reported this problem and more doubtless never sought treatment. Most soldiers and prisoners did not die from this category, though it did weaken their immune systems, making them more susceptible to other pathogens, like that causing pneumonia. Those who sought treatment were just as likely to recover at Rock Island as in their own capital. In Richmond the mortality rate among diarrhea/dysentery patients was 9.80% while at Rock Island 9.37% of these cases resulted in death.[77]

Ultimately the records for Rock Island do not support the thesis that Confederate prisoners were victimized by callous or vindictive Northern keepers. Water and food supplies appear to have been sufficient. Barracks were elevated and floored and provided with multiple coal-burning stoves and fuel. When prisoners became sick they were treated effectively enough that they got well as often (and with pneumonia more often) as ill soldiers being treated by Southern doctors in Richmond. The prisoners' lot at this facility was far from ideal, especially during a winter that set records for severity, but the argument that Union officials made life at Rock Island unduly or exceptionally harsh and lethal are sustainable only if one is willing to put their faith in postwar writing.

Perhaps the statistics that best indicate that Confederate prisoners were not victims of Northern neglect or systematic cruelty are those showing what Rock Island prisoners died of. Of the 1,589 disease fatalities 799 (over half) came from two categories: smallpox and diarrhea/dysentery. Quarantine facilities were initially inadequate but the records clearly reveal that Union officials did all they knew to do to bring smallpox under control, if not out of a sense of humanity then out of a sense of self preservation. Holding the Yankees responsible for the diarrhea/dysentery mortality is also questionable. This category was simply too common in Civil War camps to suggest that conditions at the prison were solely or uniquely responsible. Finally, with Rock Island prisoners recovering from pneumonia at a significantly higher rate than in Richmond it is difficult to conclude that pneumonia sufferers were neglected or denied medical treatment. Thus, these three disease categories that account for over 1,100 or just over 75% of all the disease deaths recorded for Rock Island do not appear to be attributable to Yankee malice or neglect.

As this chapter has argued, wartime records suggest that Union prisons in Indiana and Illinois were not intended to be places where Southern prisoners were punished. On the contrary, they were inspected regularly to assure that prisoners were treated according to the enlightened guidelines laid out in General Orders 100 and that they had sufficient food, clothing, and shelter. Deficiencies were generally, though not always, remedied in a timely manner. Sick prisoners at these facilities, judging from the mortality rates among reported cases, were treated as well in these Northern prisons as soldiers in the South's largest hospital in Richmond. If there is a case to be made that negligent officials or retaliation orders made Union prisons exceptionally hellish and lethal, it cannot be made using the prisons discussed here. The same can be said, as the next chapter shows, of the Ohio prisons.

Endnotes

1. United States War Department, *War of the Rebellion: Official Records of the Union and Confederate Armies* (Washington, D.C.: Government Printing Office, 1899; repr., Harrisburg, PA: Telegraph Press, 1971) Series II, Volume 8, 986–1002 (Hereafter cited as *OR* with all citations coming from Series II unless otherwise indicated); Lonnie Speer, *Portals to Hell: Military Prisons in the Civil War* (Mechanicsburg, PA: Stackpole Books, 1997), 67–70; "Alton in the Civil War: Alton Prison" website source, http://www.altonweb.com.

2. *OR*, Volume 5, 500, 523, 535, 569–70; Volume 6, 392–93.

3. *OR*, Volume 6, 998–99.

4. *OR*, Volume 7, 43, 81–88, 172, 175–76.

5. *OR*, Volume 7, 535–37, 813

6. *OR*, Volume 6, 392–93, 662–63; Volume 7, 468; United States Surgeon General's Office, *Medical and Surgical History of the War of the Rebellion, 1861–1865* (Washington, D.C.: Government Printing Office, 1875), Volume I, Part III, 46 (hereafter cited as *Medical and Surgical History*).

7. OR, Volume 8, 986–1002.

8. OR, Volume 6, 392–93, 662–63.

9. OR, Volume 5, 150, 285, 357, 450, 495–98; Volume 6, 61, 70, 96–97, 104–5, 160, 179, 191–92, 1123; Volume 8, 986–1002; *Medical and Surgical History*, Volume I, Part III, 30, 46, 63.

10. *OR*, Volume 8, 986–1002; *Medical and Surgical History*, Volume I, Part III, 30, 46, 63; Stewart Brooks, *Civil War Medicine* (Springfield, IL: Charles C. Thomas, 1966), 110–19, 125–27; Richard H. Shryock, *Medicine in America: Historical Essays* (Baltimore, MD: The Johns Hopkins University Press, 1966), 90–108; Bell I. Wiley, *The Life of Johnny Reb* (Baton Rouge: Louisiana State University Press, 1943), 254–55.

11. *Medical and Surgical History*, Volume I, Part III, 30, 46; Brooks, 113–17, 125–27. This health problem is covered in more detail in Chapter Eight.

12. Other diseases are discussed in Chapter Eight and also indicate that maladies such as typhus, malaria, and typhoid account for much of the remaining disease mortality. That chapter also argues that most of those deaths cannot be justly laid at Federals' feet as the work of negligent or abusive officials.

13. OR, Volume 8, 986–1002. See Chapter Four for the discussion about the South's role in killing the exchange cartel that led to the overcrowded conditions in each side's prisons.

14. George Levy discovered that not only did temperatures not reach the lows described in the article, the prisoner in question was far from an innocent lamb; he was being held after murdering a fellow prisoner. George Levy, *To Die in Chicago: Confederate Prisoners at Camp Douglas, 1862–1865* (Evanston, IL: Evanston Publishing, Inc., 1994), 41; *Confederate Veteran* (February 1900), 62–64, (December 1907), 565–66, (June 1910), 261, (June 1914), 268–70, (July 1914), 310–12, (June 1924), 218–19.

15. Levy, 6–13, 80, 149–54.

16. *Illinois in the Civil War: Camp Douglas, Illinois* at www.illinoiscivilwar.org/ campdouglas.html (08/22/2002); Speer, *Portals to Hell*, 71–72; Levy, 12–17.

17. *OR*, Volume 4, 106–8, 110, 162.

18. *OR*, Volume 4, 107–8, 129, 162, 166, 172–73, 185–86, 238, 239–40, 324–25, 353; Speer, *Portals to Hell*, 73; Lori Renee Fulton, "A Civil War Prison by the Lake: Camp Douglas in Chicago, Illinois," (master's thesis: Illinois State University, 1993), 7–42; Levy, 54–65.

19. *OR*, Volume 4, 253–54, 234–35; *Medical and Surgical History*, Volume I, Part III, 46; Levy, 18–21, 25–27, 36–37, 74–75.

20. *OR*, 110, 166, 172–73, 238; Levy, 12–13, 18–19, 22.

21. *OR*, Volume 4, 107–8; Levy, 36.

22. *OR*, Volume 4, 279; Levy 36.

23. Levy, 118.

24. *OR*, Volume 6, 4, 371–74, 417–18; Levy, 118–32.

25. *OR*, Volume 6, 6, 461–64, 489–90, 660–61, 848–51; Levy, 118–32, 134–46.

26. *OR*, Volume 6, 848–51, 908–10; Levy, 149–56.

27. *OR*, Volume 6, 417–18.

28. *OR*, Volume 6, 778–800, 804–5, 811–12, 927–28.

29. *OR*, Volume 6, 928–29, 975; Levy, 134–46, 156–60.

30. *OR*, Volume 7, 57–58, 102.

31. *OR*, Volume 7, 496–98, 694–95, 804, 840–41, 913, 959–60, 1026–27, 1067, 1104–5, 1187–1188, 1242–43; Volume 8, 44, 76, 144–45.

32. *OR*, Volume 6, 371–72, 660–61, 779–97, 848–51; Volume 7, 142–43, 496–98, 840–41, 913, 1006, 1059, 1104–5, 1187–88, 1243; Volume 8, 44, 76, 144–45; Levy, 181.

33. Levy, 149, 239–40.

34. *OR*, Volume 7, 184–85, 767, 804, 834–35, 840–41, 913, 959–60, 1026–27, 1067, 1104; Levy, 144–56, 239–40.

35. *OR*, Volume 8, 66, 76, 999–1000; *Medical and Surgical History*, Volume I, Part III, 46.

36. *Medical and Surgical History*, Volume I, Part III, 30, 46; Wiley, *Life of Johnny Reb*, 244–45, 260; McPherson, *For Cause and Comrades: Why Men Fought in the Civil War* (New York: Oxford University Press, 1997), 164–67.

37. *OR*, Volume 5, 345–46, 449–53, 498, 525, 537–39, 548–49, 686; Volume 7, 498, 1187–88, 1123, 1275; *Medical and Surgical History*, Volume I, Part III, 46.

38. *Medical and Surgical History*, Volume I, Part III, 30, 46.

39. *Medical and Surgical History*, Volume I, Part III, 30, 46.

40. For more on contemporary medical ignorance of the causes and control mechanisms for a number of infectious lethal diseases see the final chapter. *Medical and Surgical History*, Volume I, Part III, 46.

41. Robert K. Little, *A Year of Starvation Amid Plenty* (Belton, TX: n.p., 1891; repr., Waco, TX: Library Binding Co., 1966), 9–18, 23–24; *Confederate Veteran* (December 1898), 571.

42. James R. Hall, *Den of Misery: Indiana's Civil War Prison* (Gretna, LA: Pelican Publishing, 2006). The quote is taken from the book's dust jacket.

43. *OR*, Volume 6, 424–25.

44. *OR*, Volume 6, 425–26.

45. *OR*, Volume 6, 424–26, 442–43.

46. *OR*, Volume 6, 878–79.

47. *OR*, Volume 6, 878–80.

48. *OR*, Volume 6, 878–80.

49. *OR*, Volume 7, 71–72, 95–97.

50. *OR*, Volume 7, 95–96.

51. *OR*, Volume 7, 96–98.

52. *OR*, Volume 7, 554–56.

53. *OR*, Volume 7, 585, 599, 663–64.

54. *OR*, Volume 7, 694, 771, 812, 823, 842-843, 917–918, 927-928, 966, 1007–8, 1105, 1146–47, 1154–55, 1165–66, 1273.

55. *OR*, Volume 7, 693–94, 771, 812, 917–18, 1165–66.

56. *Medical and Surgical History*, Part I, Volume III, 46.

57. *Medical and Surgical History*, Volume I, Part III, 30, 46.

58. *Medical and Surgical History*, Volume I, Part III, 30, 46. A more detailed discussion of this particular category of illness is supplied in Chapter 8.

59. *Medical and Surgical History*, Volume I, Part III, 30, 46.

60. Margaret Mitchell, *Gone with the Wind* (New York: The Macmillan Co., 1969, 1936), 285–86.

61. *Southern Historical Society Paper* 1, no. 4 (April 1876): 281–89; *Confederate Veteran* (February 1898): 71–73, (January 1906): 27–32, (August 1907): 378, (July 1908): 346–47, (February 1912): 65–69, (April 1919): 130-131; J.W. Minnich, *Inside and Outside of Rock Island* (Nashville, TN: Publishing House of the M.E. Church, South, 1908), 3–4, 7–9, 16–19, 23–31.

62. Benton McAdams, *Rebels at Rock Island: The Story of a Civil War Prison* (DeKalb: Northern Illinois University Press, 2000), xiii. The *OR* gives the total

death toll as 1,860 between December 1863 and June 1865, Volume 8, 993–1002. The *Medical and Surgical History* puts the death from disease total at 1,589 between February 1864 and June 1865, Volume I, Part III, 46.

63. OR, Volume 6, 939–40; Volume 7, 24, 59, 65, 123, 472, 505–6, 600, 666–67; Volume 8, 116, 152, 216.

64. OR, Volume 7, 65, 180–81; Lafayette Rogan, *Diary* (copy), MOC; McAdams, 96–99.

65. *Medical and Surgical History*, Volume I, Part III, 46.

66. OR, Volume 6, 939, 948, 1002; Volume 7, 24, 65, 99, 377, 456, 472, 506, 666–67, 697, 880; Volume 8, 47–48, 116, 152, 216; McAdams, 45–46.

67. OR, Volume 7, 24, 65, 456, 506, 666–67, 697, 771, 880, 918; Volume 8, 47–48, 116, 152, 216; Rogan, *Diary*.

68. OR, Volume 6, 939, 948.

69. OR, Volume 6, 949; Volume 7, 24.

70. OR, Volume 7, 24, 65, 99, 506.

71. OR, Volume 6, 939, 949, 1003–4; Volume 7, 24, 99, 494.

72. OR, Volume 8, 994–1002; *Medical and Surgical History*, Volume I, Part III, 46.

73. OR, Volume 6, 938, 949, 963.

74. OR, Volume 6, 949, 1002, 1022; Volume 7, 13–15, 26, 505–7; Volume 8, 47–48.

75. *Medical and Surgical History,* Volume I, Part III, 30, 46.

76. *Medical and Surgical History,* Volume III, Part I ,30, 46.

77. *Medical and Surgical History,* Volume I, Part III, 30, 46.

−6−

FEDERAL POLICIES AT THE MAJOR OHIO PRISONS

Johnson's Island

Johnson's Island opened as an officers' prison in 1863 and operated as such for the rest of the war. Located in Sandusky Bay in Lake Erie, this facility was described in terrible terms after the war by ex-prisoners. In February 1904, James F. Crocker spoke of his experiences at Johnson's Island before a United Confederate Veterans meeting in Virginia. "My God," he exclaimed, "it was terrible." He explained to the gathering that prisoners there were intentionally starved by the Union officials as a matter of policy. "It was a cruel, bitter treatment," he said, adding to the postwar argument that the North's superior resources ought to have made Yankee prisons oases, "and that too, by a hand into which Providence had poured to over-flowing its most bounteous gifts." In 1917 ex-prisoner Henry E. Shepherd recalled life in Johnson's Island as a "grim and remorseless struggle with starvation . . . ." This was not just his experience; Shepherd claimed that for all prisoners on the Island, "relentless and gnawing hunger was the chronic and normal state."[1]

The *Official Records* indicate that during 1863 and for a significant portion of 1864 Johnson's Island had some serious problems. They also show that inept local officials rather than negligent or harsh retaliatory policies were often the culprits. Take the first commandant assigned to Johnson's Island, Lieutenant-Colonel William Pierson. For the first six

153

months of 1863 he seemed to be capable of running the camp with a reasonable degree of competence. Of course his job was not all that taxing. The exchange cartel was in effect and during that period he never had more than 350 prisoners to look after. In April, for example, the prison had only 123 prisoners and in May the number hit a low of only seventy-two. In June, though, the cartel disintegrated and the number of prisoners at the prison began to rise dramatically. By the end of August over 2,000 Confederate officers were held at Johnson's Island. And, as the numbers rose and summer turned to fall, inspectors' reports coming from the camp began to show that running a major military prison was beyond Pierson's administrative abilities.

At the beginning of October Surgeon Anthony M. Clark filed a very negative report from Johnson's Island. The prison's sanitary condition was utterly horrible, he told Hoffman. Clark complained, "The police of the whole camp, . . . is most inexcusably neglected." Garbage was allowed to pile up throughout the camp for want of an effective policy and method for hauling it out of camp. The sinks were in a filthy state as well, contributing to a very unhealthy, not to mention offensive, atmosphere. Clark also noted the need for additional hospital facilities on Johnson's Island as well as additional medical personnel. While Clark found Dr. T. Woodridge to be "a skillful practitioner of medicine," he was not a very able administrator, delegating "too much of his authority to his subordinates, . . . consequently much of the duty is carelessly performed."[2]

On October 19 Pierson heard from Hoffman, who was very unhappy about Clark's report on Johnson's Island. Though, as will be discussed more fully below, food, clothing, and shelter generally received good marks from Clark, Pierson was still in hot water with Hoffman. Johnson's Island should not be so filthy, Hoffman told the commandant. The poor sanitary state of the hospital, Hoffman admonished, "shows a very great neglect on the part of the surgeon in charge, which the commanding officer should not have tolerated." In several places Hoffman quoted directly from Clark's report to make his point. By calling "the most conspicuous deficiencies" to the commandant's attention Hoffman told Pierson he expected "immediate measures will be taken to remedy the present unsatisfactory condition of your command."[3]

A few days after Hoffman's rebuke, Pierson attempted to excuse his failures by claiming that he did not realize that the prison was going to be used so soon by so many prisoners. That excuse was lame to say the least. Johnson's Island was specifically constructed as a prisoner of war facility and with the cartel's suspension Pierson ought to have expected increasing numbers of "fresh fish" and prepared accordingly. Hoffman therefore was not at all moved by Pierson's explanation. "You have had every reason," he told the commandant, "to believe that the depot was to be occupied this winter by a large number of prisoners and it was not necessary to wait [for inspectors and superiors to order you to put the camp] in proper condition . . . ." Hoffman expected Pierson to show some initiative to get the camp cleaned up. "I have not time," Hoffman wrote, "to give you minute instructions about the many matters [associated with running a prison camp]. The responsibility for the good condition of your command is entirely upon yourself and it is expected that you will not wait for instructions, but act on your own judgement, only asking for authority when it is not already in your hands." Such communiqués, at least at this point in the depot's history, are not consistent with the more common picture of negligent and vindictive Yankee officials—inept perhaps, but not negligent.[4]

Such delegation of authority was normal and necessary. Had those instructions been given to someone other than William Pierson they may have resulted in more positive results. Unfortunately Pierson was all Hoffman had at the time. The winter of 1863–64 was unusually cold, causing prisoners to remain crowded together in their rather dirty barracks. Also, Pierson had done nothing to improve the cleanliness of either the prisoners' quarters or the hospital. On January 11, 1864, Clark reported to Hoffman that the prisoners' living areas were filthy as were the kitchens, where "all [the] utensils, and the ground around the outer doors covered with filth and slops, frozen to a depth of several inches." The sinks were still "in a filthy condition." Not only was Clark disgusted by the state of the prisoners' barracks, he had little positive to say about Johnson's Island's hospital facilities, which he described as "exceedingly dirty." The prisoners apparently had plenty of food, clothing, and shelter, but Pierson had done little if anything to improve the depot's overall sanitation. That, combined with a rising mortality rate during that winter led directly to his being replaced within a week of Clark's negative inspection report by Brigadier General Henry D. Terry.[5]

Hoffman hoped that a change in administration at Johnson's Island would solve some of the glaring sanitary problems that had constantly been reported during Pierson's tenure. To help make sure the new commandant got off on the right foot, Hoffman gave Terry some important instructions. He informed the general that as commander he and he alone was responsible for giving "the necessary and proper orders to insure that a proper state of police shall be preserved throughout the prison." To help make certain that the barracks were in good condition for future residents, in early February 1864 he told Terry that any and all repairs and upgrades in the prisoners' quarters needed to be made "as soon as practicable, as there will be prisoners enough to fill them up very soon." That same month Hoffman gave instructions about clothing for the prisoners on the Island. The Union's position had been and continued to be, he told Terry, that "prisoners will be supplied with all clothing necessary to prevent suffering, and if it is not furnished by their relatives it is to be issued by the Quartermaster's Department." Hoffman went on to tell the commandant that if there were "any cases at Johnson's Island of prisoners in summer clothing, or in clothing very much worn, so as to render it unfit for the season, will you have the kindness to order such as is proper [*sic*] issued?"[6]

Initially the change appeared to bring positive results. One February inspection report noted that "the real evils are being remedied. A rigid system of policing is established . . . ." And, most importantly, prisoner mortality was declining. Unfortunately all was still not well at Johnson's Island according to Yankee inspectors. Although one of them, Lieutenant-Colonel John F. Marsh, found clothing, food, and shelter to be satisfactory generally speaking, the same old sanitary problems remained, causing an unhealthy atmosphere to prevail at the facility. Policing remained a major problem and the sinks (which nobody seemed anxious to deal with) were "allowed to become offensive." Worse, in mid-nineteenth-century America, Marsh described Terry in a May report as "an intelligent, clever gentleman, but quite as fond of a social glass of whiskey as of attending to the duties of his command." Less than one week later Colonel Charles W. Hill replaced Terry as commandant of Johnson's Island. The removal of two commandants within five months of one another for failing to take steps to make Johnson's Island reasonably clean does not conform to the Yankee negligence theory of Confederate prisoner mortality at Johnson's Island. Prisoners apparently had sufficient food, clothing, and shelter but significantly, given the negligence charges against Union prison officials, such measures were simply not enough.[7]

Johnson's Island was getting its third commandant in a year when Colonel Hill took charge in May 1864. Understandably irritated with the inability to put a competent commandant at the post, Hoffman made it very clear to Hill that he was expected to succeed where his predecessor had failed. Prior problems, he told Hill, had stemmed from "want of good management," the implication being that Hoffman did not want Hill to be guilty of the same quality. The filthy sinks had been a source "of some embarrassment" and Hoffman urged Hill to put this at the top of his list of problems to fix. Initial reports indicated that Hill was indeed the answer to Hoffman's and Johnson's Island's prayers and in late June Hoffman congratulated Hill on his work turning the prison around and assured him that he knew Hill would ultimately "remedy all the existing evils."[8]

Those initial improvements were relative to the state of affairs before Hill took over and apparently were not as extensive as Hoffman had been led to believe, however. In mid-July, Surgeon Alexander inspected the camp and did not find anything good to say about its cleanliness. "Seeing the camp," he fumed to Hoffman, "you would not know whether to be most astonished at the inefficiency of the officer in charge of the prisoners' camp or disgusted that men calling themselves gentlemen should be willing to live in such filth." Hoffman, once again, faced the problem of a Johnson's Island commandant with no ability or interest in cleaning up the prison to provide a healthier overall atmosphere. On July 28, Hoffman wrote to Hill informing the commander how displeased he was that "the condition of the police of the depot under your command [is] in a most censurable condition . . . ." Such reports were, Hoffman let Hill know, wholly unacceptable. The result was a curt order from Hoffman that Hill was "required to institute immediately an entire and thorough reform."[9]

Hoffman's attempt to light a fire under a commandant at Johnson's Island finally appeared to work when the flame was applied to Colonel Hill. That summer, inspection reports from two different inspectors, Major Edward Scovill and Major Manning Fowler, were increasingly and consistently more favorable for all aspects of Johnson's Island. At the end of August Major Scovill reported improvements in garbage removal and he described the sinks as being "in good order," the first time something positive could be said of the latrine situation. Never again do reports from this post complain of dirty barracks, bad police, or filthy sinks.[10]

The records tend to suggest that the dirty and unhealthy environment found at Johnson's Island during 1863 and for much of 1864 was due to ineffective leadership at the camp and not because officials like Hoffman took a nonchalant attitude towards such issues. One area, however, where officials were inexcusably tardy was in providing additional hospital space when it was needed. In Clark's October 1863 report he specifically requested that more space be provided for sick prisoners at Johnson's Island. Additional reports in 1864 from other officers routinely called attention to the lack of adequate hospital space. The records do not indicate why this often-mentioned and significant problem was ignored. Miserly or vindictive Federal officials likely do not answer the question, at least not very adequately because they seemed to have been very active in trying to fix other problems at the prison. And eventually officials did act to remedy this need, but not until September 1864. The construction of a new hospital was approved that month but there can be no doubt that the new facility ought to have been provided much earlier than it actually was. Insufficient hospital space insured that ill prisoners remained in dirty barracks, compromising their ability to recover and infecting their fellow prisoners.[11]

Having shown what the problems at Johnson's Island were, it should be pointed out that other areas could be described generally in satisfactory terms for the era. This appears to have been the case for the food situation despite postwar claims of relentless struggles against gnawing hunger. It is significant that in the October 1863 report that got Pierson in so much trouble Clark told Hoffman that the prisoners' rations were inspected for quality and he described the food rations as "abundant and very good." The prisoners also had a "plentiful" supply of vegetables. While occasional reports do indicate shortages in the prisoners rations, Johnson's Island inmates do not appear to have been systematically denied an adequate amount of food. If they had been, scurvy would have shown up in the records as a key problem, which it does not. From June 1863 to June 1865, 3,571 illnesses were recorded at the prison. Of those, only 58 (1.62%) were scurvy patients. And while scurvy was blamed in the deaths of at least a few prisoners at every other camp discussed in this book, Johnson's Island did not record a single fatality from scurvy.[12]

One food-related problem that did exist for a few weeks in the spring of 1864 was the quality of the beef supply. In early May the on-site inspector reported that "The beef furnished this post is of the poorest quality and often deficient in quantity." Subsequent inspections do not mention how the problem was corrected but it apparently was, at least until late October and early November when prisoners began receiving "sour beef." Again, this was not permitted to continue. An early November report noted that the beef problem was caught and "was immediately replaced by good [beef]." Since inspectors did not ignore food problems in their reports it seems reasonable to conclude that the overwhelming majority of reports giving the rations positive reviews indicate that the rations were generally sufficient in quality and quantity, an assumption buttressed by the low incidence of scurvy.[13]

Being an officers' prison, Johnson's Island inmates tended to come from an economic class more capable of supplementing their rations through relief packages and the post sutler. In August 1863 John Dooley wrote in his diary: "Our men having plenty of money live as well in the way of eating as we ever did." If John Inger's diary is any indication, there was little change in access to food through mail and sutler in 1864. On April 19, 1864, he had "bacon, beef, sausage, butter, [and] biscuit" for dinner. On June 27 he had a "[f]ine dinner [of] boiled ham, beef, corn and flour bread, onions, lettuce and beets, pound cake, tea, strawberry preserves and butter." He does record restrictions on food through the mail and the sutler in August 1864 but they did not last long. In October he records receiving twenty-five pounds of flour, a four-pound ham, coffee, brown and white sugar, tea, raisins, tomatoes, and molasses in the mail. On Christmas Day 1864 Edmund DeWitt Patterson recorded that nearly "two hundred boxes came in by express today filled with eatables and Christmas gifts." At the end of the day he sat down with his "Mississippi friends [who shared] a nice dinner, as any one could wish for anywhere." Others were getting food by mail and in February 1865 food was again available for sale at the sutler.[14]

Postwar assertions that Yankee officials neglected to provide Confederates at Johnson's Island with adequate clothing are difficult to substantiate through contemporary records. That is not to suggest that there were not prisoners there who at times had worn-out clothing. The point is simply that the image of ragged, half-naked Rebel officers at the prison is generally inaccurate. For one thing, again because these prisoners were officers, they had greater access to better quality uniforms and multiple changes of clothing. They tended, therefore, to arrive on the island better equipped to take care of this necessity than many enlisted prisoners whose clothes saw harder service and who rarely had more than what they had on their bodies when captured. Pierson pointed that out in an August 1863 communication to Hoffman, saying, "Many of the prisoners now here have fine clothing which they brought with them." At the end of September 1863, Hoffman informed Pierson that prisoners could buy extra clothing in preparation for the coming winter and for those unable to purchase such extras Pierson could, "if recommended by the medical officer, . . . issue such extra clothing as may be necessary." In December 1863 alone Pierson reported that the Federal government had issued 1,046 pairs of pants, 1,022 shirts, 200 blouses, 270 pairs of drawers, 380 pairs of socks, 13 greatcoats, and 796 pairs of shoes to a population that averaged 1,391 prisoners between February and December 1863. Of course not all prisoners needed new clothing and during this period sutlers and family members and friends were allowed to supply clothing with virtually no restrictions whatsoever.[15]

Little changed on this front in 1864. In February Hoffman ordered Terry to make sure prisoners were furnished with a suitable set of clothes. Hoffman was tired of reports and accusations that inmates suffered in Union prisons for want of clothing. The new commandant was to see to it "that prisoners will be supplied with all the clothing necessary to prevent suffering." The following month Hoffman let Terry know that prisoners could still get clothing in the mail with the only restrictions being no uniforms or anything beyond immediate need. That was apparently ignored in some cases. In April 1864 John Inger got a coat, vest, a pair of pants, four shirts, two pairs of drawers, four collars, and two cravats in the mail. Two weeks later this well-clad Rebel received a hat, a pair of shoes, five pairs of socks, two scarves, a pair of gloves, and three more shirts. Johnson's Island officials may have ignored existing restrictions because it was in the government's best financial interest to let prisoners give, trade, or sell extra clothes to other captives—which Inger records on several occasions.[16]

Mail and sutler restrictions did not take effect at the island until late August 1864 and in November Inger reported clothing again coming in through the mail. There may have been brief periods of want for some prisoners regarding clothing but such likely resulted from factors other than a Yankee retaliation program. In October 1864 Captain L. M. Brooks, the assistant quartermaster for the area, became ill and died, causing delays in supplying the prison with a number of provisions. One inspector assured Hoffman, though, that the "delay will undoubtedly obviated the coming week." Such apparently did come to pass as the Federal government issued 423 shirts, 748 pairs of socks, 17 greatcoats, 465 pairs of drawers, and 599 pairs of shoes during November alone. And in December 1864 ice was making supplying the island difficult. The prison was out of blankets and a few other important items as a result. But officials at the depot were making every effort to overcome the difficulty as a communication from Hill makes clear. "We are getting over supplies by hand on the ice on sleds and in small boats on runners where practicable," he told Hoffman, "and can now keep some days ahead of current wants."[17]

For living quarters, Johnson's Island prisoners were housed in wooden barracks that had wooden floors and stoves. These structures were often described as in disrepair and insufficiently ventilated but they generally fit the criteria each side believed was necessary for prisoners of war, which was basic shelter from the elements. When repairs were necessary, as in mid-October 1864 when a violent storm damaged virtually every building, work to repair the barracks commenced immediately to assure the prisoners would have sufficient shelter during the coming winter. The prisoners slept two to a bunk and were supplied with straw bed ticks. The straw provided some measure of insulation and the prisoners could combine blankets and body heat to help stay warm during the night. All things considered, the officers confined at Johnson's Island had living quarters that were about as good as they would have in the field or in winter quarters. Understandably, as pointed out in Chapter Four, Union officials did not see why Southern prisoners, even officers, were entitled to living quarters that were superior to what was available to their own soldiers and officers in the field.[18]

In October 1864, as the nights began to get colder, some prisoners did experience some very uncomfortable conditions because they had no stoves in their quarters. Looking back they likely recalled the lack of stoves and attributed it to cheap officers or retaliation programs. The reality was that Captain Brooks's death not only affected the clothing issues for a short time in 1864, but it also affected the ordering and delivery of stoves for the prison. Major Thomas Linnell, who inspected the camp regularly, told Hoffman on October 16, 1864, that the lack of stoves was a problem but the quartermaster "is making every possible exertion to obtain them as fast as possible." And the stoves did arrive prior to winter's onset, though some long cold nights were endured by some prisoners until they got there. The point here, of course, is not that some prisoners suffered from the cold in 1864; it is that Northern officials acted positively to alleviate the problem and successfully solved it in a reasonably timely manner.[19]

When looking at the mortality at Johnson's Island, the comparisons to Andersonville or the arguments that life there was unduly precarious are hard to sustain. Pierson's claim in late December 1863 that "the health of the prisoners greatly improves while at this depot, so much so that there is a marked change in their appearance for the better between their arrival and departure" was an exaggeration from a man under considerable fire from his superiors at the time, but perhaps not overly so. Between July 1862 and June 1865 the total number of deaths at Johnson's Island was 235, which comes to a monthly average of just over 6, not bad at all for a stationary camp of the era where between 2,500 and just over 3,000 men were confined for an extended period.[20]

The mortality is probably not attributable to the so-called retaliation policies instituted in the spring and summer of 1864. Between May 1864 and June 1865 a total of fifty-three prisoners died at Johnson's Island. That comes to a monthly average of just over four, which is *lower* than the monthly average during the entire time the prison was in operation. No other Federal prison has such low mortality numbers. In fact, of all the major Union prisons, Confederates were most likely to walk out of Johnson's Island than any other one.[21]

A look at the records reveals that a significant percentage of the mortality recorded at Johnson's Island occurred during a four-month period in late 1863 to early 1864. Between November 1863 and February 1864, seventy-one prisoners died. According to the *Official Records*, which covers more time than *The Medical and Surgical History of the War of the Rebellion*, 235 prisoners died at Johnson's Island between June 1862 and June 1865. The seventy-one deaths represent a spike during late 1863 and early 1864 that accounted for 30.21% of all the deaths recorded at Johnson's Island in the *OR*. The reason for the spike is more mundane than conspiracies to "retaliate" against or punish Southern prisoners. Such plans were not discussed seriously in the War Department until the spring of 1864 for one thing. The simpler and more likely explanation is that as the weather got significantly colder, and that year winter set in earlier than usual. Prisoners therefore spent most of their time crowded around the barracks's stoves keeping warm. With dozens of men huddled around stoves for hours at a time coughing and sneezing on one another a spike in illness and death totals is not particularly mysterious or sinister.[22]

When the *Medical and Surgical History* is consulted one finds the usual suspects killing Confederate officers at Johnson's Island that were responsible for killing Northern and Southern soldiers and officers in their respective armies. Not surprisingly the category diarrhea/dysentery took the largest percentage of Rebel officers at the prison. Between June 1863 and June 1865, forty-six inmates or 29.48% of the 156 recorded disease fatalities for that period succumbed to diarrhea/dysentery. How many of these victims were chronic sufferers is impossible to determine with certainty but no doubt some arrived with the affliction, which became more of a problem as the war progressed and had no respect for rank.[23]

It would be impossible to prove that Union policies increased the number of diarrhea/dysentery cases at Johnson's Island. It was simply too common during the war. And since no effective cures were known at the time in America, one can hardly argue that prisoners at Johnson's Island were denied the necessary medicines that would have significantly reduced the fatalities from the post's leading killer. One important and quantifiable thing that one can say about this health issue is that Confederate officers were more likely to recover from it at Johnson's Island than at Chimborazo Hospital in Richmond. The Southern facility, according to *The Medical and Surgical History*, treated 4,644 diarrhea/dysentery cases, of which 455 or 9.80% ended in death. At Johnson's Island 1,855 of these cases were treated with 46 or 2.47% of them ending in death, significantly better than in Richmond.[24]

The next leading killer was a vague category of illness simply labeled "continued fevers," which generally included typhoid and any other disease that had fever as a symptom but that doctors could not readily identify. At Johnson's Island, twenty-six prisoners died from this category, which comes to 16.66% of the total recorded in *The Medical and Surgical History*. As with the diarrhea/dysentery category, the mortality rate was quite a bit better than that recorded in Richmond. On Johnson's Island, ninety-three prisoners were treated for this problem, with 27.95% of them resulting in death. That is a rather ghastly statistic by modern standards but in Richmond 885 or 41.11% of the 2,153 patients treated for this problem died. Obviously treating "continued fevers" during the Civil War left a great deal to be desired. The point here is that in yet another category Johnson's Island prisoners were less likely to die of a particular illness there than in their country's largest medical facility.[25]

The same held true for pneumonia. At the prison ninety-nine prisoners were treated for pneumonia. Of them, twenty-five died or 25.25% of the recorded cases. Again, that is not a statistic a modern hospital would brag about. But in the context of the mid-nineteenth century it does not seem to be proof of negligence or of a policy to deny Southern prisoners proper medical care. At Chimborazo, 583 of the 1,568 pneumonia patients treated there died, which is a mortality rate of 37.18%. That is significantly higher than at Johnson's Island.[26]

The records all seem to indicate, in fact, that regardless of the reason a prisoner wound up in Johnson's Island's medical facilities, he was very likely to make a full recovery. Between June 1863 and June 1865, 3,571 prisoners were treated for some disease at the prison. Of them 156 or 4.36% died. Put another way, 95.64% of sick prisoners treated there during that span recovered from whatever problem they were being treated for. In Richmond 2,717 of the 23,849 patients treated there died, which is a mortality of 11.39%: 2.61 times higher than at Johnson's Island. Such statistics seriously undermine the argument that Northern officials actively denied decent (for the time period) medical care or neglected to provide medicine in sufficient amounts to keep the prisoners there reasonably healthy and, more importantly, alive at this Ohio prison.[27]

Johnson's Island certainly had problems that postwar Southerners recalled and attributed to malicious Yankee policies. No doubt those prisoners living in unheated barracks in the fall of 1864 suffered significantly and assumed it was deliberate. The lack of ample hospital space until the fall of 1864 was a significant problem. And the camp's deplorable sanitary condition for most of the prison's first year was inexcusable even by the standards of the period. The remarkable incompetence of post commandants certainly guaranteed that problems went unaddressed or that solutions to them were poorly executed.

Despite these issues, contemporary evidence does not support charges of negligence or abuse at Johnson's Island. Scurvy statistics, inspection reports, and prisoners' private diaries all undermine Shepherd's claim of a "grim and remorseless struggle with starvation." By the winter of 1864, all barracks had stoves and clothing was not a problem for most prisoners. Further compromising the cruel Yankee thesis is the fact that multiple commandants were relieved for failure to clean up the prison. Finally, the high recovery rates from numerous diseases and the fact that mortality declined over time at Johnson's Island suggest that the facility was not designed to be a place of punishment.

Federal policies and guidelines like General Orders No. 100 played a big role in making Johnson's Island the least deadly of all the Union prisons. But so too did the class of prisoners held there. Officers were far more likely to either have money or to be able to get it from friends and relatives than the ordinary enlisted prisoners. They would have had, therefore, the significant advantage of being able to use the post sutler to get a larger and more varied diet than that issued by their captors. Officers' uniforms were generally of better quality and they were more likely to have changes of clothing than the common soldier. The mail and the sutler also assured that captured officers were better provided with clothing. The greater access to a more nutritious diet and better access to warmer clothing no doubt contributed significantly to prisoners' comfort and health. When combined with the evidence that Northerners were not trying to undermine prisoners' health it is no wonder that Johnson's Island was the healthiest Union prison.

Camp Chase

Speaking at Camp Chase in 1910 as part of Memorial Day celebrations there, Bennett H. Young said the prison was a typical example of Yankee prisoner of war camps, which was to say that it was a "veritable 'hell hole'" where inmates never got all the vital supplies they needed to survive even though the North was "a land of plenty and abundance . . . ." Located near Columbus, Ohio, Camp Chase, like other Northern prison camps, was described in wholly negative terms by postwar speakers and writers. The influential *Southern Historical Society Papers* used a significant amount of space in its 1876 inaugural volume to vindicate the Confederate cause by portraying the Southern leaders and soldiers as paragons of Christian virtue and their Yankee counterparts as sociopathic vandals. According to one section of the *Papers*, prisoners who escaped from Camp Chase and were recaptured "were taken out in the presence of the garrison and tortured with the thumb-screw until they fainted with pain." In March 1898 *Confederate Veteran* magazine printed a short piece by ex-prisoner W. H. Richardson. In it, Richardson said that he arrived at Camp Chase in August 1864 where he and his comrades "found an order curtailing rations to the lowest minimum to sustain life. Therefore, a constant want of necessary healthy food to sustain life fast filled those graves [at the prison]." The publication's June 1912 issue ran an article entitled "Prison Life at Camp Chase Ohio" informing readers that starvation was the norm there as was inadequate clothing and shelter. The article also claimed that one had to be very careful at all times because the guards liberally scratched their itchy trigger fingers. John Dyer recalled in 1898 that every guard "seemed to think he ought to kill a rebel, and we had to keep our eyes on them at all times to save our lives." Perhaps most sinister, though, was the accusation that Camp Chase prisoners were injected with poison on the pretext of vaccinating them against smallpox.[28]

The discussion to determine if accusations that Northern officials systematically victimized prisoners at Camp Chase begins in 1863. With the exchange cartel falling apart in the middle of that year, leading to extended confinement for Confederates there, such a starting point makes sense. One unpublished 1990 study of the prison found living conditions at Camp Chase to have been, generally, very satisfactory during 1863. Those findings were consistent with inspection reports from the fall and winter. In October Anthony M. Clark gave Camp Chase a good overall report. The barracks needed to be better ventilated, he believed, but other than that they were in "very good" condition. The barracks were supplied with stoves and plenty of wood. Prisoners' rations and bedding were also fine in Clark's view. "In reference to this camp," Clark concluded, "there is nothing to be complained of except its imperfect drainage, the non-ventilation of the barracks, and the insufficiency of hospital room." He also assured Hoffman that Colonel William Wallace, the post's commanding officer "promises to improve the drainage . . . ."[29]

In December 1863 Hoffman had gotten some reports of problems at Camp Chase. At the beginning of the month, Acting Medical Inspector J. M. Cuyler repeated Clark's concerns about insufficient hospital space at the prison. The government was also a bit concerned about rumors circulating in the South in late 1863 that prisoners at the depot were being denied adequate food, clothing, shelter, and medical care. Hoffman wanted an explanation. Colonel Wallace responded that at Camp Chase the prisoners' "subsistence is the ration daily issued to our troops, in kind and quality, but recently reduced to three-fourths, in consequence of the prisoners wasting so much . . . ." Prisoners' clothing "is of good common quality and the quantity issued to them . . . is one outer suit and a change of underclothing." Since the end of October, prisoners had been issued 200 coats, 506 pairs of pants, 500 shirts, 125 pairs of drawers, 560 pairs of shoes, and 550 pairs of socks. These Federal issues were in addition to the "300 suits of clothing, sent by friends of prisoners . . . ." As for blankets, Camp Chase prisoners at the end of 1863 had at least one blanket per man. At the end of December reports show that the 2,700 prisoners had "3,100 good and some 400 worn and inferior blankets . . . ." Wallace also included a report from Dr. I. M. Abraham, Acting Assistant Surgeon, who found the prisoners' general health to be "good as could be expected under like circumstances."[30]

Wallace's report probably reassured Hoffman to some degree but the post commandant may have had some reasons to file a positive report defending his record at Camp Chase. At the end of December 1863, Hoffman told Clark to inspect Camp Chase again along with other prisons in the West. Hoffman was particularly concerned about hospital facilities and treatment of sick prisoners because, despite Wallace's report, Clark and Cuyler had both referred to medical care as something less than ideal. "Give such directions to the surgeons in charge of hospitals in all minor matters," he told Clark on December 25, "and in those of more consequence you will consult the commanders and request the proper orders given." In those same instructions Hoffman told Clark: "When larger hospital accommodations . . . are necessary direct them to be built and . . . procure all necessary bedding and clothing for the sick . . . ." Of course Hoffman was by nature a bit careful with money and his superiors had warned him as early as 1861 to watch spending. So it is not surprising to find Hoffman follow up his initial instructions three days later with a telegram to Clark wherein Hoffman told his inspector to keep an eye on how much the necessary improvements would cost and to make sure that any spending that was recommended was truly needed. Clark was told that "it is only desirable to put things in such a condition as to make the sick as comfortable as the promptings of humanity demand." Hoffman knew that under the circumstances "it must fall far short of perfection, but it is hoped the essential will be sufficiently attained to insure that there shall be no want of comfort."[31]

At the end of the first week of January 1864, Clark told Hoffman that he found that the conditions at Camp Chase closely matched Wallace's report from the previous month. In fact, the reports from 1864 all tend to indicate that food, clothing, shelter, and medical care were not withheld or curtailed or pared down to unreasonable levels. Postwar charges of starvation rations notwithstanding, food does not appear to have been a serious problem. Inspectors that spring noted the food was of proper quality and issued in proper quantity and that food, including "pies, cakes, candies, soda water, &c" were all available from the post sutler. In August the adjutant-general of Ohio, B. R. Cowen, thought Camp Chase inmates, whom he referred to as "sleek, fat rebels," ate better than they should. He felt that the sutler's wares, food from friends, and government rations

> certainly constitute a bill of fare much more creditable to our generosity than to our proper consideration of the treatment due an enemy which has constantly violated the commonest dictates of humanity in the treatment of prisoners of war, and is an unpleasant contrast to the treatment received by our soldiers now languishing in Southern prisons.

No doubt the adjutant-general greatly exaggerated how well most Camp Chase prisoners ate, but the report does show that the prisoners had access to food from several sources and apparently were not suffering from hunger. When Charles T. Alexander inspected the prison he too found the prisoners to be eating well enough. He found the rations to be of good quality and issued in sufficient quantity. Throughout the fall and early winter of 1864, Captain F. S. Parker regularly inspected Camp Chase and found the rations to be good. On October 20, 1864, he reported that inmates got "the full amount of rations as allowed by the Commissary-General of Prisoners, and as to quality, they are the same quality as the rations issued to U.S. troops at this post and could be no better." In mid-December, Captain E. K. Allen also reported that there was nothing about the food rations to complain of at Camp Chase. Considering that inspectors, like Alexander especially, did not usually hesitate to note shortcomings about the prison, it seems reasonable to conclude that the generally favorable reports about the food situation at Camp Chase are accurate.[32]

Throughout 1864 there is a conspicuous absence of complaints of poor or insufficient clothing for Camp Chase prisoners. Since officers like Clark and Alexander reported clothing deficiencies at other prisons, the lack of any reference to clothing problems probably indicates that prisoners were not being denied clothing from one source or another. There is no record that the Federals scaled back clothing issues for prisoners at Camp Chase and Cowen's report mentions that prisoners were allowed to get clothing sent to them from friends and relatives. In fact, even postwar sources rarely mention a lack of clothing specifically at Camp Chase. Most probably had no more than the bare minimum of shoes, socks, a pair of pants, a shirt, a hat, and one or two pairs of underclothing, but that was generally all both governments' soldiers in the field had and the Federals certainly did not feel Southern prisoners were entitled to better than that.

Prisoners at Camp Chase also apparently had little to complain of in terms of living quarters in 1863 when they began arriving in larger numbers as the cartel broke down that summer. Prisoners lived in one-story buildings of wood that had wood stoves for heat. In December Wallace wrote to Hoffman, assuring him that the prisoners' living quarters were "the same as [provided for] our troops here . . . and all supplied with stoves and plenty of fuel." At the beginning of December, Brigadier-General William Orme inspected Camp Chase for the War Department and found little to complain of other than the hospital needed to be a little cleaner and the sutler needed to quit selling gin and schnapps to the prisoners. Orme found the prisoners' barracks to be sturdy enough to keep the elements out and capable of housing the nearly 3,000 prisoners without overcrowding. He also reported the barracks as being "comfortably heated by stoves." And when Clark revisited the prison at the end of 1863 he found nothing negative to report about the barracks at Camp Chase, calling them "very good." Ultimately what this evidence shows is that in 1863 the War Department expected prisoners to have protection from the wet and cold that was at least as good as any soldier in the field had access to and that it was provided.[33]

Housing did not seem to deteriorate in 1864. During the colder months the prisoners were housed in stove-heated barracks and in the warmer months wall tents were provided. Some of the original buildings were beginning to need repair during the summer of 1864 and regular reports indicate that all the necessary improvements to the prisoners' barracks were made. During the heavy campaign season the number of Confederate prisoners was rising steadily and Camp Chase was designated to handle some of the additional load. At the end of August, new barracks were under construction at Camp Chase and were reported as nearly complete. By the end of September, the prison would be able to house 7,000 prisoners according to the new commandant, Colonel William P. Richardson. With new spaces becoming available, Southern prisoners began arriving in larger and larger numbers. In August the population swelled from just under 1,900 to nearly 4,500. For the rest of 1864, the number of Confederates held at the Ohio prison remained constant at around 5,500, a number Camp Chase could accommodate reasonably well thanks to the additional barracks.[34]

During the first three months of 1865 the relatively decent housing situation changed for the worse. Crowding became a serious problem as Hood destroyed his army in the West and large numbers of prisoners arrived at Camp Chase. The additional barracks built over the summer and early fall anticipated an increase to as many as 7,000 prisoners and perhaps a little more in a pinch. Swelling the prison's population from just over 5,000 at the beginning of January to over 9,400 by month's end had not been anticipated. Why is a matter of speculation, but negligence or retaliation seems unlikely. Federal officials had doubled the post's capacity in anticipation of increasing numbers in the second half of 1864. What seems more likely is that Northern officials did not expect that such losses could be inflicted on Southern armies and the Confederate forces still remain stubbornly in the field. New barracks to hold the excessive numbers were not built in early 1865 partly because victory was perceived to be on the horizon and those in charge hoped existing facilities, though quite crowded, would hold out just a little longer. With the Confederacy's principal armies unable to mount offensive operations, its territory shrinking to include only Virginia and the Carolinas, and its major ports blocked as Fort Fisher and Wilmington fell, it is easy to see how Union officials could see the war as winding down. Also, in February exchanges began, haltingly, to resume. The issue of black prisoners had not been resolved. The South had not rescinded its policy to enslave and/or execute blacks captured in battle. But the two sides had agreed to begin exchanging those who had been held the longest, meaning that, for at least the first few weeks, only whites would be exchanged and the issue of African Americans would not have to be dealt with directly. These factors help explain why Federal officials decided that in late winter and early spring 1865 that new barracks for Camp Chase to ease crowding was an unnecessary expense. And in March the population did dip below 8,000 and in April it was back to around 5,000. It is true that crowding was a serious issue, but it was clearly not because of negligence or retaliatory policies and it was only an acute problem for about ninety days.[35]

Camp Chase did have its problems, of course, as all Northern prisons did. Drainage was a significant one and standing water was not an uncommon complaint in 1863 and early 1864 inspection reports. Such pools were breeding grounds for all sorts of harmful germs and bacteria and therefore constituted a real health hazard at the camp. And, as at other prisons, nobody seemed eager to deal with the sewage issue. It seems that at every camp finding or assigning people to keep the toilet areas for thousands of men, many of whom suffered from severe intestinal problems, proved extremely difficult. The thoroughly unpleasant job of managing the sinks was critical and there was no good reason for Clark to have had to complain in October 1863 of filthy latrines. Worse, seven months later Lieutenant-Colonel John Marsh filed a report about Camp Chase wherein he noted that "the sinks are allowed to become offensive." There can be little doubt that if Wallace and Richardson had addressed these two problems in a timely manner, as they certainly should have done, the number of sick prisoners as well as those who ultimately died of some disease at Camp Chase could have been reduced, perhaps significantly.[36]

Not until the summer of 1864 did drainage and latrine sanitation begin to improve at the camp. Captain Parker reported at the end of August: "Almost the entire camp is undergoing a change, erecting new barracks, grading and draining the ground, cleaning the sinks, and improving the condition in every possible way." The following month Parker credited Colonel Richardson and his subordinates with transforming "the camp from a detestable mud hole to a fine healthy and well-organized camp. Their untiring efforts to promote the health and well-being of the camp deserve the highest commendation." It could be argued that Parker's report was a bit over the top, but it is significant to note that other inspectors, like Alexander and Captain E. K. Allen, visited Camp Chase in the second half of 1864 and also described drainage and sewage issues as significantly better.[37]

Camp Chase was a dangerous place to be. Between February 1864 and June 1865 over 1,700 prisoners died for a ghastly monthly average of just over 102. Closer inspection of the records suggests that raw numbers may not tell the whole story. From February through September 1864, 174 prisoners died at Camp Chase, a monthly average of just under twenty-two. Fully one-quarter of those deaths were recorded in September alone. Most of the previous months recorded very low death totals with only eight in March and ten each in June and July. Thus the raw statistic showing that over 100 prisoners per month died at Camp Chase is somewhat misleading. The records clearly show that during the first eight of the seventeen months between February 1864 and June 1865, prisoners were not dropping dead by the score.[38]

But the death totals rise dramatically beginning in October 1864, nearly tripling that month from 46 to 113. For the next six months Camp Chase's death totals were in the triple digits each month with a sickening high of 499 in February 1865. One likely reason for the increase in mortality even as the camp was undergoing major improvements was the poor condition of many prisoners in the second half of 1864. When General Hood took over command of the Army of Tennessee in mid-July he attacked General Sherman around Atlanta in a determined, some say reckless, manner, losing thousands of men wounded and taken prisoner in the process. Then in November Hood drove his men into Tennessee to reclaim Nashville only to have his men thrashed at Franklin in a brave but doomed assault on the final day of that month. Exhausted survivors were then attacked and defeated by General George Thomas in mid-December, utterly destroying whatever force Hood commanded in Tennessee. These Southern soldiers had been driven hard by the pugnacious Hood throughout the summer and fall of 1864 posting a record of valor and endurance that few armies then or since could match. But it took a serious toll on their health. Many of Hood's men arrived at Camp Chase after being wounded. Others were sick and many were just plain exhausted—poor candidates for survival for most military camps at that time, much less a military prison. Inspection reports from late 1864 and early 1865 routinely refer to the hurt and dilapidated condition of the new arrivals. One January report said that *most* of the new arrivals were wounded and an early February report from Captain Allen complained about the difficulty officials at Camp Chase were having "in reviving the wasted fragments of Hood's army." Not surprisingly

January and February 1865 were the deadliest months at Camp Chase with 792 prisoner deaths, over 40% of the total deaths recorded during the entire seventeen months between February 1864 and June 1865.[39]

Additional evidence that prisoners' preexisting conditions may have accounted for a lot of the deaths at Camp Chase is found in a January 1865 report from Colonel Richardson where he says: "The prisoners received from [General George] Thomas' army have been very much exposed, and great mortality prevails. Pneumonia is the principal disease." The specific reference to pneumonia is important because it was the leading killer at Camp Chase. Of the 1,739 disease deaths cataloged in *The Medical and Surgical History of the War of the Rebellion*, 954 (54.85%) were from pneumonia. Even those coming in from Hood's army in late 1864 and early 1865 who did not have advanced cases of this disease were especially vulnerable to getting it. Many had severely compromised immune systems from being wounded or because they were worn out physically from a hard period of campaigning.[40]

The second leading killer at Camp Chase, and it was a rather distant second to pneumonia, was smallpox. This disease too is reported as being brought in by new prisoners in late 1864 and early 1865. During the second week of October, Colonel Richardson reported that "smallpox is prevailing [here] to a considerable extent, averaging this month ten cases per day." Richardson told Hoffman that all known cases were in the smallpox house, "which is entirely outside of the camp inclosure and at a considerable distance from the southeast corner of camp." All prisoners were also vaccinated against the disease. Hoffman was glad to hear that and emphasized to Richardson the need to stay on top of this particularly deadly disease that was a threat not only to the prisoners but to the Federal guards and officers as well as the local civilian population. At the beginning of November, Richardson reported that smallpox remained an issue, "but it is brought by new arrivals," causing the commandant to complain that this made his job of controlling the disease even more difficult. Throughout November and December and into January, smallpox was consistently listed as a major health problem, thanks in part to new arrivals carrying the illness and despite quarantine procedures and the vaccination program. By early March 1865, officials had brought the situation under control. On March 11, it was reported that "smallpox, which raged for a while so fearfully, through . . . vaccination, with rigid removals and care, has almost disappeared from [Camp Chase]." Unfortunately, though, 362 prisoners still died from "eruptive fevers," which were mostly smallpox cases at Camp

Chase, slightly more than 20% of the total recorded in *The Medical and Surgical History.*[41]

Given the prevalence of the diarrhea/dysentery problem in the field during the Civil War, it is also likely that many prisoners came to Camp Chase suffering from this category of disease, which ranked third for killing prisoners, taking 226 between February 1864 and June 1865. But when the fact that effective medication for this problem did not exist at the time is pointed out, holding Camp Chase personnel responsible for these fatalities seems unjustifiable. Furthermore, proving that unique conditions at the prison existed that caused prisoners to come down with this category of illness who otherwise would never have suffered or died from it is virtually impossible to do.[42]

Finally, an important point to make when attempting to determine if Confederate prisoners at Camp Chase were neglected medically or denied medical care altogether as has been charged by some writers, is that prisoners were generally less likely to die from serious illnesses at the Ohio prison than at Richmond's Chimborazo Hospital. Patients suffering from "eruptive fevers," which were smallpox cases in most instances, had a 21.84% chance of dying in Richmond where 166 of the 760 patients died. At Camp Chase, 362 of the 1,865 cases ended in death for a 19.41% mortality rate. It would certainly seem, then, that smallpox victims at Camp Chase were cared for and treated at least as well as they would have been by their own doctors in their own capital. The same is true for diarrhea/dysentery. At Chimborazo 455 of the 4,644 cases, or 9.80%, concluded with the patient's death. At Camp Chase, on the other hand, the numbers were quite a bit better. From February 1864 through June 1865, 226 of the 4,063, or 5.56%, diarrhea/dysentery cases ended in death, nearly half the mortality rate registered in Richmond. With Camp Chase prisoners recovering at better rates from two leading killers than Southern patients in the Confederacy's largest medical center, the argument that sick prisoners were neglected or denied proper medical care is difficult to sustain.[43]

Camp Chase was not as effective against pneumonia, however. At the prison, 56.75% of the reported cases (954 of 1,681) ended in death. Chimborazo's mortality rate of 37.18% (583 of 1,568) was pretty dismal as well but it was still a good deal better than Camp Chase's. The possibility that pneumonia patients were systematically neglected seems unlikely given the relatively good records treating other diseases. What is more likely, and has some evidence to support it, is that a lot of the 1,681 pneumonia patients were new arrivals with advanced cases of the disease. At the time there was little doctors could effectively do to cure acute pneumonia sufferers. There was also the large number of wounded who entered in late 1864, limiting the number of beds for pneumonia patients in the hospital. Sick prisoners who should have been admitted, and under normal circumstances probably would have been, but could walk were put in the barracks. That some of these prisoners developed serious cases of pneumonia seems likely. Concluding though, that pneumonia patients were neglected is tough. On the one hand barracks could have been reorganized so that some of them only housed pneumonia patients. And it seems reasonable that additional medical personnel could have been located and pressed into emergency service to treat the large number of sick and wounded prisoners arriving in such large numbers in late 1864 and early 1865. On the other hand, evidence exists that new arrivals had such advanced cases of the disease that they were largely beyond help. It would seem that the only safe conclusion to draw is that Camp Chase officials could have done a better job with pneumonia cases than they actually did but that circumstances largely beyond officials' control in late 1864 and early 1865 insured that pneumonia would put a large number of Southerners in Northern graves.

In the end, what is to be made of the over 1,700 deaths recorded in *The Medical and Surgical History*? Does this terrible figure prove that Union authorities neglected and abused Southern prisoners of war at Camp Chase? Probably not. The tardy drainage and sink improvements insured an unhealthy environment for an extended period that contributed to sickness and disease mortality totals as did the excessive crowding during the first three months of 1865. On the other hand, the improvements (drainage, cleaner latrines, barracks expansion) to the camp and the recovery rates from most diseases indicate that prisoners were not systematically mistreated or neglected at Camp Chase. Finally, the records indicate that a large infusion of ill, wounded, and generally broken down men from Hood's command significantly contributed to an increase in mortality at Camp Chase in late 1864 and early 1865.

Endnotes

1. James F. Crocker, *Prison Reminiscences* (Portsmouth, VA: W. A. Fiske, 1906), 24–25; Henry E. Shepherd, *Narrative of Prison Life at Baltimore and Johnson's Island* (Baltimore, MD: Commercial Printing and Stationery Co., 1917), 13–16.

2. United States War Department, *War of the Rebellion: A Compilation of the Official Records of the Union and Confederate Armies* (Washington, D.C.:

Government Printing Office, 1894; repr., Harrisburg, PA: Telegraph Press, 1971), Volume 6, 365–66. Hereafter cited as OR with all citations coming from Series II unless otherwise indicated.

3. OR, Volume 6, 395–96.

4. OR, Volume 6, 422–24, 433–44.

5. OR, Volume 6, 826–30, 841; Volume 8, 991–94.

6. OR, Volume 6, 583-854, 899, 922–23, 972.

7. OR, Volume 6, 853–54, 899–901, 922–23; Volume 7, 122, 140–41.

8. OR, Volume 7, 178, 228, 380, 415.

9. OR, Volume 7, 484–88, 504–5.

10. OR, Volume 7, 563, 592, 695, 765, 803, 839-840, 876–77, 912–13, 995–96, 1064–65, 1105–6; Volume 8, 4–5, 75–76, 112–13, 143, 182–83.

11. OR, Volume 6, 364–65, 826–30, 899–901; Volume 7, 701, 820.

12. OR, Volume 6, 364–66, 826–30; Volume 7, 122, 484–88, 695, 765, 839–40, 1021–22; Volume 8, 4–5, 75 76, 112 13; United States Surgeon General's Office, *Medical and Surgical History of the War of the Rebellion, 1861–1865* (Washington, D.C.: Government Printing Office, 1875), Volume I, Part III, 46. Hereafter cited as *Medical and Surgical History.*

13. OR, Volume 7, 122, 228, 380, 415, 456, 484–88, 592, 695, 839–40, 876–77, 912–13, 1064–65, 1105–6, 1186–87, 1211–12, 1240–41, 1274; Volume 8, 4–5, 75–76, 112–13, 182–83; Inger, 61–72, 106–9, 129–30.

14. John Washington Inger, *The Diary of a Confederate Soldier*, ed. Mattie Lou Teague Crow (Huntsville, AL: The Strode Publishers, 1977), 90–107; Edmund DeWitt Patterson, *Yankee Rebel: The Civil War Journal of Edmund DeWitt Patterson*, ed. John G. Barrett (Chapel Hill: University of North Carolina Press, 1966), 134, 151; John Dooley, *John Dooley, Confederate Soldier, His War Journal*, ed. Joseph T. Durkin (Washington, D.C.: Georgetown University Press, 1945), 138–39, 153–54; *Joseph Mason Kern Diary and Papers*, Southern Historical Collection: University of North Carolina, Chapel Hill (Hereafter cited as SHC); Philip R. Shriver and Donald J. Breen, *Ohio's Military Prisons in the Civil War* (Columbus: Ohio State University Press for the Ohio Historical Society, 1964), 27–32; Charles E. Frohman, *Rebels on Lake Erie* (Columbus: Ohio Historical Society, 1965), 20–23.

15. OR, Volume 6, 184, 330, 353, 758–60; Patterson, 134, 146–49; *Kern Diary and Papers*; Frohman, 18; Charles R. Schultz, "The Conditions at Johnson's Island Prison During the Civil War" (master's thesis: Bowling Green State University, 1960), 88.

16. OR, Volume 7, 484–88, 695, 912–13, 1064–65, 1164–65, 1186–87; Inger, 68–72, 74–77, 85, 107–9, 130.

17. *OR*, Volume 6, 972, 1036; Volume 7, 484–88, 695, 803, 839–40, 912–13, 959, 995–96, 1064–65, 1164–65, 1186–87, 1274–75.

18. *OR*, Volume 7, 959, 995–96, 1025–26, 1050–51, 1274–75.

19. Ibid.

20. *OR*, Volume 8, 986–1002; *Medical and Surgical History*, Volume I, Part III, 46.

21. Ibid.

22. Ibid.

23. *Medical and Surgical History*, Volume I, Part II, 1, 6–7, Volume I, Part III, 46; *OR*, Volume 6, 365–66, 826–30, 899–901, Volume 7, 484–88, Volume 8, 990–96.

24. *Medical and Surgical History*, Volume I, Part III, 30, 46.

25. Ibid.

26. Ibid.

27. Ibid.

28. *Southern Historical Society Papers*, Richmond, VA, Volume I (1876), 240–41; *Confederate Veteran* (March 1898), 121–22, (March 1900), 121–22, (June 1912), 294–97, (August 1916), 348–52; Joe Barbiere, *Scraps from the Prison Table at Camp Chase and Johnson's Island* (Doylestown, PA: W. W. H. Davis, Printer, 1868), 105–6, 198–99, 288–92, 320–21; John H. King, *Three Hundred Days in a Yankee Prison* (Atlanta, GA: J. P. Davis, 1904; repr., Kennesaw, GA: Continental Book Co., 1959), 71–96; John Dyer, *Reminiscences; or Four Years in the Confederate Army* (Evansville, IN: Keller Printing and Publishing Co., 1898), 36–37.

29. *OR*, Volume 6, 479–80; Jack Morris Ivy, Jr., "Camp Chase, Columbus, Ohio, 1861–1865: A Study of the Union's Treatment of Confederate Prisoners of War" (master of Military Arts and Sciences thesis, U.S. Army Command and General Staff College, 1990), 64-67.

30. *OR*, Volume 6, 682, 718, 746–48.

31. *OR*, Volume 6, 758, 773.

32. *OR*, Volume 7, 581–81, 699, 764–65, 845–46, 1017–18, 1021, 1062, 1097, 1123, 1161–62, 1235–36; Ivy, Jr., 59–83, 91–96.

33. *OR*, Volume 6, 479–80, 661–62, 746–47, 819; Ivy, Jr., 64.

34. *OR*, Volume 7, 52, 108–9, 580–81, 698–99, 764–65, 845–46, 971–72, 1123, 1161, 1235–36.

35. *OR*, Volume 8, 106, 205–6, 380–81, 999–1001.

36. *OR*, Volume 6, 479–80; Volume 7, 108–9.

37. OR, Volume 7, 580–81, 699, 765, 845–46, 877, 1062, 1097, 1123, 1161, 1235–36; Volume 8, 106, 205, 380–81.

38. OR, Volume 8, 995–98; *Medical and Surgical History*, Volume I, Part III, 46.

39. OR, Volume 7, 972, 1017–18, 1062, 1097; Volume 8, 106, 205–6, 381, 1000.

40. OR, Volume 8, 106, 381; *Medical and Surgical History*, Volume I, Part III, 46.

41. OR, Volume 7, 972, 1088, 1097, 1161, 1235–36; Volume 8, 106, 380–81; *Medical and Surgical History*, Volume I, Part III, 46.

42. *Medical and Surgical History*, Volume I, Part III, 46.

43. *Medical and Surgical History*, Volume I, Part III, 30, 46.

POINT LOOKOUT, FORT DELAWARE, AND ELMIRA

I followed old mas. Robert
For four years near about,
Got wounded in three places,
And starved at Pint Lookout.

SO WROTE THE AUTHOR OF THE POPULAR SOUTHERN TUNE, "I'm a Good Old Rebel." In all likelihood the writer did not intend to single out Point Lookout so much as to use it to represent the hardships Confederate prisoners endured in all Yankee pens because it was easier to rhyme with than Fort Delaware or Alton. Other writers over the last century and a quarter, however, have pointed to that particular prison as especially nasty. Anthony M. Keiley, an unreconstructed Rebel politician from Virginia who was no more above waving the bloody prison shirt than were others in and outside of his region, said the food was awful at Point Lookout and there was never enough of it. Prisoners were, according to Keiley, abused physically and denied adequate clothing and shelter as a matter of policy. He claimed that to get decent treatment one had to appeal to guards' greed—a congenital defect found in Northern character. Bribery was the only effective way to assure humane treatment in Federal military prisons because, according to Keiley; "Yankee soldiers are very much like ships: to move them, you must 'slush the ways.'"[1]

In 1972, a historian of the prison echoed Keiley, writing that "the prisoners at Point Lookout died from lack of sufficient food, clothing, blankets, shelter, and medical attention that the Federal Government could have provided." The Point Lookout Prisoner of War Organization's website tells visitors: "Rations were below minimal, causing scurvy and malnutrition. Prisoners ate rats and raw fish. It's recorded that one hungry Rebel devoured a raw seagull that had been washed ashore. Soap scum and trash peelings were often eaten when found." If ever there was a "Northern Andersonville," Point Lookout was certainly in the running for that title.[2]

Without question, life at Point Lookout was primitive and unpleasant. Conditions were crowded, unsanitary, and with some 4,000 deaths occurring there, potentially deadly. Of course such descriptions could and generally did apply to any Civil War military camp regardless of which side one is talking about. The important question is not whether life at the prison was difficult, but whether the prisoners there were neglected or abused as a matter of Union policy. Were officials responsible for increasing prisoners' suffering and mortality through what one commentator has described as "vindictive directives from the high command in Washington"?[3]

As was the case with most Northern prisons, Point Lookout was often described by postwar writers as a place where prisoners were starved, or nearly so, as a matter of policy. Postwar claims of prisoners gnawing on raw seagulls notwithstanding, contemporary evidence exists suggesting that food was not systematically withheld or doled out in ridiculously tiny amounts. Berry Benson of South Carolina was held for a time at Point Lookout and he recalled, "As a whole, I don't think Confederate prisoners [at Point Lookout] suffered greatly for food, tho' we had none too much truly." Four months after Point Lookout opened as a prison in August 1863, Brigadier-General Gilman Marston sent a report to Hoffman in which he assured the Commissary-General of Prisoners that the Southerners under his care received "wholesome food sufficient to insure vigorous health." On December 1, 1863, the Commissary-Sergeant, J. H. Wilkinson, noted the prisoners got plenty to eat and were fed according to official guidelines. "I would remark here in regard to the issue of vegetables," he added, "that I never knew a time during my service when Federal troops got so constant a supply of vegetables as has been issued to the prisoners here." Anthony M. Clark inspected the camp as well in December 1863 and found nothing to complain about as far as food was concerned at Point Lookout. In fact, Clark noted that prisoners even gambled some of their rations away, something it is hard to imagine starving men doing.[4]

Official reports do not note any change in the food situations during 1864. There were occasional recommendations that more vegetables be issued, but evidence that would support the claim that prisoners were placed on "starvation rations" is lacking from these reports. Henry Clay Dickinson, a Confederate captain who spent some time at Point Lookout in the middle of 1864 before being transferred to Fort Delaware, noted that the "fare at Point Lookout was better than at any other place in which I was confined." That may be faint praise, but Francis Atherton Boyle was there at the same time as Dickinson and he did not record any complaints about the quality or the quantity of the food he was issued in his diary. North Carolinian Bartlett Yancey Malone wrote in his journal that on Christmas Day 1864 bets were made at Point Lookout on an eating contest. Wagers were made by inmates on whether or not a prisoner in the 11th Alabama could consume five pounds of bacon and three two-pound loaves of bread at a single sitting. Malone did not stick around to watch the entire episode. He got bored with it after witnessing the Alabamian down half a pound of bacon and a pound of bread.[5]

The 1863 reference to gambling for food from Clark's inspection report also does not fit the image of half-starved, skeletal Southern prisoners particularly well. If a Federal report was the only evidence of gambling with food at Point Lookout it could perhaps be attributed to some sort of "Yankee bias," or as something that only went on prior to the "harsh" 1864 ration reductions. But a sketch artist's diary kept by a prisoner throughout 1864 supports Clark's observations and indicates that gambling with and for food, usually hardtack crackers, was common. This diary also depicts prisoners at Point Lookout paying for haircuts and shaves with crackers a well as trading them for things like coffee and tobacco. If food were so scarce that prisoners ate raw seagulls and lapped up soap scum, as at least one writer has claimed, the idea that they would choose to trade what precious morsels they had for a shave or a plug of tobacco is difficult to accept.[6]

On the other hand, reports of scurvy being a problem do exist and *The Medical and Surgical History of the War of the Rebellion* shows 3,312 cases of the disease between September 1863 and June 1865—167 resulting in death. In November 1863 Marston told Hoffman: "The surgeon in charge of the rebel camp informs me that many of the prisoners are afflicted with scurvy . . . ." Other 1863 reports also mention scurvy as a problem among Confederate prisoners at Point Lookout. To deal with the problem, Marston planned to issue more vegetables to the prisoners, a course of action that Hoffman endorsed. The records suggest that the scurvy problem in the latter part of 1863 was brought under some degree of control. Unfortunately, *The Medical and Surgical History* only provides the numbers of cases and deaths at various camps for the period they were in operation. It does not provide month-by-month totals, making it impossible to say definitively that scurvy was eliminated in early 1864 and for the rest of the war. But, references to scurvy from 1864 onward are difficult to find in the inspection reports. That is not to claim, of course, that no cases existed, only that they were so few in number at that point that officials did not feel they warranted mention.[7]

What can be definitively concluded from the records is that scurvy was a serious issue between September 1863 and early 1864. This is significant because that was a period of time before rations were reduced and prior to serious discussions about "retaliating" against Confederate prisoners, which did not take place until the middle of 1864. If policies hardened as 1864 wore on and were especially bad during the second half of the year, it seems reasonable to expect that references to scurvy would increase rather than disappear, which is what happened at Point Lookout according to wartime records. Combine that with the Confederate evidence that prisoners seemed to have had food enough to gamble with and use as payment for shaves and haircuts and it seems that the claim that Union officials virtually starved Point Lookout prisoners to death as long as the prison operated contains significant flaws.

Often forgotten or unacknowledged is that scurvy is not necessarily the result of an insufficient amount of food. Scurvy is caused by not taking in enough vitamins, especially Vitamin C. Full Union rations, which records indicate prisoners at Point Lookout received, were the bulkiest, most calorie-rich on the planet. Most defined a good ration as one that filled the belly. Consequently, the United States military ration during the Civil War contained a lot of meat and bread to fill the belly but made little room for vegetables and none at all for fruit. Ideas about the importance of balance and variety in one's diet were either unknown or not completely understood at the time. Officials, for example, increased fruits and vegetables to reduce scurvy cases but issuing them regularly as a preventative measure never occurred to them. The point is that unless one could get some access to fruits and vegetables through foraging, patronizing the local sutler, or from friends and relatives, it was possible to have a full stomach and still come down with scurvy.

That is exactly what happened in the late fall of 1863. Partly as a response to reports that prisoners were gambling with food at places like Point Lookout, Federal officials restricted their access to outside food sources. The restrictions also no doubt reflected the Northern officials' anger at the thought that their boys were starving in Southern prisons while Confederate prisoners were so flush with food they gambled with it. Colonel Hoffman, always concerned about money being wasted, was not happy to hear that food he had paid for was being used as gambling chips. In early November he told Marsten that since "the prisoners are bountifully supplied with provisions, I do not think it well to permit them to receive boxes of eatables from their friends." The following month the sutler was barred from selling food items to the prisoners. Thus from the end of 1863 until the early spring of 1864, prisoners at Point Lookout were restricted to the official ration that, while filling, was monotonous and nutritionally deficient. Not surprisingly scurvy is reported as a regular problem during this time.

Fortunately for the prisoners, these restrictions were not in effect for the rest of the war. In fact they were repealed in early March 1864, only four months after they were instituted. On March 3, Hoffman authorized the sutler to resume selling "salt fish, crackers, cheese, pickles, sauces, meats and fish in cans, vegetables and dried fruit, syrups [sic], lemons, nuts [and] apples." A few days later the restrictions on food from friends and relatives were lifted, allowing prisoners greater access to a better balanced, healthier diet. The result was the virtual disappearance of scurvy in inspection reports from the spring of 1864 until the end of the war.[8]

Another possible reason for scurvy besides the assumption that prisoners were systematically starved was the prevalence of diarrhea at Point Lookout. Between September 1863 and June 1865 there were 20,474 cases of diarrhea/dysentery reported at the camp, with 2,050 deaths from this category of illness. This was a particularly thorny problem at Point Lookout as the numbers clearly show. Acute cases of diarrhea were very serious health problems in the 1860s. If they did not clear up they led to dehydration. Another major problem was that if prisoners' diarrhea problems did not resolve themselves (and there were no effective treatments at the time) they significantly compromised prisoners' ability to absorb vital nutrients, like Vitamin C, as food shot through their bodies far faster than normal. That some of the 20,000 prisoners who developed cases of diarrhea, or entered the prison with chronic cases, could have wound up as scurvy patients is quite possible, showing that perhaps scurvy numbers could have been affected by variables other than "starvation rations."[9]

Point Lookout has also taken a beating in the literature on Civil War prisons for confining prisoners in tents rather than more substantial wooden barracks. One commentator has said recently that Confederate prisoners at the depot were "housed in old, worn, torn, discarded union sibley tents." This description of Confederate prisoners' tents is not inaccurate but it can be misleading. In November 1863 the United States Sanitary Commission conducted an unofficial investigation of the prison and had some unflattering things to say. However, prisoners' accommodations at this former vacation resort were given fairly good reviews. "Of their shelter there can be no possible complaint, for they all have good tents, such as wall, hospital, Sibley, wedge, shelter, hospital and wall tent flies."[10]

This observer remarked that the tents were in good condition rather than being tattered cast-offs and he reported that their interiors offered sufficient protection from the cold. He reported that "almost every tent throughout the camp has a fireplace and chimney built of brick made by [the prisoners] from the soil (which is clay) and sun baked." In December 1863 Clark commented rather extensively on the prisoners' quarters, reporting that "Nearly all of the tents are provided with fireplaces and chimneys built of bricks manufactured by the prisoners." The often-quoted Keiley memoir claims that prisoners were denied fuel for these fireplaces but that charge is inconsistent with Clark's observation that prisoners "are sent out in squads into the woods to cut down stumps, &c. In this way they procure an abundant supply, and in many of the tents they have piled away stores of it. In several tents I saw piles containing at least half a cord . . . ."[11]

In mid-May 1864, Captain Dickinson recorded in his diary that he and his comrades "were quartered in large Sibley tents, which were quite comfortable." Pictures from a prisoner's sketchbook kept from 1863 through the end of the war do not indicate that inmates' tents were dilapidated or unfit for use. One inspection report from July 1864 does describe many of the tents as "old and worn" but that was more a way of describing them as compared to "new and pristine." Had the tents been in truly deplorable condition Clark would very likely have recommended they be discontinued and newer ones supplied. He made such requisitions at other posts, making it unlikely that he would have failed to ask for changes at Point Lookout had they been necessary.[12]Regarding blankets and clothing at Point Lookout, one writer recently stated that "only one blanket among sixteen" prisoners was the norm. While there were times when some prisoners could be observed in worn clothes and without a blanket, their deficiencies may have reflected their condition upon arrival. Marston informed Hoffman in one report that "it has happened that on arrival of a large number of prisoners without blankets the quartermaster has not had enough to supply them, but it is not so now." For example, Elijah Saunders Johnson of the 15th Virginia Cavalry wrote to a Miss Fannie in June 1864 that he could use some clothes and money, "having lost everything I had in the excitement and confusion of battle . . . ." Thus there were times when prisoners lacked blankets but there is no contemporary evidence of a policy to deny blankets or clothing to Confederate captives at Point Lookout.[13]

The evidence tends to suggest that Northern authorities did quite a decent job making sure prisoners had clothes and blankets at the prison. In November 1863 the Sanitary Commission did complain about "one blanket to three men," prompting positive action from Union officials. Hoffman had little use for the Sanitary Commission, viewing it as a meddlesome and overly soft-hearted organization. But it was an organization that could not be ignored. Within days of the Commission's report Hoffman questioned Marston about the veracity of the observations regarding the blanket and clothing situation at his post. "From the report it appears that there is a great want of clothing among many of the prisoners. Though it is the desire of the War Department to provide as little clothing for them as possible, it does not wish them to be left in the very destitute condition which this report represents." Hoffman let Marston know that if the deficiencies were anything approaching what the Commission described they were to be put right immediately.[14]

At the end of 1863 Clark had noted that Point Lookout prisoners had a suit of clothes and a blanket, same as in the field. Nothing changed on this front in 1864 or 1865 according to inspection reports. Prisoners were permitted to have clothing sent from friends and relatives if they did not want to wear Yankee-issue clothes. Francis Atherton Boyle recorded in June 1864, for example, that he got shirts, shoes, pants, coat, and a pair of drawers in the mail along with fifty dollars to use at the sutler. Other prisoners also received clothing in the mail in 1864 or bought clothing from the sutler. Henry Dickinson recalled that the sutler at Point Lookout "was allowed to keep many articles of food for the more fastidious and, indeed, was only prohibited from selling boots, military clothing, and articles calculated to aid our escape." The prisoner-artist who kept a pictorial diary does show the occasional barefooted prisoner but most appear to be every bit as well-clothed as their brethren in the field. The wartime evidence thus seems to show that if a prisoner arrived in a ragged condition and in need of a blanket, as many did, especially towards the end of the war, he did not remain in that state long. If the Federals did not remedy the deficiencies, prisoners were allowed for most of Point Lookout's history to do so through express packages or through purchase at the sutler.[15]

Most of the wartime evidence indicates that the prisoners' medical care was not neglected nor were prisoners denied medical treatment. A report from the Sanitary Commission in October 1863 said that the hospital was not as clean as it should have been, blankets were insufficient, and the prisoner-patients were dirty. In December Marston answered the report, which had caused Hoffman some concern though he rarely placed much stock in reports from unofficial sources. Marston assured Hoffman: "Every bed in the hospital is supplied with two blankets. There is a laundry for cleansing the clothing of sick men and the hospital is abundantly supplied with wash basins, towels, and soap." Sick prisoners, he said, did not have to only eat the common soldiers' rations either. The surgeon was supplied with, among other food items, "soft crackers, fruit, beef extract, wine, jelly, and cordials." Concerns that there was not enough medicine on hand had been addressed, he said. "At one time," he admitted to Hoffman, "there was considerable delay in filling the surgeon's requisition for medicines, but during that period he was furnished with medicines from the general hospital [so the prisoners did not have to go untreated]."[16]

It could be argued, and quite reasonably, that Marston was putting a prettier face on the medical situation at Point Lookout than actually existed because he was under some official fire. And he did fail to mention at least one of Point Lookout's shortcomings in treating smallpox patients. Still, when Clark inspected the prison's hospital facilities in December 1863, his report tended overwhelmingly to support Marston's rather than expose it as overly rosy. When describing the policing of the hospital, Clark said it was "excellent in every particular." Sick prisoners got the same food as Union guards who were treated in the general hospital at Point Lookout. In Clark's opinion the medical personnel, especially Surgeon James H. Thompson, were doing an excellent job and were responsible for the overall good state of the prisoners' wards and care. "[T]he excellent condition of the hospital," he reported to Hoffman, "is proof sufficient of the efficiency of the surgeon in charge . . . ." At another point in his report Clark noted that most of "the patients are on iron bedsteads, the exceptions being on well-built wooden bunks. The men look clean and comfortable; the clothing is clean and in good order, though the surgeon in charge complains that until very recently it has been impossible to obtain a sufficient supply of underclothing. The quartermaster has now filled his requisitions." Some six months later, in May 1864, Henry Dickinson became very ill and was admitted to the prison hospital. "I remained in the hospital one week," he said, "and received every attention that I desired. At this hospital Dr. Hayes had medicines and sick diet furnished in abundance, and there was little control over his actions so that a sick man fared very well."[17]

Clark had nothing positive to say about the smallpox hospital, however. The set of tents constituting the quarantine area was three-quarters of a mile northwest of the prison and had guards posted to keep people away and the afflicted prisoners from leaving and spreading their disease. Clark did say that prisoners were all vaccinated and the disease did appear to be decreasing at the end of 1863. But he condemned thoroughly the officer in charge of the smallpox hospital, an assistant surgeon named Bunton. "The officer in charge of this hospital," Clark complained, "is utterly incompetent to fill his post." He found what he viewed as an "utter want of attention to police and a complete disregard of the comfort and safety of the patients." Clark contacted the surgeon in charge of that district in Maryland, a Dr. Heger, and had him inspect the smallpox hospital. Dr. Heger was upset by what Clark revealed and, according to Clark, "declared his intention of at once taking charge of the matter himself, putting the hospital into proper condition, and placing [a] competent officer in charge. That this will be . . . done, I feel assured, from the excellent effects of his administration in the camp and general hospitals." Upon reading this, Hoffman contacted Marston on December 24, 1863, expressing his concern that the smallpox hospital "seems to have been very badly conducted by Assistant Surgeon Bunton, . . . it is hoped that the hospital will be put in a satisfactory condition. Please give the matter your attention." It appears that if the concerns articulated by the Sanitary Commission were at all valid, they were successfully addressed by the end of 1863 and that officials that year acknowledged and moved positively to fix the most glaring hospital issue, which was the substandard administration of the smallpox wards. Charges of negligence in the area of medical care are difficult to sustain in light of official reports and Hoffman's reaction to the need to improve conditions for the smallpox patients.[18]

Of course the prison had its problems, the most serious being a lack of potable drinking water. In November 1863 Clark reported that there was plenty of water to be had but that a significant amount was of questionable quality, which he held as largely responsible for a lot of the diarrhea afflict-ing many of the prisoners at Point Lookout. He was no doubt correct. Contrary to the conventional image of Northern officials, they did not sit on their hands, but rather sought new sources of good water. Success was, unfortunately, not immediately achieved. In June 1864 reports were still being filed about the "injurious quality of the water" at Point Lookout. In early July, Quartermaster General Montgomery Meigs himself got involved to solve the water problems. He told Brigadier General D. H. Rucker, chief quartermaster of the Washington Depot, to "let two canal-boats be fitted with casks and pumps . . . so as to be filled with fresh water of the Potomac, [and] towed to Point Lookout, and moored at the dock."[19]

Had officials' instructions been carried out, the water problem at Point Lookout would have been solved relatively quickly. Unfortunately there was some misunderstanding on the parts of several key players and Hoffman had to find out why the prison was still experiencing water prob-lems as late as September 1864. Writing to Brigadier General Joseph K. Barnes, commander of the Saint Mary's, Maryland, district, which included Point Lookout, he told Barnes he was pleased with the generally favorable reports coming out of the prison. However, Hoffman understood that boats supplying 20,000 gallons of fresh water daily had been ordered, which led him to wonder why water "of a very bad quality" was still being reported to him. Hoffman asked Barnes to investigate whether or not fresh water was actually being brought in as ordered and how much more would be required so that it could be supplied.

After looking into the situation, Barnes reported that there had appar-ently been some sort of miscommunication between an assistant quarter-master (Captain H. E. Goodwyn) and some of the water boats' captains. There had also been, Barnes noted, some mechanical problems on some of the boats designated to haul water to the Point. They were remedied, though, and two steamers, the *Ide* and *Commodore Foote*, were set to bring at least 40,000 gallons of water to the post during the third week of October and would continue hauling water during the subsequent weeks. Barnes hoped that the boats, combined with recently dug wells that were producing good water, would effectively solve the water concerns. Apparently they did, because reports of bad water cease to appear in the records after the fall of 1864.[20]

Failing to effectively address the impure water problems at Point Lookout in a timely manner unquestionably increased sickness and mortal-ity figures there and it was unquestionably Federal officials' fault. Northern officials were not negligent; the problem was reported by government inspectors and plans were made to fix the dangerous water problems early on. Key officials on site and in Washington failed to make certain that the plans to fix the camp's leading health hazard were actually implemented. To the prisoners it made no difference that the bad water was more reflective of gross mismanagement, miscommunication, and mechanical malfunctions than Yankee apathy or vindictiveness; they suffered and died from the water's effects all the same.

In fact the bad water was responsible for most of the mortality at Point Lookout. Impure water led directly to increased numbers of diarrhea and dysentery cases. At this facility, over 20,000 cases were reported and 2,050 prisoners who reported to Point Lookout doctors with this problem died from it. That is over half (56.33%) of the 3,639 disease deaths recorded for the site in *The Medical and Surgical History*. Given the prevalence of this health problem during the Civil War, Union officials cannot be totally blamed for all these cases but there can be no doubt their failure to provide pure water regularly until late 1864 inflated (possibly significantly) the number of cases and fatalities from dysentery.

Bad water probably played a role in the 425 deaths from pneumonia, too. Though a distant second to the diarrhea/dysentery category, pneumonia was responsible for just over 11% of Point Lookout's disease deaths. With so many cases of diarrhea and dysentery, there were hundreds of prisoners whose immune systems were seriously weakened, which made contracting pneumonia all but inevitable for many of them. Impure water may not have directly caused prisoners to contract pneumonia, but it increased the numbers and deaths from it indirectly by undermining immune systems and hindering recovery.[21]

Smallpox numbers were also higher than they should have been at Point Lookout. The third leading killer at Point Lookout was "eruptive fevers," taking 333 prisoners. According to the records, 1,033 prisoners were treated for this, meaning the mortality rate was 32.23%, a good bit higher than the 21.84% found at Chimborazo. No doubt the fact that the quarantine hospital was run by a complete incompetent for much of 1863 played a role. Federal officials like Clark and Hoffman certainly thought so and that particular variable was removed from the equation before the year was out. Another problem presented itself in the summer of 1864 that doubtless affected the number of smallpox cases and fatalities. At this time, the vaccinations were discontinued because prisoners were developing "unhealthy ulcers" after being treated. This was not uncommon at the time. Vaccines were often prepared in unsterile environments leading to people being injected with more than just smallpox vaccine. Those contaminants often led to painful sores, the ones cited after the war by Lost Cause writers as proof that Yankees tried to poison them. It would seem, rather, that contaminated vaccines combined with a stoppage in administering the medicine completely until a pure batch was procured inflated mortality from smallpox at Point Lookout.[22]

In the final analysis, the evidence points to the seemingly contradictory conclusion that sickness and mortality among prisoners at Point Lookout were excessive but not because United States officials intended to punish or retaliate against Southern captives. Food, clothing, and shelter all appear to have been sufficient by contemporary standards. Medical care also seems to have been adequate. The overall prisoner recovery rate from diseases was 91.65%, which compares very favorably to Chimborazo's 88.61% rate. But in the end, the over 3,500 deaths recorded at this prison were excessive. Even though disease mortality in Civil War camps was a tragic inevitability, Federal failure to provide pure water sources until the second half of 1864 directly increased numbers of sickness and mortality beyond what one might have expected to find in a major military camp of that era.

Fort Delaware

This fort, situated on Pea Patch Island in the Delaware River, was another prison that was often written about during the Lost Cause era to show just how fiendish the Yankees could be. In 1896, J. A. Randolph submitted an article to *Confederate Veteran* recounting his experiences at that prison. It was, not surprisingly for the era, completely negative. The Yankees, he said, "put the screws to us in every way." A few years later another contributor to the magazine related how prisoners at Fort Delaware were starved and treated with an extraordinary amount of physical abuse. This writer claimed that prisoners were hung by their thumbs until they died. He also said that the Federals could sometimes get very creative with their sadistic punishments. "Sometimes," he claimed, "the prisoners were buckled hands and feet and rolled onto a stone pavement and left for hours, though the thermometer was at zero." But probably one of the most virulent treatments of life at Fort Delaware written by a former prisoner was the one written by Mississippian Lamar Fontaine in 1910. Federal officials, including Lincoln himself, were portrayed in the book as ordering cruel and inhumane conditions for Confederate prisoners of war. "You readers can imagine my sufferings, and my condition, while thus a guest of the greatest government on the face of the globe. Words and similes of the English language are too poor for me to describe it." William H. Morgan spent time at Fort Delaware in 1864 and 1865 and remained bitter about his experiences nearly a half-century later. As had many others before him, Morgan argued that the Confederacy had done all it could for Northern prisoners "while the Yankees, with plenty of supplies, their ports open to the world, less than half fed the Confederates in all their prisons, through malice and revenge." His own food, for example, he recalled as "badly cooked and scarcely sufficient in quantity to sustain life, besides being very inferior in quality."[23]

The image of Fort Delaware as a black hole of suffering has not really changed in most modern literature. One recent historian of the facility has followed the tradition of referring to Fort Delaware as the "Andersonville of the North." Lonnie Speer tended to perpetuate the picture of the prison as an unmitigated hell-hole in *Portals to Hell: Military Prisons in the Civil War*, writing, "No other prison was as dreaded by the South." According to Speer, the reason for the suffering and death at the prison was that during the last two years of the war the camp's commander, Brigadier General Albin Schoepf, allowed all sorts of "wanton acts of torture and brutality . . . ." Perhaps not surprisingly, most citations in Speer's work, and other modern writing on the prison, are mostly from (in some cases exclusively) Lost Cause-era sources.[24]

Contemporary Union and Confederate records, however, do not support the assertion that prisoners at Fort Delaware were neglected or mistreated as a matter of policy. The food situation is a good example. In January 1863 Edwin Stanton himself, the arch-fiend in many postwar accounts and in much modern writing on this subject, wanted "a competent officer to make an immediate and thorough investigation" of newspaper accounts of ill treatment of Confederate prisoners at Fort Delaware to determine if they were credible. In August 1863 Schoepf assured the Secretary of War that "The rations [at Fort Delaware] are the same as those furnished our own men. Fresh beef is issued four times per week, and fresh vegetables are given them when they can be obtained." The Federal rations during the Civil War were generous (if unbalanced) and prisoners were allowed additional food through the mail and, except for a period between December 1863 and March 1864, to buy food at the prison sutler.

One prisoner recorded in his diary during the summer of 1863 that he believed his rations to be perfectly adequate. "All together," he noted, "our condition is as well as can be expected under the circumstances." In November 1863, Augustus M. Clark filed his inspection report for Fort Delaware and he was quite complimentary overall. He found the rations sufficient in terms of both quantity and quality and that the food was generally well cooked in reasonably clean areas. The following month, Lieutenant-Colonel William Irvine visited the prison and reported his observations to Major General Ethan Allen Hitchcock. He informed the general, "I saw the men at their dinner and noticed their fare; everything served to them was as good and abundant as the rations supplied to our soldiers, including onions, potatoes, and cabbage once a day habitually." After talking with a number of prisoners, Irvine said that with few exceptions the prisoners admitted to him that there was no room for complaint about the food situation at the fort. E. L. Cox of the 68th North Carolina wrote in his diary that some prisoners grumbled about the rations being a bit short in some areas but noted, too, "there is a great deal of grumbling amongst the Soldiers who are guarding us about the Scantiness of [their] rations."[25]

Generally, though, diaries do not contain many complaints about food at Fort Delaware. One inmate recorded in late May 1864 that he "had plenty to eat" and during the first week of June the same prisoner wrote, "We all have money and plenty to eat." In August, James Robert McMichael, who was captured at Spotsylvania, wrote in his journal while at Fort Delaware, "Watermelons and beer are plentiful." On December 3, John A. Gibson of the 14th Virginia Cavalry wrote of having a "hash" consisting of "potatoes, onions, beans, and corn" and on the thirtieth he consumed whiskey "in the shape of a small apple toddy." Federal reports from 1864 and 1865 do refer to occasional seasonal problems procuring vegetables and in the summer of 1864 officials had to conduct an investigation into the beef supply because prisoners and guards were not getting all they were due from the contractor. Otherwise, the quantity and quality of the food at Fort Delaware does not appear, according to wartime records, to support the often-made postwar claim that "starvation rations" were the norm.[26]

Clothing and blankets also rarely appear in wartime documents as serious problems at the prison. Inspection reports rarely mention prisoners being destitute of clothing or blankets. When references to clothing or blanket deficiencies are found they generally indicate that only a few of the prisoners were in need and that they were new arrivals. To be sure, new arrivals often showed up in clothing nearly worn out through hard campaigning and lacking blankets, having discarded or lost them on the way to or during a battle. But between the Federal government, friends and family, and the sutler, prisoners at Fort Delaware appear to have had at least one suit of clothing, shoes, and a blanket. In September 1863, Hoffman reminded Schoepf that "As the approaching cold weather will make it necessary that the prisoners should be more warmly clad I would suggest that you forward estimates for a supply of such articles as will be needed." Schoepf apparently did so because two months later Clark inspected Fort Delaware and reported to Hoffman that "every man is well clothed and furnished with an overcoat." Another inspection by a Colonel Irvine reported that he "ascertained from the post quartermaster that about 6,000 overcoats had been issued to [the prisoners] since the 1st of September last and a corresponding amount of other clothing. Every man is furnished with whatever clothing he needs, to include for each man an overcoat and one good blanket." Weekly inspection reports from the end of 1863 through 1865 indicate that clothing needs were met as quickly as possible by the government, express packages from without, and/or the sutler.[27]

Many postwar accounts of life in Yankee prisons refer to overcrowded, dilapidated, poorly heated living quarters. But even Lost Cause-era writing does not complain overmuch about housing at Fort Delaware—which, given the caustic tone of most postwar writing on the subject, is quite a statement in itself. In April 1863 more barracks were ordered built at the prison to get ready for future prisoners. That month Hoffman added that the new barracks must "be free from the faults of the present ones." What those "faults" were he did not say specifically, but it is significant that the man often held up as a tight-fisted, callous, old grump ordered new and improved living quarters at Fort Delaware.

The problem causing Hoffman the most concern was that existing barracks were un-floored and not elevated off the ground. His orders stated that the new barracks should avoid dirt floors, "which being always very damp makes them uncomfortable and unhealthy." Though Clark did not consider Fort Delaware an ideal location for prisoners in the first place, his November 1863 report noted the barracks were sufficient for 8,000 men, six to twelve inches off the ground, and in good repair. The barracks were also heated by wood- and coal-burning stoves. During the winter and spring of 1864, Schoepf reported to Hoffman that barracks were repaired when necessary and that by March enough new barracks had been constructed to accommodate an additional 4,000 prisoners. Added to Clark's estimation that Fort Delaware could accommodate

8,000 captives in November without significant crowding, the additions made the depot capable of holding 12,000 prisoners. During only a single month of the fort's history as a prison, though, were that many prisoners quartered there.[28]

Throughout 1864 and 1865, efforts to supply clean water and make the prison both drier and more sanitary were made. Reports indicate that officials were more successful at bringing in pure water to Fort Delaware than at Point Lookout. In December 1863, Lieutenant-Colonel William Irvine told officials that water "is supplied from Brandywine Creek every day or once in two days; it is kept in large iron tanks convenient to and sufficient for all the uses of the post, the garrison included." He also reported that the tanks were "coated with a white paint and in warm weather keep the water as cool as any hydrant water. I tasted the water and found it as sweet as Potomac Creek or James River water." A year later Captain Ahl reported the the water at the prison remained of "of good quality" and of "a sufficient quantity." Drainage ditches were dug to take the standing water from the camp to reduce the damp, marshy conditions. In early October 1864 Ahl told Hoffman that the prison's drainage was "very good, having recently been much improved." Inspection reports for the rest of the war indicate that the camp remained as dry as officials could make it. Finally, moving the sinks closer to the Delaware River so that the massive amounts of raw sewage could be daily washed away was a major factor in helping to reduce cases of deaths from dysentery. In August 1864, Lieutenant R. H. Lewis reported that the "sinks are cleaned twice each day and the filth washed away by the tide." Two months later Ahl reported that the sinks were "kept clean by tide and force [water] pumps." Records for the rest of the year and into 1865 indicate that the sinks remained in a much-improved state and were not singled out as a health hazard.[29]

In terms of medical care, compelling contemporary evidence suggests Federal authorities did a good a job for the time. In August 1863, despite the rather heavy mortality that month, four Confederate surgeons confined at Fort Delaware offered a positive view of Union efforts. "In justice to the officer commanding this post we would beg leave to state that everything in his power to add to the comfort of these prisoners is being done. The sick are cared for as well as possible and new hospitals [are being] built for the accommodation of more." In November 1863 Clark was impressed by the hospital facilities at the prison and he described Dr. H. R. Silliman, the medical officer in charge, as "an energetic and competent officer." Clark found the other surgeons competent as well. "The hospital," he told Hoffman, "is in excellent condition and the patients look clean and comfortable."

When compared to Chimborazo Hospital in Richmond, Fort Delaware seems to have done quite well taking care of ill soldiers. At the Confederate facility, 11.39% of those entering the facility never came out whereas only 5.04% of the sick cases at Fort Delaware resulted in death. Not only did Fort Delaware have a superior mortality rate per reported cases than Chimborazo, the prison did a better job treating the three major killers at the post (diarrhea/dysentery, eruptive fevers, and pneumonia) than the Richmond facility. At Fort Delaware, 6.66% of all diarrhea/dysentery cases resulted in death while at Chimborazo the figure was 9.80%. Looking at the eruptive fevers category (which was dominated by smallpox), 18.20% of the cases at the prison died compared to 21.84% of those treated at the Richmond hospital. And finally, 35.54% of Fort Delaware's pneumonia patients succumbed to the illness while 37.18% of those cases died at Chimborazo.[30]

While it has been commonly assumed that overcrowded conditions and vindictive retaliation policies put the over 2,000 prisoners who died there between the spring of 1863 and June 1865 in their graves, such does not appear to be supported by the records available. Between May 1863 and May 1864, Fort Delaware housed an average of 5,655 prisoners and recorded 1,611 deaths. As the population increased between May 1864 and May 1865 by 20% to a monthly average of 7,685, the number of deaths decreased by 47% to 856. Since mortality significantly decreased as the prison became more crowded and Union policies hardened, these factors do not appear to adequately explain why Confederate prisoners perished at Fort Delaware.[31]

Medical records for the period from August 1863 to June 1865 reveal that prisoners at this prison were more likely to die in the first ten months between August and May 1864 than during the final thirteen months of the prison's history. During those initial months, 1,429 prisoners died, representing 64.98% of the 2,199 total disease deaths recorded for that span. During that particularly deadly period the water was brackish and surface drainage and sewage removal were major problems. Impure water, stagnant pools, and the presence of raw sewage provided conditions that were perfect for the organism responsible for the deadly disease dysentery. Not surprisingly this problem was referred to often in reports, especially during the second half of 1863, and was the leading killer at Fort Delaware, taking 644 prisoners' lives.[32]

Another factor in the higher mortality in late 1863 at Fort Delaware was a smallpox epidemic. Smallpox was the second-leading killer at the prison and during the late fall of 1863 the disease was raging, taking most of the 472 Southerners who would ultimately die from it there. In November Shoepf told Hoffman that since he had assumed command of the fort smallpox has "been prevailing more or less constantly." That same month he reported that "vaccine and instruments have been furnished to the Confederate surgeons, and they have been sent to the barracks to vaccinate all they can." Plans were under way to build additional quarantine areas on the New Jersey shore and "each man who comes to the post is compelled to suffer vaccination as well as each patient who enters the general hospital." By the end of 1863 Fort Delaware officials got a handle on the situation and smallpox rarely appeared again in inspection reports. But during the height of the epidemic, September to November 1863, 860 prisoners died, 39.10% of the total recorded from September 1863 to June 1865.[33]

Pneumonia, the prison's third-leading killer, took 401 prisoners. It too was a larger problem at the beginning of the camp's history than at the end. The diarrhea/dysentery sufferers would have been prime candidates for pneumonia as would those who were weakened while fighting smallpox during the fall of 1863. Another factor contributing to pneumonia totals at Fort Delaware was the broken-down state of many prisoners who arrived in the late summer and early fall of 1863. Many were men who had endured Grant's Vicksburg siege and been transported halfway across the country. Shoepf specifically mentioned this in August 1863, telling Hoffman he thought that part of the recent mortality problems could be traced to the "exhausted" state of a lot of incoming prisoners. Sheopf thought this "was the case especially with those from Vicksburg."[34]

Ultimately Fort Delaware was a place to be avoided, especially during the first nine to ten months it was operating as a prison. Initially the barracks were leaky and dirty; the water supply was impure; the camp was wet and poorly drained; sewage removal was inefficient; and smallpox stalked the grounds. That was Fort Delaware at its worst and most dangerous. It must be remembered, however, that all of these potentially lethal problems were positively addressed by Union authorities. Barracks were repaired and expanded; fresh water was amply supplied; the camp was drained more effectively; sewage removal was greatly improved; quarantine and vaccination procedures virtually eliminated smallpox. Prisoners at Fort Delaware recovered from major illnesses at a significantly higher rate than did patients at Chimborazo. Finally, and perhaps most significantly, mortality at Fort Delaware declined significantly as the war progressed, suggesting that the improvement efforts had positive effects.

Elmira

"Talk about Camp Chase, Rock Island, or any other prison as you please, but Elmira was nearer Hades than I ever thought any place could be made by human cruelty." That was what G. T. Taylor wrote for *Confederate Veteran* in 1912. He was not the first Southerner to use Elmira as the ultimate example of Yankee depravity and inhumanity towards Confederate prisoners of war, though, or the most virulent. Walter Addison was captured at the Wilderness in 1864 and recalled bitterly his experiences at Elmira in 1889. Addison wrote that the doctors at Elmira "had our poor helpless soldiers at their mercy. Often have I heard them, when gathered together in the dispensary discussing their experiences of the day, exult over the numbers of the Rebs they had put through, i.e. killed and expressing their desire to, in this way, get rid of the whole number . . . .All authority at Elmira seemed to be of this opinion." Addison went as far as to claim that in order to turn the prison into as efficient a death camp as possible, "contagious diseases were introduced into crowded prisons. I recollect in one instance at Elmira hundreds of deaths were the result of small-pox introduced by patients from Blackwell's Island, New York."[35]

In 1912 Clay W. Holmes wrote the first book-length history of Elmira. Holmes was a Northerner who was perturbed at Southern accounts of the prison that portrayed it as at least as bad as Andersonville and usually worse. He did not believe Union officials intended Elmira to be as uncomfortable and as lethal as it was and he hoped to show that in his book. What sets Holmes's book apart from others of that era was that it relied primarily on wartime records and letters obtained from former prisoners. Polemics like those appearing in *Confederate Veteran* and heard at Grand Army of the Republic meetings did not interest him and had no place in his book. For the era, it was one of the better treatments of the volatile prisoner of war issue.

Something that is interesting and quite significant about the Holmes book is that sixteen pages at the back of the book are dedicated to reprinting letters he received from twenty-seven ex-prisoners from all over the South in 1911. These letters are of varying lengths but they are extraordinarily consistent. None of the letters expresses the belief that prisoners at Elmira were consciously mistreated or neglected by the Yankees. A. F. Perkins's of Lumpkin, Georgia, said: "I think the intentions of the U.S. Government were good, and they did the best they could under the circumstances." J. R. Mills of Edison, Georgia, was at Elmira for its entire history as a prison camp and he told Holmes: "My treatment was very good there." From Mebane, North Carolina, came a letter from J. S. Johnson who said his experience at Elmira was "as good as I could expect in any prison." Not that the letter was meaning to give the impression that Elmira was a good place to spend time. Most of the letters, while expressing confidence that prisoners were supposed to be well-treated, said food was often a problem. As J. T. Hudson of Alabama said, and he was not alone, "Treatment was tolerably good for prisoners, but the food was mighty light." While these letters are but a tiny fraction of the number of prisoners who were confined at Elmira, their uniformity as well as their much milder opinion of Elmira than most Lost Cause-era writers are striking.[36]

Judging by the writing done on Elmira since the 1960s, the image of Elmira painted by the Lost Cause writers has been judged to be the more accurate one. In his article, "The Scourge of Elmira," James I. Robertson stated that Elmira was the absolute worst military prison operating during the Civil War on either side because Yankee officials "assumed an almost sadistic apathy toward the prisoners." Not only were prisoners put on bread and water diets, according to the article, but Dr. E. L. Sanger, the prison's chief medical officer, is accused and convicted of intentionally neglecting prisoners in retaliation for perceived mistreatment of Union prisoners at Andersonville in Georgia. More recently, in *Portals to Hell*, Lonnie Speer never questioned that Elmira was the worst of a bad lot and Philip Burnham has echoed the theme that conditions at the prison in New York's Chemung Valley were unnecessarily harsh and lethal. Michael Horigan's *Elmira: Death Camp of the North*, a book that garnered glowing endorsements from William C. Davis and Robertson, argues that the Federals, through neglect and "retaliation" policies, created a prison depot where the Grim Reaper strolled unmolested. Michael Gray's recent excellent study of Elmira, while far more objective and far less accusatory than most work on the prison, tends to perpetuate the idea that officials insured that conditions at Elmira were far worse than they should have been.[37]

With so many conflicting images of Elmira, finding the truth, or a reasonable facsimile of it, can be a daunting task. As with most issues, the truth probably lies somewhere between Lost Cause-era depictions and

Holmes's relatively benign one. On the one hand Elmira was by far the most lethal of all the Union prisons. Between July 1864 and June 1865, 2,927 prisoners died of some disease at Elmira. Camp Douglas and Point Lookout recorded more deaths but they were both in operation for significantly longer periods than Elmira. If a prisoner got sick at Elmira his chances of recovery were much lower than at other Northern prisons and at Chimborazo. Recovery rates at other prisons and in Richmond were all in the upper 80's and low 90's. At Elmira the recovery rate was a dismal 71.25%.[38]

By far the most common killer at Elmira was diarrhea/dysentery, which killed 1,394 prisoners: 47.62% of all disease deaths recorded in *The Medical and Surgical History of the War of the Rebellion*. Of those who came down with this particular problem, just over 30% died from it, compared with a 9.80% mortality rate per reported cases at Chimborazo. With numbers like these, if it can be shown that Northern officials, through overt policies or negligence, created an atmosphere ripe for this category of disease, then charges of inflating suffering and death at Elmira will stick. It is hard to hold officials at Elmira guilty of failing to give proper medicines for this category of disease, however, because no effective medicines existed at the time. And Elmira did not suffer from problems associated with impure water at any time in the camp's history. In fact most of the letters at the back of Holmes's book refer specifically to the good quality of the water and not a single inspection report complains of an injurious water supply as was found at Point Lookout, for example. And given the prevalence of diarrhea/dysentery in each side's field armies there can be no doubt that a lot of the prisoners entered Elmira with cases of it.[39]

One area in which officials did have the ability to exert some form of meaningful control was in cleaning up a large body of water in the middle of the prison known as Foster's Pond. This stagnant lake was a combination cesspool and garbage dump, an excellent breeding ground for dysentery. From the beginning of the camp's history inspectors cited Foster's Pond as Elmira's key health risk. In the middle of August 1864 Hoffman was told that the pond "has become offensive, and may occasion sickness unless the evil is remedied very shortly. The only remedy for this is to dig a ditch from the pond to the river so that the water will run freely through it." The same month a medical officer complained the pond received all the prison's "fecal matter hourly" and he had even gone so far as to calculate that the prisoners at Elmira "will pass 2,600 gallons of urine daily" into Foster's Pond. Not surprisingly, Captain Benjamin Munger, Elmira's inspector, complained at the end of August: "The stench arising from the stagnant water in the pond is still very offensive."[40]

Such a nasty situation was not just a problem from an olfactory perspective; it was a serious health hazard. Flies by the million were attracted to Foster's Pond. The flies landed on sewage contaminated with the organisms responsible for causing dysentery then flew away to deposit these deadly pathogens onto prisoners' food and eating utensils. The understanding that flies were common disease vectors in military camps did not exist at the time but officials did realize that stagnant ponds like the one at Elmira somehow led to high rates of sickness among those living in close proximity to them. That explains the early calls to get something done to clean up Foster's Pond.

For reasons that are difficult to nail down definitively, nothing came from the War Department or any Union official authorizing plans to fix the problem posed by the pond in August or September 1864. As late as October 20, 1864, the post's commanding officer, Colonel Benjamin Tracy, complained to Hoffman of "the [negative] effects of the pool of stagnant water in the center of camp." The ultimate result was that for several months Foster's Pond received trash and human waste and posed a direct and lethal threat to thousands of prisoners. Since officials certainly knew of the problem, ignorance cannot be the explanation. Neither is an active policy of ignoring the problem because it would be too expensive to fix or to dish out a little extra misery to Confederates a particularly likely scenario. For one thing, there is no direct evidence to support either assumption. For another, Union officials had been much more active in fixing these kinds of problems at other prisons so it seems out of character to single out Elmira and make it as unpleasant as possible by leaving Foster's Pond alone.[41]

The most recent study of Elmira, Michael Gray's *The Business of Captivity: Elmira and Its Civil War Prison*, suggests that at least part of the problem was Hoffman's notorious cost consciousness. Hoffman was anxious to remove Foster's Pond's effects but he wanted to keep expenses to a minimum, which Tracy convinced him could be done by using prison labor. On October 23, 1864, Hoffman let Tracy know that the plans for draining the pond had been approved and work began at the end of the month on this very important project. Other issues besides Hoffman's obsession with the bottom line also played roles in slowing down work on the drainage ditch. Local landowners were concerned that a ditch running through their property would damage their lands and had to be assured that their lands would be unaffected by the drainage ditch. Also, digging a ditch sounds much easier than it actually was. As Tracy explained to Hoffman, the job had "been a more serious job than was anticipated, owing to waste and quicksand in the bottom of the cutting. Through a considerable portion of the [ditch] we struck the coarse gravel of what seems to have once been the river's bottom. Through this water ran quite freely, compelling us to use the pump extensively. Quicksand was also found in places." In early January 1865 Tracy contacted Hoffman to tell him the ditch "works like a charm." Unfortunately, this project's completion was so late in coming that many prisoners had already been adversely affected by the pond's putrid presence. Though there were certain factors beyond officials' control, Hoffman's failure to appreciate the pond's unhealthy hazards and order its immediate removal or drainage is as inexplicable as it is inexcusable.[42]

While officials were slow to respond to one major contributing factor to diarrhea/dysentery, they responded relatively quickly to other environmental factors that contributed to this major disease category. Elmira, like a lot of other prison camps had problems with standing water and inefficient sewage removal. The camp's topography was not conducive to good natural drainage and whenever it rained water remained in pools all over the camp for days before evaporating, creating breeding grounds for all sorts of bacteria. Attention was called to the issue as early as the middle of August 1864 by the post's surgeon, E. F. Sanger, who noted that the "drainage of the camp is very imperfect." He recommended large drains that would collect the camp's excess water and whisk it away, keeping the camp dryer and healthier. In that same report Sanger complained that the sinks were not in good condition either. While the sinks had been removed from Foster's Pond (though prisoners were still using it as a toilet), the holes or vaults that had been built to serve as latrines were not an acceptable substitute in Sanger's opinion.

> I am satisfied from long and continued experience that vaults will not answer
> for a large number of men crowded into a limited space without drainage. The
> best and most perfect disinfectant is earth, and sinks to smell sweet must be
> dug narrow and deep and daily covered with earth, but this cannot be in the
> prisoners' barracks, as the whole ground would be dug over in a short time.
> The remedy then is to pass a current of water through this putrid matter.[43]

Unlike with Foster's Pond, work to improve Elmira's soggy environment commenced right away. Tracy's predecessor, Lieutenant-Colonel

Seth Eastman, reported to Hoffman just a week after Sanger made his observations that drainage of the camp "is being made complete." That same week in August 1864 the camp's inspector, Captain Benjamin Munger, also noted that drainage of the camp was "progressing, but incomplete." During the late summer and early fall of 1864 inspectors either gave the camp's drainage better marks or made no complaint. In early December Captain J. H. Borden observed that officials were working constantly to keep the grounds as dry as possible. His report from December 11, 1864, noted that Elmira was "undergoing new grading and draining" and that those efforts had helped improve the overall atmosphere of the grounds.[44]

Efforts to improve the sink problems were also under way in the early fall of 1864. Poor sewage removal was a common complaint at every prisoner of war camp and Elmira was certainly no exception. Poorly managed sewage areas guaranteed that disease, especially dysentery, would be a problem. In the mid to late summer of 1864 several inspectors noted that the sink issue was a major health problem. Using Foster's Pond as a massive commode was the first thing that officials at Elmira had to stop and did by the middle of August. Beginning late that summer and throughout the rest of the year sinks at Elmira consisted of sheds over vaults that were filled in and new ones dug as needed. This was not what Sanger had recommended but his idea of having ditches with water running through them taking the sewage out of camp was not acted upon; at least there is no evidence in the records that it was. Vaults were simpler, likely cheaper, and very common for military camps of the period, which were all probable reasons this mode of waste management was used at Elmira. This was not the healthiest way to manage the prodigious amount of human waste created at the prison, of course. Until the holes were covered with dirt, contaminated material drew flies in huge numbers that, in turn, contaminated everything and everyone they landed on.[45]

Determining whether Elmira prisoners were adequately fed can be a difficult job. The evidence is often conflicting. For example, Thomas Benton Alexander of Tennessee was a prisoner at Elmira and recorded in his diary in December 1864: "we have two meals a Day for breakfast Bread and meat for Dinner soup and meat." For Alexander "the two meals [were] very good Enough to live on." And a few of the former prisoners who wrote to Holmes as he was putting together his history of the camp suggested that the food at Elmira was sufficient, at least as far as they were concerned. J. R. Mills, who was at Elmira during its entire existence as a prison, wrote from Edison, Georgia: "My prison fare at Elmira was about the same as our army fare."

Most of the ex-prisoners, though, said they did not always get enough to eat. Erastus Palmer told Holmes that the "food was as good as we could expect, but there was not half enough of it. I was assured by the guard that the same rations were issued to the prisoners as to the U.S. troops stationed there. There seemed to me to be some bad leak in it somewhere before it got to us." "The food was reasonably good," another wrote, "can't say I had plenty." While most of the prisoners who wrote to Holmes did complain that food was on the scanty side at Elmira, none expressed the belief that they were victims of a policy to starve them. In fact, none suggested that food rations were so insufficient as to constitute "starvation rations" as was claimed by many Lost Cause writers. Perhaps the best observation about the amount of food issued to prisoners at Elmira came from J. S. Johnson of Mebane, North Carolina. Johnson had been captured at Petersburg and was confined at Elmira until June 1865. "Some of the prisoners," he wrote, "did not think they got enough to eat; all got the same rations, but what would satisfy one would not another."[46]

The prisoners who wrote to Holmes in 1911 and the *Official Records* suggest that food was indeed short at times at Elmira, causing some prisoners to not get all they were entitled to. That this was because the United States was actively withholding adequate amounts of food as part of a retaliation program is not well supported by the evidence. For one thing, if Federal authorities really wanted to impose gnawing hunger on Confederate prisoners they would have not only curtailed food rations sharply at Elmira, which they did not, they would have forbidden the camp's sutler from selling food items to the prisoners, which they also did not do. As former prisoner A. J. Hooper informed Holmes: "I did not live on the rations I drew entirely. I made watch chains out of horse hair, and finger rings out of gutta-percha buttons and sold them. I could buy anything from the camp sutler." Furthermore, several of the former inmates said they believed prisoners were shorted on rations because fellow prisoners who were in charge of cooking and distributing rations held out additional portions for themselves at their comrades' expense. "The food [at Elmira] was well prepared," M. T. Wade wrote, "but my appetite was much better then than it is now. I can not say I had enough, but I attribute a good deal of that to some of those 'cook-house rats,' as we called them, who were Confederates chiefly, and in charge of the cooks." J. A. Hooper told Holmes: "I think the Government furnished more rations than we actually got. The cooks and waiters were prisoners. They carried out meat in their bosoms and sold it for I have bought it from them." J. L. Williams, who had served in the 9th Alabama and was captured at the Wilderness, openly admitted to Holmes that he and James M. Gilmore of the 11th Mississippi skimmed rations from their fellow prisoners for their own consumption and profit. Williams explained that Gilmore "had a position in the dining-room and managed to 'flank' from twenty-five to thirty rations a day, and after eating all we wanted, I sold the remainder." So it would appear that at least some of the real hunger experienced at Elmira was due to the actions of selfish prisoners.[47]

Federal records also indicate that during the early fall of 1864 the beef ration was often lean and short. In October the beef issued to prisoners was described as "unfit for issue, and inferior in quality . . . ." There was also a lack of fresh vegetables in the early weeks of Elmira's existence as a prison, which caused officials to call for additional vegetables to be bought and issued to the prisoners, especially those in the hospital and barracks suffering from scurvy symptoms. Holmes made a valid point about the beef and vegetable problems at the beginning of Elmira's history. He pointed out that the summer of 1864 had been extremely dry and the local beef and vegetables had suffered as a result. One of Munger's inspection reports hints at this same problem. "The beef is very lean. Cows milked through the summer and too poor for a respectable farmer to winter are slaughtered and the beef issued to the prisoners." Holmes, though, was perhaps too willing to let Federal officials off the hook for the spindly beef the prisoners were getting during the fall of 1864. Getting decent beef and an adequate amount of vegetable matter to the prisoners may have indeed been more difficult because of certain uncontrollable natural factors like a prolonged local drought. But officials knew about this problem as early as September and there was no reason not to have been more aggressive in seeking alternative beef or pork sources. They did not and prisoners suffered as a result.

They did, albeit slowly, fix the problem, however. According to the wartime evidence, the problems were remedied by the end of 1864 and inspection reports cease to mention food shortages and references to scurvy virtually disappear. In mid-January 1865 Colonel Tracy reported that the "daily ration for each prisoner is uniformly as follows: For breakfast, eight ounces of bread, eight ounces meat; for dinner, eight ounces bread, one pint and a half soup of excellent quality, made from the meat, potatoes, onions, and beans."[48]

Clothing at Elmira was inconsistent. References to inmates not having sufficient clothing or blankets are not difficult to find, especially for those weeks when the prison opened and received a number of prisoners in various states of undress. In the summer of 1864 the Elmira *Daily Advertiser* reported that some of the new arrivals "had nothing on but drawers and shirts . . . ." In July Surgeon Charles Alexander reported shortages of "blouses, pants, blankets, shirts, [and] bootees" among the Elmira prisoners. The following month officials complained that blankets and shirts especially were needed at the depot. Throughout the fall and winter of 1864 to '65 prisoners at Elmira drew clothing and blankets from the Federals, got clothing through the mail, or bought from the sutler. These sources were not always up to the task, however, of making sure that prisoners had all they needed in this area.

Federal officials attempted to place the burden of clothing more on prisoners' friends and families to minimize the burden on the government. That had worked reasonably well at some prisons like Johnson's Island where prisoners came from a class that was more likely to have friends and family with sufficient resources. The system was not adequate for Elmira's inmates, however. In September Munger reported: "Some clothing is received daily from the friends of prisoners, but there is still great destitution." The deficiency in prisoners' clothing remained an issue, though it was improving slightly by October and early November. Munger reported in early November that some prisoners were still in need of some item or other of clothing and blankets but the shortages were not nearly as acute as they had been in September. He also noted in his report that additional clothing requisitions had been made to outfit needy prisoners, which was needed as Holmes noted in his book that the fall and winter of 1864–65 was one of the coldest the region had ever seen.

At the end of November 1864, William Jordan inspected the camp and he found that clothing deficiencies were less serious than they had been earlier. In fact he used the term "good" to describe the clothing situation for most of the prisoners and he noted that "most of the men have blankets . . . ." With a particularly bitter winter setting in that year at Elmira, however, the fact that officials were working to issue heavier clothing and blankets to prisoners in need did nothing to help those who were in need at that moment. These prisoners no doubt suffered considerably from the cold until the Union officials came through for them with more blankets, which they eventually did. In early December Colonel Tracy reported that "a large amount of clothing and 4,000 blankets has just been received and the articles will be issued immediately . . . ." The number of blankets received and issued is significant. A previous report had noted that some 1,600 prisoners had either worn out blankets or none at all. That 4,000 were ordered indicates that Elmira officials intended not only to insure that prisoners had blankets and blankets in good condition but that prisoners who would arrive at the depot without blankets or with worn ones would have a new good one to use at the camp. This kind of planning was remarkable because it was so rare during the war. During the week of December 11, 1864, 2,500 jackets, 2,000 pairs of pants, 3,011 shirts, 1,126 pairs of drawers, 6,065 pairs of socks, and 3,938 blankets were issued to the 8,000 prisoners. Not all of that 8,000 were in need of an article of clothing, of course, and others had been able to get clothing and blankets through the mail or at the sutler. Thus Captain J. H. Bordan, another of Elmira's inspecting officers, was able to finally describe the prisoners' clothing and blanket situation by the end of the year as "comfortable" for the first time in the prison's history. To be sure, there was a considerable lack of efficiency filling prisoners' clothing needs at Elmira. But, ultimately, they were filled suggesting that inefficiency and perhaps incompetent or even dishonest quartermasters and government contractors were more to blame for clothing deficiencies than an overt program or policy to deprive Confederate prisoners of blankets and clothing. This is perhaps best illustrated by Hoffman's dressing down of Tracy in February 1865 over reports of clothing deficiencies among some of the prisoners at Elmira. That month Hoffman reminded Tracy,

> The regulations, to which your attention has before been called, prescribe the mode of procuring clothing for prisoners, and if at any time there was an insufficiency on hand to meet the demands, it must be attributed to a want of attention on the part of the commanding officer whose duty it is to see that timely requisitions are made for such clothing as may be required . . . .[49]

Holmes brought up another possible reason why clothing was a problem at Elmira in late 1864/early 1865. There was apparently some confusion about who was responsible for clothing prisoners. Confederate officials, concerned that their prisoners were not being treated properly, asked if they could sell Southern cotton in the North and have the proceeds go towards procuring clothing for prisoners held in Union prison camps. As this would ease the spending burdens on the Federals' part, it was agreed to. Colonel Tracy was informed on December 12, 1864, in fact, by the War Department: "By mutual agreement between the U.S. and Rebel authorities a large amount of cotton has been shipped for New York and an officer designated to receive and dispose of it, the proceeds to be applied to the purchase of clothing, etc., for the comfort of Rebel prisoners of war. In view of this fact, it is desirable that no more clothing shall be provided by the Government than is absolutely demanded by the ordinary dictates of humanity." Unfortunately for many at Elmira that meant that they would have to wait until the cotton was disposed of and the clothing and blankets obtained and distributed. This wound up taking a long time—too long in Tracy's opinion. During the first week of January 1865, Tracy contacted the Commissary-General of Prisoners to say that many of those at his prison were still waiting on clothing and blankets and requested that his earlier requisitions for clothing be filled "unless the department is advised that supplies will be speedily forwarded by the Rebel authorities." Not until February did the Confederate-procured items arrive for needy Rebels at Elmira.[50]

When Elmira was reopened as a prison in the summer of 1864, housing was, of course, a major concern. The existing barracks that had been used by Union recruits would again be used to house prisoners but there was only enough room in them for about half the number that would ultimately arrive at Elmira. These additional prisoners, about 5,000 in number, were housed in tents, as were the guards. The tents were not the tiny "dog tents" but rather commodious A-frames. J. H. Michaels, formerly of the 27th South Carolina, recalled in 1911 that he transferred to Elmira in late July 1864 and was "quartered in Barrack No. 8. After the barracks were filled the new arrivals were put in 'A' tents. The men built mud chimney's at the end of the tent." But the climate made tents a short-term solution to housing needs and Lieutenant-Colonel Eastman requested permission to begin work on more permanent barracks for both prisoners and guards in August 1864. Typical of Hoffman's decision-making, since the need and expense were not immediate, he replied on September 8, 1864, to Eastman that barracks "for the guard, or additional ones for the prisoners, will not be put up at present. Sibley tents can be estimated for in October."[51]

The location of the prison alone dictated that more substantial wooden barracks with stoves be erected to help keep the prisoners (and the guards for that matter) better protected from the cold. Furthermore, Hoffman was specifically warned by Eastman that obtaining the necessary amount of wood would be difficult, making it even more necessary to begin work on barracks as soon as possible to have the men sheltered by winter's onset. But such was not to be and an especially cold winter set in earlier than expected with extremely uncomfortable results for thousands of Confederate prisoners. In late September Captain Munger warned that the "weather is cold for the season, and those in tents especially suffer." Tracy reinforced Munger's observation, stating flatly to Hoffman that "Barracks should be erected instead of tents." Based on these recommendations from men on the site Hoffman should have moved more quickly to order barracks built at Elmira. Only after the need was too well documented to ignore were measures approved to begin building barracks. On October 3, 1864, Hoffman informed Tracy that he was free to "order the erection of shed barracks for the prisoners of war at the Elmira depot." It should be pointed out that the Federal guards were not going to get better, more expensive quarters than the prisoners. Hoffman made it clear that the guards' quarters "will be built after the style of those directed for the prisoners, and in every way the closest economy will be studied." The barracks were to be off the ground, which was more sanitary, and the roofs "should be covered with the patent felt roofing, which is much warmer than the shingle roof." Finally, many prisoners could begin to look forward to getting into more substantial and warmer living quarters.[52]

Work began immediately after receiving Hoffman's approval but the barracks went up slowly. Though the cause is not altogether clear, obtaining wood in proper quantity became a very real problem. During the first week of November, Colonel Tracy informed Hoffman that the building projects at Elmira "progress slowly" largely because of the shortage of wood. He assured Hoffman, though, that whatever problems existed in that area had been overcome and plenty of wood "is now being supplied and we hope to have no further delay." Two weeks later Tracy told Hoffman: "Six of the new barracks for the use of the prisoners are completed and occupied. Four others will soon be done." By the second week of December over 7,000 of the nearly 8,500 prisoners at Elmira had been moved from tents to elevated wooden barracks that were heated by stoves. By New Year's Day 1865 all the prisoners were in barracks.[53]

Life in the barracks was much better, obviously, than trying to fend off the cold and elements outside in a tent no matter how good the tent. Most of the prisoners who wrote to Holmes recalled that the barracks were quite good and comfortable as a general rule. J.A. Hooper recalled: "We slept three in a bunk on one blanket and covered with two. They finally allowed us two blankets for each man." Other comments from former prisoners about the barracks included recollections like: "Barracks were good enough"; "The barracks were good"; "We had good wards to live in; two good stoves in each ward; good bunks to sleep in . . . "; and "The barracks were moderately comfortable for that climate." Of course, the barracks would not have been defined as comfortable by modern standards. They were not insulated, the bunks were hard, and even with two wood- or coal-burning stoves the interiors must have been quite cold when temperatures dipped well below freezing and stayed there for much of the winter of 1864/65.[54]

Where Elmira seems to really stand out as a death trap is in the area of medical care. Of the nine major Northern prisons examined in this book, most posted recovery rates from various diseases that were as good, or better, than for the same diseases at Chimborazo Hospital in Richmond. Elmira's disease mortality rates, on the other hand, were significantly worse than for the Confederate hospital. *The Medical and Surgical History of the War of the Rebellion* shows that at Chimborazo 2,717 of the 23,849 patients treated died of their illness for a mortality rate per reported case of 11.39% or an 88.61% recovery rate. At Elmira between July 1864 and June 1865, 2,927 of the 10,178 prisoners treated there died for a mortality rate of 28.75% or a recovery rate of only 71.25%. Even by mid-nineteenth century standards such statistics were alarming.[55]

These sorts of numbers could indeed suggest, as at least one recent Elmira historian has, that Southern prisoners' medical needs were neglected, which, in turn, caused excessive mortality among Confederates held at the depot. But such raw statistics have to be combined with other evidence to more accurately determine whether or not Union officials took the callous position towards prisoners' health needs at Elmira that they have stood accused of for so long. When Elmira opened in the summer of 1864 mortality and scurvy issues became serious almost immediately. In late August the surgeon in charge of the camp, E. F. Sanger, recommended more vegetables to be issued to help with the scurvy problems and he complained that there was a lack of space for all the sick at Elmira. The following month both Munger and Tracy expressed their concerns that scurvy remained a problem and that the diet in the hospital was inadequate to restore the patients' health. In the middle of October disease mortality was still alarming, causing Tracy to write to Hoffman:

> The mortality in this camp is so great as to justify, as it seems to me, the most
> rigid investigation as to its cause. If the rate of mortality for the last two
> months should continue for a year you can easily calculate the number of pris-
> oners there would be left here for exchange. I have, therefore the honor to

request that a thorough investigation be made into all the probable causes of disease in this camp, including the sufficiency of the present diet and clothing to maintain the standard of health in this climate, the effects of the pool of stagnant water in the center of the camp, and the competency and efficiency of the medical officers on duty here. It seems to me that such an investigation, conducted by competent men, would do much do discover the cause and remedy the evil.

Hoffman was in agreement, telling Tracy a few days later that his request to investigate the mortality problems at Elmira had been forwarded to Stanton "with the recommendation that a medical inspector be ordered to investigate the causes of the unusual sickness among the prisoners of war at Elmira." The officials at Elmira and even Hoffman himself appear to have taken an active interest in disease control and prevention even if they were not terribly successful. This would seem to undermine, or at least call into question, accusations of "sadistic apathy."[56]

The prisoners writing Holmes about their experiences at Elmira at the beginning of the twentieth century also recalled that they either got reasonably decent medical treatment at Elmira or believed that Federal officials did the best they could for the sick prisoners held there. J. L. Camp wrote that he did not recall the food or barracks being more than the bare minimum but while he was in Elmira's hospital he said he was "cared for all right. I think Elmira did everything for the prisoners which could be expected." W. P. Whitesides told Holmes he thought the "sick were well cared for as to food, quarters, and good beds; plenty of stimulants, but a good deal of it drank by the doctor; still there was plenty for the sick." W. W. Edwards, who had served in the 6th Alabama, was confined to the hospital at Elmira for nearly two weeks where he said he was "very well cared for." "Never was in the hospital," M. A. Bunch wrote from Meigs, Georgia, "but had a friend who was, and he was pleased." A former member of the 14th Alabama, J. T. Hudson, replied to Holmes briefly that his memories of Elmira included that "the food was mighty light. I never was in the hospital. The sick were very well cared for." Finally, Isaac Kale wrote from Claremont, North Carolina: "The barracks were not so very comfortable. The food was very light, not as plenty as it should have been. [But] I was in the hospital and well treated." Though the statistics show that the physicians at Elmira were far from successful at dealing with a host of diseases, the prisoners who wrote Holmes all indicate that they believed that at the time they were treated well, medically speaking.[57]

Several factors combined at Elmira to increase disease mortality. Part of the problem was the large percentage of diarrhea/dysentery cases that occurred at Elmira. Over 40% of all the disease cases recorded in *The Medical and Surgical History* were from that category, which was higher than for most other Northern prisons. There was no effective treatment for this particular problem and when it did not clear up on its own, death often resulted. Even if one did survive a bad case of diarrhea/dysentery, one's immune system was significantly compromised because of the body's inability to absorb vital nutrients. The result was heightened susceptibility to diseases like the prison's second-leading killer, pneumonia, which took 773 (26.40%) of all prisoners who died of a disease at Elmira.

Another, more serious, problem that directly affected recovery from sickness at Elmira was the lack of hospital space. As early as August 1864, Eastman noted the need for additional hospital space, telling Hoffman that it "will be necessary to erect three more [hospital wards] as soon as lumber can be obtained." Until they were built, though, many ill prisoners remained in the general population, which was an unwholesome, unsanitary place. Captain Munger complained at the end of August that on "the 20th instant 226 were reported sick in hospital and a larger number in quarters. Many of those in quarters are unable to attend sick call, and in some cases had not been visited by a surgeon in four days." In such a situation, ill prisoners did not fully recover and new cases of sickness were cropping up all the time, putting a severe strain on hospital space. By the end of September there was still not sufficient space to get sick Southerners out of the tents and barracks, which detrimentally affected their ability to recover. At the end of September Tracy noted, "Hospital accommodations insufficient at present. New wards being built."

References to sick in the quarters diminished as winter approached and reports indicate that sick prisoners were removed from the general population so that they would have a better chance at recovery. At the end of November Tracy reported, "I have the honor to report that six hospital wards were erected at the camp previous to September 8, 1864, when more being deemed necessary, authority was granted to erect as many hospital wards as were deemed indispensably necessary, ... Under this authority two wards have been constructed and are now in use. One more is needed and will be constructed as soon as possible, making in all nine wards, besides six old barracks which have, under my orders, been converted into convalescent wards." Though hospital space was pushed to capacity for the fall and early winter of 1864, prisoners were no longer treated in the barracks.

When beds were unavailable in the hospital in late 1864, prisoners were laid on straw in the wards until one became available. It was far from ideal but it was an improvement over remaining in tents or in the barracks. By the beginning of 1865 Elmira seemed to finally have sufficient and reasonably clean hospital space for the prisoners. Tracy reported at the beginning of January that new hospital wards were finally all completed and "are now very comfortable."[58]

When evaluating life at Elmira there can be no doubt that it was probably the worst of all the Union prisons. It was easily the deadliest. At times adequate food was a problem and the prisoners did not always have enough clothing and blankets. Those who lived in tents during the late fall and early winter of 1864 suffered tremendously and must have wondered how they would ever keep from freezing to death before moving into more substantial housing. Inadequate hospital space was a problem for much of the second half of 1864 and the sanitary conditions, especially while Foster's Pond remained a putrid presence, left a great deal to be desired. Unquestionably, life at Elmira was bleak and precarious.

Retaliatory policies and "sadistic apathy" do not sufficiently account for Elmira's lethal conditions or the uncomfortable living conditions many endured. Given the positive and relatively timely efforts to drain the camp and improve sewage removal, the Foster's Pond fiasco seems more reflective of a tragic error on Hoffman's part than negligence or vindictiveness. This seems especially likely in view of the other sanitation improvements Hoffman did authorize and his order to investigate the heavy mortality at Elmira. Barracks ought to have been provided before winter set in but since the guards also lived in tents during the chilly fall of 1864 and occupied barracks of comparable quality as the prisoners', it cannot be said that Confederate prisoners' quarters were exceptionally deficient by the era's standards. And while food and clothing shortages did exist, they were episodic rather than chronic.

Establishing what made Elmira uniquely lethal is difficult. Blaming Northern malice is too simplistic and ignores evidence that Federal officials undertook significant improvement projects at the site. Certainly poor sanitary conditions contributed to dysentery totals during the second half of 1864 but improvement programs belie malicious intent. Perhaps the answer lies in the prison's location. For most of the time this former Union training facility was a prison the captives stayed in their tents and barracks to escape from the unusually long and bitter winter of 1864–65. Thousands of dirty men huddling together around stoves and fireplaces for such long periods created an environment ideal for spreading germs. Not surprisingly, slightly over 74% of the mortality at Elmira was attributed to dysentery or pneumonia, two diseases that thrive in crowded, unhygienic conditions.

Endnotes

1. William L. Fagan, ed., *Southern War Songs* (New York: M.T. Richardson & Co, 1890), 361–62; Anthony M. Keiley, *In Vinculis; or The Prisoner of War* (Petersburg, VA: Daily Index Office, 1866), 5–6, 146–47; *Southern Historical Society Papers*, Richmond, VA (Volume I), 156–61, 259–70.

2. Edwin W. Beitzell, *Point Lookout Prison Camp for Confederates* (n.p.: by author, 1972), 176; "Point Lookout Prison Camp for Confederates," at http://members.tripod.com/~PLPOW/prisonhis.htm, (accessed 12/23/1998).

3. United States War Department, *War of the Rebellion: A Compilation of the Official Records of the Union and Confederate Armies* (Washington, D.C..: Government Printing Office, 1894; repr., Harrisburg, PA: Telegraph Press, 1971) Series II, Volume 8, 991–1002 (hereafter cited as OR with all citations being from Series II unless otherwise indicated); Beitzell, 176.

4. OR, Volume 6, 643–44, 742; Berry Benson, *Berry Benson's Civil War Book: Memoirs of a Confederate Scout and Sharpshooter*, ed. Susan Williams Bensen (Athens: University of Georgia Press, 1992), 94.

5. *Diary of Henry C. Dickinson, CSA* (Denver, CO: The Williamson-Haffner, Co, unreadable date of publication); *Francis Atherton Boyle Diary*, Southern Historical Collection, University of North Carolina, Chapel Hill (hereafter referred to as SHC); *Bartlett Yancey Malone Diary*, SHC; *Elijah Saunders Diary*, Eleanor Brokenbrough Library, Museum of the Confederacy, Richmond, VA (hereafter referred to as MOC); James T. Meade, *Journal of Prison Life* (Torrington, CT: Rainbow Press, 1987), 4.

6. *Sketches from Prison: A Confederate Artist's Record of Life at Point Lookout Prisoner-of-War Camp, 1863–1865* (Baltimore, MD: Maryland State Park Foundation, 1989).

7. OR, Volume 6, 763; Volume 7, 379, 399–400, 449–50, 835; Volume 8, 462–63; *Medical and Surgical History*, Volume I, Part III, 46.

8. OR, Volume 6, 473, 489, 575–81, 625, 644–45, 741–45, 1014–15, 1036.

9. *Medical and Surgical History* Volume I, Part II (entire volume is dedicated to diarrhea because the problem during the Civil War was so large); Volume I, Part III, 46; Bell I. Wiley, *The Life of Johnny Reb: The Common Soldier of the Confederacy* (Baton Rouge: Louisiana State University Press, 1943), 90–107, 247–53; Richard H. Shryock, *Medicine in America: Historical Essays* (Baltimore, MD: The Johns Hopkins University Press, 1966), 90–108; H. H.

Cunningham, *Doctors in Gray: The Confederate Medical Service* (Baton Rouge: Louisiana State University Press, 1958, 1993), 175–88; Stewart Books, *Civil War Medicine* (Springfield, IL: Charles C. Thomas, 1966), 114–17, 125–27.

10. *OR*, Volume 6, 368–69, 390, 575–81, 644–46, 740–45, 763–64.

11. Ibid.

12. *OR*, Volume 6, 390, 448–50, 577, 740–45, 962, 1023; *Diary of Capt. Henry C. Dickinson, CSA*, 26; *Sketches from Prison*.

13. *OR*, Volume 6, 585, 763–68, 1036; Volume 7, 153–55, 448–50; Volume 8, 462–63; *Elijah Saunders Johnson Diary*, MOC.

14. *OR*, Volume 6, 575–81, 585, 644–45.

15. *OR*, Volume 6, 740–45, 763, 1014–15, 1036; Volume 7, 448–50; Dickinson, 28, 45; *Francis Atherton Boyle Diary*, SHC; *Bartlett Yancey Malone Diary*, SHC; *Sketches from Prison; Elijah Saunders Johnson Diary*, MOC.

16. *OR*, Volume 6, 575–81, 644–45.

17. *OR*, Volume 6, 645–46, 740–45, 753–54, Volume 7, 153–55, 379, 399–400, 448–50; Volume 8, 133–34, 462–63; Dickinson, 26.

18. *OR*, Volume 6, 743–45, 753–54.

19. *OR*, Volume 6, 575-581, 741-745, Volume 7, 399–400, 440, 448–50.

20. *OR*, Volume 7, 399–400, 440, 448–50, 835, 962, 984–85, Volume 8, 462–63.

21. *Medical and Surgical History*, Volume I, Part III, 30, 46.

22. *OR*, Volume 6, 740–45, 753–54; Volume 7, 448–50.

23. *Confederate Veteran* (November 1896), 387; (November 1910), 516; Lamar Fontaine, *The Prison Life of Major Lamar Fontaine* (Clarksdale, MS: Daily Register Print, 1910), 3–4, 12–18; William Henry Morgan, *Personal Reminiscences of the War of 1861–5* (Lynchburg, VA: J. P. Bell Co., 1911), 225, 237–48, 255–61.

24. W. Emerson Wilson, *Fort Delaware* (Newark: University of Delaware, 1957), 15; Speer, *Portals to Hell*, 143–47; Brian Temple, *The Union Prison at Fort Delaware: A Perfect Hell on Earth* (Jefferson, NC: McFarland and Company, Inc., 2003).

25. *OR*, Volume 5, 220–21; Volume 6, 215–16, 516–18, 651–53, 1039–41; Volume 7; *Peters Family Papers*, SHC; *James H. Franklin Diary*, MOC; *E. L. Cox Diary*, VHS; Dale Fetzer and Bruce Mowday, *Unlikely Allies: Fort Delaware's Prison Community in the Civil War* (Mechanicsburg, PA: Stackpole Books, 2000), 59–60.

26. *OR*, Volume 6, 1040–41; Volume 7, 495, 664–65, 695, 766, 836, 909–10, 956–57, 1023, 1187, 1301–2; Volume 8, 40, 80, 112, 143; *Paul Agalus*

McMichael Papers, SHC, *Rufus Barringer Papers*, SHC, *James Robert McMichael Diary*, SHC; *John C. Allen Diary*, MOC, *James Mackey Diary*, MOC, *Joseph W. Mauck Diary*, MOC; *John A. Gibson Diary*, VHS, *E. L. Cox Diary*, VHS; W. W. Ward, *"For the Sake of My Country": The Diary of Col. W. W. Ward*, ed. R. B. Rosenburg (Murfreesboro, TN: Southern Heritage Press, 1992), 25–39, 40, 45, 65; Fetzer and Mowday, 59–67, 78-87, 98–99.

27. OR, Volume 5, 220–21; Volume 6, 215–16, 235, 309–10, 516–18, 651–53, 1040; Volume 7, 421, 664–65, 695, 766, 836, 909–10, 956–57, 1023, 1187, 1301–2; Volume 8, 40, 80, 112, 143; Ward, 25–39; *James Taswell Mackey Diary*, MOC; *Elijah Saunders Johnson Diary*, MOC; *Thomas Pickney Diary*, MOC; *James Henry Franklin Diary*, MOC; *Henry Robinson Berkeley Diary*, VHS, *E. L. Cox Diary*, VHS; "Prison Times," handwritten newspaper from Fort Delaware, SHC, *Paul Agalus McMichael Papers*, SHC; Fetzer and Mowday, 59–67, 78–87, 92–93, 98–99.

28. OR, Volume 5, 220–21, 457, 467, 481, 484, 492–93, 502, 538, 586; Volume 6, 80–81, 88, 105–6, 216, 235, 281, 516–18, 651–53, 716; Volume 7, 664–65, 695, 766, 836, 909–10, 956–57, 1023, 1187, 1301–2; Volume 8, 40, 80, 112, 143.

29. OR, Volume 6, 651–53; Volume 7, 421, 664–65, 695, 766, 836, 910, 956–97, 1023, 1187, 1301-2; Volume 8, 40, 80, 112, 143; Fetzer and Mowday, 99–100.

30. *Medical and Surgical History*, Volume I, Part III, 30, 46, 63, 70–71; OR, Volume 5, 467; Volume 6, 215, 435, 477, 1041; Volume 7, 421.

31. *Medical and Surgical History*, Volume I, Part III, 30, 46, 63, 70–71; OR, Volume 8, 990–1002; Fetzer and Mowday, 115–19.

32. Ibid.

33. *Medical and Surgical History*, Volume I, Part III, 30, 46; OR, Volume 8, 1039–41; Fetzer and Mowday, 115–19.

34. OR, Volume 5, 467; Volume 6, 215, 435, 477, 1041; Fetzer and Mowday, 62–65, 77, 120.

35. *SHSP* (Volume I, 1876), 235, 259–60, 264; *Confederate Veteran* (July 1912), 327; Walter D. Addison, "Recollections of a Confederate Soldier of the Prison-Pens of Point Lookout, Md., and Elmira, New York," (SHC and *Elmira Prison Camp On-Line Library*); Keiley, 134–47; G. W. D. Porter, "Nine Months in a Northern Prison," www.tennessee-scv.org/4455/index.htm.; W. A. Wash, *Camp, Field, and Prison Life* (St. Louis: Southwestern Book and Publishing Co., 1870), viii–ix.

36. Clay W. Holmes, *The Elmira Prison Camp: A History of the Military Prison at Elmira, N.Y., July 6, 1864–July 10, 1865* (New York: G. P. Putnam's Sons, 1912), 326–40.

37. Robertson, "The Scourge of Elmira," in *Civil War Prisons*, ed. William B. Hesseltine (Kent, OH: Kent State University Press, 1995, 1972), 80–97; Speer, *Portals to Hell*, 241–48; Philip Burnham, "The Andersonvilles of the North," in *With My Face to the Enemy: Perspectives on the Civil War*, ed. Robert Cowley (New York: Berkely Books, 2001), 369–72, and *So Far From Dixie: Confederates in Yankee Prisons* (New York: Taylor Trade Publishing, 2003); Michael Horigan, *Elmira: Death Camp of the North* (Mechanicsburg, PA: Stackpole Books, 2002), 17–20, 58, 70–95; Michael P. Gray, *The Business of Captivity: Elmira and Its Prison Camp* (Kent, OH: Kent State University Press, 2001), 100–3, 161.

38. *Medical and Surgical History*, Volume I, Part III, 30, 46.

39. *Medical and Surgical History*, Volume I, Part III, 30, 46; *OR*, Volume 7, 466, 1003; Holmes, 326–40.

40. *OR*, Volume 7, 603–4, 676–77.

41. *OR*, Volume 7, 603–5, 677, 1003–4, 1025, 1042–43; Gray, 3, 13, 27, 40, 57–58.

42. *OR*, Volume 8, 3–4; Gray, 57–58; Holmes, 43–57; Horigan, 52–53, 74–76.

43. *OR*, Volume 7, 603–5.

44. *OR*, Volume 7, 603–5, 676–77, 682, 1004, 1124, 1146, 1184–85, 1213, 1240, 1272–73; Volume 8, 3–4, 39.

45. *OR*, Volume 7, 465–66, 603–5, 676–77, 878, 1092–94, 1104, 1124, 1146, 1167, 1184–85, 1213, 1240, 1272; Volume 8, 3–4, 39.

46. Holmes, 326–40; *Thomas Benton Alexander Diary*, University of Notre Dame Rare Books and Special Collections; Horigan, 68–71.

47. Holmes, 326–40.

48. *OR*, Volume 7, 466, 682–83, 878, 996–97, 1003–4, 1104, 1124, 1146, 1167, 1173–74, 1184–85, 1213, 1240, 1272–73; Volume 8, 3–4, 39, 76–77; Holmes 88–104; Horigan, 68–71.

49. *OR*, Volume 7, 466, 560, 584, 676–77, 878, 1065, 1104, 1124, 1146, 1167, 1184–85, 1213, 1240, 1272; Volume 8, 3–4, 39, 195–96, 209; Gray, 62–65.

50. Holmes, 70–76.

51. *OR*, Volume 7, 157, 450–51, 465–66, 560, 584, 692–93; Gray, 2–3, 58–61, 105, 157; Holmes, 58–69, 105–6, 332.

52. *OR*, Volume 7, 878, 918–19; Holmes, 58–69, 105–6.

53. *OR*, Volume 7, 157, 450–51, 465–66, 560, 584, 692–93, 786, 878, 918–19, 1065, 1104, 1124, 1134–36, 1146, 1167, 1173, 1237, 1272–73; Volume 8, 3–4, 39; Gray, 2–3, 8, 58–61, 105, 157; Holmes, 58–69, 105–6.

54. *OR*, Volume 8, 3–4, 39; Holmes, 326–40.

55. *Medical and Surgical History*, Volume I, Part III, 30, 46.

56. OR, Volume 7, 676–77, 682–83, 692–93, 878, 997; James I. Robertson, "The Scourge of Elmira," in *Civil War Prisons*, ed. William B. Hesseltine (Kent, OH: Kent State University Press, 1962, 1995), 80–98; Gray, 47–51; Horigan, 22–47, 58–69.

57. Holmes, 326–40.

58. OR, Volume 7, 465–66, 560, 676–77, 692, 878, 997, 1104, 1146, 1167, 1173–74, 1213, 1237, 1240, 1272–73; Volume 8, 3–4.

-8-

THE OMNIPRESENT SPECTER
OF DISEASE

PREVIOUS CHAPTERS ARGUED THAT UNION OFFICIALS generally did a decent job of providing Confederate prisoners with adequate food, clothing, shelter, and medical care. Many still question, however, how that could have been so when 12 % of the South's soldiers died in captivity. The reason many have concluded that such a statistic was excessive is that mortality in Confederate prisons, which operated under severe material constraints, was not much higher at 15.5 %. The North, on the other hand, was practically bursting with material resources and was virtually untouched by the war's destructiveness. Given the respective resource disparities between North and South, many commentators have assumed that a starker contrast between the regions' military prisons should have existed as well. A 3.5 % difference has not seemed significant enough, leading many to continue following the well-worn path leading to the conclusion that Yankee officials were negligent or abusive in their treatment of Southern prisoners.

The assumption of a direct connection between resources and disease mortality ignores several crucial factors directly affecting Confederate prisoners' mortality. Death by disease was extremely common during the Civil War. Disease deaths were more common than combat deaths and especially problematic when the armies remained in one place for extended periods of time. Assuming that disease mortality would not have been an enormous problem in Union prisons is simply unrealistic. Contemporary medical ignorance of the microscopic causes of infectious diseases precluded effective treatment and control of them. Further, the treatments that were available at the time either made existing health problems worse or were practically useless. And, many prisoners arrived in Union prisons severely injured and/or in sub-par physical condition, making them prime targets for a host of lethal pathogens. When all of these variables are taken into account it becomes clear that most of the mortality found among Confederate prisoners during the Civil War was tragically inevitable rather than induced by Yankee policies.

During the Civil War, death came from many directions. While the battlefield was a dangerous and horrifying place, it was not the place most likely to take soldiers' lives. Death from a wide variety of diseases was twice as likely to kill soldiers during that conflict as enemy shot and shell. That was largely because American physicians had no idea how to deal effectively with a host of infectious diseases. Doctors generally did not know what caused most diseases in the first place. That situation led to treatments and preventive measures that amounted to little more than guesswork. This lack of effective treatments or control mechanisms for such major killers as dysentery, typhoid, pneumonia, and smallpox assured that disease mortality would be significant during the Civil War.

To give some idea as to just how antiquated the American medical profession was in 1861, Harvard's medical school did not own a single stethoscope and Surgeon General Thomas Lawson viewed medical books as useless encumbrances. He believed, as did many of his colleagues, that doctors should learn their trade in apprentice fashion from a practicing physician. This is not a bad idea by itself, but it tended to discourage new and perhaps more effective ideas about the causes and treatment of infectious diseases among American physicians. Thus, while Europeans like Louis Pasteur and Joseph Lister were discovering the microscopic culprits for many diseases and how they were spread in the 1860s, Americans remained ignorant of them. New doctors simply followed in their mentors' footsteps, believing that people became ill because of noxious miasms floating through the air. This prevailing theory of disease origin insured the spread of many diseases in all military camps because it precluded the notion that people or insects actually carried and spread the infectious diseases responsible for over half the deaths in the Civil War.[1]

As one writer has aptly put it, "In the life of the average soldier, conditions were perfect for the rampant spread of a long list of afflictions which could decimate a regiment even before it tasted the smoke of its first battle.

Between disease and the Civil War soldier, there was not a fair fight." The 4th Ohio Infantry's experience in 1862 certainly supports that assessment. That unit reported over 800 men fit for duty in July 1862 but listed a mere 120 as fit for duty a few months later in November despite minimal combat casualties (one killed and ten wounded). The diarrhea/dysentery category killed or seriously debilitated most of those 680 Buckeyes who were downgraded from fit to unfit during that period. Similar stories can easily be found in other units in both armies during the war.[2]

In the fall of 1862, Julia Wheelock learned first-hand what a problem disease was for Civil War armies. Wheelock was from Michigan and in September 1862 she traveled to Virginia to make sure that her brother, who had been wounded at Antietam, was being cared for. Unfortunately her brother did not recover from his wounds. But Julia, like so many other women during the war, remained with the ill and wounded soldiers to do what she could to comfort other Michigan boys who would otherwise not have received much kindly attention from an overworked medical staff. There was certainly plenty for her to do in her first months in the hospitals in northern Virginia and Washington. In January 1863 she noted in her diary that the 26th Michigan "suffered much from sickness," with "pneumonia, measles, typhoid fever, and smallpox [doing] fearful work in the regiment." The 26th Michigan was not the only regiment in the Army of the Potomac fighting the legions of deadly microscopic enemies at the beginning of 1863. Dr. Daniel Holt was attached to the 121st New York and he recorded in his diary many of the same experiences Wheelock did. "The health of the regiment is bad," he wrote. "Death is upon our track, and almost every day sees its victim taken to the grave. Yesterday two, and to-day two more were consigned to their last resting place, and still the avenger presses harder and harder . . . ."[3]

So prevalent were lethal infectious diseases, they could affect military operations very directly. During his first attempt to take Vicksburg in July 1862, over one-half of Ulysses S. Grant's troops were on the sick lists. Pierre G. T. Beauregard's decision to abandon the critical railroad town of Corinth, Mississippi, without a fight was due, at least partially, to the fact that over one-third of his army was stricken with various illnesses and no relief appeared in sight. At the end of the Peninsula Campaign, General George McClellan, suffering from dysentery himself, got his army away from Harrison's Landing as much to escape the malaria, dysentery, and typhoid running rampant through his camps as to get away from Robert E. Lee.[4]

Serious diseases did not respect rank, as Jack D. Welsh has shown in two excellent studies of the medical histories of Union and Confederate generals. Welsh pointed out that over half of the Confederacy's generals experienced some significant illness during the war. From May through July 1863 Braxton Bragg suffered from chronic diarrhea, which "culminated in a general breakdown of his physical condition. He reported that he had recovered in July but in fact was in such poor health that he was barely able to continue his duties." Richard Ewell had malaria in the summer of 1862, "fever" in the winter of 1863, and severe diarrhea in the spring of 1864. Edmund Kirby Smith had typhoid in June 1862 and acute dysentery in August 1864. A. P. Hill never seemed to be entirely well. Even Robert E. Lee was seriously ill on several occasions. He had a bad cold in April 1863 and at Gettysburg he had diarrhea "and possibly a recurrence of malaria." The following spring Lee had to deal with a bout of dysentery. Welsh argues also that the estimation that half of the South's generals had some serious illness at least once during the war "is doubtless an underestimation, as illnesses were rarely mentioned in the *Official Records* or the men were treated by unit surgeons in camp and the event never documented."[5]

Union generals' medical histories were better documented and Welsh found that three-fourths of the 583 Northern generals in Ezra Warner's *Generals in Blue* were ill enough to have to see the surgeon at some point during their service. Ambrose Burnside, along with many of his men, suffered from a terrible case of diarrhea in the spring of 1862. John Buford contracted typhoid fever in 1863 and died of it that December. Dan Butterfield, the composer of "Taps," also caught typhoid in July 1862 and could not get out of bed for three months. Joshua Chamberlain contracted malaria in August 1863 and in November "collapsed with malaria-like symptoms." As a result, he was furloughed and on sick leave until the following June. The first half of 1862 was particularly hard on Henry Halleck who contracted measles in January and a raging case of diarrhea that summer. George Meade was stricken with pneumonia twice during the war, in January 1863 and again the following January. Finally, future president James A. Garfield may have been one of the sickest generals in the Union army. He was seriously ill so often it is truly amazing he survived the war at all. In April 1862 he suffered from a severe case of dysentery that by August had contributed to his losing forty-three pounds. The medical records of Northern and Southern generals illustrate very clearly how pervasive and dangerous disease was during the Civil War.[6]

The major problem was simple ignorance of what caused most diseases. Believing as people did at the time in the miasm theory of disease transmission, nobody had the faintest idea that people or insects were the primary means by which most lethal infectious diseases were spread. Smallpox was the only exception but, as will be discussed below, the understanding that people transmitted the deadly disease did little to mitigate its lethal effects. As a result, attention to proper personal and environmental hygiene was lax in Civil War army camps and in Union prisons. Most people in mid-nineteenth-century-America simply did not see the need to be all that scrupulous about proper (by modern standards) personal cleanliness, except to keep from offending others' nasal passages. Such consideration was rare in military camps, however.[7]

When one looks at how Civil War-era physicians and Americans viewed disease origin and treatment the mystery of the high disease mortality in the war's camps disappears. By examining specific killers such as diarrhea/dysentery, pneumonia, and smallpox to name a few that will be discussed below, one discovers why a Civil War soldier was more likely to die in a hospital bed or the surgeon's tent rather than on the field of battle. I hope that by showing how many diseases stalked Civil War camps and just how little was known about how to effectively fight them, the disease deaths found in Northern military prisons will appear less as shocking examples of neglect or apathy and more as the tragically inevitable fortunes of war that they were.

The records often lump diarrhea cases with dysentery cases because they appeared to be so similar to contemporaries. Most prisoners who died in Federal prisons, though, likely died from dysentery. This killer took thousands of Southern prisoners and weakened many more because of the poor sanitation and hygiene habits that were so common in Yankee prisons. The report of Camp Morton's surgeon, Morton J. Kipp, from July 1864 that "Dysentery is prevailing to a considerable extent and is of a very malignant character" is not at all uncommon.[8]

Most soldiers/prisoners likely contracted amebic dysentery. This form of the disease is caused by a one-celled animal that lodges in the intestine and eventually enters the circulatory system through ruptured blood vessels. This process creates abscesses throughout the body, leading to death upon entrance into the liver, lungs, and brain. The body attempts to get rid of the pernicious organism via the intestinal tract, making it vitally important that people wash their hands after visiting the sinks or latrines to prevent spreading the organism to others. When such hygienic procedures are not observed (and they were not) the chances for transmission to others directly by hand-to-hand contact are very good. Infected people who fail to wash their hands after relieving themselves may also spread the disease indirectly by coming into contact with others' food and cooking and eating utensils.

Adequate control practices were rarely, if ever, observed in Federal prisons because nobody understood the various ways people could spread dysentery. Even if they did, it is difficult to imagine how Federal prison officials could have enforced hand-washing rules. Robert E. Lee was said to have lamented the filthy habits of his soldiers, saying once, "They are worse than children, for the latter can be forced [to be cleaner]." Furthermore, because one did not report to the hospital unless one was terribly unwell, generally defined as being unable to get out of bed, dysentery victims tended to remain among the general population, thus constituting a severe health hazard to the rest of the post. Researchers must remember too that contemporary attitudes towards illness in the 1860s were quite different from modern ones. Being sick was so common that it was not cause for concern unless one was unable to get and remain vertical for any period of time. Most people at that time, as one historian has observed, "did not consider themselves victims but accepted what happened and carried on with their lives." It was not uncommon, in fact, for soldiers and officers to stay on duty with fevers, diarrhea, or unhealed wounds. Until dysentery carriers became severely debilitated they remained, often without realizing it, a danger to thousands of their comrades. No doubt part of the reason had to do with the limited and often inadequate hospital space in Union prisons. But, part of the reason infected individuals remained in their barracks was because they knew that seeing the doctor did not always help and, as often as not, made a bad situation worse.[9]

Amebic dysentery was also carried to thousands of Confederate prisoners by flies, which were extremely common in the unsanitary military camps of the Civil War. A Louisiana soldier camped in Virginia in 1861 complained about the fly problem that plagued soldiers' living quarters in his journal, saying:

> When we open our eyes in the morning, we find the canvas roofs and walls of our tents black with [flies] . . . . It needs no morning reveille then to rouse the soldier from his slumbers. The tickling sensations about the ears, eyes, mouth, nose, etc., caused by microscopic feet and inquisitive suckers of an army

numerous as the sands of the sea shore will awaken a regiment of men from innocent sleep to wide-awake profanity more promptly than the near beat of the alarming drum.

Another Southern soldier wrote, "I get vexed at them and commence killing them, but as I believe forty come to every one's funeral I have given it up as a bad job." Annoying as they were, they were not believed to pose any health risk. Rather, flies were just considered another unpleasant facet of army life to be endured along with bad food, long marches, and getting shot at. Not until 1898 did Walter Reed demonstrate the dangers flies posed to military camps as disease vectors.[10]

Flies spread the disease by landing on contaminated feces, picking up the microbes responsible for it, and depositing them wherever they happen to land—on prisoners' faces and hands, on cooking and eating utensils, or directly on prisoners' food. In Federal prisons, and most military camps at the time, sewage and garbage disposal procedures left a great deal to be desired. With thousands of men thrown into a single area in an era when sewers with running water were the exception rather than the rule, where waste disposal measures were barely worthy of the name, flies were omnipresent. A sink or latrine was little more than a ditch to catch waste. "When its edges were clean," one historian has noted, "and earth was thrown into it once a day, it was considered adequate, even though it repelled its users, and would be condemned today."[11]

Several prisons attempted to improve sewage disposal practices to mitigate what must have been horrendous stenches, especially in the warmer months. Camp Douglas employed soil boxes that some poor unfortunate individuals had to empty outside the camp daily. At Point Lookout and Fort Delaware, sinks were constructed over areas where the tide came in periodically to wash much of the sewage away. Despite Northern officials' attempts to deal with malodorous sinks, flies descended on the camps and constituted a constant and dangerous presence. The result was considerable mortality from dysentery and typhoid.

The fact should also be mentioned that soldiers and prisoners, out of modesty or laziness or because they were understandably disgusted by the sinks' effluvia, did not always use the designated areas. This contributed mightily to the fly problems. Virginia private Richard Waldrop wrote home in December 1863 that when he rolled up his bedding one morning he found he had been "lying in . . . something . . . that didn't smell like milk and peaches." Similar scenes played out in Union prisons, as an inspection report from Point Lookout makes nauseatingly clear: "in many places excrement was found in the division streets." At Alton in April 1864, the sinks overflowed, causing human waste matter to saturate the ground near the hospital kitchen until the problem was corrected.[12]

It seems likely that many, perhaps most, Confederate prisoners who contracted amebic dysentery did so as a result of contaminated food or eating utensils. Cooking areas in Northern prisons were often described as in "great disorder and miserable police . . . ." At Johnson's Island an inspector reported that "their [the prisoners'] pork is hung everywhere, greasing everything near it; sometimes it is in the mess-room, then on a shelf in the kitchen, again on the floor." Not surprisingly, diarrhea/dysentery, was listed as responsible for more mortality there than any other disease (46 deaths or 30% of the total of 156). And this was the case at an officers' prison where presumably the inmates were more likely to practice better hygiene.

Most soldiers, and officers too apparently, took a very cavalier attitude towards the purity of their eating utensils, rations, and food preparation areas and often had cause to regret it. John Billings recalled that when Civil War soldiers finished their meals, the dishes "were tossed under the bunk to await the next meal." If soldiers did bother to clean them, simple scraping with a knife followed by a wiping out with leaves or straw was all that was done. "As to knife and fork," according to Billings, "when they got too black to be tolerated—and they had to be of a very sable hue, it should be said—there was no cleansing process so inexpensive, simple, available, and efficient as running them vigorously into the earth a few times." When meat and bread was issued with worms and maggots, new recruits may have cringed for a time, but as they became veterans they simply scooped them out and ate their rations. James Franklin of the 4th Alabama, when describing the dining tables at Fort Delaware, recorded in his diary that "you catch yourself wondering how much grease would be made if the filthy tables were all scraped." In such an environment contaminated flies must have done a great deal of damage.[13]

These variables were also responsible for helping to spread typhoid among Confederate prisoners. Typhoid was especially difficult to control because those who survived a bout with it appeared healthy to the naked eye but in reality remained infectious for months or even years, passing the disease on to countless others who were not so lucky. Not until the 1880s did physicians discover that otherwise asymptomatic people could be deadly typhoid carriers. Also, hospital space was at a premium in Union prisons and typhoid carriers returned to the general populations when their fever abated and they could get up and move about. General Grant experienced this first-hand in 1862 when his army suffered an epidemic of typhoid after taking Fort Donelson. The practice of putting men back on duty or in the general prison population simply because their fever had disappeared, common during the Civil War, led to tragic results for hundreds of Southerners who died of "fever" in Union prison camps.[14]

Unknown to physicians during the Civil War, the microorganisms responsible for typhoid can persist in the individual for months or years without causing obvious problems to the carrier. Carriers shed these potentially deadly pathogens during urination and defecation. Without scrupulous hand-washing afterward, they can transmit typhoid to a considerable number of people—particularly if they live in a confined or restricted environment such as a prison camp. "Typhoid Mary" infected over 200 people while employed as a cook and is perhaps the most famous example of how an outwardly healthy person could pose a serious danger to those around them without ever really being aware of the danger they pose. Less well-known is the case that occurred in 1937 in Croyden, a neighborhood of London, where 310 people contracted typhoid and forty-three died from it when a carrier working on water pipes in that area contaminated the water supply by urinating on nearby ground. As recently as 1940 a study showed that in upstate New York only 17 % of chronic typhoid carriers were known as such. Nobody should be surprised that typhoid fever, or just fevers, which were often typhoid, is listed in numerous inspection reports. But since officials did not know to implement hand-washing regulations (even if they could be enforced) or that typhoid survivors could be, and often were, quite dangerous to others, the deaths attributed to this category cannot be attributed to negligent Yankees.[15]

Pneumonia is another excellent example of the importance of personal and environmental cleanliness in mitigating disease. It was the second leading killer of Southern prisoners. In Union prisons, pneumonia accounted for 5,042 deaths, which was 21 % of the total known to have died from disease, a significant number indeed. Pneumonia is spread very easily in a variety of ways. The disease's causative agent, diplococcus pneumonia, is present in the throat and nasal passages of healthy people. When people cough, sneeze, or even shout, vast quantities of minute droplets are thrust into the air from those passages, which is the medical reason behind polite people's practice of covering their mouths and noses when they cough or sneeze. It is highly doubtful that even had prisoners understood that pneumonia is spread by droplet infection would they have bothered to observe proper social etiquette regarding sneezing and coughing. As mentioned in the previous chapter, prisoners at Fort Delaware spit so much tobacco juice on their barracks' floors that officials had to threaten to cut off the supply if they did not cease that filthy practice, making it difficult to imagine that they were terribly careful about where or on whom they sneezed. It is quite easy to envision, on the other hand, prisoners huddled around barracks stoves during winter months coughing and sneezing on one another and passing around their germs and bacteria.[16]

The common sleeping practice known as "spooning" also contributed to pneumonia's spread. When two or more soldiers "spooned" they lay facing the same direction (like spoons in a drawer) combining body heat and blankets for added warmth. Sleeping areas in military barracks at the time were designed to accommodate two, sometimes three, soldiers per bunk. Prison barracks were no different. Spooning was a very good way to make cold winter nights a bit more bearable but it was also an excellent way to pass along germs and bacteria.[17]

In addition to this direct mode of transmission, pneumonia, like dysentery, may also be spread indirectly. Droplets containing the causative agent can settle on blankets, floors, furniture, and eating utensils becoming part of the dust. Shaking out a blanket or, more rarely, sweeping a floor, stirs up this dust, which can be inhaled by others and infect them. This may sound far-fetched and to a degree it is because healthy individuals' immune systems are quite capable of fighting off pneumonia's agents. But many prisoners arrived in sub-par health, and had access generally to a nutritionally poor diet, which combined to compromise immune systems and make captives increasingly vulnerable to contracting pneumonia.[18]

Contemporary ignorance of proper personal and area hygiene practices was also directly responsible for the contraction and spread of typhus. Wherever individuals who rarely bathe or launder their clothes congregate, body lice are common. Like flies, lice tended to be viewed as harmless, if incredibly annoying. One veteran remembered that everyone, regardless of background, got lice during their military careers. Most were embarrassed the first time the pests were discovered, but over time one veteran explained, "The feeling of intense disgust aroused by the first contact with these creepers soon gave way to hardened indifference, as a soldier realized the utter impossibility of keeping free from them . . . ." Since many old veterans joked that when soldiers did finally take the time to bathe they often found old shirts and socks thought long since lost, the presence of lice is easy to understand. These nasty little creatures went by a variety of nicknames— graybacks, zouaves, Bragg's bodyguard, to name a very few—and were parodied in the soldiers' prayer:

Now I lay me down to sleep,
While graybacks o'er my body creep,
If I should die before I wake,
I pray to God their jaws to break.[19]

While Americans during the Civil War viewed lice as harmless, modern medical personnel have discovered that lice pose a rather serious health hazard as potential typhus vectors. Worse, they often carry the most lethal form of that disease, epidemic or classic typhus. A body louse becomes infected when feeding from an infected host. The contaminated louse then jumps to another host who may contract the disease. Infected lice excrete rickettsiae in their feces and they defecate as they feed and the infective material remains on the skin unless it is washed off. Since bathing was a low priority for most soldiers at the time, the contaminated matter remained on the skin and was often rubbed into a louse's bite wound or existing abrasion or cut when a prisoner scratched his skin. Given the prevalence of the body louse in military camps and typhus's characteristic high fever, it is reasonable to conclude that a significant number of Confederate prisoners' vaguely defined "fevers" were cases of classic typhus. A table in *The Medical and Surgical History of the War of the Rebellion* (which is not complete) shows the maladies that killed Southern prisoners at the nine major prisons discussed in this book. Of the 18,808 disease deaths listed, 1,109 were from a category defined simply as "continued fevers." How many were typhus cannot be determined with any certainty, but it is reasonable to conclude that, given the prevalence of lice, a lot of them were.[20]

Another less common but still potentially deadly form of typhus that likely existed in the camps was endemic or murine typhus. The fleas from rats spread this particular form of the disease in the same basic manner as epidemic typhus. Wherever rats and humans live in close proximity murine typhus will be found. And rats were rather abundant in Northern prison thanks to lax garbage disposal habits. Not that rats were found only in Union prisons, though. They were universally found wherever soldiers giving little thought to where they tossed their garbage stayed for long periods of time. The trenches of World War I are a good example of how large numbers of men living in less than sanitary conditions draw rats in great numbers.

Northern officials tried to make the prisoners do a better job cleaning their barracks and properly disposing of garbage. Unfortunately they were about as successful as most officers in the field were at getting soldiers to police their camps properly. Consequently prisons were often described as "infested in all parts by immense numbers of rats." The result was that many of the Southern prisoners suffering from "fevers" had contracted endemic typhus. If this illness did not kill a prisoner it did weaken him significantly, making him more susceptible to diseases like pneumonia.[21]

Even when doctors did have some idea, usually mistaken, of how an illness or physical ailment operated, the treatment often exacerbated the problem or was practically useless. Nowhere did this reality result in greater mortality than with diarrhea. Often this problem was a symptom of dysentery but in many cases it was not. And though diarrhea is not an infectious disease, it was responsible for putting thousands of Confederate prisoners in early graves. One should remember that this held true for Confederate and Union soldiers in the field as well, where diarrhea was extremely common and actually increased in frequency as the war progressed.

Diarrhea sufferers who went to see doctors for treatment were subjected to a variety of "cures." Lead acetate, sulfuric acid, calomel, and silver nitrate, which, as one historian has aptly described it, "bear about the same relationship to diarrhea as gasoline to a blazing fire," were commonly administered. Ultimately the best chance one had of getting over diarrhea during the Civil War was to steer clear of doctors and hope for the best. In many cases the problem did correct itself. In thousands of others, however it did not and soldiers in the field and in prisons died from problems directly related to having a bad bout of diarrhea.[22]

One reason for that was foods' uncomfortably quick trip through the intestinal tract, which did not allow prisoners' bodies to absorb water into the blood, eventually leading to dehydration. Diarrhea also caused prisoners to lose minerals vital to their bodies' chemical welfare because food did not stay in the digestive system long enough. Unfortunate individuals listed as being "chronic" sufferers, and they were legion during the Civil War, became quite weak and especially susceptible to catching an infectious disease such as pneumonia due to their severely compromised immune systems. In the North's nine major prisons, there were 65,586 cases of diarrhea/dysentery reported and though 58,192 of those cases survived their bout with diarrhea, many of those survivors became prime targets for other diseases. In fact, one report from Fort Delaware specifically stated that most of the pneumonia patients also had diarrhea. It seems safe to conclude, then, that diarrhea/dysentery was directly or indirectly responsible for much of the mortality found in Union prisons. It seems equally safe to conclude that Union officials were not responsible for diarrhea/dysentery in Northern prisons. It was too common a problem in Civil War camps and contemporary treatments could actually make the problem worse.[23]

Smallpox was another disease that doctors believed they understood but were ultimately ineffective against. Smallpox was lumped into the category of "eruptive fevers," which included measles and chickenpox. Most of the eruptive fever deaths that occurred in Union prisons were probably smallpox, however, as that disease is mentioned far more often in prison reports than either measles or chickenpox. This deadly illness hit some facilities harder than others. For example, at Alton, smallpox accounted for 537 deaths or 36.90 % of the 1,455 prisoners who died of disease there between September 1862 and June 1865. This claimed more lives than any other malady, even diarrhea/dysentery, which took 229 prisoners. At the other end of the spectrum, smallpox took only seventeen prisoners at Johnson's Island between June 1863 and June 1865, or 10.89 % of the 156 who died there. Most prisons fell somewhere in between but none escaped this pernicious disease.[24]

Smallpox was one of the few diseases that doctors understood to be communicated by humans. Vaccine and quarantine procedures were known and employed. Unfortunately, they were often ineffective and tardy. At the time, the practice of preventative measures through vaccination was practically unknown in the United States. One went to the doctor to fix an existing problem, not to guard against problems that may never appear. Massachusetts was the only state to enact a compulsory smallpox vaccination law in 1855, but the law allowed so many exemptions that it may as well not have existed.[25]

Smallpox began appearing in the camps and vaccination procedures were implemented to combat the disease. Prisoners were vaccinated against smallpox at every Federal prison camp but the medicines' effects were often negligible. Contemporary smallpox vaccines were primitive and of limited value. Usually prepared from smallpox scabs, a sound enough procedure, by the time they were administered they were often too old to have any of the virus left, rendering them useless. In addition to the age problem, contamination from preparation in unsterile environments further compromised the vaccines' effectiveness.[26]

The records clearly indicate that prisoners in every Northern camp were vaccinated against smallpox and that those exhibiting the tell-tale rash were quarantined to limit this terrible disease's death toll. The Yankees were certainly not negligent when dealing with this illness, if for no other reason than that they were terrified of getting it themselves. Tragically, their efforts were not only compromised by the vaccines' limitations, but their quarantine efforts were often too late. Officials and doctors during the Civil War did not understand smallpox's sub-clinical nature. They did not know, in other words, that smallpox victims were actually most contagious during the day or two prior to the rash's appearance. The upshot of this is that smallpox carriers were routinely in the general populations, spreading this deadly sickness not because Federal officials neglected to quarantine them but because nobody knew they were ill, much less carrying and spreading a lethal disease. Once it became obvious a prisoner had smallpox he was generally isolated quickly. But that was after a lot of damage had already been done.[27]

Alton offers a good example of how smallpox could be a major killer despite Federal efforts to control it. In January 1863, an additional surgeon was assigned to that post to help deal with the problem that had "increased within the past week from 6 to about 100 cases." Though additional medical personnel were assigned to the camp to deal with the smallpox outbreak and though prisoners were vaccinated, the disease raged for much of 1863 with lethal results. In July 1863 an inspection report noted that smallpox was a key health hazard and had been killing prisoners with alarming regularity for over eight months. "Smallpox," the report stated, "has become an almost established disease in the prison. It first appeared in December last, since which time the prison has scarcely been free from it." The result was that at Alton, smallpox was the leading killer of Confederate prisoners.[28]

An additional problem that faced Alton may have been that the quarantine hospital for smallpox patients was not far enough from the prisoners to be as effective as it could have been. Ideally a smallpox house would have been constructed outside the prison compound. This was not done until late 1863 to early 1864, but not because Northern officials were unconcerned about the problem. The local civilian population resisted the erection of a smallpox hospital outside the prison walls because they felt safer if there was a physical barrier between them and the infected prisoners. Officials eventually overcame the resistance and a pest house was built outside the prison walls, though still very close to the compound. Whether or not better quarantine facilities helped bring the smallpox situation at Alton under control is difficult to say with any kind of quantifiable certainty. However, once such facilities became available, smallpox did diminish significantly in inspection reports from mid-1864 through the end of the war.[29]

The story was similar at Camp Douglas where "prisoners were vaccinated as speedily as possible" in the spring of 1863. Camp Douglas battled smallpox more or less continuously until the war ended, losing 823 prisoners to the disease. At Fort Delaware, despite strenuous efforts to fight smallpox, during the period between September 1, 1863, and the middle of December alone there were 526 cases of smallpox with 177 fatalities. That prison appeared to win its battle with smallpox in 1864. In March, camp officials reported that the disease had "entirely disappeared from the island." Unfortunately, the positive claim was short-lived, as smallpox reappeared that August. At Camp Chase in late 1864 and early 1865 smallpox cases averaged ten per day despite vaccination and quarantine procedures there. And at Elmira, the North's most infamous pen, smallpox took 388 prisoners.[30]

The evidence in the wartime records is quite clear that Federal officials did all they knew to do to treat and control smallpox in their prisons. The tragic fact was that in the 1860s that was not enough. By the end of the war, 3,453 Southern prisoners died in the North's nine major prisons from eruptive fevers, most of which were smallpox cases. That is a very significant percentage of the total number of disease fatalities recorded in those prisons. According to *The Medical and Surgical History*, 18,808 Southerners perished from an identifiable disease, with slightly over 18 % of them dying from eruptive fevers. The position that Union officials were somehow directly or indirectly responsible for this significant percentage of disease deaths is simply not supported by the evidence available.[31]

Contemporary misunderstanding, if not downright ignorance, of the importance of a balanced and varied diet also played a significant role in undermining Confederate prisoners' health. Most captives did not have access to nutritional foods on a regular basis. This was especially true for those who did not have friends and family who could send food to them through the mail or who lacked money to use at the prison sutlers. But the problem of malnutrition faced by so many Rebel prisoners did not reflect a callous or neglectful attitude on the Federals' part. As most Americans did at the time, Federal officials thought a good ration was one that was high in calories and filled up the belly. Quantitatively speaking, the Federal rations that the prisoners received were exceptionally generous. Surgeon General William Hammond boasted that the United States Army "had the most abundant food allowance of any soldiers in the world." Even after Congress reduced rations in June 1864 for soldiers and prisoners, Union rations were 20 % larger than British soldiers received and almost double those of French soldiers at the same time.[32]

Of course greater bulk did not translate into a healthy, well-balanced diet. The official ration, while providing plenty of meat and bread, did not include a lot of vegetables, especially greens, and did not contain fruit at all. The Northern government did make an effort during the war to get soldiers and prisoners more vegetables by issuing dehydrated, pressed cakes of beans, carrots, beets, onions, and whatever other vegetable or vegetable-like matter was handy. These unappetizing cakes were officially called desiccated vegetables but the soldiers who had to consume them generally referred to them as "desecrated vegetables" or "baled hay." The intention was good. Desiccated vegetables seemed a good way to provide vegetables to the soldiers out of season and perhaps limit scurvy among troops and prisoners. The major problem, though, was that the drying process robbed the vegetables of a lot of their nutrients, most importantly Vitamin C—the most effective scurvy deterrent.[33]

There can be no doubt that poor diets and medical ignorance contributed significantly to Confederate prisoner mortality. But there were other factors beyond the Yankees' control that also led directly to increased mortality in Union prison camps. Southern prisoners who arrived after having been wounded on the battlefield were likely to either die from their injuries or, as in Stonewall Jackson's case, contract an infectious disease like pneumonia because of their weakened state. This could be a significant number when one considers that after the Battle of Gettysburg alone the Army of the Potomac captured nearly 7,000 Confederates who were too seriously wounded to retreat with Lee's army.[34]

It is impossible to determine with any accuracy what sort of medical attention wounded Rebels received from their captors. About the only thing that is probably certain is that wounded Confederates were treated only once Union boys had been taken care of. After huge engagements like Gettysburg, that could be a considerable and dangerous amount of time. Often during the Civil War, wounded soldiers lay on or around the battlefield for hours or even days before getting critically important first aid. During the time between being wounded and getting medical treatment the wound was highly susceptible to infection. Modern soldiers are issued sterile dressings to guard against bacteria and germs. All the Civil War soldiers had were dirty, sweaty rags and shirts to dress their wounds. Many times by the time a wounded soldier received medical attention infection had often already set in, often with tragic results. But even if a soldier got quick medical attention, which prisoners rarely did, the chances for infection remained unacceptably high because field hospitals and surgeons' instruments were far from sterile. Those unfortunate enough to have to endure amputation were especially likely to develop a post-operative infection that could weaken or even kill them. This was still the era of the theory of "laudable puss" when oozing wounds were thought to be signs of improvement rather than the signs of infection that they actually were.[35]

In December 1863, Lieutenant-Colonel William Pierson, commandant at Johnson's Island, called Hoffman's attention to another set of pre-existing conditions that, contrary to recent claims that most prisoners arrived in "perfectly healthy" condition, applied to many Confederate prisoners: poor health upon arrival. These prisoners were particularly vulnerable to contracting one of the various diseases that stalked Civil War prison camps. Pierson had been reprimanded by Hoffman for some poor inspection reports so his December communication was designed to defend his job performance. But he made a very important point nonetheless when he told Hoffman, "In considering the mortality it should be taken into consideration that many came here after great exposure in camp, on marches, and on the battlefield; many wounded, many sick on their arrival, and many very much emaciated." The defensive Pierson was not alone. Several months earlier, an inspection report described new prisoners' physical condition at Camp Douglas as "wretched." And a Fort Delaware official told Hoffman, "It should be remembered that these men were not in full health when received upon the island." After the war, a contributor to *The Medical and Surgical History* supported the idea that many Confederate prisoners were likely to arrive at Union prisons in sub-par physical condition. The Confederate records were spotty, he said, but the figures that were available "indicate that the Confederate sick-rate was considerably greater than that of the Union forces, and that dirrhoea [*sic*], dysentery, and pulmonary affections, exceedingly prevalent on both armies, were more prevalent among the southern troops."[36]

Historians since then have consistently maintained that Confederate soldiers were more likely to contract an infectious disease than their Union counterparts. Being more likely to come from rural areas, they were less likely to have had any of the so-called childhood diseases like measles and chickenpox. Consequently, they had no natural immunity to them and were very likely to get them when they joined the service. But the Confederacy's increasing inability to feed its soldiers adequately as the war dragged on played a larger role in undermining Southern soldiers' health in the field and at the time of capture. One Confederate soldier complained that his corn meal was "sour, dirty, weevil-eaten, and filled with ants and worms, and not bolted." The Army of Northern Virginia's medical director, Lafayette Guild, said that the poor quality of the rations and the insufficient quantity were "the prime source of disease" among Lee's soldiers. The romantic Lost Cause image of the lean Rebel soldier defending his land and way of life while living on a handful of unbolted cornmeal and a few ounces of fatty pork is not a postwar fabrication. When looking at sickness and mortality in Union prisons one must keep in mind that many captives arrived hurt, ill, and/or malnourished.[37]

Another variable that affected the health of new arrivals was that the Confederacy's need for manpower, especially during the war's final two years, made it increasingly difficult to be choosy about whom it accepted into military service. The shortage of soldiers forced the Confederate government to adopt in 1862 the first draft law in American history, which made all men up to age thirty-five eligible for combat duty—unless one was an owner or an overseer of twenty or more slaves. As the war dragged on, the South pushed the age limit for active duty to fifty, illustrating just how desperate the Confederacy was. Medical inspection of recruits, rare and cursory enough to let women into the service, virtually disappeared. Given these circumstances, few were turned away in 1864 and 1865 for health reasons, though many certainly should have been. One Southern regimental surgeon complained in April 1864 that because Richmond was sending anybody it could find into the service, there "was more sickness in this regiment than in the balance of the division." The number of sickly late-war recruits who wound up in Federal prisons is impossible to determine. But it seems reasonable to conclude that some members of this group were found in all Union prisons and pushed sickness and mortality rates up.[38]

Confederate prisoners' health was also compromised by physical and psychological stress. Modern researchers have concluded that stress plays a direct role "in the onset or exacerbation of all physical illness—from a cold to AIDS." Another researcher has concluded that those "who must cope with stress are more likely to get ill than people who experience little stress." So direct, in fact, is the connection between stress and sickness that a new field, psychoneuroimmunology (PNI) has emerged. PNI researchers have discovered that during stressful periods the body secretes adrenal hormones called glucocorticoids, which weaken the immune system by inhibiting the production of T-cells. T-cells are among a category of white blood cells that fight bacteria that invade the body. The fewer T-cells the body produces the more likely it is that the person will contract an infectious disease. One study showed that this happened at a medical school during exam periods where the stress of important tests reduced T-cell production and increased the number of students reporting to the infirmary.[39]

James McPherson has been one leading historian who has documented the connection between stress and Civil War soldiers' health. He has demonstrated very clearly that Yankees and Rebels both suffered from what today would be called combat stress reaction and post-traumatic stress disorder. Soldiers on both sides endured prolonged exposure to combat, long marches, and living conditions that offered little protection from the worst Mother Nature could dish out. Such stressful conditions seriously compromised many soldiers' health and broke others' completely. The effects were worse when the armies were most active in the spring and summer months, when marching and combat were most frequently experienced. In 1862, for example, during Stonewall Jackson's famous Valley Campaign, Confederate soldiers marched roughly 350 miles and fought five battles in a single month. An officer from the 27th Virginia observed shortly after the campaign, "[I am] in a state of exhaustion . . . . I have never [seen] the Brigade so completely broken down and unfit for service." Things only got more stressful for Jackson's men as they moved from the Shenandoah Valley to Richmond to help throw George McClellan's forces back from the gates of Richmond during the Seven Days' Battles. After the Seven Days', a South Carolinian commented on one his comrades' broken condition. Though his friend had not been physically injured in the fighting, he had "almost lost the entire use of his hands and legs and is almost as helpless as poor little Johnnie."[40]

During the war's final two years the soldiers' stress actually increased. From 1861 through 1863 campaigning and fighting could be fairly regular but generally after major battles the armies withdrew and did not engage each other again for weeks or even months. This general ebb and flow of stressful events changed dramatically when Grant and Sherman assumed leading roles in formulating and executing plans for breaking Southern resistance. Both men believed that the only way to defeat the South was through constant pressure on the enemy's resources and manpower. The result was that the major armies in the eastern and western theaters were in almost daily contact with each other. Oliver Wendell Holmes, Jr., serving in the Army of the Potomac, wrote that the prolonged stress of life in and around the Petersburg trenches had caused "many a man [to go] crazy since this campaign began from the terrible pressure on mind and body." A Confederate wrote from Georgia that Sherman was putting so much pressure on them that "sleeping has been almost out of the question—fighting all day & marching during the night." There can be little doubt that many soldiers on both sides captured during the war's final year were, to use a bit of modern slang, stressed out. These men were not good candidates for survival in enemy prison camps.[41]

Adding to the problem was the fact that getting away from the pressures found in the field did not necessarily translate into decreased stress levels. Being held by the enemy actually was an additional stressor. One thing scientists have found is that stress levels often rise or fall based on a person's perception of the amount of control they have over their lives. When people feel like they generally control what happens to them, they are less likely to show significant levels of stress. These people are also healthier physically. On the other hand, people who feel that they have little to no control over their lives tend to show higher levels of stress and tend to be less physically fit. Prisoners had no control over what happened to them. They were under the complete control of the enemy. Added to that stressful situation was not having any idea how long their incarceration would last. The idea that they could be trapped in an enemy prison for years must have weighed heavily on many prisoners' minds.[42]

To this point this chapter has argued that much of the sickness and mortality found in Northern prisons can be attributed to factors other than neglect or abuse. Admittedly, a lot of the evidence, while compelling, is difficult to quantify. This is not the case, however, when looking at recovery rates from illness in the various prisons. When examining statistics from *The Medical and Surgical History* for the North's nine major prisons, 90.36% of Confederate prisoners who were treated for some sort of illness recovered. When Elmira's recovery rate (77.3%) is removed as the glaring anomaly that it was, the overall recovery rate at the eight remaining prisons rises to 92.43%. Three of the sites—Johnson's Island, Fort Delaware, and Alton—posted recovery rates above 95% while three others—Camp Douglas, Camp Chase, and Point Lookout—had recovery rates of at least 90%. Rock Island and Camp Morton were not far behind with recovery rates of 88.2% and 86.8% respectively. These rates would not be anything to boast about today, but for the time period they were not bad at all and show that Union officials took their medical duties towards Southern prisoners seriously and posted pretty decent records as a general rule.[43]

That becomes more clear when recovery rates at the North's major prisons are compared to the South's major hospital, Chimborazo Hospital in Richmond, before supply shortages became a serious issue. From 1861 through December 1862, 11.39% of the cases treated at the Richmond facility resulted in death—an 88.61% recovery rate. Six of the North's nine major prisons posted better recovery rates than that and only Elmira's was significantly worse. The wartime evidence, while spotty in places, suggests strongly that Confederate soldiers who got sick were at least as likely to recover when treated in Yankee prisons as they were in the largest hospital in their nation's capital. In fact, McPherson has pointed out, "Confederate prisoners were 29% less likely to die in Yankee prisons than to die of disease in their own army . . . ." The point should also be made here that since only one Union prison, Elmira, posted much lower recovery rates for various diseases than Chimborazo, charges that Southern prisoners died because the Yankees neglected sick prisoners or denied them medicines altogether as part of a vast and destructive retaliation program seem to run counter to the available facts.[44]

Finally, if one consults wartime records one will find that the three deadliest diseases in Northern prisons were the same three that killed the most Confederate soldiers in the field and in Southern hospitals: diarrhea/dysentery, pneumonia, and smallpox. The biggest killer, diarrhea/dysentery, had no effective cure at the time, making it difficult to prove that prisoners who died from this extremely common malady were victims of Northern apathy. Smallpox was one of the big three and killed thousands despite vaccination and quarantine procedures. And generally speaking, pneumonia victims recovered about as often in captivity as they did at Chimborazo. It would seem, then, that Southern soldiers who died from these maladies did not do so because they were neglected. If Yankee officials cannot be held responsible for causing the mortality attributed to these three categories, then they are exonerated of responsibility for the vast majority of deaths that occurred in their prisons.

Diarrhea/dysentery .... 5,965 deaths or 31.7% of the 18,808 recorded

Pneumonia .... 5,042 deaths or 26.8% of the 18,808 recorded

Smallpox .... 3,453 deaths or 18.35% of the 18,808 recorded

OR

14,460 deaths or 76.88 % of the 18,808 recorded

If one adds the 1,147 prisoners who died of "other diseases," Union officials could stand absolved of 15,607 deaths or 82.98% of the 18,808 recorded in *The Medical and Surgical History* at the nine major prisons. That does not seem unreasonable. If one cannot prove what a person actually died of, one cannot hold someone guilty of causing the death. In other words, one cannot be charged with murder (much less convicted of it) without adequate proof that a murder actually took place.[45]

Ultimately when attempting to assess why Confederate prisoners died in captivity, one must keep in mind a number of things. One must also consider the contemporary medical ignorance of most diseases' causation and, therefore, of effective control mechanisms. Perhaps the most important thing to remember is that disease mortality during the Civil War was high only by modern standards. Grisly as it may sound, the American Civil War was the healthiest conflict fought to that time in the Western world. One must also consider that the overall 12% mortality rate was not out of line for large military camps, especially stationary ones, in the mid-nineteenth century as the case of the Army of the Potomac illustrated in May 1864. The army "impressed observers as healthy despite its 11.41% disease morbidity rate for the month." In the end, Northern officials appear to have done the best they could at the time for Confederate prisoners of war. Tragically that was often not enough.[46]

Endnotes

1. James M. McPherson, *Battle Cry of Freedom: The Civil War Era* (New York: Oxford University Press, 1988), 485–87; Stewart Brooks, *Civil War Medicine* (Springfield, IL: Charles C. Thomas, 1966), 9, 125–27; Peter Joseph, ed., *The Wounded River: The Civil War Letters of John Vance Lauderdale, M.D.* (East Lansing: Michigan State University Press, 1993), 20–21; George W. Adams, *Doctors in Blue: The Medical History of the Union Army in the Civil War* (New York: Henry Schuman, 1952), 222–23; Richard H. Shryock, *Medicine in*

America: Historical Essays (Baltimore, MD: The Johns Hopkins University Press, 1966), 90–108; Paul E. Steiner, *Disease in the Civil War: Natural Biological Warfare in 1861–1865* (Springfield, IL: Charles C. Thomas, 1968), 39–41; James I. Robertson, *Tenting Tonight: The Soldier's Life* (Alexandria, VA: Time-Life Books, 1984), 78–83.

2. Joseph, 20–21; Shryock, 90–108; Adams, 222–23; Steiner, 28–36; Brooks, 106–12.

3. Julia S. Wheelock, *The Boys in White: The Experience of a Hospital Agent In and Around Washington* (New York: Lange and Hillman, 1870), 39, 78, 241; James M. Grenier, Janet L. Coryell, and James R. Smithers, eds., *A Surgeon's Civil War: The Letters and Diary of Daniel M. Holt, M.D.* (Kent, OH: Kent State University Press, 1994), 33–36, 58–59, 63, 68–71, 75, 106, 127, 146, 243–44; Steiner, 28–36.

4. Steiner, 26–49; McPherson, *Battle Cry of Freedom*, 486–88.

5. Jack D. Welsh, *Medical Histories of Confederate Generals* (Kent, OH: Kent State University Press, 1995), xii–xv, 18–19, 23, 63–65, 99–101, 134–35, 198–99

6. Jack D. Welsh, *Medical Histories of Union Generals* (Kent, OH: Kent State University Press, 1996), xiv–xvii, 46, 50, 63–64 123–24, 145–46, 209–10, 225–26, 300–1.

7. Robert E. Denney, *Civil War Medicine: Care and Comfort of the Wounded* (New York: Sterling Publishing Co., Inc., 1994), 7–8; Joseph, 20–21; Steiner, 4–5; Brooks, 6–9; Adams, 202–4.

8. United States War Department, *War of the Rebellion: Official Records of the Union and Confederate Armies* (Washington, D.C.: Government Printing Office, 1899; repr., Harrisburg, PA: Telegraph Press, 1971) Series II, Volume 5, 133–35; Volume 6, 424–26; Volume 7, 513 (hereafter cited as *OR* with all references from Series II unless otherwise indicated).

9. United States War Department, *War of the Rebellion: Official Records of the Union and Confederate Armies* (Washington, D.C.: Government Printing Office, 1899; repr., Harrisburg, PA: Telegraph Press, 1971), Series II, Volume 5, 133–35; Volume 6, 424–26; Volume 7, 513, 1093–94 (hereafter cited as *OR*, with all references from Series II); H. H. Cunningham, *Doctors in Gray: The Confederate Medical Service* (Baton Rouge: Louisiana State University Press, 1958, 1993), 166–67; Gaylord W. Anderson and Margaret G. Arnstein, *Communicable Disease Control* (New York: Macmillan, 1953), 187–90; United States Public Health Service, *The Control of Communicable Diseases in Man* (Washington, D.C.: Government Printing Office, 1950), 40–41; Carl C. Dauer, Robert F. Corns, and Leonard M. Schuman, *Infectious Diseases* (Cambridge, MA: Harvard University Press, 1968), 25; McPherson, *Battle Cry*

of Freedom, 486–88; Bell I. Wiley, *The Life of Johnny Reb: The Common Soldier of the Confederacy* (Baton Rouge: Louisiana State University Press, 1943), 252; Welsh, *Medical Histories of Union Generals*, xviii; Brooks, 115–16, 125–27; Shryock, 90–108; Adams, 194–230.

10. Wiley, *The Life of Johnny Reb*, 248–49; Cedric A. Mims, *The Pathogens of Infectious Diseases* (New York: Academic Press, Inc., 1977), 33–36; Deward K. Grissom, *Communicable Diseases* (Dubuque, IA: William C. Brown, Co., 1971), 15–16; Dauer, Corns, and Schuman, 9–16.

11. Adams, 204.

12. *OR*, Volume 6, 740–45, 826–29, 848, 851, 967–70; Volume 7, 52, 84–86, 172, 465–66; Mims, 33–36; Grissom, 15–16; Anderson and Arnstein, 189–90; U.S. Public Health Service, 40–41; Dauer, Corns, and Schuman, 9–16; Wiley, *The Life of Johnny Reb*, 248–49; Adams, 204.

13. *OR*, Volume 6, 281, 364–66, 371–74, 479–80, 575–78, 826–29, 878–80, 967–70; Volume 7, 84–86, 172, 484–87, 492, 691–92, 1091–94; *The Medical and Surgical History*, Volume I, Part III, 46; James H. Franklin, *Diary*, Museum of the Confederacy, Richmond, Virginia; John D. Billings, *Hardtack and Coffee: The Unwritten Story of Army Life* (Boston, MA: George M. Smith and Co., 1887; repr., Lincoln: University of Nebraska Press, 1993), 76–77; Steiner, 6; Robertson, *Tenting Tonight*, 85–87.

14. Welsh, *Medical Histories of Union Generals*, xvii; Joseph, 20–22; Adams, 222–23.

15. *OR*, Volume 5, 205–6; Volume 6, 281, 364–66, 371–74, 392–93, 575–78, 682, 878–80, 967–70, 1039–41; Volume 7, 448–50, 497–98, 580–81, 1235; Macfarlane Burnet and David O. White, *Natural History of Infectious Disease* (London: Cambridge University Press, 1972), 125–26; Mims, 39, 228; Anderson and Arnstein, 168–70; U.S. Public Health Service, 144–46; Adams, 203; Brooks, 125–27; Joseph, 20–21; Welsh, *Medical Histories of Union Generals*, xvii.

16. Brooks, 118–19, 125–27; Shryock, 90–108.

17. John H. Gibson, *Diary*, Virginia Historical Society, Richmond, Virginia; Wiley, *The Life of Johnny Reb*, 56, 254–55; McPherson, *Battle Cry of Freedom*, 486–87; Brooks, 118–19, 125–27; Shryock, 90–108; Billings, 49, 78.

18. *Medical and Surgical History*, Volume I, Part III, 46; Burnet and White, 122, 124–26; Anderson and Arnstein, 335–36; Imperato, 203–97; Brooks, 118–19; Steiner, 6, 26–49, 116, 132; Joseph, 20–21.

19. Billings, 79–83; Wiley, *The Life of Johnny Reb*, 251.

20. *OR*, Volume 5, 132–35, 216–17; Volume 6, 392–93, 479–80, 682, 967–70; Volume 7, 84–86, 484–87; United States War Department, *The Medical and*

Surgical History of the War of the Rebellion (Washington, D.C.: Government Printing Office, 1870), Volume I, Part III, 46–47; Guy P. Youmans, *The Biological and Clinical Basis of Infectious Diseases* (Philadelphia, PA: W. B. Saunders Co., 1986), 685; Wiley, *The Life of Johnny Reb*, 251; Billings, 79–83; Anderson and Arnstein, 449–51; Imperato, 589–90; U.S. Public Health Service, 146–47; Dauer, Corns, and Schuman, 108–9.

21. *OR*, Volume 5, 133–35, 216–17; Volume 6, 365–66, 479–80, 826–30; Volume 7, 554–56; *Medical and Surgical History*, Volume I, Part III, 46; Imperato, 593–94; Youmans, 688; Cunningham, 166–67.

22. Brooks, 117.

23. *Medical and Surgical History*, Volume I, Part III, 46. The table on that page only covers the North's nine major prisons and does not include figures for the entire war. It does, however, contain figures for most prisoners' deaths: 18,808 of the 23,591. Erwin D. Cyan, *Vitamins in Your Life* (New York: Simon and Schuster, 1974), 165–66; Ronald R. Watson, ed., *Nutrition, Disease Resistance, and Immune Function* (New York: Marcel Dekker, Inc., 1984), 35–43; Wiley, *The Life of Johnny Reb*, 247; Wiley, *The Life of Billy Yank: The Common Soldier of the Union* (Baton Rouge: Louisiana State University Press, 1952), 238–46, Robertson, *Tenting Tonight*, 85–87; Billings, 130–37; Brooks, 113–17; Adams, 206–13, Shryock, 90–108; Steiner, 6, 42, 116, 124–28; Mims, 195, 248–50 Grierson, Coryell, and Smithers, 58–59, 63, 71, 75, 106, 127, 146, 243–44.

24. *Medical and Surgical History*, Volume I, Part II, 36–37; Volume I, Part III, 46.

25. Dauer, Corns, and Schuman, 78; Denney, 7

26. Adams, 219-220; Brooks, 120.

27. *OR* Volume 5, 282, 444, 449–53, 495, 497–98, 537; Volume 6, 70, 391, 422–35; Grimes, 303; U.S. Public Health Service, 119–21; Imperato, 348–50.

28. *OR*, Volume 5, 150, 285, 357, 450, 495–98; Volume 6, 61, 96, 104–5, 392–93, 967–70; The *Medical and Surgical History*, Volume I, Part III, 46.

29. *OR*, Volume 6, 160, 179, 1123; Volume 7, 536–37.

30. *The Medical and Surgical History*, Volume I, Part III, 46; *OR*, Volume 5, 108, 345–46, 449–53, 495, 504, 537, 686, Volume 6, 422, 435, 637, 736, 740–45, 825, 1000–1; Volume 7, 665, 686–87, 1272–73.

31. *The Medical and Surgical History*, Volume I, Part II, 36–37; Volume I, Part III, 46.

32. Wiley, *The Life of Billy Yank*, 224–27; Adams, 206–13; Billings, 108–12, 138–39.

33. Robertson, *Tenting Tonight*, 86–87, Cyan, 150–63; Denney, 9–10; Adams, 206–13; Brooks, 106–12; Joseph, 20–22; Mims, 248–50; William C. Davis,

Rebels and Yankees: The Fighting Men of the Civil War (New York: Salamander Books, 1989), 189.

34. Stephen Sears, *Gettysburg* (New York: Houghton Mifflin Co., 2003), 498.

35. *Medical and Surgical History*, Volume I, Part II, 36–37, Volume I, Part III, 46; Herbert M. Schiller, "Health and Medicine," *Encyclopedia of the Confederacy*, ed. Richard N. Current (New York: Simon and Schuster, 1993), Volume 2, 755–56; Edward L. Munson, "The Army Surgeon and His Work," in *The Photographic History of the Civil War: Prisons and Hospitals* (Secaucus, NJ: The Blue and Grey Press, 1987), 231–32.

36. Sanders, 5; *OR*, Volume 5, 282, 343–46, 449–53, 497–98, 537; Volume 6, 391, 422, 435, 1039–41; Volume 7, 1240; Volume 8, 990–1001; *Medical and Surgical History*, Volume I, Part II, 36–37, Volume I, Part III, 63, 70–71, 885–86.

37. McPherson, *Battle Cry of Freedom*, 486–88; Wiley, *The Life of Johnny Reb*, 90–107, 246–47; Cunningham, 163, 175–80; Denney, 9–11; Brooks, 9, 20–21, 106–10; Steiner, 119–28; Welsh, *Medical Histories of Confederate Generals*, xii–xv.

38. *Medical and Surgical History*, Volume I, Part III, 63, 70–71; *OR*, Volume 5, 282, 343–46, 449–53, 497–98, 537; Volume 6, 391, 422, 435, 1039–41; Volume 7, 1240; Volume 8, 990–1001; McPherson, *Battle Cry of Freedom*, 326; Wiley, *The Life of Johnny Reb*, 90–107, 244–46, 250–60; Robertson, *Tenting Tonight*, 79–80; Denny, 11; Brooks, 9, 20–21; Shryock, 90–108; Steiner, 26–49; Cunningham, 163–65.

39. Robert H. Lauer, *Social Problems and the Quality of Life*, 7th Ed. (Boston: McGraw-Hill, 1998), 511–18; Robert E. Emery and Thomas F. Oltmans, *Essentials of Abnormal Psychology* (Upper Saddle River, NJ: Prentice-Hall, 2000), 217–39; Mims, 250–54.

40. James McPherson, *For Cause and Comrades: Why Men Fought in the Civil War* (New York: Oxford University Press, 1997), 164; Cunningham, 163, 170–73; Mims, 250–54.

41. McPherson, *For Cause and Comrades*, 164–67; *Medical and Surgical History*, Volume I, Part III, 70–71, 885–86.

42. *Medical and Surgical History*, Volume I, Part III, 70–71, 885–86; Emery and Oltmans, 224; Lauer, 515–18.

43. *The Medical and Surgical History*, Volume I, Part III, 46.

44. *Medical and Surgical History*, Volume I, Part III, 30, 46; McPherson, *Ordeal by Fire: The Civil War and Reconstruction*, 3rd ed. (Boston: McGraw Hill, 2001), 485–92.

45. *Medical and Surgical History*, Volume I, Part II, 2–7, 31, 36-37; Volume I, Part III, 45–47, 191, 209.

46. *Medical and Surgical History*, Volume I, Part II, 1–7, 26–28, 36–37; Volume I, Part III, 11, 30, 45–47, 63–64, 70–71, 885–86; Duncan, 390–407; McPherson, *Battle Cry of Freedom*, 484–87; Wiley, *The Life of Johnny Reb*, 250–60; Dauer, Corns, and Schuman, 25, 80, 174–75; Shryock, 90–108; Denny, 7, 11; Adams, 194–230; Brooks, 6, 9, 20–21, 106–12; Steiner, 26–49; Joseph, 19–22; Geriner, Coryell, and Smiters, 58–59, 63, 71, 75, 106, 127, 146, 243–44.

CONCLUSION

THIS STUDY DOES NOT CLAIM TO BE THE LAST WORD on Federal policies or living conditions in Yankee prisons during the Civil War. Neither has it sought to portray Union prisons as pleasant places to have been confined. Rather, this study has sought to demonstrate why the predominately negative impression of Union authorities' policies and actions towards Confederate prisoners as neglectful, apathetic, and deliberately cruel is in need of serious reevaluation. The evidence supporting the prevailing stereotype of the cruel and negligent Yankee comes almost exclusively from the postwar writing of Southerners who, like their Northern counterparts, exploited the prisoner of war issue to achieve a number of goals. Rarely was one of those goals the objective accounting of life in Federal prisons during the war. This study has shown why researchers should heed the advice James Ford Rhodes gave nearly a century ago and treat postwar memoirs by ex-prisoners with extreme skepticism and rarely (if ever) as reliable primary source material.

Perhaps the most important misconception I have sought to clear up is the one surrounding the North's decision to suspend the prisoner exchange cartel in mid-1863. This decision has been held up for generations as the ultimate proof of Yankee callousness and calculation. The Union government did not, as has been so often claimed, suspend the agreement because doing so would weaken the Southern war effort by increasing the manpower disparity between North and South. The evidence suggests strongly that the decision was prompted by the Davis administration's policy to enslave or kill black soldiers and execute the white leaders of African American soldiers. From 1863 through 1865 Northern officials responded to Southern pleas to resume exchanges by telling them consistently that all prisoners held at that point would stay incarcerated until the Confederacy rescinded its inequitable policies regarding black prisoners and allowed them to be exchanged under the 1862 cartel on the same basis as whites. That Confederate officials viewed black soldiers as illegitimate was their right, of course, but Washington was not obliged to fight the war on its enemy's terms. Ultimately the Federals had the right to use black soldiers to save the country and Confederate authorities even decided, too late, to do the very same thing. It is also very difficult to argue that Northern authorities did not have a duty to protect their soldiers from being enslaved or killed if they were captured in battle. They did that the only way they could, by imposing a meaningful sanction (suspension of the exchange cartel) on the Confederacy to persuade the enemy to alter a particular policy.

Northern officials were far from perfect. They certainly made their fair share of mistakes in this area. At a number of the prisons, officers were placed in charge who were grossly incompetent or even lazy, making conditions worse than they should have been. The most glaring and consistent problem with Northerners' management of their prisoner of war facilities, though, was their failure to anticipate potential problems and deal with them as effectively as possible before they became serious. After the cartel broke down, for example, and the South was showing a fierce determination to cling to their right to treat blacks any way they saw fit, Union authorities should have realized that they would be responsible for increasing numbers of prisoners for an extended period of time. They did not do that, however. Rather than prepare for increasing numbers by, say, expanding barracks at existing facilities and scouting out new sites, they reacted to problems such as crowded living quarters on the fly. The same was the case with scurvy cases. Officials knew that fruit and vegetables were effective preventatives but increased amounts were rarely, if ever, provided until scurvy was actually reported as a problem. As a final example of failing to take what we would today call a pro-active approach was the way Foster's Pond at Elmira was handled. True, landholders in the area were part of the problem cleaning up that stagnant body of water, but by that late stage of the war Union officials did not need to be told by inspectors that the pond was an environmental hazard at the camp. They ought to have realized that ahead of time and begun work to mitigate its unhealthy effects months earlier than they actually did.

Such examples of inefficiency and poor planning have tended to become trees obscuring researchers' view of the forest here. Taken as a whole, Federal prisoner of war policies and conditions in their prisons were quite humane and enlightened for the time. General Orders 100, for example, was considered humane enough to form the basis for many later international agreements on the subject of prisoners of war. And while incompetent officers were sometimes placed in charge of the camps, they were never allowed to remain in their positions. The existence of a regular and meaningful inspection system for every prison as well as compelling evidence that conditions in Union prisons did improve over time points to the conclusion that Federal officials intended to treat Confederate prisoners as well as possible under the circumstances throughout the war, not just in its earlier stages. As for the 1864 "retaliation program," the restrictions associated with that were not only too short-lived to have been responsible for substantially increasing death and discomfort in Union prisons, at many facilities most of the mortality recorded there took place before the program was even discussed in the spring of 1864. Finally, and perhaps most significantly, in most Yankee prison camps Confederates were more likely to recover from communicable camp diseases like pneumonia, smallpox, and dysentery in those facilities than in their own country's major medical facility.

If being a Confederate prisoner during the Civil War was unpleasant and potentially dangerous, and it was both of those things, it was not because the Yankees went out of their way to make it so. If Confederate prisoners were victims of anything, it was the time in which they lived. Contemporary ignorance about nutrition and the true causes of most infectious diseases made conditions in Civil War armies' camps and Union prisons very unhealthy. Primitive living conditions were the norm in both; unbalanced, nutritionally deficient diets were the norm in both; ineffective, primitive medical treatment was the norm in both; disease mortality was the norm in both. Confederate suffering and death in Union prisons were truly tragic aspects of America's Civil War, but the wartime evidence strongly points to the conclusion that they were far more attributable to the misfortunes of war than to systematic Yankee cruelty or neglect.

APPENDIX A

RECOVERY RATES FROM DISEASE AT THE NINE MAJOR UNION PRISONS AND AT CHIMBORAZO HOSPITAL[1]

Facility	Number of Diseases Treated	Number of Deaths from Disease	Recovery Rate
Johnson's Island	3,571	156	95.64%
Fort Delaware	43,571	2,199	94.96%
Alton	28,766	1,455	94.95%
Camp Douglas	68,809	3,929	94.29%
Camp Chase	23,946	1,739	92.74%
Chimborazo Hospital	23,849	2,717	88.61%
Rock Island	13,453	1,589	88.19%
Camp Morton	8,863	1,175	86.75%
Point Lookout	43,571	3,639	85.33%
Elmira	10,178	2,927	71.25%

1. *Medical and Surgical History of the War of the Rebellion, Volume I, Part III,* 30, 46.

APPENDIX B

LEADING KILLERS OF CONFEDERATE PRISONERS OF WAR AT THE INDIVIDUAL CAMPS[1]

Prison	#1 Killer	#2 Killer	#3 Killer	Percentage of total Disease Mortality at Site
Alton	Eruptive Fevers (Smallpox) 537 deaths	Pneumonia 276 Deaths	Diarrhea/Dysentery 229 Deaths	71.6% (1,042 of 1,455)
Camp Chase	Pneumonia 954 Deaths	Eruptive Fevers 362 Deaths	Diarrhea/Dysentery 226 Deaths	88.67% (1,542 of 1,739)
Camp Douglas	Pneumonia 1,290 Deaths	Eruptive Fevers 823 Deaths	Diarrhea/Dysentery 690 Deaths	71.69% (2,817 of 3,929)
Camp Morton	Pneumonia 495 Deaths	Diarrhea/Dysentery 315 Deaths	Malarial Fevers 119 Deaths	79.06% (929 of 1,175)
Elmira	Diarrhea/Dysentery 1,394 Deaths	Pneumonia 773 Deaths	Eruptive Fevers 388 Deaths	87.29% (2,555 of 2,927)
Fort Delaware	Diarrhea/Dysentery 644 Deaths	Eruptive Fevers 472 Deaths	Pneumonia 401 Deaths	68.98% (1,577 of 2,199)
Johnson's Island	Diarrhea/Dysentery 46 Deaths	Continued Fevers 26 Deaths	Pneumonia 25 Deaths	62.17% (97 of 156)
Rock Island	Eruptive Fevers 436 Deaths	Pneumonia 397 Deaths	Diarrhea/Dysentery 363 Deaths	75.26% (1,196 of 1,589)
Point Lookout	Diarrhea/Dysentery 2,050 Deaths	Pneumonia 425 Deaths	Eruptive Fevers 333 Deaths	77.16% (2,808 of 3,639)

LEADING KILLERS OF CONFEDERATE PRISONERS OF WAR AT THE 9 MAJOR PRISONS

#1 Killer	#2 Killer	#3 Killer	# and % of 18,808 Disease Fatalities
Diarrhea/Dysentery 5,965 Deaths (31.7%)	Pneumonia 5,042 Deaths (26.8%)	Eruptive Fevers 3,453 Deaths (18.3%)	14,460 Deaths 76.8% of Total

---

1. *Medical and Surgical History of the War of the Rebellion, Volume I, Part III*, 30, 46.

BIBLIOGRAPHY

Unpublished Primary Sources

Adams, Richard H. Jr. Papers. Virginia Military Institute.

Allen, Henry Archibald, Papers. University of Virginia.

Allen, John C. Diary. Virginia Historical Society, Richmond, Virginia.

Allen, Matthew Wood. Journal. Virginia Historical Society, Richmond, Virginia.

Alston, Trudy. Diary. Southern Historical Collection, University of North Carolina.

Bagby, Robert Anderson. Diary. Museum of the Confederacy, Richmond, Virginia.

Barber, Flavel C. Papers. Lilly Library, Indiana University, Bloomington, Indiana.

Basinger, William Starr. Papers. Virginia Historical Society, Richmond, Virginia.

Bell, John. Papers, University of Virginia.

Berkeley, Henry Robinson. Papers. Virginia Historical Society, Richmond, Virginia.

Bingham, Robert. Papers. Southern Historical Collection, University of North Carolina.

Bird Family Papers. Virginia Historical Society, Richmond, Virginia.

Bowden, John Malachi. Papers. Duke University.

Boyle, Francis Atherson. Works. Southern Historical Collection, University of North Carolina

Branch Family Papers. Hargrett Rare Book and Manuscript Library, University of Georgia Libraries.

Britton Family Papers. Virginia Historical Society, Richmond, Virginia.

Brown, Thomas W., Jr. Letters. Duke University.

Bullock Family Papers. University of Kentucky.

Burnley, Pattie. Papers. Kentucky Historical Society.

Burrows, Francis Asbury. Papers. University of South Carolina.

Caldwell, Eliza F. Papers. Duke University.

Camp Chase, Ohio. Papers. Virginia Historical Society, Richmond, Virginia.

Carrington Family Papers. Virginia Historical Society, Richmond, Virginia.

Carter, John C. Papers. Ohio Historical Society.

Cave, Richard. Papers. University of Virginia.

Cheeseborough, Esther B. Papers. University of South Carolina.

Cocke Family Papers. Virginia Historical Society, Richmond, Virginia.

Coleman Family Papers. Virginia Historical Society, Richmond, Virginia.

Collins, John Overton. Papers. Virginia Historical Society, Richmond, Virginia.

Colwell, Porter T. Correspondence. Ohio Historical Society.

Couper, John. Family Papers. Georgia Historical Society.

Cox, E.L. Papers. Virginia Historical Society, Richmond, Virginia.

Confederate States – Army – Miscellany. Prison Papers, 1861-65. Collection #1184. Duke University.

Cumming Family Papers. Augusta State University, Augusta, Georgia.

Davis, Wilbur Fisk. Papers. University of Virginia.

Davis, William Jonathan. Papers. Filson Historical Society.

Deaton, Noah. Letters. Duke University.

De Wolf, Mark. Letters. Southern Historical Collection, University of North Carolina.

Ditto, Captain William L. Collection. Rutherford B. Hayes Presidential Center, Freemont, Ohio.

Douglas, Charles Achilles. Papers. Virginia Historical Society. Richmond, Virginia.

Dunn, John D. Papers. Duke University.

Eames, William Mark. Papers. Tennessee State Library and Archives.

Edwards, Leroy Summerfield. Correspondence. Virginia Historical Society, Richmond, Virginia.

Ellis, Henry M. Letters. Vermont Historical Society.

Finney Family Papers. Virginia Historical Society, Richmond, Virginia.

Forsberg, August. Memoir. Collection #109. Washington & Lee University.

Frary, George Spencer. Diary. Western Reserve Historical Society.

Fuller, Joseph Pryor. Papers. Southern Historical Collection, University of North Carolina.

Gibson, John Alexander. Diary. Virginia Historical Society, Richmond, Virginia.

Gordon, D.E. Diary. Museum of the Confederacy, Richmond, Virginia.

Gorman, John. Papers. Duke University.

Gramling Civil War Diary. Special Collections, Robert Manning Strozier Library, Florida State University.

Green, Adeline Burr Davis. Papers. Duke University.

Greer, William Robert. Papers. Duke University.

Gunn, James M. Diary. Museum of the Confederacy, Richmond, Virginia.

Guy, John Henry. Diary. Virginia Historical Society, Richmond, Virginia.

Haigh, William H. Papers. Southern Historical Collection, University of North Carolina.

Hairston, Elizabeth Seawell. Papers. Southern Historical Collection, University of North Carolina.

Hamlin, Theodore P. Papers. Southern Historical Collection, University of North Carolina.

Haws, Samuel H. Diary in Katherine Heath Hawes Papers. Virginia Historical Society, Richmond, Virginia.

Holladay Family Papers. University of Virginia.

Holliday, B. T. "The Account of My Capture." Southern Historical Collection, University of North Carolina.

Holloway, John William. Papers. Virginia Historical Society, Richmond, Virginia.

Jameson, James H. Letters. Virginia Military Institute.

Johnson, Elijah Saunders. Diary. Museum of the Confederacy, Richmond, Virginia.

Johnson's Island Prison Collection. Rutherford B. Hayes Presidential Center, Freemont, Ohio.

Jones, Benjamin Anderson. Papers. Virginia Historical Society, Richmond, Virginia.

Jones, George William, Letters. Duke University.

Jones, Madison P. Letters. Auburn University.

Joyner Family papers. Southern Historical Collection, University of North Carolina.

Kern, Joseph Mason. Papers. Southern Historical Collection, University of North Carolina.

Killen, William E. Diary. Cleveland Public Library.

Kinsey, Joseph. Papers. East Carolina Manuscript Collection, East Carolina University.

Lambeth, Joseph Harrison. Diary. Virginia Historical Society, Richmond, Virginia.

Langhorne, James Henry, Diary, Volume 2. Virginia Historical Society, Richmond, Virginia.

Mackey, Daniel N. Letters. Duke University.

Mackey, James Taswell. Diary. Museum of the Confederacy, Richmond, Virginia.

Malone, Bartlett Yancey. Diary. Southern Historical Collection, University of North Carolina.

Mauck, Joseph W. Diary. Museum of the Confederacy, Richmond, Virginia.

McIntosh, Hattie. Papers. Southern Historical Collection, University of North Carolina.

McLaughlin-Jordan Papers. Indiana Historical Society.

McMichael, James Robert. Diary. Southern Historical Collection, University of North Carolina.

McMichael, Paul Agalus. Papers. Southern Historical Collection, University of North Carolina.

Mebane and Graves Family Papers. Southern Historical Collection, University of North Carolina.

Miley, George Washington. Papers. Virginia Historical Society, Richmond, Virginia.

Morris, William Groves. Papers. Southern Historical Collection, University of North Carolina.

Murphy, Virgil S. Diary. Southern Historical Collection, University of North Carolina.

Murrell Family Papers. University of Georgia.

Nelson Family Papers. Virginia Polytechnic and State University.

Oldham, Van Buren. Diaries. University of Tennessee, Martin.

Peters Family Papers. Southern Historical Collection, University of North Carolina.

Peyton, George Quintis. Diary. University of Virginia.

Pierce Family Civil War Papers. Indiana Historical Society.

Pinckney, Thomas. Diary. Museum of the Confederacy, Richmond, Virginia.

Printup, Daniel S. Papers. Duke University.

Pope Family Papers. Virginia Historical Society, Richmond, Virginia.

Richardson and Farrar Family Papers. Southern Collection, University of North Carolina.

Riddle Family papers. Virginia Historical Society, Richmond, Virginia.

Robertson, Reuben. Papers. Duke University.

Rush, John W. Papers. Auburn University.

Saunders, John Hubbard. Papers. Southern Historical Collection, University of North Carolina.

Sawyer, Lemuel. Papers. Duke University.

Simms, William Henry. Diary and Papers. Southern Historical Collection, University of North Carolina.

Stamp, J. B. Memoirs. Auburn University.

Stegman, George H. Collection. Virginia Military Institute.

Stonewall Register, 1865. Prisoners' Newspaper at Fort Delaware (?). Georgia Historical Society.

Street, John Kennedy. Papers. Southern Historical Collection, University of North Carolina.

Taylor, John. Papers. University of South Carolina.

Taylor Family Papers. Virginia Historical Society, Richmond, Virginia.

Thomas, James A. Letters. Filson Historical Society.

Thompson, Jeff M. Papers. Southern Historical Collection, University of North Carolina.

Thompson, Samuel. Papers. Southern Historical Collection, University of North Carolina.

Tyron Family Papers. Filson Historical Society.

Watson, W. J. Diary. Southern Historical Society, University of North Carolina.

Wells, James T. Papers. University of South Carolina.

Westcoat, Joseph Julius. Diary. Duke University

Williams Family Papers. Virginia Historical Society, Richmond, Virginia.

Wolfe Family Papers. Virginia Historical Society, Richmond, Virginia.

Woods, William G. Letters. Duke University.

Woody, Robert and Newton D. Papers. Duke University.

Wren, George Lovick Pierce. Diary. Emory University.

Published Primary Sources

Abbott, Allen O. *Prison Life in the South*. New York: Harper and Brothers, 1866.

Addison, Walter D. "Recollections of a Confederate Soldier of the Prison-Pens of Point Lookout, Md., and Elmira, New York," San Francisco: n.p., 1889. This article can be found by accessing the *Elmira Prison Camp Online Library*.

Anderson, James. "A Captured Confederate Officer: Nine Letters from Captain James Anderson to his Family." Ed. George M. Anderson. *Maryland Historical Magazine* 76 (Spring 1981): 62–69.

Andrews, Samuel J. M. *Sufferings of Union Soldiers in Southern Prisons*. Bowie, MD: Heritage Books, 1996/1870.

Ashe, S. W. *The Trial and Death of Henry Wirz*. Raleigh, NC: E. M. Uzzell, 1908.

Barbiere, Joe. *Scraps from the Prison Table at Camp Chase and Johnson's Island*. Doylestown, PA: W. W. H. Davis, 1868.

Benson, Berry. *Berry Benson's Civil War Book: Memoirs of a Confederate Scout and Sharpshooter*. Ed. Susan William Bensen. Athens, GA: University of Georgia Press, 1992.

Boggs, Samuel S. *Eighteen Months a Prisoner Under the Rebel Flag*. Lovington, IL: by author, 1887.

Boyle, Francis Atherton. "The Prison Diary of Adjutant Francis Atherton Boyle, CSA." Ed. Mary L. Thornton. *North Carolina Historical Review* 39 (Winter 1962): 58–84.

Brownell, Josiah C. *At Andersonville*. Glen Cove, NY: Glen Cove Public Library, 1981/ 1867.

Caudill, Benjamin E. *Surrender Hell: The Diary of Col. Benjamin E. Caudill*, CSA. The Dalles, OR: S. Combs, 1997.

Chamberlayne, John Hampden. *Ham Chamberlayne – Virginian. Letters and Papers of an Artillery Officer in the War for Southern Independence, 1861–1865*. Richmond, VA: Press of the Deitz Printing Co., 1932.

Chesebrough, David B. *"God Ordained This War": Sermons on the Sectional Crisis, 1830–1865*. Columbia: University of South Carolina Press, 1991.

Chipman, Norton Parker. *The Tragedy of Andersonville: Trial of Captain Henry Wirz, the Prison Keeper*. Sacramento, CA: by author, 1911.

Clark, Reuben G. *Valleys of the Shadow: The Memoir of Confederate Captain Reuben G. Clark, Company I, 59th Tennessee Mounted Infantry*. Ed. William B. Clark. Knoxville: University of Tennessee Press, 1994.

Cotton is King and Pro-Slavery Arguments: Comprising the Writings of Hammond, Harper, Christy, Stringfellow, Hodge, Bledsoe, and Cartwright. Ed. E. N. Elliot. Augusta, GA: Pritchard, Abbott, and Loomis, 1860; repr., New York: Johnson Reprint Co., 1968.

Crocker, James F. *Prison Reminiscences*. Portsmouth, VA: W. A. Fiske, 1906.

Davis, Jefferson. *The Rise and Fall of the Confederate Government*. Abridged. New York: Collier Books, 1961.

———. *"Fiction Distorting Fact": The Prison Life, Annotated by Jefferson Davis*. Ed. Edward K. Eckert. Macon, GA: Mercer University Press, 1987.

———. "Andersonville and other War Prisons." *Belford's Magazine* (Jan. 1890): 161–78; (Feb. 1890): 337–53.

Dedication of the Monument at Andersonville, Georgia, October 23, 1907, in Memory of the Men of Connecticut who Suffered in Southern Military Prisons. Hartford, CT: State of Connecticut, 1908.

Demon of Andersonville. Philadelphia: Barclay and Co., 1885.

Dickinson, Henry Clay. *Diary of Capt. Henry C. Dickinson, CSA. Morris Island, 1864–1865*. Denver, CO: Press of Williamson-Haffner Co., 1910 or 1919.

Dooley, John. *John Dooley, Confederate Soldier, His War Journal*. Ed. Joseph T. Durkin. Washington, D.C.: Georgetown University Press, 1945.

Dyer, John W. *Reminiscences; or Four Years in the Confederate Army*. Evansville, IN: Keller Printing and Publishing Co., 1898.

Ellis, John E. "A Louisiana Prisoner of War on Johnson's Island, 1863–1865." Ed. Martina Buck. *Louisiana History* 4 (Summer 1963): 233–42.

Fagan, William L., ed. *Southern War Songs*. New York: M.T. Richardson and Co., 1890.

Faust, Drew Gilpin, ed. *The Ideology of Slavery: Proslavery Thought in the Antebellum South, 1830–1860*. Baton Rouge: Louisiana State University Press, 1981.

Ferguson, Joseph. *Life-Struggles in Rebel Prisons*. Philadelphia: by author, 1865.

Fitzhugh, George. *Cannibals All! or Slaves Without Masters*. Ed. C. Vann Woodward. Cambridge, MA: Harvard University Press, 1960

Fontaine, Lamar. *The Prison Life of Major Lamar Fontaine*. Clarksdale, MS: Daily Register Print, 1910.

Frost, Griffin. *Camp and Prison Journal*. Quincy, IL: Quincy Herald Book and Job Office, 1867; repr., Iowa City, IA: Press of Camp Pope Bookshop, 1994.

Fuzzlebug, Fritz. [John J. Dunkle]. *Prison Life During the Rebellion*. Singers Glen, VA: Joseph Funk's Sons, Printers, 1869.

Glazier, Willard W. *The Capture, the Prison Pen, and the Escape*. Hartford, CT: H. E. Goodwin, 1868.

Goss, Warren Lee. *The Soldier's Story of His Captivity at Andersonville, Belle Isle, and Other Rebel Prisons*. Boston: Lee and Shepherd. 1869.

Hagan, John W. *Confederate Letters of John W. Hagan*. Ed. Bell I. Wiley. Athens: University of Georgia Press, 1954.

Hamlin, Augustus Choate. *Martyria: or Andersonville Prison*. Boston: Lee and Sheperd, 1866.

Hernbaker, Henry, and John Lynch. *True History: Jefferson Davis Answered. The Horrors of the Andersonville Prison Pen*. Philadelphia: Merrihew and Son, 1876.

Hill, Louis, ed. *Poems and Songs of the Civil War*. New York: Gramercy Books, 1990.

Houston, Thomas D. *Captain Thomas D. Houston Prisoner of War Letters*. Ed. Charles W. Turner. Verona, VA: McClure Printing Co., 1980.

Howe, Thomas H. *Adventures of an Escaped Union Prisoner from Andersonville Prison in 1864*. San Francisco, CA: Crocker and Co., 1886.

Huffman, James. *Ups and Downs of a Confederate Soldier*. New York: William E. Rudge's Sons, 1940.

Inger, John Washington. *The Diary of a Confederate Soldier*. Ed. and annotated by Mattie Lou Teague Crow. Huntsville, AL: The Strode Publishers, 1977.

Isham, Asa Brainerd. *Prisoners of War and Military Prisons*. Cincinnati, OH: Lyman and Cushing. 1890.

Jones, C. W. *In Prison at Point Lookout*. Martinsville, VA: The Bulletin, 1899.

Jones, John William. *Confederate View of the Treatment of Prisoners: Compiled from Official Records and other Documents*. Richmond, VA: Southern Historical Society, 1876.

Keen, Joseph S. *Experiences in Rebel Military Prisons at Richmond, Danville, Andersonville*. Detroit, MI: Detroit Free Press, 1890.

Keiley, Anthony M. *In Vinculis; or the Prisoner of War*. Petersburg, VA: Daily Index Office, 1866.

Kellogg, Robert H. *Life and Death in Rebel Prisons*. Hartford, CT: L. Stebbins, 1865.

King, John Henry. *Three Hundred Days in a Yankee Prison*. Atlanta, GA: J.P. Davis, 1904; repr. Kennesaw, GA: Continental Book Co., 1959.

King, John R. *My Experience in the Confederate Army and in Northern Prisons*. Clarksburg, WV: Stonewall Jackson Chapter, No. 1333, United Daughters of the Confederacy, 1917.

Leon, Louis. *Diary of a Tar Heel Confederate Soldier*. Chapel Hill, NC: Academic Affairs Library, 1998.

Lewis, Samuel E. *The Treatment of Prisoners of War, 1861–1865*. Richmond, VA: William Ellis Jones, Book and Job Printer, 1910.

Little, Robert Henry. *A Year of Starvation Amid Plenty*. Belton, TX: n.p., 1891; repr, Waco, TX: Library Binding Co., 1966.

Long, Lessel. *Twelve Months in Andersonville*. Huntington, IN: Thad and Mark Butler, 1886.

The Lost Cause: An Illustrated Journal of History Devoted to the Collection and Preservation of the Late Confederacy. Louisville, KY: Courier-Journal Job Printing Co., 1898. (serial)

McElroy, John. *Andersonville: A Story of Rebel Military Prisons*. Toledo, OH: D. R. Locke, 1879.

McGuire, Hunter, and George L. Christian. *The Confederate Cause and Conduct in the War Between the States*. Richmond, VA: L. H. Jenkins, 1907.

Meade, James T. *Journal of Prison Life*. Transcribed by Gordon and Anna Meade Minnigerode. Torrington, CT: Rainbow Press, 1987.

Minnich, J. W. *Inside and Outside of Rock Island*. Nashville, TN; Dallas, TX: Publishing House of the M.E. Church, South, 1908.

Morgan, W. H. *Personal Reminiscences of the War of 1861–5*. Lynchburg, VA: J. P. Bell and Co., 1911.

Murray, George W. *The Life and Adventures of Sgt. G. W. Murray*. Minneapolis, MN: Herald Publishing Co., 1872.

Murray, J. Ogden. *The Immortal Six Hundred: A Story of Cruelty to Confederate Prisoners of War*. Winchester, VA: The Eddy Press Corporation, 1905.

Newlin, William H. *An Account of the Escape of Six Federal Soldiers from Prison at Danville, Va*. Cincinnati, OH: Western Methodist Book Concern, 1887.

Oates, Sergeant. *Prison Life in Dixie*. Chicago: Central Book Concern, 1880.

Page, James Madison. *The True Story of Andersonville: A Defense of Major Henry Wirz*. New York: Neale Publishing Co., 1908.

Patterson, Edmund DeWitt. *Yankee Rebel: The Civil War Journal of Edmund DeWitt Patterson*. Ed. John G. Barrett. Chapel Hill: University of North Carolina Press, 1966.

Pennsylvania at Andersonville, Georgia: Ceremonies at the Dedication of the Memorial. C. E. Aughinbaugh: Printer to the State of Pennsylvania, 1909.

Peters, James Conrad. *Diary of a Confederate Sharpshooter*. Ed. and annotated by Jack L. Dickinson. Charlestown, W.V.: Pictorial Histories Publishing Co., 1997.

Phillips, M.V.B. *Life and Death in Andersonville, or, What I Saw and Experienced During Seven Months in Rebel Prisons*. Chicago: T. B. Arnold, 1887.

Poe, James T. *The Raving Foe. The Civil War Diary of Major James T. Poe, CSA*. Eastland, TX: The Longhorn Press, 1966.

Pollard, Edward A. *Observations in the North. Eight Months in Prison and on Parole*. Richmond, VA: E.W. Ayers, 1865.

———. *The Lost Cause*. 1866: repr., New York: Gramercy Books, 1994.

Porter, G.W.D. "Nine Months in a Northern Prison," *Annals of the Army of Tennessee* (July 1878): at www.Tennessee-SCV.org/4455/Index.htm.

Putnam, George Haven. *A Prisoner of War in Virginia 1864–1865*. New York: G. P. Putnam's Sons, 1912.

Purvis, Joseph Edward. "A Confederate View of Prison Life: A Virginian in Fort Delaware, 1863." Ed. Walter L. Williams. *Delaware History* 18 (Fall/Winter 1979): 226–35.

Roach, Alva C. *The Prisoner of War and How Treated*. Indianapolis, IN: Railroad City Publishing House, 1865.

Rogan, Lafayette. *Diary of Lafayette Rogan, CSA: Prisoner of War at Rock Island Prison Barracks*. West Point, NY: US Army Military Institute, 1938.

Russell, George G. *Reminiscences of Andersonville Prison. A Paper Read by Comrade Geo. G. Russell Before Post 34, G.A.R.* Salem, MA: Observer Steam Book and Job Printers, 1886.

Rutherford, Mildred Lewis. *Facts and Figures, Myths and Misrepresentations: Henry Wirz and the Andersonville Prison*. Athens, GA: s.n., 1921.

Ryan, Milton Asbury. *Experiences of a Confederate Soldier in Camp and Prison in the Civil War, 1861–1865*. Located at *www.IZZY.NET/~michaelg/maryan.htm*.

Sabre, Gilbert E. *Nineteen Months a Prisoner of War*. New York: American News Co., 1865.

Shepherd, Henry E. *Narrative of Prison Life at Baltimore and Johnson's Island, Ohio*. Baltimore, MD: Commercial Printing and Stationery Co., 1917.

Spencer, Ambrose. *A Narrative of Andersonville*. New York: Harper and Brothers, 1866.

Stamp, J.B. "Ten Months in Northern Prisons." *Alabama Historical Quarterly* 18 (Winter 1956): 486–98.

Stearns, Amos Edward. *Narrative of Amos E. Stearns*. Worchester, MA: F. P. Rice, 1887.

Stephens, Alexander H. *Recollections of Alexander H. Stephens*. Ed. Myrta Lockett Avery. New York: Doubleday, Page, and Co., 1910; repr., New York: Da Capo Press, 1971.

Stevenson, R. Randolph. *The Southern Side; or, Andersonville Prison*. Baltimore, MD: Trumbull Brothers, 1876; repr., New Market, VA: John M. Bracken, 1995.

Sturgis, Thomas. *Prisoners of War, 1861–'65*. New York: Knickerbocker Press, 1912.

Toney, Marcus B. *The Privations of a Private*. Nashville, TN: by author, 1905.

Tyler, William N. *Memoirs from Andersonville Prison*. Rockford, IL: Rockford Gazette Print, 1887.

———. *The Dispatch Carrier*. Port Byron, IL: Port Byron *Globe* Print, 1892.

Unknown Artist. *Sketches from Prison. A Confederate Artist's Record of Life at Point Lookout Prisoner-of-War Camp, 1863–1865*. Baltimore: Maryland State Park Foundation, 1989.

Vaughter, John B. *Prison Life in Dixie*: Chicago: Central Book Concern, 1880.

Ward, William Walker. *"For the Sake of My Country": The Diary of Col. W. W. Ward*. Ed. R. B. Rosenburg. Murfreesboro, TN: Southern Heritage Press, 1992.

Wash, W.A. *Camp, Field, and Prison Life*. St. Louis: Southwestern Book and Publishing Co., 1870.

Williamson, James J. *Prison Life in the Old Capitol*. West Orange, NJ: by author, 1911.

Wilson, Clyde N., ed. *The Essential Calhoun: Selections from Writings, Speeches, and Letters*. New Brunswick, NJ: Transaction Publishers, 1992.

Magazines and Periodicals

Century Magazine, 1865–1920.

Confederate Veteran. Nashville, TN: 1893–1932.

De Bow's Review. New Orleans, LA: 1846–61.

The Land We Love. Charlotte, NC: 1866–69.

Southern Historical Society Papers. Richmond, VA: 1876–1915.

Southern Literary Messenger. Richmond, VA: 1834–63.

Official Documents

United States Adjutant-General's Office. *General Court Martial Orders #607*.

United States Congress. Joint Committee on the Conduct of the War. *House of Representatives Report #67: Returned Prisoners*. New York: Johnson Reprint Corporation, 1970.

———. *Rebel Barbarities: Official Accounts of the Cruelties Inflicted Upon Union Prisoners and Refugees*. New York: Johnson Reprint Corporation, 1970.

———. *Trial of Henry Wirz. House Executive Document #23*.

United States Quartermaster's Department. *The Martyrs Who, For Our Country, Gave Up Their Lives in the Prison in Andersonville, GA*. Washington, D.C.: Government Printing Office, 1866.

United States Sanitary Commission. *Narratives of Privations and Sufferings of the United States Officers and Soldiers While Prisoners of War in the Hands of the Rebels*. Philadelphia: King and Baird Publishers, 1864.

United States Surgeon General's Office. *Medical and Surgical History of the War of the Rebellion, 1861–1865*. Washington, D.C.: Government Printing Office, 1875.

United States War Department. *War of the Rebellion: Official Records of the Union and Confederate Armies*. Washington, D.C.: Government Printing Office, 1899; repr.,Harrisburg, PA: Telegraph Press, 1971.

Secondary Sources

Adams, George Washington. *Doctors in Blue: The Medical History of the Union Army in the Civil War*. New York: Henry Schuman, 1952.

Anderson, Gaylord W. and Margaret Arnstein. *Communicable Disease Control*. New York: Macmillan Company, 1952.

Andrews, J. Cutler. *The North Reports the Civil War*. Pittsburgh, PA: University of Pittsburgh Press, 1955.

———. *The South Reports the Civil War*. Princeton, NJ: Princeton University Press, 1970.

Beitzell, Edwin W. *Point Lookout Prison Camp for Confederates*. n.p.: by author, 1972.

Beringer, Richard E., Herman Hattaway, Archer Jones, and William N. Still, Jr. *Why the South Lost the Civil War*. Athens: University of Georgia Press, 1986.

Billings, John D. *Hardtack and Coffee: The Unwritten Story of Army Life*. Boston, MA: George M. Smith and Co., 1887; repr., Lincoln: University of Nebraska Press, 1993.

Boles, John B. *The South Through Time: A History of an American Region*. Englewood Cliffs, NJ: Prentice Hall, 1995.

Bordley, James and A. Mcgehee Harvey. *Two Centuries of American Medicine, 1776–1976*. Philadelphia: W.B. Saunders Company, 1976.

Boycott, J.A. *Natural History of Infectious Disease*. New York: St. Martin's Press, 1971.

Brooks, Stewart. *Civil War Medicine*. Springfield, IL: Charles C. Thomas, 1966.

Burnet, Macfarlane, and David O. White. *Natural History of Infectious Disease*. London: Cambridge University Press, 1972.

Burnham, Philip. *So Far from Dixie: Confederates in Yankee Prisons*. Lanham, MD: Taylor Trade Publishing, 2003.

Byrne, Thomas. *Elmira's Civil War Prison Camp, 1864–1865*. Elmira, NY: Chemung County Historical Society, 1989.

Cash, Wilbur J. *The Mind of the South*. New York: Alfred A. Knopf, 1941; repr., New York: Vintage Books, 1991.

Catton, Bruce. *Reflections on the Civil War*. Ed. John Leekley. New York: Berkley Books, 1981.

———. *The Civil War*. Ed. Richard M. Ketchum. New York: American Heritage Publishing Company, 1960.

———. "Prison Camps of the Civil War." *American Heritage Civil War Chronicles* (Fall 1992): 47–52.

Conference on Civil War Medicine. *Civil War Medicine*. Frederick, MD: Triad Media Group, 1993 (4 audio cassettes).

Connelly, Thomas L., and Barbara L. Bellows. *God and General Longstreet: The Lost Cause and the Southern Mind*. Baton Rouge: Louisiana State University Press, 1982.

Constant, George W. "'Death before Dishonor:' The 'Immortal 600' – Human Shields 130 Years before Saddam Hussein" *http://www.del.net/ort/fort/imort /html*.

Cooper, William J., Jr. *Jefferson Davis, American*. New York: Alfred A. Knopf, 2000.

Cooper, William J., Jr., and Thomas E. Terrill. *The American South*. New York: Alfred A. Knopf, 1990.

Cowley, Robert, ed. *With My Face to the Enemy: Perspectives on the Civil War*. New York: Berkley Books, 2001.

Crozier, Emmet. *Yankee Reporters, 1861–1865*. New York: Oxford University Press, 1956.

Cunningham, H. H. *Doctors in Gray: The Confederate Medical Service*. Baton Rouge: Louisiana State University Press, 1993.

Current, Richard N., ed. *Encyclopedia of the Confederacy*. New York: Simon and Schuster, 1993.

Cyan, Erwin D. *Vitamins in Your Life*. New York: Simon and Schuster, 1974.

Dauer, Carl C., Robert F. Corns, and Leomont M. Schuman. *Infectious Diseases*. Cambridge, MA: Harvard University Press, 1968.

Davis, David Brion. *Antebellum American Culture: An Interpretive Anthology*. Lexington, MA: D.C. Heath and Co., 1979.

Davis, William C., ed. *Fighting for Time*. Volume 4, *The Image of War, 1861–1865*. Garden City, NY: Doubleday and Co., 1983.

———, ed. *Rebels and Yankees: The Fighting Men of the Civil War*. New York: Salamander Books, 1989.

Davis, William C., and Bell I. Wiley, eds. *Civil War Album: Complete Photographic History of the Civil War, Fort Sumter to Appomattox*. New York: Tess Press, 2000.

Dearing, Mary R. *Veterans in Politics: The Story of the G.A.R.* Baton Rouge: Louisiana State University Press, 1952.

Denney, Robert E. *Civil War Prisons and Escapes: A Day-by-Day Chronicle*. New York: Sterling Publishing Co., 1993.

———. *Civil War Medicine: Care and Comfort of the Wounded*. New York: Sterling Publishing, 1995.

Duncan, Louis C. *The Medical Department of the United States Army in the Civil War*. n.p.: n.d.: repr., Gathersburg, MD: Olde Soldier Books, Inc., 1987.

Dunn, Beverly Charles. *Major-General Montgomery Cunningham Meigs*. n.p., 1914.

Eaton, Clement. *The Growth of Southern Civilization, 1790–1860*. New York: Harper and Row, 1963.

Elmira in the Civil War: Training Camp of the Blue, Prison Camp of the Gray. New York: n.p., 1991.

Emery, Robert E. and Thomas F. Oltmanns. *Essentials of Abnormal Psychology*. Upper Saddle River, NJ: Prentice-Hall, 2000.

Escott, Paul D. *After Secession: Jefferson Davis and the Failure of Confederate Nationalism*. Baton Rouge: Louisiana State University Press, 1978.

Evans, Josephine King. "Nostalgia For a Nickel: The Confederate Veteran." *Tennessee Historical Quarterly* 48 (1989): 238–44.

Everett, Edward T. "Pennsylvania Newspapers and Public Opinion, 1861–1862." *Western Pennsylvania Historical Magazine* 44 (1961): 21–31.

Faust, Drew Gilpin. The Creation of Confederate Nationalism: Ideology and *Identity in the Civil War South*. Baton Rouge: Louisiana State University Press, 1988.

Fermer, Douglas. *James Gordon Bennett and the New York Herald: A Study of Editorial Opinion in the Civil War Era, 1854–1867*. New York: St. Martins Press, 1986.

Fetzer, Dale and Bruce Mowday. *Unlikely Allies: Fort Delaware's Prison Community in the Civil War*. Mechanicsburg, PA: Stackpole Books, 2000.

Flory, William E.S. *Prisoners of War: A Study in the Development of International Law*. Washington, D.C.: American Council on Public Affairs, 1942.

Ford, Lacy K. *Origins of Southern Radicalism: The South Carolina Upcountry, 1800– 1860*. New York: Oxford University Press, 1988.

Foster, Gaines M. *Ghosts of the Confederacy: Defeat, the Lost Cause, and the Emergence of the New South, 1865–1913*. New York: Oxford University Press, 1987.

Franklin, John Hope. *The Militant South, 1800-1861*. Cambridge, MA: Harvard University Press, 1956.

Freeman, Frank R. *Microbes and Minie Balls: An Annotated Bibliography of Civil War Medicine*. Rutherford, NJ: Fairleigh Dickinson University Press, 1993.

Freidel, Frank. "The Loyal Publication Society: A Pro-Union Propaganda Agency." *Mississippi Valley Historical Society* 26 (1939–1940): 259–76.

Futch, Ovid L. *History of Andersonville Prison*. Gainesville: University of Florida Press, 1969.

Gallagher, Gary W. *The Confederate War: How Popular Will, Nationalism, and Military Strategy Could Not Stave Off Defeat*. Cambridge, MA: Harvard University Press, 1997.

Gallagher, Gary W., and Alan T. Nolan, eds. *The Myth of the Lost Cause and Civil War History*. Bloomington: Indiana University Press, 2000.

Gerster, Patrick, and Nicholas Cords, eds. *Myth and Southern History*. Vol. 1, *The Old South*, 2nd ed. Urbana: University of Illinois Press, 1989.

Gray, Michael P. *The Business of Captivity: Elmira and Its Civil War Prison*. Kent, OH: Kent State University Press, 2001.

Grimes, Deanna E. *Infectious Diseases*. St. Louis, MO: Mosby-Year Book, 1991.

Greiner, James M., Janet L. Coryell, and James R. Smither, eds. *A Surgeon's Civil War: The Letters and Diary of Daniel M. Holt, M.D.* Kent, OH: Kent State University Press, 1994.

Grissom, Deward K. *Communicable Diseases*. Dubuque, IA: William C. Brown Co., 1971.

Hall, James R. *Den of Misery: Indiana's Civil War Prison*. Gretna, LA: Pelican Publishing, 2006.

Heidler, David S. and Jeanne T. Heidler, eds. *Encyclopedia of the American Civil War*. Santa Barbara, CA: ABC-Clio, 2000.

Hemmerlein, Richard F. *Prisons and Prisoners of the Civil War*. Boston: Christopher Publishing House, 1934.

Hesseltine, William B. *Civil War Prisons: A Study in War Psychology*. Ohio State University Press, 1930; repr.; New York: Frederick Ungar Publishing Co., 1971.

———, ed. *Civil War Prisons*. Kent, OH: Kent State University Press, 1995.

Holmes, Clayton Wood. *The Elmira Prison Camp: A History of the Military Camp at Elmira, N.Y., July 6, 1864–July 10, 1865*. New York: G. P. Putnam's Sons, 1912.

Horigan, Michael. *Elmira: Death Camp of the North*. Mechanicsburg, PA: Stackpole Books, 2002.

Hundley, Daniel Robinson. *Prison Echoes of the Great Rebellion*. New York: S. W. Green, 1874.

Imperato, James P. *The Treatment and Control of Infectious Diseases in Man*. Springfield, IL: Charles C. Thomas, 1974.

Jenkins, William Sumner. *Pro-Slavery Thought in the Old South*. Chapel Hill: University of North Carolina Press, 1935.

Johnson, Charles Beneulyn. *Muskets and Medicine, or, Army Life in the Sixties*. Philadelphia: F. A. Davis, Co., 1917.

Joseph, Peter, ed. *The Wounded River: The Civil War Letters of John Vance Lauderdale, M.D.* East Lansing: Michigan State University Press, 1993.

———. *Civil War Battlefield Medicine.* n.p.; repr., Springfield, IL: Department of Medical Humanities, Southern Illinois University, 1994.

Joslyn, Mauriel P. *Immortal Captives: The Story of the 600 Confederate Officers and the United States Prisoner of War Policy.* Shippensburg, PA: White Mane Publishing Co., 1996.

Keen, Nancy. "Confederate Prisoners at Fort Delaware." *Delaware History* 13 (1968): 1–27.

Keller, Morton. *The Art and Politics of Thomas Nast.* New York: Oxford University Press, 1968.

Kelly, Dennis. *A History of Camp Douglas, Illinois, Union Prison, 1861–1865.* Atlanta, GA(?): National Park Service, Southeast Region, 1989.

Kennedy, Stetson. *After Appomattox: How the South Won the War.* Gainesville: University of Florida Press, 1995.

Key, Jack D. U.S. *Army Medical Department and Civil War Medicine.* Albuquerque, N.M.: Lovelace Foundation for Medical Education and Research, 1958.

Kirwin, Albert D., ed. *The Civilization of the Old South: Writings of Clement Eaton.* Lexington: University of Kentucky Press, 1968.

Lauer, Robert H. *Social Problems and the Quality of Life.* 7th ed. Boston: McGraw-Hill, 1998.

Levy, George. *To Die in Chicago: Confederate Prisoners of Camp Douglas, 1862–1865.* Evanston, IL: Evanston Publishing, 1994.

Lewis, John B. "The Reminiscences of a Civil War Surgeon, John B. Lewis." *Journal of the History of Medicine and Allied Sciences* 21 (1966): 47–58.

Lumpkin, Katherine Du Pre. *The Making of a Southerner.* New York: Alfred A. Knopf, 1947.

Marvel, William. *Andersonville: The Last Depot.* Chapel Hill: University of North Carolina Press, 1994.

Maxwell, William A. *Lincoln's Fifth Wheel: The Political History of the United States Sanitary Commission.* New York: Longmans and Green, 1956.

McAdams, Benton. *Rebels at Rock Island: The Story of a Civil War Prison.* DeKalb: Northern Illinois University Press, 2000.

McConnell, Stuart. *Glorious Contentment: The Grand Army of the Republic, 1865–1900.* Chapel Hill: University of North Carolina Press, 1992.

McKitrick, Eric L., ed. *Slavery Defended: The Views of the Old South.* Englewood Cliffs, NJ: Prentice-Hall, Inc., 1963.

McPherson, James M. *The Negro's Civil War*. New York: Vintage Books, 1965.

———. *Battle Cry of Freedom: The Civil War Era*. New York: Oxford University Press, 1988.

———. *For Cause and Comrades: Why Men Fought in the Civil War*. New York: Oxford University Press, 1997.

———. *Ordeal by Fire: The Civil War and Reconstruction*. 3rd ed. Boston: McGraw Hill, 2001.

McPherson, James M., and William J. Cooper, Jr., eds. *Writing the Civil War: The Quest to Understand*. Columbia: University of South Carolina Press, 1998.

Miller, Randall M., Harry S. Stout, and Charles R. Wilson, eds. *Religion and the American Civil War*. New York: Oxford University Press, 1998.

Mims, Cedric A. *The Pathogens of Infectious Disease*. New York: Academic Press, 1977.

Mitchell, Reid. *Civil War Soldiers*. New York: Viking, Penguin, 1988.

Neely, Mark E., Harold Holzer, and Gabor S. Boritt. *The Confederate Image: Prints of the Lost Cause*. Chapel Hill: University of North Carolina Press, 1987.

Nevins, Allan. *The War for the Union: War Becomes Revolution, 1862–1863*. New York: Charles Scribner's Sons, 1960.

Oratory in the New South. Baton Rouge: Louisiana State University, 1979.

Osterweis, Rollin G. *The Myth of the Lost Cause, 1865–1900*. Hamden, CT: The Shoe String Press, 1973.

Owsley, Frank Lawrence. "The Irrepressible Conflict," in *I'll Take My Stand: The South and the Agrarian Tradition*. Baton Rouge: Louisiana State University Press, 1977.

Perman, Michael, ed. *Major Problems in the Civil War and Reconstruction*. Lexington, MA: D.C. Heath and Co., 1991.

"Point Lookout Prison Camp for Confederates." at

http://members.tripod.com/~PLPOW//prisonhis.htm.

Pressly, Thomas J. *Americans Interpret Their Civil War*. Princeton, NJ: Princeton University Press; repr., New York: The Free Press, 1966.

Radford, John P. "Identity and Tradition in the Post Civil War South." *Journal of Historical Geography* 18 (1992): 91–103.

Reynolds, Donald E. *Editors Make War: Southern Newspapers in the Secession Crisis*. Nashville, TN: Vanderbilt University Press, 1966.

Rhodes, James Ford. *History of the United States*. Vol. 5, 1864–1866. New York: The Macmillan Company, 1912.

Robertson, James I. *Soldiers Blue and Gray*. Columbia: University of South Carolina Press, 1988.

———. *Tenting Tonight: The Soldier's Life*. Alexandria, VA: Time-Life Books, 1984.

Sanders, Charles W., Jr. *While in the Hands of the Enemy: Military Prisons of the Civil War*. Baton Rouge: Louisiana State University Press, 2005.

———. "'A Most Horrible National Sin': The Treatment of Prisoners in the American Civil War." *North and South* 9, no. 5 (Oct. 2006): 12–29.

Sears, Stephen. *Gettysburg*. New York: Houghton Mifflin Co., 2003.

Segars, J. H., ed. *Andersonville: The Southern Perspective*. Atlanta, GA: Southern Heritage Press, 1995.

Shalhope, Robert E. "Thomas Jefferson's Republicanism and Antebellum Southern Thought." *Journal of Southern History* 42, no. 4 (Nov. 1976): 529–56.

Shannon, Fred Albert. *The Organization and Administration of the Union Army, 1861– 1865*. 2 vols. New York: Longmans and Green, 1956.

Shriver, Phillip R. and Donald J. Breen. *Ohio's Military Prisons in the Civil War*. Columbus: Ohio State University Press for the Ohio Historical Society, 1964.

Shattuck, Gardiner H., Jr. "Appomattox as a Day of Blessing: Religious Interpretations of Confederate Defeat in the New South Era." *Journal of Confederate History* 7 (1991): 1–18.

Shryock, Richard Harrison. *Medicine in America: Historical Essays*. Baltimore, MD: The Johns Hopkins University Press, 1966.

Silber, Nina. *The Romance of Reunion: Northerners and the South, 1865–1900*. Chapel Hill: University of North Carolina Press, 1993.

Silver, James W. *Confederate Morale and Church Propaganda*. New York: W. W. Norton, 1957.

Simpson, John A. "The Cult of the Lost Cause." *Tennessee Historical Quarterly* 34 (1975): 350–61.

Speer, Lonnie. *Portals to Hell: Military Prisons in the Civil War*. Mechanicsburg, PA: Stackpole Books, 1997.

———. *War of Vengeance: Acts of Retaliation Against Confederate POWs*. Mechanicsburg, PA: Stackpole Books, 2002.

Stampp, Kenneth. *The Era of Reconstruction, 1865–1877*. New York: Vintage Books, 1965.

Starr, Louis M. *Bohemian Brigade: Civil War Newsmen in Action*. Madison: University of Wisconsin Press, 1987.

Steiner, Paul Eby. *Physician-Generals in the Civil War: A Study in Nineteenth Mid-Century Medicine*. Springfield IL: Charles C. Thomas, 1966.

———. *Disease in the Civil War: Natural Biological Warfare in 1861–1865.* Springfield, IL: Charles C. Thomas, 1968.

Sydnor, Charles S. *The Development of Southern Sectionalism, 1819–1848.* Baton Rouge: Louisiana State University Press, 1948.

Tate, Allen. *Jefferson Davis: His Rise and Fall.* New York: Minton, Balch, and Co., 1929; repr., New York: Kraus Reprint Co., 1969.

Taylor, William R. *Cavalier and Yankee: The Old South and American National Character.* Cambridge, MA: Harvard University Press, 1979.

Temple, Brian. *The Union Prison at Fort Delaware: A Perfect Hell on Earth.* Jefferson, NC: McFarland Co., 2003.

Thomas, Emory M. *The Confederate Nation, 1861–1865.* New York: Harper Torchbooks, 1979.

Thompson, Holland, ed. *The Photographic History of the Civil War.* Vol. 4, *Soldier Life and Secret Service and Prisons and Hospitals.* n.p.: 1911; repr., Secaucus, NJ: The Blue and Grey Press, 1987.

United States Public Health Service. *The Control of Communicable Diseases in Man.* Washington, D.C.: Government Printing Office, 1950.

Vinson, J. Charles. *Thomas Nast, Political Cartoonist.* Athens: University of Georgia Press, 1967.

Wade, Linda R. *Prison Camps of the Civil War.* Edina, MN: Abdo and Daughters, 1998.

Walker, Gary C. *Civil War Tales,* Vol. 2. Roanoke, VA: A and W Enterprises, 1994.

Ward, Geoffrey. *The Civil War: An Illustrated History.* New York: Alfred A. Knopf, Inc., 1990.

Warren, Robert Penn. *The Legacy of the Civil War: Reflections on the Centennial.* New York: Vintage Books, 1964.

Watson, Ronald R., ed. *Nutrition, Disease Resistance, and Immune Function.* New York: Marcel Dekker, 1984.

Weaver, Richard M. *The Southern Tradition at Bay: A History of Postbellum Thought.* Ed. George Core, M. E. Bradford, George Gore. Washington, D.C.: Regnery Publishing, 1989.

Welsh, Jack D. *Medical Histories of Union Generals.* Kent, OH: Kent State University Press, 1996.

———. *Medical Histories of Confederate Generals.* Kent, OH: Kent State University Press, 1995.

Wheelock, Julia S. *The Boys in White: The Experience of a Hospital Agent in and Around Washington.* New York: Lange and Hillman, 1870.

Wiley, Bell I. *The Life of Billy Yank: The Common Soldier of the Union.* Baton Rouge: Louisiana State University Press, 1952.

————. *The Life of Johnny Reb: The Common Soldier of the Confederacy.* Baton Rouge: Louisiana State University Press, 1943.

Williams, T. Harry. *Romance and Realism in Southern Politics.* Baton Rouge: Louisiana State University Press, 1966.

Williamson, Mary L. *A Confederate Trilogy for Young Readers, The Life of Gen. Robert E. Lee, Lt. Gen. T. J. "Stonewall" Jackson, Major Gen. J.E.B. Stuart.* n.p.: 1895, repr., Harrisonburg, VA: Sprinkle Publications, 1989.

Wilson, Charles Reagan. *Baptized in Blood: The Religion of the Lost Cause, 1865–1900.* Athens: University of Georgia Press, 1980.

Wilson, W. Emerson. *Fort Delaware.* Newark: University of Delaware, 1957.

Woodford, Arthur M. "Johnson's Island: The Story of a Yankee Prison." *Bulletin of the Detroit Historical Society* 28, no. 1 (Fall 1971): 4–10.

Wyatt-Brown, Bertram. *Southern Honor: Ethics and Behavior in the Old South.* New York: Oxford University Press, 1982.

Youmans, Guy P. *The Biological and Clinical Basis of Infectious Diseases.* Philadelphia: W. B. Saunders Co., 1986.

Theses and Dissertations

Bangert, Elizabeth C. "The Press and the Prisons: Union and Confederate Newspaper Coverage of Civil War Prisons." Ph.D. diss., College of William and Mary, 2001.

Dale, Corinne Howell. "The Lost Cause: Myth, Symbol and Stereotype in Southern Fiction." Ph.D. diss., University of Michigan, 1978.

Durant, Susan Speare. "The Gently Furled Banner: The Development of the Myth of the Lost Cause, 1865–1900." Ph.D. diss., University of North Carolina, 1972.

Evans, Josephine King. "Confederate Veteran: The Bible of the Lost Cause." Masters thesis, University of South Florida, 1988.

Ferguson, L. Gilbert. "A Study of Civil War Prisoner Policy." Masters thesis, Mississippi College, 1994.

Fulton, Lori Renee. "A Civil War Prison by the Lake: Camp Douglas in Chicago, Illinois." Masters thesis, Illinois State University, 1993.

Gardner, Douglas Gibson. "Andersonville and American Memory: Civil War Prisoners and Narratives of Suffering and Redemption." Ph.D. diss., Miami University, 1998.

Gray, Michael P. "Extremities of War: A Case Study of the Prison Camps Established at Elmira, N.Y. and Andersonville, GA." Masters thesis, East Stroudsburg University, 1991.

———. "The Business of Captivity in the Chemung Valley: Elmira and its Civil War Prison." Ph.D. diss., Kent State University, 1998.

Ivy, Jack Morris, Jr. "Camp Chase, Columbus, Ohio, 1861–1865: A Study of the Union's Treatment of Confederate Prisoners of War." Masters of Military Art and Science Thesis, U.S. Army Command and General Staff College, 1990.

Jabbs, Theodore H. "The Lost Cause: Some Southern Opinion between 1865 and 1900." Masters thesis, University of North Carolina – Chapel Hill, 1967.

Koerting, Gayla M. "The Trial of Henry Wirz and Nineteenth Century Military Law." Ph.D. diss., Kent State University, 1995.

Kublanza, Joan Marie G. "A Comparative Study of Conditions at Two Civil War Prison Camps: Camp Douglas, Chicago, Illinois and Camp Sumter, Andersonville, Georgia." Masters thesis, DePaul University, 1979.

Parker, Elizabeth Leonard. "The Civil War Career of Henry Wirz and its Aftermath." Masters thesis, University of Georgia, 1948.

Rasner, Gustav C. "The Effect of the Breakdown of the Prisoner Parole and Exchange Cartel." Masters thesis, Baylor University, 1986.

Roberts, Nancy A. "The Afterlife of Civil War Prisons and Their Dead." Ph.D. diss., University of Oregon, 1996.

Schultz, Charles R. "The Conditions at Johnson's Island Prison During the Civil War." Masters thesis, Bowling Green State Universtiy, 1960.

Simpson, John A. "A Vindication of the 'Lost Cause': The Confederate Veteran Magazine, 1893–1913." Masters thesis, University of Arkansas, 1974.

Snell, William Halsey, Jr. "Union and Confederate Treatment of Prisoners of War During the American Civil War." Masters thesis, University of Southern Mississippi, 1992.

West, Deborah B. "Image of the South as Presented by Selected Northern Magazines,1865–1880." Masters thesis, Florida State University, 1959.

Wolfson, Nathan Zevi. "The Trial of Henry Wirz." Masters thesis, University of California, 1940 or '49.

Video

"*Hellmira, 1864-1865: The Andersonville of the North.*" WSKG Telecommuncations Council, 1993.

INDEX

A

Alexander, Charles T.: inspects Alton, 112, 114; inspects Camp Chase, 167–68, 170; inspects Camp Douglas, 125; inspects Camp Morton, 135, 136; inspects Elmira, 201, 204; inspects Johnson's Island, 157; inspects Rock Island, 143

Alton (prison), Illinois, 109–18; clean water issues, 113–14; crowded conditions, 110, 114, 117–18; diarrhea/dysentery, 116–17; food/rations, 100, 111, 113, 117–18; Hendrickson, T., commandant, 110–11; Kincaid, G. W., commandant, 111; living quarters, 110, 112, 114, 117; medical care, 112, 114–17; pneumonia, 116; Weer, William, commandant, 111–13; Copeland, Joseph T., commandant, 112; inspected by Freedley, 115; sanitation issues, 111–13; smallpox, 115–16, 230–31. *See also* inspections by Alexander, Clark, Marsh, and Orme

Andersonville, 2, 7, 9–17, 20–22, 64; inadequate shelter provided, 12–13; Northern claims of starvation at, 7–8, 12, 14, 17–18, 21; postwar charges of abuse, 7, 10–12, 14, 16; as proof of

Southern inferiority, 9–10, 15–18, 22; Republican exploitation of for political advantages, 20–21; South's defense of, 32–36; torture and murder by physicians, 11–12; unhealthy location, 13–14; used to liberalize veterans' pension policies, 18–20, 58–59; Wirz, Henry, 9–11, 14, 32–36

B

Beauregard, P. G. T., 91, 220

Belle Isle, Richmond, Virginia, 2, 7, 13, 16, 21, 59, 97

black prisoners, 4–5, 86, 89–95, 169–70, 244–45

Bragg, Braxton, 92, 220

Butler, Benjamin, 86, 91–93

C

Cameron, Simon, 74

Camp Chase, 165–74, 247, 249; clothing, 166–68; diarrhea/dysentery, 172–74; food/rations, 77, 166–68; inspection by I. M. Abraham, 166; inspected by E. K. Allen, 168, 170; inspected by J. M. Cuyler, 166; inspected by F. S. Parker, 167, 170; living quarters, 165–66, 168–70, 174; medical care, 82, 166–67, 171–74, 237; pneumonia, 170–74;